Proceedings of the Ninth International Symposium on

Human Aspects of Information Security & Assurance (HAISA 2015)

Mytilene, Greece
1-3 July 2015

Editors

Steven Furnell
Nathan Clarke

Centre for Security, Communications & Network Research
Plymouth University
United Kingdom

ISBN: 978-1-84102-388-5

Preface

It is now widely recognised that technology alone cannot provide the answer to security problems. A significant aspect of protection comes down to the attitudes, awareness, behaviour and capabilities of the people involved, and they often need support in order to get it right. Factors such as lack of awareness and understanding, combined with unreasonable demands from security technologies, can dramatically impede their ability to act securely and comply with policies. Ensuring appropriate attention to the needs of users is therefore a vital element of a successful security strategy, and they need to understand how the issues may apply to them and how to use the available technology to protect their systems.

With the above in mind, the Human Aspects of Information Security and Assurance (HAISA) symposium series specifically addresses information security issues that relate to people. It concerns the methods that inform and guide users' understanding of security, and the technologies that can benefit and support them in achieving protection.

This book presents the proceedings from the 2015 event, held in the city of Mytilene, in Lesvos, Greece, during July 2015. A total of 25 reviewed papers are included, spanning a range of topics including user attitudes and awareness, management and modelling of security, and the suitability of technologies that people are expected to use. All of the papers were subject to double-blind peer review, with each being reviewed by at least two members of the international programme committee.

We would like to thank the authors for submitting their work and sharing their findings, and the international programme committee for their efforts in reviewing the submissions and ensuring the quality of the resulting event and proceedings. We would also like to thank the local organising committee for making all the necessary arrangements to enable this symposium to take place. Special thanks go to Dr. Christos Kalloniatis (University of the Aegean) as the local host, for organising the venue and other facilities. Thanks are also due to Dr Paul Dowland for his assistance on producing the proceedings and managing the conference submission system. Final thanks are due to Emerald (publishers of the sponsoring journal, *Information & Computer Security*) as an ongoing supporter of the event.

Steven Furnell and Nathan Clarke
Symposium Co-Chairs, HAISA 2015

Lesvos, July 2015

International Programme Committee

Peter Bednar	University of Portsmouth	United Kingdom
William Buchanan	Edinburgh Napier University	United Kingdom
Jeff Crume	IBM	United States
Adele Da Veiga	University of South Africa	South Africa
Dorothy Denning	Naval Postgraduate School	United States
Ronald Dodge	United States Military Academy	United States
Paul Dowland	Plymouth University	United Kingdom
Jan Eloff	SAP	South Africa
Simone Fischer-Huebner	Karlstad University	Sweden
Stefanos Gritzalis	University of the Aegean	Greece
John Howie	Cloud Security Alliance	United States
William Hutchinson	Edith Cowan University	Australia
Murray Jennex	San Diego State University	United States
Andy Jones	Edith Cowan University	Australia
Vasilios Katos	Bournemouth University	United Kingdom
Sokratis Katsikas	University of Piraeus	Greece
Costas Lambrinoudakis	University of Piraeus	Greece
Fudong Li	Plymouth University	United Kingdom
Javier Lopez	University of Malaga	Spain
George Magklaras	University of Oslo	Norway
Haris Mouratidis	University of Brighton	United Kingdom
Maria Papadaki	Plymouth University	United Kingdom
Malcolm Pattinson	University of Adelaide	Australia
Corey Schou	Idaho State University	United States
Rossouw von Solms	Nelson Mandela Metropolitan University	South Africa
Kerry-Lynn Thomson	Nelson Mandela Metropolitan University	South Africa
Theodore Tryfonas	University of Bristol	United Kingdom
Kim Vu	California State University	United States
Jeremy Ward	Hewlett Packard	United Kingdom
Merrill Warkentin	Mississippi State University	United States
Zihang Xiao	Palo Alto Networks	United States
Wei Yan	Trend Micro	United States
Louise Yngstrom	Stockholm University	Sweden
Ibrahim Zincir	Yasar University	Turkey

Contents

An Ontology for a National Cyber-Security Culture Environment

N. Gcaza[1], R. von Solms[1] and J. van Vuuren[2]

[1] PO Box 77000, Nelson Mandela Metropolitan University, Port Elizabeth 6031, South Africa
[2] Council for Scientific and Industrial Research, Meiring Naude Road, Pretoria, 0001 South Africa
e-mail: {Noluxolo.Gcaza; Rossouw.VonSolms}@nmmu.ac.za; jjvvuuren@csir.co.za

Abstract

The modern-day use of cyberspace has created a world that is increasingly relying on online services to operate. Nevertheless, cyberspace has a 'dark side'; as there are many risks associated it. This 'dark side' has called for safety and security measures to be implemented through cyber security. As such, cultivating a supportive culture is perceived to be an important contributing factor to cyber security. For this reason, many nations aspire to cultivate a culture of cyber security amongst all the users of cyberspace. However, what is lacking currently is a well-defined and delineated definition of the cyber-security culture domain. To define this domain, this paper proposes a national cyber-security culture ontology.

Keywords

Cyber Security, Cyber-Security Culture, Ontology

1. Introduction

At the inception of cyberspace, "…no one, perhaps, could have clearly foreseen that and how the Internet would someday become a veritable platform for globalized criminal activities" (Moses-Òkè 2012, p.1). Nowadays, cyberspace is a 'playground' for criminal activities, such as cybercrime, fraud, identity theft, phishing and more. A report compiled by the RSA (RSA 2014) on criminal activities, reported that in the year 2013, organisations lost about $5.9 billion to phishing attacks. The RSA foresees more sophisticated and pervasive cybercrime trends in future, which include mobile threats and malicious software.

Such security implications of cyberspace called for the establishment of cyber-security measures. Von Solms and van Niekerk (2013, p.5) define cyber security as "…the protection of cyberspace itself, the electronic information, the [Information and Communication Technologies] ICTs that support cyberspace, and the users of cyberspace in their personal, societal and national capacity, including any of their interests, either tangible or intangible, that are vulnerable to attacks originating in cyberspace".

Cyber security came into the spotlight in 2007, when Estonia became one of the first countries to experience a cyber-attack on its national assets (Dlamini et al. 2011). This attack called for national attention, owing to the high level of dependence of the Estonian government services on cyberspace. As a result, Estonia drafted a cyber-security policy, in order to avoid future incidents of the same kind (Dlamini et al. 2011).

As it is, over 50 nations, such as the United States (US), the United Kingdom (UK) and Australia have followed suit by drafting and implementing strategies and policies that outline how each nation intends to approach cyber security (Klimburg 2012). According to Pfleeger (2012), cyber security is the prevention and protection of cyber attacks by means of both technology and a human-centred approach. However, for a long time, technology-centred solutions such as anti-virus software, encryption, firewalls and more have been used in isolation. Up until it was acknowledged that in isolation, such solutions are not sufficient to mitigate the cyber-security risks. One of the reasons for this was that many users perceive these security measures as an obstacle (Pfleeger & Caputo 2012).

This user perception is often attributed to the difficulty of the security measure, and/or mistrust and misinterpretation of the security measure (Virginia Tech 2011). Additionally, a user-resistant behaviour was observed in a study that revealed that when users are prompted to change their passwords, the prompt was ignored or delayed; since the users perceived this security measure as being a waste of time (Pfleeger & Caputo 2012). Users often lack the awareness of cyber-security risks, making them easy targets for exploitation. Furthermore, humans are deemed as a threat not only to themselves, but also to others – and to national security at large (Dlamini & Modise 2012).

Due to the above-mentioned observations concerning the human factor, a more human-centred approach (i.e. a cyber-security culture) to cyber security is an imperative. Van Niekerk and von Solms (2010, p.476) view the establishment of a culture as the "...key to managing the human factor". However, what is lacking currently is a well-defined and delineated definition of the cyber-security culture domain. Therefore, the primary objective of this paper is to propose an ontological approach for formally defining a national cyber-security culture domain.

2. Cyber Security

The International Telecommunications Union (ITU) regards the creation of a cyber-security culture as an essential approach to cyber security (International Telecommunication Union, 2008). Recognizing this, many developed nations, such as the US, the UK and Canada are striving to cultivate such a culture amongst their respective citizens (Kortjan & von Solms 2014). South Africa (SA), in particular, has outlined the creation of a culture of cyber-security as a major objective of its draft cyber-security policy framework (SA Government gazette 2011).

One of the pillars of such a culture comprises awareness and education (Ghernouti-Hélie 2010). However, it is found that even users who possess more cyber-security knowledge do not necessarily act differently to those who lack any form of cyber-security awareness (Al-shehri 2012). Regardless, of the fact that the awareness level of the user positively affects the user behavior, there is still an apparent gap between the user awareness levels and respective practices and behavior (Furnell et al. 2008). Therefore, "cyber security needs the development of a cyber-security culture and acceptable user behaviour in the new reality of cyberspace..." (High-Level Experts Group (HLEG) 2008, p.103).

Having realized the role of cultivating a culture in pursuing cyber security it is important to formally and precisely define what is meant by a cyber-security culture. Even though the concept of fostering a cyber-security culture is used extensively, research that focuses particularly on cyber security culture is still at its infancy, and knowledge on the subject is not clearly bounded and defined. However, because of the relationship between information security and cyber security, it is reasonable to make the assumption that what applies in information security culture may also apply to cyber security culture.

Schein (1992, p.17) defines information security culture as a "pattern of shared basic assumptions that the group learned as it solved its problems of external adaptation and internal integration, that has worked well enough to be considered valid and, therefore, to be taught to new members as the correct way to perceive, think, and feel in relation to those problems". Similarly, in information security Schlienger and Teufel (2002) refer to the culture within the organization as that which "should support all activities in such a way that information security becomes a natural aspect in the daily activities of every employee".

Both the latter and former information security culture definitions deal with altering the behavior of users by instilling a certain way to "naturally behave" in daily life, a way that subscribes to certain information security assumptions. This is precisely the ultimate aim of the envisaged cyber security culture. A security culture considers the social, cultural, ethical aspects of a user in order to change the overall security behavior. Moreover, such a culture is cultivated over time and is evident in the behavior of users (Schlienger & Teufel 2002). There is, however, a lack of a clear definition of a security culture. Even though research that promotes the benefits of cultivating a security culture exists, supportive literature is lacking (da Veiga et al. 2007).

Consequently, in an attempt to formally define and represent a national cyber security culture domain, an ontological approach is proposed in this paper. Through such an approach, the aim is to better formalise cyber security culture, from a national point of view. Further details on this ontology are provided in the following section.

3. An Ontology for Knowledge Representation

The definition most cited of an ontology in the context of computer science was proposed by Gruber who defined an ontology as: "an explicit specification of a conceptualization" (Gruber 1993, p17). An ontology enables one to conceptualize a specific subject in a formal and explicit manner (Gruber 1993). It is also defined as "a technology that provides a way to exchange semantic information between people and systems. It consists of an encoded, common domain vocabulary and a description of the meaning of terms in the vocabulary" (Grobler et al. 2012, p.220). An ontology can be used to define and formalize a domain that is not explicitly defined (Fenz et al. 2009). Moreover, with this approach, the existing knowledge can be mapped together, in order to present a holistic view of a particular domain (Fenz & Ekelhart 2009). For these reasons, an ontological approach is appropriate for defining and formalizing the domain of a cyber-security culture.

In general, an ontology consists of two components: a descriptive component and a reasoning component (Grobler et al. 2012). The descriptive component captures the domain from the perspective of the domain experts; and it presents the domain information in a manner that is comprehensible to humans, and one that can be processed by computers. The reasoning component enables the ontology to make new deductions from the existing facts. From the descriptive angle, an ontology generally uses the following terms (Noy & McGuinness 2001):

- A domain – the subject area that is modelled by the ontology.
- Classes and subclasses – concepts embodied in the domain.
- Individuals – those typical of the class.
- Properties – it defines the relationships between two classes.
- Restrictions – a feature used to define and describe a class that is based on the relationships among the class participants.

From the perspective of ontology, Davis, Shrobe and Szolovits (1993, p.17), argued that if something is a surrogate (a substitute), it enables one to "determine [the] consequences by thinking rather than acting, that is, by reasoning about the world rather than taking actions". As such, with the use of ontology, one can draw inferences and reason about the world – without having to act. Additionally, the authors acknowledge that a surrogate is not immune to errors. Nevertheless, the main goal of knowledge representation is not perfection; but rather it is to create an ontology that fulfils its purpose, one which has the least amount of errors (Davis et al. 1993).

To develop such an ontology, it is important for one to have a clear understanding of the domain of interest, the classes, the individuals, the properties and restrictions. Such information can be acquired with the aid of the existing body of knowledge. Brinson, Robinson and Rogers (2006) attempted to define and formalize the cyber-forensic domain. These authors studied the existing knowledge on traditional forensics; and they argued towards a formal curriculum for cyber forensics. Another instance of an ontological approach is that of Wali, Chun and Geller (2013). These authors maintain that online cyber-security-educational resources are scattered; and this makes it difficult for users to locate the right learning resources at the right time. Consequently, they developed a cyber-security ontology with the aid of the existing cyber-security textbooks and security ontologies.

Likewise, Grobler, van Vuuren and Leenen (2012) also developed an ontology in their attempt to define and formalize a conceptualization of the cyber-security strategic environment domain. According to these authors, the use of an ontology for the cyber-security strategic environment could contribute to the development, implementation and roll out of a national cyber-security policy in SA. Furthermore, Fenz and Ekelhart (2009) also used an ontology in their attempt to formalize and holistically present information-security knowledge. According to these authors, they were driven by the apparent lack of any unified and well-defined information-security-risk-management process. In developing this ontology, the existing information-security best practices and standards were considered.

From the above-cited instances, it is evident that an ontological approach can be used to define, formalize and holistically present the knowledge of a domain that is rather poorly defined. Noy and McGuiness (2001) summarise the reasons for developing an ontology, as follows: To share a common understanding of the structure of information among people or software agents; to enable the re-use of domain knowledge; to make domain assumptions explicit; to distinguish domain knowledge from the operational knowledge; and to analyze this domain knowledge.

In the context of this study, an ontological approach would contribute to formalizing a national cyber-security culture domain. It could assist in eliminating the vagueness of the vocabulary that exists in the domain of cyber security. It could further ensure the integration and interoperability of concepts in the domain at hand. It would play a fundamental role in ensuring the complete and holistic conceptualization of the domain of a cyber-security culture. The following section will discuss this proposed ontology for the domain of a national cyber-security culture.

4. A National Cyber-Security Culture Domain

The previous section provided an overview of ontology; this section will introduce the proposed ontology for a national cyber-security culture domain. It will provide an overview of the knowledge base represented by the ontology; and it will further provide a brief on the development of the ontology.

4.1. Knowledge Base

As an initial attempt to model a national cyber-security culture domain, a study on cyber-security culture, focusing on awareness and education, was used as a foundation. This study was published in 2013 as an academic dissertation in fulfilment of the requirements for the Master of Technology degree (Kortjan 2013); and it was also published in a journal (Kortjan & von Solms 2014). Furthermore, additional sources were consulted, in order to gather additional information regarding the other constituents of a cyber-security culture.

In summary, in the above-mentioned academic dissertation, it was reasoned that a cyber-security culture has pillars; one of these pillars comprises awareness and education. This pillar was delineated in three forms: Awareness Campaigns; Formal Education; and Workforce Education. In terms of the Awareness campaigns, which were the main focus of the study, a national cyber-security awareness and education campaign entitled *iWiseMzansi* was suggested for SA. The name *iWiseMzansi* suggests an informative SA, hence the 'i', and a cyberwise SA, and hence the name 'wise'. "Mzansi" is an accepted name that refers to SA. It was further proposed that *iWiseMzansi* could reach the people of SA through sub-campaigns and initiatives that should include the following:

- *iWiseMzansi* Month – an annual cyber security-centred event aimed at all South African citizens.
- *iWiseMzansi* Community Outreach – an initiative intended to give everyone an opportunity to lend a helping hand and to participate in spreading cyber-security awareness and education to communities.
- *iWiseMzansi:* For All – an all-encompassing cyber-security educational website for the general public of SA.
- *iWiseMzansi:* For Schools – aimed at learners in primary and secondary schools, to ensure that cyber security forms part of the school curriculum.

It was further reasoned that for this pillar to stand, it has to be resourced, with a delineated target audience; and finally, it must have dedicated role-players with active roles. As previously mentioned, additional sources were consulted, in order to gather additional information on the other constituents of a cyber-security culture. Along with other useful deductions from these sources, additional cyber-security pillars were extrapolated, such as: Research and Development; Cyber-Security Measures; and Capacity Development (Wamala 2011; High-Level Experts Group (HLEG) 2008; Klimburg 2012).

The aforesaid pillars basically depict the following: to cultivate a cyber-security culture amongst users. Over and above the need for basic awareness and education, there has to be a strong component of research and development in order to be able to determine the current behavioural norms and other related factors. Additionally, as with information security, clear cyber-security assumptions and related measures need to be in place. Finally, the necessary capacity and various capabilities also need to be considered.

The information modelled in the proposed ontology for a national domain of a cyber-security culture is described in this section. Accordingly, the subsequent subsection presents this proposed ontology.

4.2. The Ontology

Reflecting on the existing knowledge, as previously discussed, the ontology was developed and implemented by using Protégé, an open-source ontological editor. Figure 1 presents the proposed ontology.

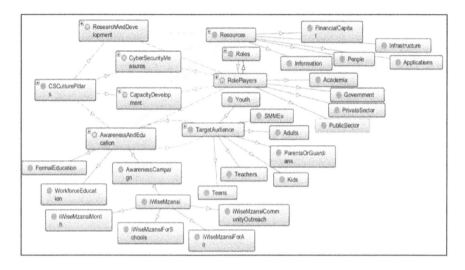

Figure 1: National Cyber-Security Culture Domain

Figure 1 presents the proposed high-level ontology model for a national cyber security culture domain. The concepts and relationships presented in the ontology will be elaborated in the development phases, in order to highlight the ontology model. The development the proposed ontology included the following phases that were adapted from Noy and McGuinness (2001): Defining classes in the ontology; arranging the classes in a taxonomic (subclass–superclass) hierarchy; defining the properties (relationships); and describing the permissible values for these slots; and defining individuals. These phases will be expanded further in the following subsections.

4.2.1. Classes and Taxonomic hierarchy

As previously mentioned, the domain at hand is that of a national cyber-security culture. The main classes of the domain are: *CSCulturePillars* (CS = Cyber Security), *ResearchandDevelopment*, *CyberSecurityMeasures*, *CapacityDevelopment*, *AwarenessandEducation*, *Resources*, *RolePlayers*, *Roles*, *and TargetAudience*. In the ontology these classes are arranged in a taxonomic hierarchy. Therefore some of these main classes have subclasses, which have further subclasses as well, as listed below:

- The *AwarenessandEducation* class has subclasses *AwarenessCampaigns*, *FormalEducation* and *WorkforceEducation*.

- The subclass *AwarenessCampaigns* also has a subclass *iWiseMzansi*.
- The subclass *iWiseMzansi* also has subclasses *iWiseMzansiMonth*, *iWiseMzansi*CommunityOutreach, *iWiseMzansiforAll* and *iWiseMzansiForSchools*.
- The *Resources* class has subclasses: *People, Information, Applications, Infrastructure* and *FinancialCapital*.
- The *RolePlayers* class has subclasses: *Academia, Government, PrivateSector, and PublicSector*.
- The *TargetAudience* class also has subclasses: *Kids, Teenagers, Youth, ParentsorGuardians, Adults, Teachers* and *SMMEs* (Small, Medium and Micro-sized Enterprises).

4.2.2. Relationships

It can be observed in Figure 1 that all the classes have a particular link to some or other class within the ontology. This link represents the relationships (properties) in which each class participates. These relationships are shown in Figure 2 below.

Figure 2: Defined Object Properties

As previously mentioned, an ontology has reasoning abilities. As such, the automated reasoner in Protégé can make inferences in the ontology by using the classes defined, as well as the properties in Figure 2.

4.2.3. Individuals

The last phase in the development of an ontology model is the identification of the individuals, as the instances of a class. The individuals that can be created in this proposed ontology are those of *the iWiseMzansi* class, i.e. iWiseMzansi Week, iWiseMzansi Community Outreach, iWiseMzansi: For All and iWiseMzansi: For Schools.

At this stage, the proposed ontology for the national cyber-security culture domain is still a high-level ontology that has only presented the descriptive components of the domain. Even so, it can be said that from a descriptive point of view, an explicit and formal conceptualization of the domain has been presented. Following are some concluding remarks and future plans from the study.

5. Conclusion and Future Work

It has come to the attention of many nations that although cyberspace offers many positive benefits, it also brings with it a number of safety and security implications. In recognition of this, implementing a culture of cyber-security is increasingly becoming a global pursuit. However, what is lacking currently is a well-defined and delineated definition of the cyber-security culture domain itself. Accordingly, this paper has proposed an ontology whereby this environment can now be formally defined.

In the future, further data on a cyber-security culture will be gathered in order to add depth to the ontology. A general morphological analysis (GMA), which is "simply an ordered way of looking at things" (Ritchey 2011, p.7), will be employed, in order to obtain more insights on the cyber-security culture from the relevant experts. The GMA will take place early in 2015. This technique is employed to define, the structure, and to analyze the complex issue of the policy driven, such as a cyber-security culture (Ritchey 2011). As such, the reasoning end of the ontology will be incorporated when the lower levels of the ontology have been added.

6. References

Al-shehri, Y., 2012. Information Security Awareness and Culture. *British Journal of Arts and Social Sciences*, 6(1), pp.61–69.

Brinson, A., Robinson, A. & Rogers, M., 2006. A cyber forensics ontology: Creating a new approach to studying cyber forensics. *Digital Investigation*, 3(2006), pp.37–43.

Davis, R., Shrobe, H. & Szolovits, P., 1993. What is in a Knowledge Representation? *AI Magazine*, p.21.

Dlamini, I.Z., Taute, B. & Radebe, J., 2011. Framework for an African Policy Towards Creating Cyber-Security Awareness. *Security*, pp.15–31.

Dlamini, Z. & Modise, M., 2012. Cyber-security awareness initiatives in South Africa: a synergy approach. In *7th International Conference on Information Warfare and Security*. USA: Academic Conferences International.

Fenz, S. & Ekelhart, A., 2009. Formalizing information security knowledge. *4th International Symposium on Information, Computer, and Communications Security - ASIACCS '09*, p.183.

Fenz, S., Pruckner, T. & Manutscheri, A., 2009. Ontological mapping of information security best-practice guidelines. Lecture Notes in Business Information Processing, 21, pp.49–60.

Furnell, S., Tsaganidi, V. & Phippen, A., 2008. Security beliefs and barriers for novice Internet users. *Computers & Security*, 27(7-8), pp.235–240.

Ghernouti-Hélie, S., 2010. A National Strategy for an Effective Cybersecurity Approach and Culture. In *2010 International Conference on Availability, Reliability and Security*. Ieee, pp. 370–373.

Grobler, M., van Vuuren, J. & Leenen, L., 2012. Implementation of a Cyber Security Policy in South Africa: Reflection on Progress and the Way Forward. *ICT Critical Infrastructures and Society*, pp.215–225.

Gruber, T.R., 1993. A Translation Approach to Portable Ontology Specifications by a Translation Approach to Portable Ontology Specifications. *Knowledge Acquisition*, 5(April), pp.199–220.

High-Level Experts Group (HLEG), 2008. *ITU Global Cybersecurity Agenda High-Level Experts Group (HLEG) Global Strategic Report*, Geneva, Switzerland.

International Telecommunication Union, 2008. *Global Security Report*.

Klimburg, A., 2012. National cyber security framework manual 1st ed. Alexander Klimburg, ed., Tallinn: NATO CCD COE Publications.

Kortjan, N., 2013. *A Cyber Security Awareness and Education Framework for South Africa*. Nelson Mandela Metropolitan University.

Kortjan, N. & Von Solms, R. 2014. A conceptual framework for cyber-security awareness and education in SA. *South African Computer Journal, 52, 29-41.*, 2014(52), pp.29–41.

Moses-Òkè, R., 2012. Cyber capacity without cyber security: A case study of Nigeria's national policy for information technology (NPFIT). *The Journal of Philosophy, Science & Law*, 12, pp.1–14.

Van Niekerk, J.F. & Von Solms, R., 2010. Information-security culture: A management perspective. *Computers & Security*, 29(2010), pp.476–486.

Noy, N.F. & McGuinness, D.L., 2001. Ontology Development 101 : A Guide to Creating Your First Ontology, Available at: http://protege.stanford.edu/publications/ontology_development/ontology101.pdf.

Pfleeger, S.L. & Caputo, D.D., 2012. Leveraging behavioral science to mitigate cyber-security risk. *Computers & Security*, 31(2012), pp.597–611.

Ritchey, T. 2011. General Morphological Analysis (GMA). In Risk, Governance and Society (Vol. 17, pp. 7–19).

RSA, 2014. *The current state of cybercrime: An Inside Look at the Changing Threat Landscape*, Available at: www.emc.com/rsa.

SA Government gazette, 2011. Draft National Cybersecurity-Policy Framework for South Africa. , p.33. Available at: http://www.cyanre.co.za/national-cybersecurity-policy.pdf.

Schein, E., 1992. *Organizational culture and leadership. 2nd edn. Jossey- Bass; 1992* 2nd Edition, San Francisco: Jossey-Bass.

Schlienger, T. & Teufel, S., 2002. Information security culture – from analysis to change. In *In Security in the Information Society*. US: Springer, pp. 191–201.

Von Solms, R. & van Niekerk, J., 2013. From information security to cyber security. *Computers & Security*, (2013), pp.1–6.

Da Veiga, A., Martins, N. & Eloff, J.H.., 2007. Information security culture – validation of an assessment instrument. *Southern African Business Review*, 11(1), pp.147–166.

Virginia Tech, 2011. When users resist. *Pamplin: College of Business Magazine*. Available at: http://www.magazine.pamplin.vt.edu/fall11/passwordsecurity.html [Accessed Nov 11, 2014].

Wali, A., Chun, S.A. & Geller, J., 2013. A Boot-strapping Approach for Developing a Cyber-security Ontology, Using Textbook-Index Terms., *2013 International Conference on Availability, Reliability and Security*, pp.569–576.

Wamala, F., 2011. *ITU National Cybersecurity Strategy Guide*, Geneva, Switzerland.

An Information Security Culture Model Validated with Structural Equation Modelling

N. Martins and A. Da Veiga

University of South Africa, PO Box 392, UNISA 0003, South Africa
e-mail: martin@unisa.ac.za; dveiga@unisa.ac.za

Abstract

Information security culture must be considered as part of the information security programme to direct employee behaviour. Such a culture can contribute to the protection of information and minimise the risk that employee behaviour poses. This paper proposes a theoretical model, i.e. an information security culture model (ISCM) with four mechanisms (i.e. management, policies, awareness and compliance) that potentially influence information security culture positively. ISCM is based on the information security culture assessment (ISCA) questionnaire dimensions that are correlated with the theoretical mechanisms (dimensions). The theoretical model is validated through structural equation modelling (SEM) using empirical data derived from an ISCA assessment. This research produces a sound theoretical information security culture model, which is supported by the empirical study and further confirms the research hypothesis that management, policies, awareness and compliance contribute to an information security-positive culture as represented by the validated model.

Keywords

Information security culture, theoretical model, empirical model, policies, awareness, management, compliance

1. Introduction

An information security-positive culture is an important aspect to address when implementing controls to protect organisational information (Furnell & Clarke, 2012; Furnell & Thomson, 2009; Ruighaver, Maynard, & Chang, 2007; Schlienger & Teufel, 2005). An information security-positive culture is evident when information is processed in a secure manner by employees, at all times, whilst preserving the integrity, availability and confidentiality of information and abiding by privacy requirements. This can suffice only when employees exhibit compliance behaviour in line with regulatory requirements and organisational policies. Employees need to have a positive attitude towards the processing of information in order to exhibit acceptable behaviour, which will become the manner in which information is processed over time that postulates in the culture. Employees will be able to comply only if they are supported by management and if there are adequate processes and technology safeguards in place to facilitate such compliance. A combination of people, process and technology safeguards will, together, aid in inculcating an information security-positive culture. Such a culture can also be referred to as a "healthy" or "strong" information security culture. This culture guides employees to behave in a certain manner, depicts what is important for the organisation to protect information and defines how employees should interact with information and what they should strive for (Plunkett and Attner 1994). If employees have shared beliefs and values around the aforementioned concepts they develop a group sense of how to process information securely, which they can use as reference to direct their own interactions with information (Plunkett and Attner 1994).

However, risk is introduced if the organisational culture is not conducive towards the protection of information. In such a culture, employee behaviour – still considered as one of the main threats to the protection of information (PwC 2014, Ponemon 2013) – could lead to information security incidents and breaches. As such, organisations require guidance to "inculcate" or "develop" a strong information security culture whereby the protection of information becomes "the way things are done" in the organisation. In this research we propose to use an information security culture assessment (ISCA) questionnaire (Da Veiga & Martins, 2015) in a study to confirm the theoretical model by means of an empirical model that can serve as guidance for organisations to influence the information security culture positively.

2. Background

There are various mechanisms that influence the development of organisational culture, which is a combination of internal (e.g. organisational processes and tangible assets) and external mechanisms (social system and regulators or competitors) (Plunkett and Attner 1994). It is generally recognised that management plays a significant role in influencing an organisational culture (Johnson & Goetz, 2007). Similarly, employees play a role as they need to accept the culture which is facilitated through training (Plunkett and Attner, 1994), such as induction and annual information security compliance training.

Various researchers have investigated an information security culture and the mechanisms that could potentially influence the culture and behaviour of employees (Schlienger and Teufel 2005; Thomson et al. 2006; Kraemer, Carayon, & Clem, 2009; Ruighaver et al. 2007; Van Niekerk and Von Solms 2010; Furnell and Thompson 2009; Van Niekerk and Von Solms, 2010; Furnell & Rajendran, 2012). Management, policies, awareness and compliance are some of the prominent mechanisms that could potentially influence information security culture – see table 1. For the purposes of this research, individual employee mechanisms such as intrinsic and extrinsic motivation (Padayachee 2012, Furnell & Rajendran, 2012) and mechanisms external to the organisation, for example national culture (Hoffstede 1980), are excluded.

Mechanisms influencing information security culture	Description
Management (Hu, Dinev, Hart, & Cooke, 2012; Johnson & Goetz, 2007; Knapp, Marshall, Rainer, & Ford, 2006; Wilderom, Van den Berg, & Wiersma, 2012)	Management or leadership in the organisation play a critical role in forming the desired culture. They need to define the organisation's information security strategy and lead by example.
Information Security Policies (Vroom and Von Solms 2004, ISF 2000, Boxand Pottas 2013)	Employees' knowledge and perception of information security policy rules and procedures could influence the information security culture positively. The information security policy is a critical cornerstone to direct the information security culture and serve as a foundation to create shared values and beliefs.
Awareness and Training (Nosworthy 2000, Thomson et al. 2006, Parsons et al. 2014, Herold 2011, Da Veiga and Martins 2015)	Information security awareness and training is implemented to educate employees to understand the risk to information and the relevant controls to use and abide by. Training and awareness has been proven to have a positive impact on the information security culture over time.
Compliance (Parsons et al. 2014)	The workforce's knowledge of information security policy and procedures will have a positive impact on the attitude towards the information security policies and compliance. In an organisation where there is a strong or healthy information security culture one would expect compliance as a visible trait of the culture.

Table 1: Factors influencing information security culture

The following hypotheses are subsequently identified:

H1: Management has a positive and strong influence on policies

H2: Policies have a positive and strong influence on awareness

H3: Awareness has a positive and strong influence on compliance

H4: Management, policies, awareness and compliance contribute to an information security-positive culture as represented by a validated model

Although researchers have investigated what mechanisms could influence the information security culture there is no empirical research where a validated and reliable information security culture instrument has been deployed to derive data to develop a structural equation model for information security culture.

The information security culture assessment (ISCA) (Da Veiga & Martins, 2015) tool is an example of a validated assessment instrument whereby a survey is conducted in the organisation to measure the level of information security culture. In previous research it has been empirically proven that ISCA can be deployed successfully to monitor and improve the information security culture. There is, though, a need to understand the influence between the various constructs (sub-dimensions) in ISCA in order to understand the critical mechanisms (dimensions) that influence the information security culture positively.

In the next section we propose a conceptual model for information security culture and validate it using empirical data through structural equation modelling (SEM). The objective is to further improve the ISCA by understanding the underlying influences of the constructs in the questionnaire and how it influences the development of an information security-positive culture.

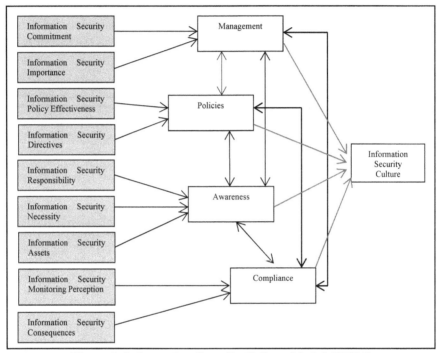

Figure 1: Information Security Culture Model (ISCM)

3. Information Security Culture Model (ISCM)

The constructs of ISCA were used to develop the conceptual Information Security Culture Model (ISCM). The ISCA is comprised of 45 statements across nine constructs. Figure 1 portrays the ISCA constructs that could influence the factors identified in table 1 which, in turn, could influence the information security culture.

The model proposes that the information security culture constructs on the left have a positive influence on the mechanisms, namely management, policies, awareness and compliance. These four mechanisms have a positive influence on each other and in turn have a positive influence on the information security culture. The possible relationships between the constructs will be tested statistically and discussed in the next sections to determine whether the proposed theoretical information security culture model is valid and could influence information security culture.

4. Research method and data collection

An ISCA was conducted in 2013 in an international organisation. The convenience sampling method (Brewerton and Millward 2001) was used to distribute the electronic ISCA to the employees. The required sample size for the overall data and biographical areas were calculated using the method of Krejcie and Darryl (1970) which allows for a marginal error of 5% and confidence level of 95%.

Three hundred and seventeen responses were required and 2 159 employees participated, giving a 38,7% response rate from the 8 220 employees. Seventy-six per cent of the participants were non-managerial employees, 20.8% were managers, and 2.4% executives. Only 14.8% worked in IT and the remainder of the respondents in other business functions. Responses were received across 13 business units and 12 countries.

5. Data analysis and results

5.1. Factor analysis and reliability

To reduce the dimensionality of the data, Principle Axis Factoring (PAF) with IBM SPSS Statistics 22 was used to examine patterns of correlations among the questions used to measure the respondents' perceptions regarding information security.

The factorability of the correlation matrix was investigated using Pearson's product-moment correlation coefficient. Preliminary distribution analyses indicated that the assumptions of normality, linearity and homoscedasticity were not violated. The correlation matrix demonstrated a number of coefficients of 0.3 and above. The Kaiser-Meyer-Olkin value was 0.968, well above the recommended minimum value of 0.6 (Kaiser, 1970, 1974) and the Bartlett's Test of Sphericity (Bartlett, 1954) reached statistical significance, $p<.001$. Thus, the correlation matrix was deemed factorable.

The ISCA is comprised of questions measuring information security knowledge and culture. The information security culture questions are measured using a 5-point Likert scale, question 19 (Q19) to question 72 (Q72). These 52 questions were initially subjected to PAF and seven of the variables demonstrated very little contribution to the solution with communalities of less than 0.3. These variables were left out of the analysis one by one to see the effect of each. This resulted in a seven-factor solution with two variables (Q47 and Q52) having only loadings of less than 0.3. Thus, it was decided to exclude Q47 and Q52 from the analysis. The remaining 45 variables resulted in a seven-factor solution, explaining 51.42% of the variation in the data.

Due to the large sample, it was decided to allow factor loadings of 0.3 and higher since increasing this cut-of value to 0.4 would result in many more questions that would need to be excluded from the solution. Promax rotation, a rotation method that allows for correlation among the latent factors, was performed. Excluding factor loadings of less than 0.3 resulted in a reasonably simple structure (Thurstone, 1947), with each of the seven factors showing a number of strong loadings, although there are a number of cross-loading situations that need careful interpretation.

Two dimensions were subjected to second-order factor analysis to determine if they could be further analysed. The second-order factor analyses revealed two sub-factors for each of the two dimensions. Each of the extracted factors demonstrates acceptable (or almost) internal consistency as illustrated by the Cronbach's alpha coefficients between 0.909 and 0.545 as shown in table 2. All the values meet the minimum accepted criteria and are above 0.5 (Nunnally & Bernstein, 1994). This analysis confirms the internal consistency and reliability of the ISCA questionnaire.

Factors (Constructs)	Description	Cronbach's Alpha
F1 – Information Security Commitment	Commitment from an organisational, divisional and employee perspective regarding the protection of information and implementation controls.	0.909
F2 – Information Security Importance	The perceived importance of information security by management which includes executives and a divisional perspective.	0.863
F3 – Information Security Responsibility	Information security responsibility from an end-user perspective.	0.779
F4 – Information Security Necessity	Information security necessity is established by focusing on specific concepts such as people, time, money and the impact of changes.	0.847
F5 – Information Security Policy Effectiveness	Assesses the perception of whether the information security policy is understandable and practical and whether it was successfully communicated.	0.848
F6 – Information Security Monitoring Perception	The perception regarding monitoring and disciplinary action.	0. 625
F7 – Information Security Assets	Assesses users' perceptions of the protection of information assets in hard copy and electronic format.	0.915
F8 - Information Security Directives	The perception as to whether the organisation has clear directives for the protection of employee and client information.	0.888
F9 - Information Security Consequences	Assesses the perception pertaining to recording of and actions taken in the event of non-compliance.	0. 545
Overall		0.849

Table 2: Cronbach's alpha coefficients for the ISCA constructs

5.2. Structural equation modelling (SEM)

SEM has been described as a collection of statistical techniques that allows examination of a set of relationships between one or more independent variables, and one or more dependent variables, either discrete or continuous in both independent and dependent cases (Tabachnick & Fidell, 1983). A confirmatory factor analysis

(CFA) was conducted in order to develop and specify the measurement model (Hair et al., 2010). The AMOS (Analysis of Moment Structures) computer program was used to conduct the CFA. The CFA was conducted using the nine factors identified during the PAF. Once the measurement model has been specified, its validity needs to be determined, which depends on establishing acceptable levels of goodness-of-fit. According to Hair et al. (2010), goodness-of-fit (GOF) indicates how well the specified model reproduces the observed covariance matrix among the indicator items. These results are portrayed in table 3. Except for the chi-square index, all the other GOF indices were at a recommended level (Hair et al., 2010).

Indices	Value	Accepted
Chi-square (CMIN)	4057.386	No
Ratio of CMIN to its degrees of freedom (df)	792	Yes, good fit
P-value	0.000	-
Goodness-of-fit index (GFI)	0.914	Yes, good fit
Root mean square error of approximation (RMSEA)	0.044	Yes, good fit
Incremental fit index (IFI) - Bollen's IFI	0.934	Yes, good fit
Tucker Lewis index (TLI)	0.928	Yes, good fit
Comparative fit index (CFI)	0.934	Yes, good fit

Note: Conventional cut-off: Good fit is indicated by GFI>= .90; TLI, IFI and CFI>= .90 (Garson, 2010)

Table 3: Goodness-of-fit indices for the overall measurement model

The information security culture structural equation model developed is portrayed in figure 2.

6. Discussion

The first hypothesis, namely that management has a positive and strong influence on policies, is confirmed. The second hypothesis, namely that policies have a positive and strong influence on awareness, is also confirmed. The third hypothesis, namely that awareness has a positive and strong influence on compliance, is also confirmed. The last hypothesis, namely that management, policies, awareness and compliance contribute to the measurement of information security culture represented by a validated model, was also confirmed. The results of the SEM provide an indication as to where researchers can focus their information security efforts when they intend to enhance the information security of an organisation by using ISCM.

The results of the SEM model confirm the existence of the four main dimensions (or mechanisms) namely, policies, management, awareness and compliance, (2nd order latent constructs) and nine sub-dimensions (9 ISCA constructs) as depicted in Figure 1. In this model, the focus was on the overall relationships between the different sub- dimensions of the four main dimensions which are in line with the theory and proposed hypothesis. The results of the standardised regression weights, correlations and covariances are all significant. The results of the squared multiple correlations (curved arrows) in figure 2) indicate very high correlations between the main dimensions of management and policies (.95) and awareness and compliance (.76). There are, however, lower correlations between policies and compliance (.63) and management and awareness (.62). This is important for management to take note of as it indicates that management has a high influence on policies and that by focussing on providing adequate direction, and though management support, the information security culture can be positively influenced. Similarly, if employees are aware of information security requirements they will behave in a more compliant manner.

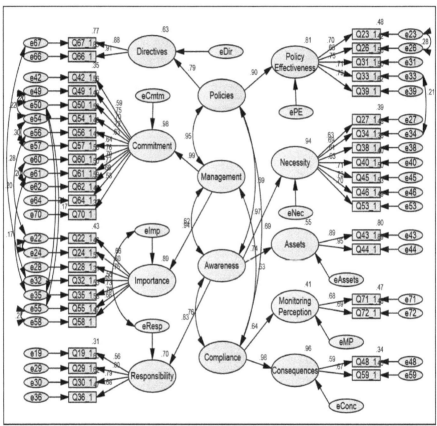

Note: → Regression weights (straight lines), ∩ Correlations (curved lines), 0.00 Squared multiple correlations (figures above the circle)

Figure 2: Information Security Culture Structural Equation Model (SEM)

In interpreting the relationship (standardised regression weights as indicated by the straight results on the arrows in figure 2) between the main dimensions and sub-dimensions, most indicate positive to high relationships. The highest relationships are between management and commitment (.99) and importance (.89), policies and policy effectiveness (.90), compliance and consequences (.98). In other words, if management is committed and perceive information security as important they can influence the culture positively. The lowest relationships are between compliance and monitoring perception (.64) and awareness and assets (.63) and necessity (.69). This could indicate that compliance is not necessarily influenced by employees' perception on whether they are comfortable if they are being monitored, thus, they might still exhibit compliance behaviour irrespective of their perception regarding monitoring. Also, employee awareness about the protection of information is not necessarily influenced by distinguishing between hard copy and electronic information. The low relationship between awareness and necessity could indicate that awareness is not necessarily influenced positively through perceptions relating to the necessity of adequate resources to protect information, or employees' views on change, as measured through this dimension. As organisational culture represents a common perception held by the organisation's members (Martins and Martins, 2010) it is important to note that each organisation's culture will differ. This will subsequently have an impact on each organisation's information security culture.

7. Conclusion

This research proposed a theoretical information security culture model (ISCM) with the objective of identifying mechanisms that could positively influence the information security culture. The theoretical model was validated using structural equation modelling (SEM) to assist in answering the hypothesis. The research methodology chosen for this research produced a sound theoretical information security culture model which was supported by the empirical study. The exploratory factor analysis produced a reliable factor structure which was confirmed by the SEM confirmatory factor analysis. The SEM methodology enabled the researchers to test and confirm the main dimensions and sub-dimensions influencing information security culture. This ISCM can be used by researchers and organisations to direct their information security initiatives to be in line with the four main dimensions, namely management, policies, awareness and compliance, in order to positively influence information security culture. Their efforts can successfully be monitored by conducting the ISCA survey which will also benchmark data to monitor improvements and developmental areas.

8. References

Bartlett, M.S. (1954), "A note on the multiplying factors for various chi square approximations", *Journal of the Royal Statistical Society*, Vol. 16, No. B, pp296 – 298.

Brewerton, P. and Millward, L. (2002), *Organizational research methods*, Sage Publications, London, ISBN 9780761971009.

Box, D. and Pottas, D. (2013)," Improving information security behaviour in the healthcare context", Procedia Technology, Vol. 9, No. 2013, pp1093 – 1103.

Catell, R.B. (1966), "The scree test for the number of factors", *Multivariate Behavioral Research*, Vol.1, pp245 – 276.

Da Veiga, A., and Martins, N. (2015), Improving the information security culture through monitoring and implementation actions illustrated through a case study, *Computers & Security*, Vol. 2015, No. 9, pp162–176.

Furnell, S., and Clarke, N. (2012). Power to the people? the evolving recognition of human aspects of security. Computers and Security, 31(8), 983–988.

Furnell, S., and Rajendran, A. (2012), "Understanding the influences on information security behaviour", *Computer Fraud and Security*, Vol. 2012, No. March, pp12–15.

Furnell, S., and Thomson, K. L. (2009), "From culture to disobedience: Recognising the varying user acceptance of IT security", *Computer Fraud and Security*, Vol. 2009, No. 3, pp5–10.

Garson, G.D. (2010), "Structural equation modeling example using WinAMOS: the Wheaton study", http://faculty.chass.ncsu.edu/garson/PA765/structur.htm , (Accessed 10 January 2015).

Hair J. F. Jr., Black W. C., Babin B. J., Anderson R. E. And Tatham R. L. (2006). Multivariate data analysis (6th Ed.). Prentice Hall. New Jersey.

Herold, R. (2011), *Managing an information security and privacy awareness and training program*, Taylor and Francis Group, Boca Raton.

Hoffstede, G. (1980), *Culture's consequences: International differences in work-related values*, Sage Publications, Beverley Hills, ISBN 9783423508070.

Hu, Q., Dinev, T., Hart, P., and Cooke, D. (2012), "Managing employee compliance with information security policies : The Critical role of top management and organizational culture ", *Decision Sciences Journal*, Vol. 4, No. 4, pp615–660.

Information Security Forum (ISF). *Information security culture – A preliminary investigation.* s.l.; 2000.

Johnson, M. E., and Goetz, E. (2007), "Embedding information security into the organization", IEEE Security and Privacy, Vol. 2007, No. 5, 16–24.

Kaiser, H. F., (1970), "A second-generation little Jiffy", *Psychometrica*, Vol. 35, No.4, pp410–415.

Kaiser, H. F., (1974)," An index of factorial simplicity", *Psychometrica*, Vol.39, No.1, pp 31–36.

Knapp, K. J., Marshall, T. E., Rainer, R. K., and Ford, F. N. (2006), "Information security: management's effect on culture and policy", Information Management and Computer Security, Vol. 14, No. 1, pp24–36.

Kraemer, S., Carayon, P., and Clem, J. (2009), "Human and organizational factors in computer and information security: Pathways to vulnerabilities", Computers and Security, Vol. 28, No. 7, 509–520.

Krejcie, R.V., Morgan, D.W. (1970), "Determining sample size for research activities", Educational and Psychological Measurement, Vol. 30, No. 1970, pp607-610.

Martins, N, and Martins, E. C. (2004). *Organisational culture*. In S. P. Robbins, & G. Roodt (Eds.), Organisational behaviour: Global and Southern African perspectives. Cape Town: Pearson Education South Africa.

Nosworthy, J.D. (2000), "Implementing information security in the 21st century – do you have the balancing factors?", Computers and Security, Vol. 19, No. 4, pp337-347.

Nunnally, J. & Bernstein, I.H. (1994). Psychometric theory (3rd ed.). New York: McGraw-Hill.

Padayachee K. (2012), "Taxonomy of compliant information security behaviour", Computers and Security, Vol. 2012, No. 31, pp673-80.

Parsons, K., McCormac, A., Butavicius, M., Pattinson, M., and Jerram, C. (2014), "Determining employee awareness using the Human Aspects of Information Security Questionnaire (HAIS-Q)", Computers and Security, Vol. 2014, No. 42, pp165–176.

Plunkett, W.R and Attner, R.F. (1994), *Introduction to management*, fifth edition, International Thomson Publishing, California, ISBN: 0534933211.

Ponemon Institute. (2013), "Cost of data breach study: Global analysis benchmark research sponsored by Symantec", http://www.symantec.com, (Accessed 10 June 2014).

PricewaterhouseCoopers (PwC). (2014), "The global state of information security survey",http://www.pwc.com/gx/en/consulting-services/information-security-survey/download.jhtml, (Accessed 10 June 2014).

Ruighaver, A. B., Maynard, S. B., and Chang, S. (2007), "Organisational security culture: Extending the end-user perspective", *Computers and Security*, Vol. 2007, No. 26, pp56–62.

Schlienger, T. and Teufel, S. (2005), "Tool supported management of information security culture: An application to a private bank", in Sasaki, R., Okamoto, E. and Yoshiura, H., (eds) *Security and privacy in the age of ubiquitous computing*, Kluwer, Japan.

Tabachnick, B.G. and Fidell, L.S., (2007), *Using multivariate statistics (5th Ed.)*. Pearson Education, Boston, ISBN: 0205459382

Thomson K., Van Solms R. and Louw L. (2006), "Cultivating an organisational information security culture", *Computer Fraud and Security*, Vol. 2006, No. 10, pp 7-11.

Thurstone, L.L. (1947), *Multiple factor analysis*, University of Chicago Press, Chicago, Libraries Australia ID23945090.

Van Niekerk, J. F., and Von Solms, R. (2010). "Information security culture: A management perspective", *Computers and Security*, Vol. 2010 No. 29, pp. 476–486.

Vroom, C. and Von Solms, R. (2004), "Towards information security behavioural compliance", *Computers and Security*, Vol. 2004, No. 23: 191-198.

Wilderom, C. P. M., Van den Berg, P. T., and Wiersma, U. J. (2012), "A longitudinal study of the effects of charismatic leadership and organizational culture on objective and perceived corporate performance", *Leadership Quarterly*, Vol. 23, No. 5, pp835–848.

The Influence of Information Security Policies on Information Security Culture: Illustrated through a Case Study

A. Da Veiga

College of Science, Engineering and Technology, School of Computing, University of South Africa, P.O. Box 392, UNISA 0003, South Africa (email: dveiga@unisa.ac.za)

Abstract

An information security-positive culture is required in organisations where employees process information in line with its confidentiality, sensitivity and privacy requirements. The information security policy serves as a critical cornerstone in guiding employee behaviour to direct the protection of information. Employees must be aware of and understand the information security policy requirements they have to abide by in order to process information securely and thereby contribute to an information security-positive culture.

This study outlines a case study over eight years in which empirical research was conducted to examine the level of information security culture between employees who had read the information security policy and employees who had not read the policy. It was found that the overall information security culture average scores were significantly more positive for employees who read the information security policy when compared with employees who had not, illustrating the positive impact of the policy on the information security culture in the context of an Information Security Culture Assessment (ISCA). The study confirms theoretical research stating the importance of information security policies as part of an information security programme and the governance of information to instil an information security-positive culture.

Keywords

Information security policy, information security culture, assessment, survey, awareness, behaviour, empirical data

1. Introduction

One of the top priorities of organisations in managing information and minimising risks to it is having a written information security policy (PwC 2014). This policy provides the formal direction and intent of management for the protection of information in the organisation. It outlines the framework for setting control objectives and controls to be implemented to mitigate risk to information (ISO/IEC 27001 2013).

The information security policy is implemented through a combination of people, processes and technology controls. From a people perspective, the policy directs the manner in which employees process information and establishes a baseline from which ethical decisions are made when dealing with organisational information. The policy influences the way in which employees interact with information assets and ultimately directs their behaviour to be compliant with legislative, regulatory and contractual requirements.

The information security policy is a critical success factor to establish an information security-positive culture in an organisation. Employees' knowledge and perception of information security policy rules and procedures influence information security behaviour and potentially the information security culture (ISF 2000, Box and Pottas 2013). The more aware employees are of the information security policy and procedures, the more positive their attitude becomes towards it, resulting in risk-averse behaviour (Parsons et al. 2014). If an information security-positive culture is present, it will improve the information security (Bulgurcu et al. 2010) and enable an environment in which information is protected from a people, process and technology perspective.

2. Aim of the paper

This study aimed to determine whether awareness of the information security policy has a significant influence on instilling an information security-positive culture. A contribution of this research is to provide empirical evidence to confirm literature perspectives indicating that the information security policy could influence the information security culture positively. Another is to provide empirical evidence that an information security-positive culture can be inculcated over time through the awareness and understanding of the information security policy. In support of the aforementioned the research explored the following research question:

- Do employees that have read the information security policy have a stronger information security-positive culture compared to those who have not?

3. Background

There are various studies that aim to establish how to influence employees to comply with information security policies. It is generally concluded that one of the internal influences on policy compliance is the organisational culture. The organisational culture influences the effective implementation of the information security policy as it impacts the perception employees have about information (Knapp et al. 2009). As part of this theory, awareness and training are regarded as two of the processes required to govern the implementation of the information security policy. Von Solms and Von Solms (2004) suggest that policies can in turn define the organisational culture using continuous education and communication. Thomson, Von Solms and Louw (2006) propose the information security shared tacit espoused values (MISSTEV) model. The aim of this model is to instil behaviour that is in line with the information security policy and that could lead to the cultivation of an information security culture.

Apart from awareness and training, there are various other factors that also influence perceptions of employees' compliance with information security policies. Herath and Rao (2009) identify three facts that influence policy compliance, namely threat perceptions about the severity of breaches, organisational commitment, social influences and resource availability. Cross-cultural differences can also influence ethical decision making (Hoffstede 1980, Jackson 2000), the normative belief system of employees (Pahnila et al. 2007), the perception of senior management commitment and users' personal values and standards of conduct (Leach 2003), the use of rewards to motivate compliance (Bulgurcu et al. 2010) and the readability and understandability of the policy language (Goucher 2012) are all factors that could potentially influence employees' compliance with information security policies.

More recently, Padayachee (2012) proposed a taxonomy for compliant information security behaviour by considering extrinsic (e.g. regulatory requirements) and intrinsic (e.g. employee competence, their commitment, ethical values, personality, values and attitude) motivations. A crucial conclusion from Ifinedo's (2014) research is that attitude towards compliance has the greatest effect on information security policy compliance. Similarly, Siponen et al. (2014) argue that employees' perceived severity, vulnerability, self-efficacy, normative beliefs and attitude have a positive and significant impact on their intention to comply with information security policies and procedures.

While these studies focus on factors that influence or motivate employees to comply with the information security policy, some dimensions have not yet been tested empirically. One such dimension is the influence of awareness of the information security policy on the information security culture by comparing the culture of employees who have read the policy with those who have not, within the context of an Information Security Culture Assessment (ISCA) (Da Veiga and Martins 2014).

ISCA can be used to assess employees' attitude towards policy compliance and information security culture aspects. The outcome can be used to determine if there is a strong information security culture present in the organisation. A strong information security culture postulates that employees exhibit compliance behaviour, have coherent values towards protecting information and thus minimise the threat of the human element to information.

4. Development of an information security culture

To understand what impact an information security policy has on the information security culture, how such a culture develops must be understood. The development of an organisational culture can be leveraged off to ascertain how an information security culture develops. An organisational culture develops where executives and management develop a vision and strategy for the organisation. The vision and strategy are often depicted in organisational policies and procedures. Employee behaviour will become evident as guided by the vision, strategy and policies. Over time an organisational culture emerges that encapsulates the vision and strategy as well as the experiences employees had when implementing them. This culture will incorporate specific organisational behaviour (Hellriegel et al. 1998).

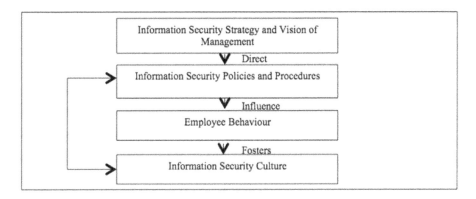

Figure 1: Development of an information security culture

Similarly, an information security culture develops in an organisation in the same way an organisational culture develops, see Figure 1. The board is responsible for ensuring that information assets are managed effectively and should approve the organisation's information security strategy (King III). The board will delegate responsibility for implementing information security and management needs to demonstrate their commitment and buy-in. They will provide the direction and intent for the protection of information through the information security policy. They could, for instance, state in the policy that information is regarded as a valuable business asset whose integrity, confidentiality and availability must be maintained throughout the information life cycle. The policy will govern employee behaviour. In turn, employees will respond to the policy as influenced by extrinsic and intrinsic factors. The information security culture that emerges could be conducive to the protection of information or hamper it. It is therefore crucial to assess the information security culture that has emerged and to determine whether it is in line with the initial information security strategy and vision of management.

The ISCA can aid management in conducting a reality check and taking corrective action to redirect the information security culture. Statistical analysis of the ISCA data can provide insight into the factors that have to be included to influence employees' perception of and attitude towards the information security policy and ultimately contribute to an information security-positive culture.

5. Research methodology

This research study comprised a quantitative study in which a survey was conducted at 4 intervals over 8 years in an international organisation as described in the paragraphs below.

5.1. Measuring instrument

To establish the impact of an information security policy on the information security culture, a validated information security culture instrument (questionnaire) must be used to measure the level of information security culture, as well as to monitor the impact of the interventions. For the purpose of this study the information security culture assessment (ISCA) questionnaire was used. This questionnaire is a validated information security culture questionnaire that has been adapted for industry purposes of which the reliability is between 0.764 and 0.877 (Da Veiga and Martins 2015).

The ISCA has 9 dimensions (constructs), one of which specifically relates to the information security policy. In total ISCA has 44 information security culture related statements that are used to assess information security culture. Seven of these statements relate to the information security policy. The information security culture statements are rated on a 5-point Likert scale (Strongly Disagree, Disagree, Unsure, Agree, Strongly Agree) to assess the employees' degree of agreement or disagreement with the statement (Dillon et al. 1993).

In total 15 yes/no questions are included in ISCA to gauge the information security awareness of certain concepts and to draw correlations with the information security culture statements. The ISCA's yes/no statements were customised for the case study organisation and 3 additional yes/no statements pertaining to the information security policy were added. This resulted in a total of 18 information security awareness statements ISCA questionnaire.

The ISCA also includes biographical questions (e.g. business units, countries and job levels) to segment the data for intervention and comparison purposes.

5.2. Case study organisation

The case study organisation operates across 12 countries and has one overarching Group Information Security Policy. In order to determine the effectiveness of the information security programme in the organisation, various methods were employed by the Group ISO, e.g. the implementation of technology and process safeguards, governance, risk assessments, monitoring, auditing and country self-assessments.

There was also a need to determine whether there is a positive information security culture in the organisation and how employees perceive information security requirements that they have to conform with. As such, ISCA was incorporated in the information security programme.

5.3. Sample

The ISCA was deployed in the case study organisation in 2006 to measure the level of information security culture present in the organisation. A number of interventions were identified as a result of the 2006 ISCA, some of which related to the information security policy. After the interventions were implemented, a second ISCA was needed to determine if they had a positive impact on the information security culture. This cycle was repeated four times as depicted in Figure 2.

The organisation employed 3 927 employees in 2006, which increased to 8 220 employees in 2014. The convenience sampling method (Brewerton and Millard 2001) was used whereby the survey was distributed electronically to all employees in the organisation across all 12 countries.

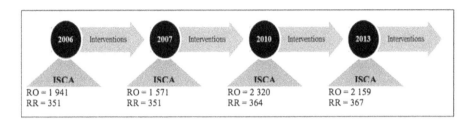

Figure 2: ISCAs and interventions over 8 years (RO – responses obtained, RR – responses required)

Each of the ISCAs was conducted over a period of 4 to 5 weeks to give employees time to respond to the survey. The required sample was calculated for each ISCA occasion based on a marginal error of 5% and a confidence level of 95%, to ascertain the findings across the organisation (Krejcie and Morgan 1970). For each of the ISCA occasions an adequate number of responses were obtained in line with the 95% confidence level.

5.4. Statistical analysis

Survey software, namely Survey Tracker (2014) was used to distribute the electronic questionnaire and to conduct the statistical analysis. The SPSS (2013) software package was used to conduct t-tests to determine the significant differences between the results of the group of employees who had read the information security policy compared with those who had not (Brewerton and Millward 2002). Regression analysis was further used to determine the most important focuses of each year (Da Veiga and Martins 2015).

The overall information security culture rating or score was determined (i.e. the average of all the items across the constructs) for the organisation as a whole and for the biographical groups such as the countries, departments and job levels. The lowest and highest items were identified per biographical group to identify developmental areas and action plans for the organisation.

The information security policy related statements in the ISCA that were below the accepted cut-off of 4.00 for the mean were identified and specific action plans defined to address them. As the information security culture level was also monitored, the average scores for the ISCA dimensions were tracked and compared as well as any constructs that were identified as developmental areas.

5.5. Results

5.5.1. Overall information security culture

The information security culture mean improved from one assessment to the next with the most positive results in 2013, as illustrated in Table 1. This mean represents the information security culture level in the organisation as assessed using the nine constructs of ISCA. The mean for the 2013 ISCA was the most positive when compared with the mean of the other years indicating that the information security culture improved from 2006 to 2013. The means of the 4 ISCA occasions illustrate the value of conducting the ISCA over a period of time to monitor the impact of the interventions and change in information security culture.

In 2010 a decline in the results was observed, which could have related to the business restructuring that occurred during that period. However, the results in 2013 improved to above the cut-off of 4 for the mean.

ISCA occasion	Actual responses	Overall Information Security Culture Mean	Overall Information Security Culture in %
ISCA 4 – 2013	2 159	4.10	83.6%
ISCA 3 – 2010	1 320	3.76	75.7%
ISCA 2 – 2007	1 571	4.00	81.7%
ISCA 1 – 2006	1 941	3.89	75.7%

Table 1: Overall information security culture overall averages

The results indicate that the information security culture that was fostered became more positive over time. One reason for the improvement is attributed to training and awareness initiatives (Da Veiga and Martins 2014). The second could be related to the implementation of the action plans.

After the 2010 ISCA a focused awareness programme regarding the information security policy was implemented. This constituted monthly e-mails explaining specific requirements in the information security policy. A brochure was also compiled with a summary of the policy in easily understandable language. The location of the policy and the importance of reading it were emphasised in the communications.

These activities might have positively influenced the overall information security culture average score from 2010 to 2013. However, to examine the actual impact of the awareness and communication interventions of the information security policy on the information security culture further comparison analysis was conducted as discussed in the next paragraph.

5.5.2. More positive overall information security culture for employees who had read the policy compare to those who had not

To further explore if having read the information security policy results in a more positive or stronger information security culture the data of all the information security culture constructs measured were segmented between the group of employees who had read the policy and those who had not. This was possible as a question was added in the ISCA questionnaire where employees had to indicate whether they had read the policy or not.

The overall information security culture mean was calculated for each of the two groups and compared. An important finding is that the overall information security culture mean of the employees who had read the policy (4.10) in 2013 was higher compared with those who had not (3.94).

Table 2 exhibits the overall information security culture in percentage for the group of employees who had read the policy compared to those who had not. For each year that the ISCA was conducted (i.e. 2006, 2007, 2010 and 2013) the information security culture percentage is more positive for the group who had read the policy than the group who had not. (It is important to note that the percentage in Table 2 indicates the overall information security culture and not the frequency of employees who have read the policy).

Data segmentation	Overall information security culture in %			
	2013	2010	2007	2006
Group that read policy	83.6%	79.6%	85.6%	82.0%
Group that did not read policy	76.6%	69.5%	75.0%	68.1%

Table 2: Information security culture for read and not read policy

The information security culture it thus more positive, as measured through ISCA, for the group of employees who had read the policy compared to the group of employee who had not read the policy. The information security culture score therefore indicates that reading the information security policy has a positive impact on the information security culture of employees.

5.5.3. Significant differences of individual statements for employees who had read the policy compare to those who had not

The positive influence of an information security policy on the information security culture was further illustrated in the significant differences of individual statements in the ISCA of the employees who had read the policy compared with those who had not. The results of the t-tests indicated that all 44 statements in the ISCA were significantly more positive for employees who had read the policy compared with those who had not.

Employees who had read the information security policy had an improved understanding of it. They also believed that the policy was practical and applicable to their working environment during the execution of their daily tasks. They were significantly more positive that management and colleagues complied with the policy. For all the abovementioned concepts, they were significantly more positive compared with employees who had not read the policy.

In an information security-positive culture fewer information security incidents would be expected. This is confirmed in the data in that fewer employees who had read the information security policy shared their passwords (89.8%) compared with those who had not read it (85.1%). Another example is that more employees who had read the policy protected data when taking it off site (54.8%) compared with employees who had not read it (45.3%). Similarly, 74.2% of employees who had read the policy took care when talking about confidential information in public places compared with 69.6% of employees who had not read it.

5.5.4. Increase in numbers who had read the policy compared to those who had not

The frequency of employees who had read the information security policy increased from 1 057 employees in 2006 to 1 381 employees in 2013. The awareness and communication interventions could have contributed to motivate employees to read the information security policy. More employees (70.3%) who had read the information security policy knew where to get a copy of it compared with those who had not (46.8%) for the 2013 data.

Interestingly, a total of 96.9% of employees knew that the organisation had an information security policy. A total of 35.9% of employees had still not read the policy and 30% did not know where to get a copy of it. Further awareness and communication interventions for specific biographical groups need to be conducted to improve this. An advantage of the ISCA is that the job levels, countries and business units can be identified with low frequencies of employees who had read the information security policy in order to be targeted through initiatives.

6. Discussion and limitations

This research study makes a contribution to the information security discipline and specifically in relation to the human threat to information protection. It strongly supports the notion that reading the information security policy has a positive influence on the information security culture. This is confirmed through the data derived from an information security culture assessment (ISCA) that was conducted at 4 intervals over 8 years across 12 countries.

The data analysis showed the group of employees who had read the information security policy had a stronger information security culture based on the more positive overall mean of ISCA and the individual statements that were significantly more positive than the group who had not read the policy. This provides empirical evidence that employees who read the information security policy have a stronger information security-positive culture compared with those who do not.

An information security policy plays a critical role in directing an information security-positive culture. The implication for organisations is that an information security policy is imperative, but if employees have not read it or understood it, it will not be effective in directing their behaviour, influencing their attitude towards policy compliance or fostering an information security-positive culture. At least one in every three organisations still does not have written information security or privacy related policies in place and up to 24% do not have an acceptable usage policy in place (Protiviti 2014). This not only introduces risk to the protection of information, but could also have legal implications and ultimately inculcate an information security culture that is not beneficial towards the protection of information.

The value of ISCA has been illustrated in this research in that the information security culture is influenced positively by addressing the developmental areas identified in the assessment. Information security policy awareness was one critical developmental area. By having an increased number of employees that have read the information security policy, the overall culture is influenced positively.

As discussed earlier, there are numerous factors that influence employees' willingness to comply with the information security policy. Similarly, there are also various factors that influence the development of an information security-positive culture. A limitation of this research study is that external factors that could potentially influence the information security culture were not considered, for example, national culture.

7. Conclusion

The results of this study provide statistical evidence that the information security culture of employees who had read the information security policy are significantly more positive when compared with employees who had not. Reading the information security policy contributes to influencing the information security culture positively. Over time a stronger information security-positive culture is developed.

Awareness of an information security policy contributes in fostering an information security-positive culture. In such an environment fewer information security incidents from a human perspective and more risk-adverse behaviour would be expected. This study emphasises the value of awareness initiatives regarding the information security policy and serves as a motivation to prioritise having an adequate policy and communicating it to employees. This will help as a motivation to eliminate the gap between the percentage of organisations that do not have awareness initiatives in place regarding their information security policy and those that do.

Although this study focused only on the influence of information security policies, further research will examine the influence of other factors on the development of an information security culture such as leadership and trust. The influence of national culture will also be explored in future work to develop an ISCA tool that considers factorial invariance across countries.

8. References

Box, D. and Pottas, D. (2013)," Improving information security behaviour in the healthcare context", *Procedia Technology*, Vol. 9, No. 2013, pp1093 – 1103.

Brewerton, P. and Millward, L. (2002), *Organizational research methods*, Sage Publications, London, ISBN 9780761971009.

Bulgurcu, B., Cavusoglu, H. and Benbasat, I. (2010), "Information security policy compliance: an empirical study of rationality-based beliefs and information security awareness", *MIS Q*, Vol. 34, No. 3, pp523-48.

Da Veiga, A. and Martins, N. (2014)," Information security culture: a comparative analysis of four assessments", in *Proceedings of the 8th European Conference on IS Management and Evaluation*, Vol. 8, No. 2014, pp49–57.

Da Veiga, A. and Martins, N. (2015). "Improving the information security culture through monitoring and implementation actions illustrated through a case study", *Computers and Security*, Vol. 49, No. 2015, pp162-176.

Dillon, W.R., Madden, J.T. and Firtle, N.H. (1993*), Essentials of marketing research*, IRWIN, Boston, ISBN: 0256081123.

Goucher, K.R.W. (2012), "Health service employees and information security policies: an uneasy partnership?" *Information Management & Computer Security*, Vol. 20, No. 4, pp296 – 311.

Hellriegel, D., Slocum, Jr. J.W. and Woodman, R.W. (1998), *Organizational behavior*, Eighth edition, South-Western College Publishing, Pennsylvania , ISBN 0538880244.

Herath, T. and Rao, H.R. (2009), "Protection motivation and deterrence: a framework for security policy compliance in organisations", *European Journal of Information Systems,* Vol. 18, No. 2009, pp106-25.

Hoffstede, G. (1980), *Culture's Consequences: International Differences in Work-related Values*, Sage Publications, Beverley Hills, ISBN 9783423508070

Ifinedo, P. (2014), "Understanding information systems security policy compliance: an integration of the theory of planned behaviour and the protection motivation theory", *Computers & Security*, Vol. 31, No. 2011, pp83-95.

Information Security Forum (ISF). *Information security culture – A preliminary investigation.* s.l.; 2000.

ISO/IEC 27002. (2013), *Information technology – Security techniques – Code of practice for information security management.*

Jackson, T. (2000), "Management ethics and corporate policy: a cross cultural comparison" *Journal Management Studies*, Vol. 37, No. 2000, pp349-69.

King Code of Governance for South Africa. (2009), Institute of Directors Southern Africa, http://www.iodsa.co.za/?kingIII, (Accessed 9 October 2014).

Knapp, K.J., Morris, R.F., Marshall, T.E. and Byrd, T.A. (2009), " Information security policy: an organizational-level process model", Computers & Security, Vol. 28, No. 2009, pp493-508.

Krejcie, R.V., Morgan, D.W. (1970), "Determining sample size for research activities", *Educational and Psychological Measurement*, Vol. 30, No. 1970, pp607-610.

Leach, J. (2003), "Improving user security behavior", *Computers & Security*, Vol. 22, No. 8, pp 685–92.

Padayachee, K. (2012), "Taxonomy of compliant information security behavior", *Computers & Security,* Vol 31, No. 2012, pp673-680.

Pahnila, S., Siponen, M. and Mahmood, A. (2007), "Employees' behaviour towards IS security policy compliance". In, *40th Hawaii International Conference on System Sciences (HICSS 07),* Hawaii, USA.

Parsons, K., McCormac, A., Butavicius, M., Pattinson, M. and Jerram, C. (2014), "Determining employee awareness using the Human Aspects of Information Security Questionnaire (HAIS-Q)", *Computers & Security*, Vol. 42, No. 2014, pp165-176.

PricewaterhouseCoopers (PwC) (2014), *The Global State of Information Security Survey,* http://www.pwc.com/gx/en/consulting-services/information-security-survey/download.jhtml, (Accessed 10 Dec 2014)

Protiviti. (2014), *IT Security and Privacy Survey,* http://www.protiviti.com/itsecuritysurvey, (Accessed 11 Dec 2014).

Siponen, M., Mahmood, A. and Pahnila, S. (2014), "Employees' adherence to information security policies: an exploratory field study", *Information & Management*, Vol. 51, No. 201, pp217–224.

SPSS version 22 (2013), IBM Software Group, ATTN: Licensing, 200 W. Madison St. Chicago, IL; 60606, U.S.A.

Survey Tracker (2014), Training Technologies Inc., https://www.surveytracker.com/ (Accessed 7 June 2014).

Thomson, K., Van Solms, R. and Louw, L. (2006), "Cultivating an organisational information security culture", *Computer Fraud and Security,* Vol. October, pp7-11.

Von Solms, R. and Von Solms, B. (2004), "From policies to culture", *Computers & Security*, Vol. 23, No. 2004, pp275-279.

A Cyber Security Culture Fostering Campaign through the Lens of Active Audience Theory

R. Reid and J. van Niekerk

Nelson Mandela Metropolitan University, Port Elizabeth, South Africa
s208045820@live.nmmu.ac.za, Johan.VanNiekerk@nmmu.ac.za}

Abstract

The South African Cyber Security Academic Alliance's (SACSAA) cyber security educational campaign aims to foster a cyber -safe and -secure culture amongst South Africa's youth. Previous work shows that the campaign is fostering a cyber security culture amongst its audience. However, it has not determined if the *developing* culture aligns with the *desired* cyber security culture that the campaign *expected* to foster. The target audience's interpretation of the campaign's educational messages meanings can affect a developing cyber security culture; possibly resulting in it not aligning with the campaigns preferred culture. This paper examines the audience's interpretative role in developing a cyber security culture, through the lens of active audience theory. The objective is to enable early detection of deviations between the campaigns objectives and its actual results within the audience.

Keywords

Cyber security culture, cyber security education, Active Audience Theory, Action Research, Case study, SACSAA, Public understanding of security

1. Introduction

In our technology- and information-infused world cyberspace is an integral part of modern-day society. In both personal and professional contexts cyberspace is a highly effective tool in and enabler of most people's daily digitally-transposed activities (Klimburg 2012; Siponen 2001; De Lange & Von Solms 2012). Several countries governments have recognized the many potential benefits that the adoption of the Internet and ICT may have for their country's welfare (Klimburg 2012). Therefore, in many of these countries, citizens are being actively encouraged to adopt these technologies. The resultant rapid adoption of cyber technologies and services has had some very positive results e.g. providing users access to many beneficial and convenient services and utilities. However, it has also had some negative and often *unintended* consequences. A prominent, problematic consequence is that the citizens are becoming increasingly technology dependent whilst also becoming increasingly vulnerable to cyber threats (Furnell et al. 2007).

As the number of *active* cyberspace users increases, so too does the chances of a cyber threat finding a vulnerable target also increase. Most users are not significantly aware of or secured against the cyber threats targeting them. To avoid becoming victims of cyber threats these cyber citizens urgently need to acquire the security- and safety- skills necessary for safe activity within cyberspace (Siponen 2001).

All cyber users who are exposed to the risks and need to be educated about cyber security. However, this education is particularly important for children who interact with cyberspace from an early age (De Lange & Von Solms 2012). A cyber security culture if instilled amongst the youth may become an integral part of all their daily activities throughout their increasingly technology infused lifetime. Additionally these children may further foster the culture by passing it on to their own children in the future. Therefore, it is particularly important that campaigns which target the youth are effective at communicating the right cyber security themed messages. The campaigns should present the messages in a way that enables the children to understand the message as the campaign's content intends it to be understood.

In South Africa, the South African Cyber Security Academic Alliance (SACSAA) runs an annual campaign which aims to raise school children's awareness about vital cyber security and safety behaviours. Ideally the campaign aims to aid in the fostering of cyber security culture amongst cyber citizens. This paper asks: "Is the developing cyber security culture, the culture which we intended to foster?"

This paper aims to use active audience theory as a lens to determine whether the SACSAA Cyber Security Campaign's target audience has been unambiguously and uncritically interpreting the meaning off the educational campaign's awareness themes (messages) as they were intended to be imposed by the campaign creators. Detecting if the audiences interpretation deviates from the campaign's intended result may make it easier to identify necessary adjustments for future campaigns.

The remainder of this paper is structured as follows: Section 2 provides more detail about the SACSAA Campaigns. Section 3 provides a preliminary explanation of the active audience theory paradigm. The research design used to meet this papers aim is outlined in Section 4. Section 5 presents the findings of the paper. Finally our work is concluded in Section 6 and limitations of the research are presented in Section 7.

2. The SAACSAA Campaign

The South African Cyber Security Academic Alliance (SACSAA) consists of research groups from three well-known South African Universities (SACSAA 2011).The main objective of SACSAA is "to campaign for the effective delivery of Cyber Security Awareness throughout South Africa to all groupings of the population"(SACSAA 2011). Ultimately, SACSAA intends to aid in the fostering of a societal cyber security culture via education. This paper will focus on the data gathered from the SACSAA campaign activities involving the youth. SACSAA has officially run an annual educational cyber security campaign targeting the youth since 2012 (2011 had a pilot study). The campaign consists of two components: an education campaign and a poster contest.

The campaign aims to first raise the youth's general awareness of the need for cyber security in their digital activities. There are six main thematic messages in the campaign: "Keep your private information private"; "Be nice online"; "Stay legal"; "Trust an adult"; "Protect your PC", "Stranger Danger". A wide variety of cyber security and safety topics within these themes have been covered each year. Mass media is used to distribute messages and cultural forms (information) to large, widely dispersed, heterogeneous audiences (Munday & Chandler 2011). The campaign presents each topics content using multiple mass media modes including: digital media (awareness posters, videos, SACSAA website and online resources), printed media (awareness posters, informational pamphlets, educational games (Reid & Van Niekerk 2013)) and finally public events (interactive school visits).

Each year the campaign has been modified to increase effectiveness of the successive campaign's results and scalability. Changes and additions to the campaign have included the use of pedagogical theory, use of multimedia and interactive presentations and multimodality in the campaign material, increased contextual customization, increased teacher involvement, inclusion of SACSAAs branding logos and mascots. Detailed about the modifications and results from 2011 until 2013 are available in previous work (Van Niekerk et al. 2013; Reid & Van Niekerk 2014). In 2014 the campaign was adapted to be more teacher-oriented, and a cyber security school curriculum was provided.

The poster contest is the instrument used to measure the campaign's effect on the involved youth's awareness levels. Learners are invited to create and submit a hand-crafted or digital poster showing an awareness message (as they understand it) for one or more of the campaign's topics. Participation is voluntarily. Evaluations of past campaign iterations competition posters has shown that the majority of participants have internalized (learned from) campaign messages. Posters indicated internalization was: "partial" if the learner depicting the message as it was given; "moderate" if the lesson was rephrased into the learner's own words; or "full" if the lesson was shown to be contextualized by the learner. It is possible that the raised awareness levels (shown by internalization), and any resultant behaviour modifications could enable the fostering of a culture amongst these participants.

This research aims to determine if the cyber security culture being fostered by the SACSAA campaign aligns with how the culture messages were intended to be being interpreted. The role of the audience in this process has yet to be examined. It is the author's opinion that active audience theory could be used to understand the role of the campaign's target audience's in fostering a cyber security culture. This opinion is due to the campaign's use of mass media and its purpose of communicating with and having a message understood by an audience (television has the same purpose).

3. Active Audience theory paradigm

In cultural studies dealing with television and mass media, understanding the relationship between a media "text" and it's audience (audience research) (Barker, 2012). In this field, the role of the audience is therefore a research focus. This paper examines the active audience paradigm. Active audience theory examines the active, interpretative role of audience when they "make meaning" from the media content (Hall, 1980; Munday & Chandler, 2011). This paradigm suggests that it should not be assumed that audiences develop a culture by uncritically accepting the 'textual' meaning of a programme (Barker, 2012).

The aim of a media "text" is typically to communicate a message with a specific meaning. The process of communication consists of a circuit of a complex structure of relations namely: production >> circulation >> distribution/consumption >> reproduction of a message (Hall, 1980).

Within this circuit of communication, messages are sent between parties. Typically, the message has a meaning, which the sender tries to convey when constructing and producing the message. However, as the message moves within the circuit, it is not guaranteed that each level interprets the meaning of the message similarly. This is because the meaning of a message is polysemic and an audience is seldomly passive.

The active audience theory paradigm argues media has a preferred message to communicate to their audience, but media audiences do not passively accept information and its imposed meanings from a structured text (Munday & Chandler, 2011). Stuart Hall's encoding/decoding model (see Figure 1) illustrates this by showing the discourses of the meaning of the text between its producer (encoder) and the reader (encoder) (Hall, 1980).

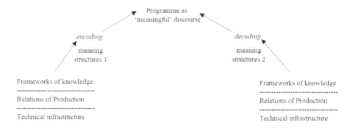

Figure 1: Meaningful Discourse (Hall, 1980)

Within the circuit of communication the encoding/decoding model shows that audiences are active and knowledgeable producers of the meaning a texts delivered message within their personal and social contexts (Barker, 2012). The producer (encoder) encodes meaning in a certain way, while the reader (decoder) decodes it differently according to their own personal knowledge and contextual frames of interpretation. It cannot be assumed that the meaning of a program, text or any other communication has a fixed interpretable meaning, which can unerringly be recognized by any audience. Instead how the audience makes sense of a texts meaning is "the product of a negotiation between the audience and the text in a particular context of reception" (Munday & Chandler, 2011).

In brief, different audiences may accept different textual meanings, based on how the "text" is constructed and communicated. *Texts*(the messages) are polysemic (can have multiple meanings)(Hall, 1980). Often only some of the meanings will be accepted by an audience (Barker, 2012). The audiences decoding will typically fall into one of the following three hypothetical decoding positions as proposed by Hall:

- "The dominant-hegemonic encoding/decoding" where the decoder accepts the messages 'preferred meanings" which a text is attempting to impose (Hall, 1980);
- "A negotiated code" position wherein the decoder acknowledges the legitimacy of the theory of the hegemonic decoding, but adapts it interpretation based on particular circumstances or context (Hall, 1980);
- "An oppositional code were audience members understand the preferred encoding may reject it and decode the text in contrary ways" (Hall, 1980).

All positions are the result of the whole communication process and the decoders (audience) producing their own meaning of the message. For the purposes of this paper, a fourth decoding position could be "null" wherein where the audience members did not understand/accept/ process the message clearly.

Due to the campaigns use of mass media, the authors believe it is possible to apply the encoding/decoding model to the campaign's audience. The decoding position espoused by the majority of the SACSAA audience's takes could indicate what type of culture is developing. This could then allow measurement of whether the fostered culture aligns with SACSAA's intended culture formation.

4. Research design

This research examines a case study of the annual SACSAA educational campaign. This campaign has been running since 2011. Its target audience is the all South African youth. However, thus far data has only been gathered from the numerous schools in the Nelson Mandela Metropolitan area who have been increasingly exposed to the campaign. This paper aims to determine if a culture which has developed over time amongst an audience, matches the campaign's desired culture. Part of the campaign's enhancements over the years has been the customization of the material to fit the issues of each particular school. Therefore, in order to measure an effect on an audience and its culture it would be best to examine one particular audience and context i.e. one school which has been exposed to the campaign for several successive years. Therefore, for the purposes of this paper only data gathered from the single school to have participated in every campaign since 2012 until 2014 (last complete campaign) will be used. This school will be referred to as 'School A'.

'School A' is a convenient and purposive sample for the analysis purpose of this paper. Firstly, it is a convenience sample as the data was "available to the researcher by means of its accessibility" (Bryman, 2012). The researchers have been gathering data for a number of successive years for research purposes. Secondly, this sample is also purposive as the sample participants were specifically selected "so that those sampled are relevant to the research questions that are being posed" (Bryman, 2012). Over the years the campaign material and approach has altered and improved. The students within 'School A' have been exposed to all of the involved culture fostering and measurement activities. The sample is believed to be representative of the SACSAA campaign's overall target audience because: the participants are all primary school children; their age ranges between 6 and 15; members of both genders participated; and different ethnic groups were represented. Due to ethical considerations no identifying data apart from participant age was captured.

A content analysis; as described by Krippendorff (2004); was done to determine if the audiences interpretation of the material aligned with the subject-expert and educator's intended key messages for each campaign topic. A content analysis can be conducted on texts and artifacts (Hodder, 1994). The researchers consider the SACSAA competition posters to be iconic cultural artifacts, which provide information about the culture of their creators. Therefore the analysis was conducted on the competition posters gathered from 'School A'. The aim was to determine if the learner's interpretation and internalization of the educational message matched, closely related (generally agreed with minor differences in interpretation) or opposed the campaign's intended meanings. For this analysis the following questions were asked for each poster: Firstly, *"What topic(s) do the message(s) in the poster cover?"* and secondly, *"What position within Hall's encoding/decoding theory did the audience member (poster creator) take once they decoded the campaign's message (in the researcher's opinion)?"* Each of these questions and the analysis process for answering them will briefly be elaborated upon in the next two subsections.

4.1. Posters per topic

This question was to determine which specific topics were considered more important by the learners. The campaign covered all of its topics well, however, it placed emphasis (considerable content) on the issues it considered critical issues. These thematic issues messages are: promoting anti-cyber-bullying, personal pc and information protection, and staying legal online. The percentage of posters covering a topic will be compared to the ratio of the campaign's content which covered the topic. The difference between the percentages could indicate a match or difference rating covered issues importance from the audience's and campaign's perspective.

4.2. Poster creators decoding position on the related campaign topic's message (according to Hall's encoding/decoding theory)

This question was asked to determine if the way the participant interpreted the message of the material aligned with how the campaign intended it to be understood. The participant's interpretation of the campaign topic(s)'s message(s) (as the show it in their poster) was categorized as having one of the following positions: the dominant-hegemonic decoding position; a negotiated coded position; or an oppositional coded position. These positions meaning according to Stuart Hall are explained in Section 3. In order to determine which of these positions a poster belonged to, the following questions were asked as an evaluation matrix:

- Does the posters *textual message* support the related campaign topic(s) message?
- Does the posters *graphical message* (examples/warnings) support the related campaign topic(s) message?

- What overall impression (in the researcher's opinion) does the poster give of the participant's interpretation of the related campaign topic(s) message?

The answers to these questions were selected to be one of the following: strongly supports related campaign topic's message; partially/vaguely supports related campaign topic's message; opposed related campaign topic's message; undeterminable. If two or more questions were answered as strongly supporting the related campaign topic's message the poster was classified as having accepted the dominant-hegemonic decoding interpretive position. Likewise, if two or more questions were answered as strongly opposing the related campaign topic's message the poster was classified as having accepted an oppositional coded interpretive position. Other combinations of answers resulted in the poster being classified as having accepted a negotiated coded interpretive position, unless two or more question was answered as 'undeterminable' in which case the posters was classified as having a "null" or "undetermined" position. "Null" position posters were typically considered impossible to interpret without further information. An example of the results of using this matrix may for classification purposes is shown by Figure 2.

a) Dominant-hegemonic decoding of campaign topic messsage   b)Oppositional coding of campaign topic's message

Figure 2: Examples of classification of poster interpretaion positions

An example of a poster which is categorised as accepting the dominant-hegemonic (preferred) encoding/decoding of the campaign's message for the topic of cyberbullying is shown in figure 2a. The text strongly supports prevention and stopping of cyber bullying and provide tips on how to do this. The graphics strongly support the message e.g. it shows the consequences (emotional pain) of the cyber bullying on the victim and the platforms this bullying may occur on. Overall the posters strongly suggests that the participant agrees with the campaigns objective of promoting the prevention of being a cyber-bully and/or victim of cyber bullying. In contrast to figure 2a, figure 2b shows an example of a poster which is categorised as representing an oppositional coded interpretative position for cyber bullying topic. The textual message was classified as being oppositional as it did not discourage cyber bullying in anyway, instead it seemed to say cyberbullying is inevitable and consequences should be disregarded. The graphical pictures illustrated an example of cyber bullying but did not indicate it should be stopped or that it was bad, therefore they were also classified as being oppositional. Overall the poster seemed to promote cyber-bullying rather discourage it.

The remainder of this paper will discuss the results of the quantitative analysis. It will then conclude with the papers findings in terms of its aim.

5. Analysis and results

This analysis aims to determine if the culture being fostered amongst this audience matches the campaign expected resultant culture. Historically, School A has had 240 learners voluntarily participate in the poster completion (50 learners in 2012, 102 learners in 2013, 90 learners in 2014). Some posters represented multiple themes and topics. The distribution of the posters per campaign topic is shown in figure 3.

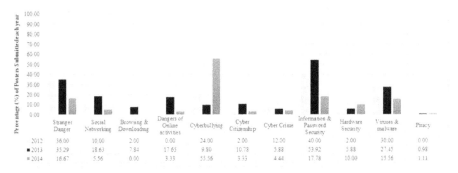

Figure 3: Percentage of each year's posters showing a particular topic

Based on Figure 3, the audience has shown a high rate of acceptance of messages relating to the dangers of interacting with strangers online, keeping their personal information (and passwords) private and secure and prevention of cyber bullying. Contrastingly they are do not accept the message of anti-piracy. These four messages were equally focussed on as serious issues in all of the campaign material, as they are issues which are strongly associated to children's cyber activities. The audience seems to agree with the campaign about the importance personal and asset security and safety; however, they reject the campaign's view that piracy and infringement of others individuals/entities property rights should be stopped (particularly if they benefit from the infringement). An informal tally done by School A's teachers found that the majority of the learners had pirated one or more series, film and/or game.

Further analysis evaluated the position of the audiences decoding an interpretation of the campaign topics messages as previously discussed. Figure 4 shows that the majority of learners accepted the campaign's preferred (dominant-hegemonic) interpretation of message for their chosen topic. Additionally the remainder of the posters positions were categorized as having accepted a negotiated coding position. It is very rare for the posters to be categorized as opposing the message or being undeterminable. This trend is visible in three successive years' posters.

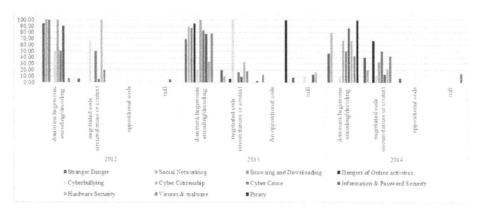

Figure 4: Message Decoding Position (%) per annum's poster ratio in topic area

Generally, this analysis has determined firstly, that the audience places similar ratings of importance on particular topic messages with the campaign; secondly, the majority of the audience is accepting/partially accepting the campaign's message meaning as the campaign prefers them to be understood. Therefore, this analysis concludes, that the culture being by the campaign amongst this audience closely aligns with the campaign's desired culture.

6. Conclusion

The campaign's audience has been actively producing meaning from the materials messages. The majority of the audience is decoding the campaign's messages and accepting the campaign's preferred message meanings. These findings were particularly strong for messages which strongly related to the participants perceived personal/asset security. However, the findings also indicated that the audience preferred to negotiate or reject messages that they did not perceive to have a negative consequence for themselves e.g. messages relating to piracy. Overall, this paper concludes that the majority of the cyber security culture developing amongst this audience matches the culture which the campaign material aims to foster. This outcome could improve further, if future work establishes how to encode material to encourage audiences to accept the campaign's less preferred messages.

7. Limitations of this research

Firstly, all conclusions drawn from the qualitative analysis of the posters may be in some measure biased by the researcher's interpretation of each poster. Secondly, the overall campaign message rejection or negotiation may not be completely measured from the data as learners were only required to include a minimum of one campaign message in their artefact as they understood it.

8. Acknowledgements

The financial assistance of the Vodacom/NMMU and National Research Foundation (NRF) scholarships towards this research is hereby acknowledged. Opinions expressed and conclusions arrived at are those of the author and are not necessarily to be attributed to the sponsors.

9. References

Barker, C., 2012. Television, Texts and Audiences. In *Cultural Studies*. SAGE, pp. 325–360.

Bryman, A., 2012. *Social Research Methods*, Oxford University press.

Furnell, S., Bryant, P. & Phippen, A., 2007. Assessing the security perceptions of personal Internet users. *Computers & Security*, 26(5), pp.410–417.

Hall, S., 1980. Encoding/decoding. In *Culture, Media, Language: working papers in cultural studies*. London, Hutchinson: Centre for Contemporary Cultural Studies, pp. 128–137.

Hodder, I., 1994. *The interpretation of documents and material culture*, Thousand Oaks: Sage.

Klimburg, A. ed., 2012. *National Cyber Security Framework Manual*, NATO CCD COE Publicaions.

Krippendorff, K., 2004. *Content Analysis: An Introduction to Its Methodology*, SAGE. Available at: http://tinyurl.com/qxpuy4w.

De Lange, M. & Von Solms, R., 2012. An e-Safety Educational Framework in South Africa. In *Proceedings of the Southern Africa Telecoms and Network Applications Conference*.

Munday, D. & Chandler, R., 2011. *A dictionary of media and communication* 1st ed., Oxford: Oxford University Press. Available at: http://tinyurl.com/qds6e5q.

Van Niekerk, J., Thomson, K.-L. & Reid, R., 2013. Cyber Safety for School Children: A Case Study in the Nelson Mandela Metropolis. In *8th IFIP WG 11.8 World Conference on Information Security Education*. Auckland, New Zealand: Springer, pp. 103–112.

Olivier, M.S., 2009. *Information Technology Research: A Practical guide for Computer Science and Informatics* 3rd ed., Pretoria, South Africa: Van Schaik Publishers.

Reid, R. & Van Niekerk, J., 2013. Back to basics: Information security education for the youth via gameplay. In *8th IFIP WG 11.8 World Conference on Information Security Education*. Auckland, New Zealand: Springer, pp. 1–10.

Reid, R. & Van Niekerk, J., 2014. Towards an Education Campaign for Fostering a Societal, Cyber Security Culture. In *8th International Symposium on Human Aspects of Information Security & Assurance*. Plymouth, United Kingdom: Centre for Security, Communications & Network Research Plymouth University, pp. 174–184.

SACSAA, 2011. South African Cyber Security Academic Alliance (SACSAA). *cyberaware.org.za*. Available at: http://www.cyberaware.org.za/.

Siponen, M., 2001. Five dimensions of information security awareness. *ACM SIGCAS Computers and Society*, 31(2), pp.24–29.

Enlighten Information Morals through Corporate Culture

A. Alumubark, N. Hatanaka, O. Uchida and Y. Ikeda

Graduate School of Informatics
Tokyo University of Information Sciences, Chiba, Japan
e-mail : h14001aa@edu.tuis.ac.jp; {hatanaka, o-uchida, ikeyuki}@rsch.tuis.ac.jp

Abstract

The leakage of secret information has increasingly become a social problem. Information leaks typically result from the targeting of specific organizations or persons and are based on a variety of factors. One factor common to the majority of leaks is the relationship between corporate culture and information morals. Organizations that lack robust standards of information morals are at a greater risk of information leaks. This paper aims to identify the causes of information leaks by applying organization theory and statistical analysis to assess the impact of corporate culture on information leaks and information morals. Furthermore, the relationship between organizational objectives and social values is discussed in order to propose a clear assessment process of corporate culture.

Keywords

Information Morals, Information Security, Security Incidents

1. Introduction

Information security begins and ends with people, while incidents and accidents involving the leakage of personally identifiable information show no sign of significant decline, e.g. the Dai Nippon Printing Co., Ltd. and the Benesse Holdings, Inc. leakage incidents. In order to understand the cause of information leaks, it is necessary to investigate the relationship between individuals and organizations. The research presented will assess the impact of corporate culture on information security incidents, information morals and the interrelationship between people and organizations. This research will also reveal that information security incidents are attributed to unaddressed information security vulnerabilities and the disharmony between organizational objectives and social values. This paper will then propose how to improve information morals through corporate culture.

2. Lack of Function Concerning Information Morals

Increasing information security is a challenge. Many organizations protect their information assets by focusing on security breaches and extended expenses related to security technologies; however, it is impossible to eliminate incidents and accidents simply by applying security technologies. It is important to identify other factors that generate incidents and accidents in the organization. There exists a widespread disconnect between the people that comprise organizational structures and the standards of information morals established by the organization. Previous research on this issue have focused on some features of corporate culture, however most of them have not succeed to identify the causes of information security incidents and improve information morals through corporate culture.

In this research, identify the defects of corporate culture that contribute to information security incidents and propose an assessment process to improve information morals within an organization. The goals of this paper are as follows:

- Determine the effects of corporate culture on information security incidents.
- Describe the impact of organizational hierarchy on corporate culture.
- Describe the impact of corporate culture on information morals.
- Establish a process for the assessment of corporate culture and its impact on information morals.

The research procedure was as follows:

- Develop a survey questionnaire concerning with information morals and corporate culture.
- Apply covariance structure analysis to extract factors of corporate culture from survey data through an exploratory factor analysis.
- Induce (variables) concerned with the organizational variable.

3. The Defects of Hierarchical Organization

Barnard (1938) studied the strengths and weakness of hierarchical organizational structures. He considered that the strengths of the hierarchical organizational structure related to the ability of leaders and swift actions. Those factors lead the hierarchical organization to success in the Industrial Age. He considered the weaknesses to be disparities in the distribution of wages and prestige among different positions, which lowered employee morale. He called those shortcomings "the inverse function of the hierarchical organizational structure" and considered them to be a major cause of scandals and accidents. The following points ought to be considered as defects of the status system and the hierarchical organization.

1. Deficiencies in the Status System (Barnard, 1938)
   - Hierarchies distort the true value of individuals in a status system.
   - The circulation of the position of the elite is unfairly limited; the ability to strengthen the exclusive positions by a specific person becomes a problem.
   - The system of distribution, such as equitable positions, functions, and responsibilities, is distorted; there is discrimination in the distribution of wages, honor, and prestige based on status.

2. Deficiencies in the Hierarchy (Barnard, 1938)
   - The administrative functions are exaggerated, and the function of morals is hampered.
   - It is an excessive symbolization function. The major issue is that the status and the true value of individuals are often confused.
   - Though it is indispensable in the cohesiveness and coordination of organizations, the hierarchy reduces the resilience and adaptability of organizations.

Barnard (1938) presented an organizational structure involving multiple layers of subcontractors as a "lateral organization," which referred to collaboration as a whole, without any formal upper-level organizations or leaders (Mano, 1989). He categorized the lateral organization into shareholders, creditors, consumers, raw material suppliers, and local governments, and subcontractors fall within the category of raw material suppliers. Furthermore, he emphasized that it is also possible to prevent information security incidents and accidents through the practical application of the lateral organization.

3.1. Sympathizing with Corporate Objectives and Social Values

Simon (1945) considers against the productivity of concept, which is determined by the relationship between the inputs and outputs of Taylorism, that organizations can increase their value, prevent corporate incidents and scandals, and increase the loyalty of their employees only when their objectives and social values are consonant. In the cases of Dai Nippon Printing Co., and Benesse Corp., the information security incidents occurred due to disharmony between social values and organizational objectives within a hierarchical structure.

3.2. The Organizational Cause of Incidents

The "administrative principles" of the organization were presented by Simon (1945). They relate to the challenges organizations face while resolving incidents. By comprehensively considering the following points, it is conceivable that suggestions can be obtained for improving efficiency and preventing organizational incidents.

Administrative efficiency is increased by the following:

1. By specializing works in a group.
2. By arranging the members to the hierarchy of the authority.
3. By limiting the span of control at small numbers of persons at any level of the hierarchy.
4. By grouping the employees according to the sort of work they do.

Consideration must be given, however, to the adverse affects of those factors since they cause organizational incidents. Nevertheless, those factors do correlate positively with efficiency. In other words, overall business efficiency results from improvements in organizational efficiency and productivity. Considering that the organization can be a hotbed of incidents, it appears necessary to confirm not only the activities and the decision-making of the organization, but also the effectiveness and the limitation of the hierarchy as in the collaboration method.

The similarities between scandals and incidents were observed through the collected data on 140 Japanese organizations in which information security incidents took place from 2006 to 2014. The data were collected from reliable websites in Japan, IPA`s archives (Information Technology Promotion Agency), and investigated these incidents cause with (Simon 1945) suggestions. It was seen that similar scandals and incidents had similar causes, the cause by social value or corporate culture.

4. The Relationship between Corporate Culture, Information Morals, and Information Security Incidents

Hofstede (2010) considers culture to be comprised of two primary elements. "Culture one" is comprised of civilization, or "refinement of the mind," and encompasses elements of society and culture such as education, literature, and art. "Culture two" is a broader conception of the word, and is related to the patterns of thinking, feeling, and acting in which individuals engage. Individuals living and operating within the same social environment tend to share these elements.

Shover and Hochstetler (2002) found that variations within the culture of an organization affect many elements of organizational performance. These include effectiveness in goal attainment and failing to comply with approved standards of conduct. Generally, there is high intra-organizational cultural uniformity. Thus, whether failing to comply with standards or legitimate, such behaviors reinforce one another (Shover & Hochstetler 2002). In line with these findings, Da Veiga and Eloff (2010) assert that an organization's approach to information security must focus on the moral behavior of employees. Gebrasilase and Lessa (2011) state that information security culture is comprised of a set of information security characteristics that are valued by the entirety of the organization. This emphasizes the effect that corporate culture has on the information morals of employees.

Van Niekerk and Von Solms (2010) researched information asset security and found that, whether due to negligence or intent, employees are its greatest threat. To ensure against the threat of negligence, it is essential that organizations establish a culture of information security and clear information morals. By establishing those standards, human factors that generate risk to information security are minimized and managed. The accomplishment of this goal, however, is not so simple (Alfawaz, 2010). Alfawaz (2010) noted the difficulty in understanding the complex, dynamic, and uncertain characteristics related to employees who perform information security activities, whether authorized or unauthorized. Information security management is influenced by individual and group behaviours alike, and must be managed as such.

Modern business and industry experts have increasingly demanded a stronger focus on information security. Information security must be incorporated into organizational strategies to be effectively addressed, but there is no clear blueprint through which a firm may achieve a corporate structure that supports organizational culture (Kayworth & Whitten, 2010). The values that are associated with organizational culture are manifested in the practices and activities within the organization in relation to information security management (Alfawaz et. al., 2010).

Focusing on information security within organizations is a comprehensive process. Kayworth and Whitten (2010) conducted qualitative research comprised of interviewing 21 information security executives from 11 organizations, and found that information security strategies are complex. Generally, those strategies incorporate not only IT products and solutions, but also social alignment and organizational integration mechanisms. The strategies are often managed through the institution of a control-based compliance model (Hedstrom, 2011).

Mitigation of information security threats depends on determining their sources. Often, such threats stem from organizational insiders. Insiders can cause greater damage due to their position; thus, they must be identified and subsequently targeted by countermeasures. Information security countermeasure strategies are a means of addressing particular threats (Coles-Kemp, 2010). The socio-technical approach is a means to achieve three objectives: achieving a balance between security essentials and the need to enable the business, maintaining compliance, and ensuring that the strategy is appropriate for the organizational culture (Kayworth &Whitten, 2010).

Employees are central to the protection of organizational information, which has prompted the study of so-called "security culture." By embedding security culture into the corporate culture, employee behaviors that protect the information of the organization are positively influenced (Lim, 2010). This positive reinforcement of moral behavior helps to lower the risk of information leaks. Employee compliance is one of the more difficult facets of information security, highlighting the importance of enforcement. One way to directly control and observe employee behavior in relation to information security is by monitoring employee computers (Green & D'Arcy, 2010). To measure employee behavior related to information security, Padayachee (2012) studied the extrinsic and intrinsic motivations that influenced employees' propensity to compliant information security behavior. Employee behavior in this regard is comprised of a set of core information security activities that must be adhered to by end-users to promote security.

5. Factors Influencing Corporate Culture and Information Morals

Covariance structure analysis was applied for comparisons through statistical testing of the effects of the latent variables (corporate cultural type) on the observed variables. Factors and issues related to scandals were proposed by the research group at Hitotsubashi University (Hoshino, 2008). While there are already case studies that have discussed scandals within organizations in Japan, we attempted to use these factors to explain the similarities between information incidents and scandals.

5.1. Questionnaire Design

A questionnaire for an IT department of IMAM institute in Tokyo was developed in both Japanese and English format. The distribution method was in site of IMAM institute and it was conducted in 8 November 2014. 184 answers were received, the sample details of the survey results shown in Table 1. The survey consisted of two parts. Part one, gathered information on employee demographics, using multiple-choice questions that allowed the researcher to examine such factors as department age, job duties, and background of information security experience. In part two, 43 observed variables were classified into eight categories. The observed variables concerned with the section "Culture of fraud and neglect of violation in the workplace" were measured on a 5-point Likert scale (1: None, to 5: Frequently). Other observed variables were measured on a 5-point scale (1: Disagree, to 5: Agree).

Participant's Answers		100%
Participant's age	20 or under	3
	21 – 30	24
	31 – 40	37
	41 – 50	31
	51 – 60	5
Participant's gender	Male	81
	Female	19
Job duties	Leader	1
	Manager	2
	Employer	91
	Contractor	6
Education level	Graduate School	48
	Collage	43
	Other	9
I have violated by a virus to my computer		78
I have looked into a password of another person		36
I have shared my password to another person		14

Table 1: Summary of survey results

5.2. Exploratory Factor Analysis

An exploratory factor analysis was applied to extract factors. Eight factors were extracted from the 43 observed variables. All coefficient alpha values were more than 0.8, which indicates that observed variables were positive. Through the results of the exploratory factor analysis, variables concerned with information security incidents have been induced. Results are shown in Table 3 and 4. The results indicate that all eight factors are valid for confirmatory factor analysis.

Latent variables	Number of Questions	Contribution Ratio	Coefficient Alpha
Culture of fraud and neglect of violation	8	0.846	0.802
Trust in the workplace	5	0.875	0.820
Sectarian behavior	9	0.906	0.905
Belonging scale	5	0.856	0.811
Moral leadership	3	0.676	0.894
Leadership at the workplace level	4	0.718	0.894
Development of compliance system	3	0.618	0.827
Other single indicators	6	0.862	0.849

Table 2: Summary of exploratory factor analysis

	Factor							
	1	2	3	4	5	6	7	8
Compliance7	**.911**	.065	.026	.061	-.059	.011	-.019	-.084
Compliance6	**.884**	-.020	-.070	-.014	.048	.004	-.035	.055
Compliance5	**.651**	-.037	.017	-.077	.005	.190	.114	-.069
Trust1	.023	**.826**	-.029	.062	.007	-.014	-.002	-.066
Trust3	.021	**.821**	.015	-.004	-.010	-.070	.040	.031
Trust4	-.029	**.749**	-.008	-.053	.016	.081	-.016	.121
Belonging4	-.185	.055	**.875**	-.017	-.040	.074	.040	-.036
Belonging5	.119	.033	**.850**	-.015	.026	-.015	-.030	-.064
Belonging3	.049	-.135	**.742**	.045	.032	-.061	.018	.156
Sectarian7	-.081	-.052	-.073	**.901**	.024	.084	.129	-.034
Sectarian6	.113	-.010	.144	**.814**	-.029	-.067	-.083	.029
Sectarian2	-.020	.082	.009	**.771**	.041	-.008	-.067	.026
Culture_fraud3	.026	-.007	.001	-.087	**.963**	.033	-.057	-.014
Culture_fraud2	-.006	-.063	-.069	.117	**.654**	-.076	.085	.153
Culture_fraud7	-.039	.102	.095	.056	**.560**	.029	-.005	-.177
Moral2	.045	-.001	.006	.052	.010	**.821**	.117	.027
Moral3	.112	-.011	.002	-.018	-.018	**.812**	-.101	.122
Other3	.015	.000	.010	.034	.008	.085	**.890**	-.114
Other1	.196	.066	.023	-.061	-.004	-.168	**.537**	.234
Leadership4	-.044	.075	.025	.014	-.007	.160	-.037	**.752**

(Extraction Method: Principal Axis Factoring)

Table 3: Results of exploratory factor analysis

No	Induced Variables
1	Have you ever made false reports in your workplace?
2	The information transfer between members is performed widely and smoothly.
3	The subordinate who does not give a present (gift) to the manager has a disadvantage regarding promotions.
4	When incidents or accidents occur, the concern is more of "whose responsibility it is" than of "what the cause is."
5	The managers in my workplace behave as a moral model for others.
6	The manager shows enough leadership at work.
7	I am aiming to establish a compliance (legal and ethical compliance).
8	The work objective of each person is clear every day.

Table 4; Results of induced variables

5.3. Confirmatory Factor Analysis

The results of the confirmatory factor analysis were induced and are shown in Figures 1. As a result, the most influential are "Sectarian behaviour" and "Belonging scale." The more "sectarian behaviour" increases, the higher "culture of fraud and neglect of violation in the workplace" rises. Furthermore, the greater level of "moral leadership" demonstrated by the administration, in combination with an increase in "trust in the workplace," the lower "culture of fraud and neglect of violation in the workplace" becomes. It also shows that "other single indicators" give certain effects, but the influence is small compared to the variables mentioned above. In addition, it has been shown that "culture of fraud and neglect of violation in the workplace" decreases in organizations that score higher in "development of compliance system." Its influence, however, is limited.

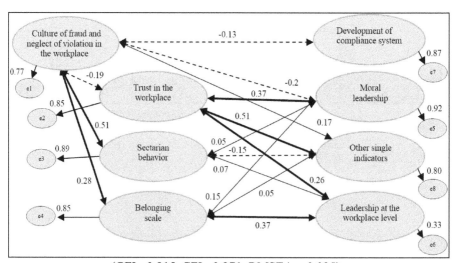

(GFI= 0.915, CFI= 0.971, RMSEA = 0.035)

Figure 1: Result of confirmatory factor analysis

6. Improvement of Information Morals

In order to launch assessments of information security incidents and improve the standards of information morals, the designer of the organizational structure must specify the elements and aspects of corporate structure that may improve or degrade corporate culture. Next, the designer or planner evaluates and supposes the change to the aspects of corporate culture. This process is proposed as "the assessment process of corporate culture." For example, consider an employee in an IT department who lost a USB containing sensitive information. In this case, the employee lost the confidence of customers by failing to consider the importance of protecting customers' information. The employee did not uphold the moral duty to protect customers' personal data. This had the effect of degrading the department`s corporate culture. Thus, it was necessary for the department's management to educate and discipline that employee. The above illustration is shown in the assessment process of corporate culture in Table 5. The proposed assessment process is as follows:

Process 1   Specifying and identifying the elements and corporate culture aspects that characterize the organization.

Process 2   Assessing and supposing the change to corporate culture after organizations activities.

Process 3   Establishing the objectives induced from and consistent with organizational policy by management.

Process 4   Setting measurable targets that are induced from the objective itself.

Process 5   Measuring the performance of the organization's activities.

	Past	Present					Future
Organization	Incidents	Aspect		Impact	Objectives	Target	Performance
IMAM Inst, IT Dept	An employee lost his USB memory contains information (Name, Address, Contact numbers)	Agent	The employee has not awareness of the importance of job's information.	The employee disregards the leak of job's information	The employee aware that the job's information is protected from missing or losing	Limit the amount of confidential information stored on portable medium (USB) to only the minimum necessary. Itself to achieve level is 80%.	The employee takes into consideration the importance of protecting job's information. Performance level is 25%.
		Organization's Objectives	The objectives are ambiguity, not acceptable by organization members, itself not to achieve, lack of information security, etc.	The employee has not the responsibility to the job duty, comply with organization policy, etc.	Management sets a policy as job's information are not leaked out of the organization.	Each member of IT deparment required to read and understand the information security policy. Itself to achieve level is 100%.	The employee contributing to his deparment, and has awareness of deparment strategies. Performance level is 70%.
		Management	The management has not invest the equipment and the training program to employee, enlightenment activities.	The unwanted and unexpected events which are suddenly occurred in the organization leaved alone.	Management invest the budget. Maked policy are well-known, and understood.	Each member of IT deparment required to attend the training program, frequently measure the response of staff with the awareness program. Itself to achieve level is 100%.	Management take secret information seriously also takes the necessary awareness or training program. Performance level is 90%.
		Interaction between Agents	Management and employee did not share the organizational value.	The shared organizational value are degrade, collapsed, etc.	The shared organizational value will be improved.	The information of unwanted and unexpected events are provided through the hierarchy, interaction between agents. Itself to achieve level is 100%.	The information of unwanted and unexpected events are provide. Performance level is 20%.

Table 5. Assessment Process of Corporate Culture

7. Conclusion

Prevention of information security incidents within the organization has become a very important topic. In this research, moral concerns of corporate culture have been operationally defined by a questionnaire. By utilizing the survey data, it was investigated how factors that influence information morals in the workplace can be affected by management actions and the overall corporate structure.

The results showed that sectarian behaviour, belonging scale, moral leadership, and other single indicators have a powerful influence on corporate culture and moral behavior. Development of compliance systems has only a limited effect on the culture of fraud and neglect of violation in the workplace, and it does not have a very strong influence on information morals.

An assessment process of corporate culture has been proposed in order to maintain high standards of information morals and prevent incidents such as information leaks. The process has been made visible by showing how to create the table included herein as Table 5. Through the application of this assessment process, one may discover areas of corporate culture that adversely affect the standards of information morals within the organization.

8. References

Alfawaz, S., Nelson, K., & Mohannak, K. (2010, January). Information security culture: a behavior compliance conceptual framework. In *Proceedings of the Eighth Australasian Conference on Information Security*, Volume 105 (pp. 47-55).

Barnard, I., "The Functions of the Executive.", *Harvard University Press*, 1938.

Coles-Kemp, L., & Theoharidou, M. (2010). Insider threat and information security management. *In Insider Threats in Cyber Security* (pp. 45-71). Springer US.

Da Veiga, A., & Eloff, J. H. (2010). A framework and assessment instrument for information security culture. *Computers & Security*, 29(2), 196-207.

Gebrasilase, T., & Lessa, L. F. (2011). Information Security Culture in Public Hospitals: The Case of Hawassa Referral Hospital. *The African Journal of Information Systems*, 3(3), 1.

Greene, G., & D'Arcy, J. (2010, June). Assessing the Impact of Security Culture and the Employee-Organization Relationship on IS Security Compliance. In *5th annual symposium on information assurance* (ASIA'10) (p. 1).

Hedstrom, K., Kolkowska, E., Karlsson, F., & Allen, J. P. (2011). Value conflicts for information security management. *The Journal of Strategic Information Systems*, 20(4), 373-384.

Hofstede, G. (2010). Culture and Organizations: Software of the Mind. *New York, NY: McGraw-Hill*.

Hoshino, T., Arai, K., Hirano, S., & Yanagisawa, H. (2008). An empirical analysis of organizational climates of misconduct. *Hitotsubashi University*, 2(2): 157-177.

Kayworth, T., & Whitten, D. (2010). Effective information security requires a balance of social and technology factors. *MIS Quarterly Executive*, 9(3), 2012-52.

Lim, J. S., Ahmad, A., Chang, S., & Maynard, S. (2010). Embedding information security culture emerging concerns and challenges. *PACIS 2010 Proceedings*, Paper 43.

Mano, "The Meaning of the Concept of Lateral Organization in C.I. Barnard's Theory", *Hokkaido University Economic Studies*, 39-1, June, 1989.

Padayachee, K. (2012). Taxonomy of compliant information security behavior. *Computers & Security*, 31(5), 673-680.

Shover, N., & Hochstetler, A. (2002). Cultural explanation and organizational crime. *Crime, Law, & Social Change*, 37, 1-18.

Simon, H. A., "Administrative Behavior", *The Free Press*, 1945.

Van Niekerk, J. F., & Von Solms, R. (2010). Information security culture: A management perspective. *Computers & Security*, 29(4), 476-486.

Examining Attitudes toward Information Security Behaviour using Mixed Methods

M. Pattinson[1], M. Butavicius[2], K. Parsons[2], A. McCormac[2] and C. Jerram[1]

[1]Adelaide Business School, University of Adelaide, Australia
[2]Defence Science and Technology Organisation, Edinburgh, Australia
e-mail: {malcolm.pattinson; cate.jerram}@adelaide.edu.au; {marcus.butavicius;
kathryn.parsons; agata.mccormac}@dsto.defence.gov.au

Abstract

This paper reports on a mixed-method research project that examined the attitudes of computer users toward accidental/naive information security (InfoSec) behaviour. The aim of this research was to investigate the extent to which attitude data elicited from repertory grid technique (RGT) interviewees support their responses collected via an online survey questionnaire. Twenty five university students participated in this two-stage project. Individual attitude scores were calculated for each of the research methods and were compared across seven behavioural focus areas using Spearman product-moment correlation coefficient. The two sets of data exhibited a small-to-medium correlation when individual attitudes were analysed for each of the focus areas. In summary, this exploratory research indicated that the two research approaches were reasonably complementary and the RGT interview results tended to triangulate the attitude scores derived from the online survey questionnaire, particularly in regard to attitudes toward Incident Reporting behaviour, Email Use behaviour and Social Networking Site Use behaviour. The results also highlighted some attitude items in the online questionnaire that need to be reviewed for clarity, relevance and non-ambiguity.

Keywords

Information Security (InfoSec), InfoSec Behaviour, Repertory Grid Technique (RGT), Theory of Planned Behaviour, Attitude, Mixed Methods, Hybrid

1. Introduction

1.1. Background

There is a growing body of literature (Schneier 2004, Vroom and von Solms 2004, Stanton, Stam et al. 2005, Pattinson and Anderson 2007, Trček, Trobec et al. 2007) that asserts that a more effective means of reducing information risk within an organisation is to address the behaviour of computer users in parallel with, and not instead of, addressing hardware and software solutions. This human behavioural approach to managing information security (InfoSec) supports Schneier's (2004) claim that "...the biggest security vulnerability is still that link between keyboard and chair" (p. 1).

As a result, management are starting to focus on human behavioural solutions to achieve the purported benefits that a positive change in computer user behaviour can have on the security of their computer systems even though very little rigorous research has been conducted to-date to confirm this management practice. This is borne out by Abraham's (2011) "extensive literature review on information security behavior in the context of factors affecting security behavior (sic) of users in organizational environments" (p. 1). In this review she cites a paper by (Thomson and von Solms 1998) as one of a small number of studies that "recognized the effects of users' attitudes in shaping security behaviour" (p. 5).

The research described in this current paper focuses on behavioural information security. More specifically, it examines the attitudes that computer users have towards accidental/naïve behaviour. Examples of accidental/naïve behaviour include: leaving a computer unattended; opening unsolicited email attachments; using guessable passwords; not reporting security incidents; and accessing dubious web sites.

1.2. Aims

The aim of this research was to investigate the extent to which attitude data elicited from repertory grid technique (RGT) interviewees support their responses collected via an online survey questionnaire. In other words, is the online survey questionnaire, on its own, a reliable instrument for extracting the attitudes of computer users toward various types of accidental/naive InfoSec behaviour?

The objectives of this research were to:

- Develop and distribute an online survey questionnaire for University students to complete
- Analyse the data and calculate an attitude score for each participant for each type of behaviour
- Interview the same students using the semi-structured interviewing method known as the Repertory Grid Technique(RGT)
- Analyse the data and calculate an attitude score for each participant for each type of behaviour
- Compare the results and report on the extent to which the interview results supported the survey results.

The structure of this paper is as follows. The next section outlines the justification for this research and this is followed by a summary of the most relevant literature and the theories that underpin the research. The research methods deployed are then discussed. Finally the results are explained, findings are discussed and conclusions are presented.

2. Justification for this research

This paper reports on research that is motivated by the need to measure the attitudes of employees toward InfoSec behaviour so that intervention strategies can be implemented that will improve attitudes and mitigate risk-inclined behaviour. Figure

1 below shows the logic hierarchy of how this will lead to a higher level of security of the information system assets within an organisation.

Figure 1: Logic hierarchy of this current research

The Crossler, Johnston et al. (2013) paper titled *Future directions for behavioral information security research* highlights the need for research that addresses better methods of collecting, eliciting and measuring security-related data, particularly attitude data. Furthermore, this paper also calls for research that differentiates between insider deviant behaviour and insider misbehaviour. This current research contributes to both these requests by firstly, using a mixed-method research approach and secondly, by focusing on only accidental/naive behaviour.

3. Theoretical Issues & Literature

3.1. Overview

There is a considerable amount of research literature on the subject of general human behaviour (Ajzen and Fishbein 1973, Ajzen 1991, Brown 2005). Although there are numerous publications relating to the interaction between humans and computer systems, (commonly known as human-computer interaction (HCI)) (Myers, Hollan et al. 1996, Zhang, Benbasat et al. 2002, Olson and Olson 2003, Parsons, McCormac et al. 2014), there is very little rigorous research devoted to factors that may influence safe/unsafe user behaviour. It has only been in the last decade that literature has emerged out of the InfoSec discipline that discusses the impact of individual behaviour whilst using a computer (Leach 2003, Stanton, Stam et al. 2005, Trček, Trobec et al. 2007).

The theoretical framework that underpins this current research is a component of Ajzen's (1991) Theory of Planned Behaviour (TPB) that claims that attitude towards behaviour is positively associated with intended behaviour. (Refer the shaded areas in Figure 2 below). The other antecedents of the TPB that are claimed to influence intended behaviour include subjective norms and perceived behavioural control, (non-shaded areas), however these are not within the scope of this study.

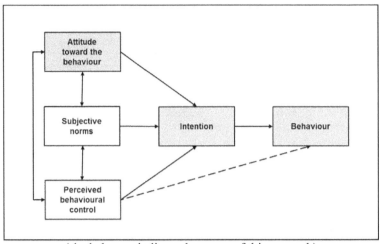

(shaded areas indicate the scope of this research)

Figure 2: Theory of Planned behaviour

Many studies have been conducted since (Fishbein and Ajzen 1975) and (Ajzen 1991) developed the theories of reasoned action (TRA) and planned behaviour (TPB) in an attempt to understand peoples' intentions to engage in a variety of activities. These theories are based on the assumption that intentional behaviour is directly related to actual behaviour (Fishbein and Ajzen 1975).

3.2. Human Behaviour

The disciplines of economics and social psychology have generated a large amount of literature, research and knowledge relating to human behaviour within organisations. In these studies, numerous theories have been espoused, many phenomena have been analysed and reported on and many concepts and principles have been developed. Examples are the Risk Homeostasis theory (Wilde 1994, Wilde 1998), the Bystander Effect theory (Darley and Latane 1968), the theory of Reasoned Action (Ajzen and Fishbein 1973) and the theory of Planned Behaviour (Ajzen 1991), to name a few. However, these studies have largely ignored the behaviour of people when they are working at a computer, particularly accidental/naive behaviour that relates to the security of an organisation's information systems.

3.2.1. Information Security (InfoSec) behaviour

Information security behaviours have been categorised in different ways by numerous studies (Stanton, Stam et al. 2005, Pattinson and Anderson 2007, Parsons, McCormac et al. 2014). For example, Stanton, et al (2005) refer to risk-averse behaviours as 'Aware Assurance' or 'Basic Hygiene'; naive behaviours as 'Dangerous Tinkering' or 'Naïve Mistakes': and risk-inclined behaviours as 'Intentional Destruction' or 'Detrimental Misuse'. For the purposes of this research and this paper, the term "InfoSec behaviour" refers to the full spectrum of behaviours by people who make significant use of computers as part of their job. As shown in Table 1 below, these behaviours range from deliberate risk-averse behaviours to deliberate risk-inclined behaviours.

Risk-averse behaviour (deliberate)	Naïve behaviour (accidental)	Risk-inclined behaviour (deliberate)
Always log-off when computer unattended	Leaving a computer unattended	Installing/using unauthorised software
Disallow email attachments from unknown sources	Opening unsolicited email attachments	Create & send SPAM email
Install more than one anti-virus software package & update regularly	Not installing anti-virus software	Writing & disseminating malicious code
Change password regularly	Sharing ID's & passwords	Hacking into other people's accounts
Vigilant in recognizing and approaching unauthorized personnel	Not being vigilant re unauthorised personnel	Giving unauthorized personnel access to authorized precincts
Back up work regularly	Not backing up work often enough	Theft or destruction of hardware or software
Always report security incidents	Not reporting security incidents	Conducting fraudulent activities
Install firewall	Accessing dubious web sites	Executing games on company equipment

Table 1: Examples of InfoSec behaviours (Pattinson and Anderson 2007)

The research described in this paper is focussed only on accidental/naive behaviours, examples of which are shown in the middle column of Table 1 above.

3.3. Attitude toward Behaviour

Although the concept of "attitude" is both complex and has been defined in many different ways by different researchers (Schrader and Lawless 2004), the psychology literature has essentially reached agreement on the concept of "attitude toward behaviour" or at least toward intended behaviour generally. This concept is universally understood as an overall feeling of a behaviour being favourable or unfavourable (Ajzen and Fishbein 2000). Other descriptions that are used include behaviour that is liked or dis-liked; desirable or un-desirable; good or bad; or behaviour that is viewed positively or negatively. This research project is concerned with information security behaviour, or more specifically, accidental/naïve behaviour of computer users. For the purposes of this paper, attitudes toward this type of behaviour are perceived as the extent to which a behaviour has the potential to put an organisation's information assets at risk. In other words, is the behaviour considered to be safe or unsafe, less risky or more risky, or likely to cause a low impact or a high impact?

3.4. Repertory Grid Technique (RGT)

The RGT is a cognitive technique that was developed by, and is grounded in George Kelly's Personal Construct Theory (1955). It is a method of interviewing in which interview participants divulge their perceptions, thoughts and views about a particular situation, object or event. The RGT has been used for a wide variety of applications within different domains such as in psychology studies (Bannister 1981, Armsby, Boyle et al. 1989) and in management research (Tan 1999). In terms of relevance to this paper, the RGT has also been applied in the information technology domain by Tan and Hunter (2002) who used it to investigate "the personal constructs that users and IS [information systems] professionals use to interpret IT [information technology] and its role in organizations" (pp. 53). Similarly, Whyte et al (1996) used the RGT to analyse factors that affect information systems "success". They interviewed business people and elicited their thoughts and opinions regarding factors that contribute to the "success" of the information systems they use.

Any number of psychological tools and techniques could be adapted to study the impact that user attitude has on accidental/naïve behaviour. However, Kelly's (1955) personal construct theory and the RGT appear to be ideally suited to the aims of this research and to the qualitative nature of the information being sought. This argument is supported by Hair *et al* (2009) who conclude that the RGT was an excellent tool to use within qualitative interviews because it enabled the elicitation of both hidden as well as tacit knowledge from interviewees. Other reported advantages of the RGT are that it can keep socially desirable responses to a minimum (Fransella, Bell et al. 2004) and minimise researcher bias (Jankowicz 2004). The RGT is also advantageous compared to other elicitation techniques because it facilitates both qualitative and quantitative data analysis (Curtis, Wells et al. 2008).

4. Research Methods

4.1. Overview

The research approach described in this paper is a mixed-method (that is, hybrid) research approach (Johnson and Christensen 2008). This particular mixed-method research design is a two-stage sequential design which incorporates an initial quantitative stage (online questionnaire) followed by a hybrid qualitative/quantitative stage (RGT interviews). The main reason for using a mixed-method approach for this project was to develop a complementary picture and to compare and triangulate results (Plano Clark and Badiee 2010). Furthermore, the topic being examined is "attitudes", that is, what humans think or feel about something, and in this project, it is their attitude toward accidental/naive risky behaviour of computer users. Therefore, it was appropriate that a quantitative stage should be followed by a qualitative (well, hybrid really) stage.

Participants were university students who were recruited via email. Most of the students were less than 30 years of age and had part time jobs. There were approximately equal number of males and females spread across all levels of university courses.

4.2. Stage 1

In this Stage, 122 students undertook a web-based survey that was accessible within a specific computer laboratory on the University campus. This online Qualtrics survey consisted of demographic questions; computer usage questions; personality and cognitive questions; and knowledge, attitude and behaviour questions. Refer Parsons, McCormac et al. (2014) for a more detailed explanation of this survey. The survey took approximately 40 minutes to complete for which participants were paid $30.

Participants were asked to rate 21 statements relating to their attitude towards computer-based behaviour on a 5-point rating scale ranging from "Strongly disagree" to "Strongly agree". Three statements were posed for each of the seven focus areas, namely, Password Management (PM), Email Use (EM), Internet Use (IU), Social Networking Site Use (SNS), Mobile Computing (MC), Information Handling (IH) and Incident Reporting (IR).

Approximately half of the statements were expressed in negative terms and questions were presented in random order of focus area. Each participant recorded 21 scores between 1 and 5. Negative questions were reversed prior to analysis. High scores represent a more favourable and better attitude toward InfoSec behaviours. Conversely, low scores represent an unfavourable and poor attitude. (Refer Table 2 in Section 5).

4.3. Stage 2

In this Stage, 25 participants from the pool of 122 who completed Stage 1, agreed to be interviewed by the researcher using the Repertory Grid Technique (RGT). The objective of these semi-structured interviews was to elicit the thoughts and views pertaining to their attitude toward information security (InfoSec) behaviours. Each interview took approximately 45 minutes and each participant was paid a further $30 for their involvement.

For these RGT interviews, a set of elements was required that represented this research's topic of interest, which was *"Attitudes toward information security behaviours"*. Although there are many approaches to developing such elements, it was decided to make these elements risk-inclined, accidental/naïve behaviours, using one from each of the seven focus areas used in Stage 1. The RGT interviews were then conducted with the supplied elements for the sole purpose of eliciting bi-polar constructs from interviewees that represented their thoughts, views and attitudes about InfoSec behaviours. This method uses the techniques of triading, laddering and pyramiding to extract appropriate and useful information from interviewees whilst ensuring researcher bias is eliminated and socially desirable responses are minimised (Stewart, Stewart et al. 1981). Interviewees were specifically asked *"What word or phrase would you use to describe the behaviour"*. On average, seven bi-polar constructs were generated by each participant before saturation was reached.

Figure 3 below shows a typical filled-in RGT individual interview sheet with the seven elements as columns and eight elicited bipolar constructs as rows (construct number 10 was supplied by the researcher). The 7 x 8 matrix of numbers are the element-construct scores out of 5 whereby "1" represents the left-hand side construct and "5" represents the right-hand side construct. For example, the interviewee of Figure 3 thought that behaviour number 6, "Inserting an unfamiliar DVD or USB into a Uni computer" was relatively "Less harmful to information" and scored it a "4" as shown circled in red.

REPERTORY GRID INTERVIEW 1	1. Using weak, guessable passwords	2. Opening email attachments from unknown senders	3. Viewing inappropriate web sites on a Uni computer	4. Posting sensitive Uni information on FaceBook using a Uni computer	5. Using a laptop to do Uni work in a public place	6. Inserting an unfamiliar DVD or USB into a Uni computer	7. Not reporting security incidents	01_1002 Interviewee / University of Adelaide Organisation / 19/05/2014 3 pm Date 5
1. Inconsiderate of other people's safety	2	1	4	3	3	4	5	Inconsiderate of own safety
2. Easier to identify as dangerous	1	2	3	3	4	4	5	Harder to identify as dangerous
3. More harmful to information	1	3	5	1	3	4	2	Less harmful to information
4. Larger impact on me	1	1	4	4	4	5	5	Larger impact on others
5. Unfamiliar environment	5	5	4	4	2	4	4	Familiar environment
6. More negligent	2	3	2	1	4	1	1	Less negligent
7. Harm felt by Uni	5	4	1	2	2	1	3	Harm felt by students
8. More likely to cause technology damage	2	2	1	3	1	4	5	More likely to cause physical damage
9.								
10. Overall, less risky	4	3	2	3	1	5	4	Overall, more risky

Figure 3: A sample filled-in repertory grid interview sheet

The set of 25 repertory grids consisting of 204 constructs needed to be reduced into a more manageable set of attitudes and this was done via a formal categorisation process in accordance with Jankowicz's (2004) core categorisation method (pp. 149). In order to analyse the raw grid data in a grounded theory manner, a set of themes (i.e. categories) needed to be developed (Cassell and Walsh 2004). There are numerous approaches to doing this, for example, one could use categories from the research literature. However, it was decided to use Osgood's (1957) three basic dimensions of responses to semantic differential constructs that have been used to "measure" attitude. The three dimensions, namely, Evaluation, Potency, and Activity (EPA) have been used in a variety of studies, in particular, studies about attitudes (Heise 1970, Kervyn, Fiske et al. 2013). In this current study, constructs were categorised as:

- EVALUATION (E): if the construct refers to behaviours as being good-bad, accidental-deliberate, sensible-foolish, responsible-careless etc.
- POTENCY (P): if the construct refers to behaviours as being less risky-more risky, low impact-high impact, few affected-many affected etc.

- ACTIVITY (A): for all other types of construct that could not be coded as "E" or "P", including inappropriate constructs such as 'knowledge of policy-unaware of policy'.

After this core categorisation process, each interviewee's construct ratings across the seven behaviours were converted to a score that represented their attitude towards these behaviours. This was calculated by multiplying the mean of all the ratings for his or her "E" constructs by the mean of all the ratings for his or her "P" constructs represented by:

$$Attitude = \frac{\sum_{i=1}^{n} E_i}{n} \quad X \quad \frac{\sum_{i=1}^{m} P_i}{m}$$

where E_i = i^{th} construct categorised as "E", n = number of E constructs in the grid, P_i = i^{th} construct categorised as "P", m = number of P constructs in the grid. Overall results were calculated as the mean of the focus area scores.

All constructs categorised as "A" were not used in this study.

5. Results

5.1. Stage 1

Table 2 below shows how five of the 25 participants scored the attitude questions in the online questionnaire between 1 and 5 for each of the seven focus areas. A high score (maximum = 5) indicates that the participant thought that the behaviour was bad and harmful. This represents a favourable and good attitude. Conversely, a low score (minimum = 1) indicates that the participant thought the behaviour was not so bad and quite harmless. This represents an unfavourable and poor attitude towards behaviours. The "overall" score for each individual is simply the mean of all focus area scores.

Participant Number	Participant ID	PM	EM	IU	SNS	MC	IH	IR	Overall
1	01-1002	5	5	1	4	1	5	1	3.11
2	01-1004	5	4	2	4	2	2	3	3.14
3	01-1005	5	3	1	4	3	2	1	2.71
4	01-1008	5	4	3	4	2	2	1	3.00
5	01-1009	4	4	3	4	2	4	2	3.29

Table 2: Sample Attitude Scores from Online Questionnaire

5.2. Stage 2

Table 3 below shows the calculated RGT interview scores for five of the 25 interviewees for each focus area. A high score (maximum = 25) indicates that the interviewee thought that the behaviour was bad and harmful. This represents a favourable and good attitude. Conversely, a low score (minimum = 1) indicates that the interviewee thought the behaviour was not so bad and quite harmless. This represents an unfavourable and poor attitude towards behaviours. The "overall" score for each interviewee is simply the mean of the focus area scores.

Interviewee Number	Interviewee ID	PM	EM	IU	SNS	MC	IH	IR	Overall
1	01-1002	12.0	10.0	9.0	18.0	8.8	12.3	10.5	11.50
2	01-1004	2.0	12.0	16.0	16.0	2.5	13.5	10.0	10.29
3	01-1005	25.0	18.0	7.5	10.0	15.0	25.0	14.0	16.36
4	01-1008	13.5	7.0	20.0	16.0	3.0	7.5	22.5	12.79
5	01-1009	15.0	10.0	5.0	10.0	16.0	15.0	5.0	10.86

Table 3: Sample Attitude Scores from Repertory Grid Technique (RGT) interviews

5.3. Summary of Results

The attitude scores for each of the two research methods were compared using Spearman product-moment correlation coefficient. The results for the individual attitudes toward each of the seven focus-area behaviours, showed small (rho > .10) to medium sized (rho > .30) correlations (Cohen 1988) between the two research methods, for most of the focus-area behaviours. This was achieved by comparing the individual scores for the seven attitude statements (items) in the questionnaire with the individual raw scores for each of the seven behaviours in the RGT interview (RGT elements).

Behaviour Focus Area	Spearman correlation coefficient (rho)	Sig. (two-tailed)	Coefficient of determination
Password Management	.015	.946	0.02%
Email Use	.175	.423	3.06%
Internet Use	.013	.953	0.02%
Social Networking Site Use	.215	.325	4.62%
Mobile Computing	.161	.463	2.59%
Information Handling	-.148	.500	2.19%
Incident Reporting	.364	.088	13.25%

Table 4: Spearman product-moment correlations

More specifically, the attitude of participants toward the behaviour of Reporting Security Incidents indicated a medium positive correlation between the survey questionnaire and the RGT interviews. For the other behaviours there was a small positive correlation between the two studies except for the behaviour Information Handling, which had a small negative correlation. Table 4 above also shows the coefficient of determination which indicates how much variance between the two studies that each of the seven attitudes share and although these percentages of variance are small, the results are encouraging and warrant further examination.

6. Limitations

1. The sample size of 25 participants was probably the reason that the levels of statistical significance (which suggest how much confidence one should have in the results), did not reach the traditional $p < .05$ levels. However, the strength of the relationships (rho) between the two sets of results was encouraging given the small sample size.

2. This research project involved university students as participants that are not representative of typical employees despite the fact that most of them had part time jobs. Future research will need to involve a more representative cross-section of employed people.

3. In retrospect, the design of the semi-structured RGT interviews could have been more aligned to the attitude statements in the survey questionnaire. Although they were similar, perhaps they needed to be identical.

4. The wording of some of the attitude statements in the survey questionnaire may have been ambiguous to participants. This observation has highlighted the need for constant updating to accommodate different populations, new behaviours and up-to-date hardware and software terminology.

7. Conclusions and future directions

The aim of this research was to investigate the extent to which attitude data elicited from repertory grid technique (RGT) interviewees support their responses collected via an online survey questionnaire. In other words, is the online survey questionnaire, on its own, a reliable instrument for extracting the attitudes of computer users toward various types of accidental/naive InfoSec behaviour?

In summary, the two research approaches were reasonably complementary and the RGT interview results tended to triangulate the attitude scores derived from the online survey questionnaire, particularly in regard to attitudes toward Incident Reporting behaviour, Email Use behaviour and Social Networking Site Use behaviour. The results also highlighted some attitude items in the online questionnaire that need to be reviewed for clarity, relevance and non-ambiguity.

This study contributes to the challenge of developing a reliable instrument that will assess individual InfoSec awareness (ISA) since attitude, (together with knowledge) is usually a principal component of ISA. Senior management will be better placed to design intervention strategies such as training and education of employees if individual attitudes are known. This, in turn, will not only improve attitudes but will mitigate risk-inclined behaviour making for a more secure environment.

8. References

Abraham, S. (2011). Information Security Behaviour: Factors and research directions. AMCIS 2011 Proceedings - All Submissions. Paper 462.

Ajzen, I. (1991). "The theory of planned behaviour." Organisational Behaviour and Human Decision Processes **50**(2).

Ajzen, I. and M. Fishbein (1973). "Attitudinal and normative variables as predictors of specific behaviour " Journal of Personality and Social Psychology **27**(1): 41-57.

Ajzen, I. and M. Fishbein (2000). "Attitudes and the attitude-behavior relation: Reasoned and automatic processes." European review of social psychology **11**(1): 1-33.

Armsby, P., A. Boyle and C. Wright (1989). "Methods for assessing drivers' perception of specific hazards on the road." Accident Analysis & Prevention **21**(1): 45-60.

Bannister, D. (1981). "Personal construct theory and research method." Human Inquiry: A Sourcebook of New Paradigm Research, John Wiley & Sons Ltd, New York, USA.

Brown, S. (2005). "Relationships between risk-taking behaviour and subsequent risk perceptions." British Journal of Psychology **96**(2): 155-164.

Cassell, C. and S. Walsh (2004). Repertory Grids. Essential Guide to Qualitative Methods in Organizational Research. C. Cassell and G. Syman. London, England, Sage Publications Ltd: 61-72.

Cohen, J. W. (1988). Statistical power analysis for the behavioral sciences. Hillsdale, New Jersey, USA, Lawrence Erlbaum Associates.

Crossler, R. E., A. C. Johnston, P. B. Lowry, Q. Hu, M. Warkentin and R. Baskerville (2013). "Future directions for behavioral information security research." Computers & Security **32**(0): 90-101.

Curtis, A., T. Wells, P. Lowry and T. Higbee (2008). "An Overview and Tutorial of the Repertory Grid Technique in Information Systems Research." Communications of AIS **2008**(23): 37-62.

Darley, J. M. and B. Latane (1968). "Bystander intervention in emergencies: diffusion of responsibility." Journal of personality and social psychology **8**(4p1): 377.

Fishbein, M. and I. Ajzen (1975). Belief, attitude, intention and behavior: An introduction to theory and research.

Fransella, F., R. Bell and D. Bannister (2004). A Manual for Repertory Grid Technique. West Sussex, England, John Wiley & Sons Ltd.

Hair, N., S. Rose and M. Clark (2009). "Using qualitative repertory grid techniques to explore perceptions of business-to-business online customer experience." Journal of Customer Behaviour **8**: 51-65.

Heise, D. R. (1970). "The semantic differential and attitude research." Attitude measurement: 235-253.

Jankowicz, D. (2004). The Easy Guide to Repertory Grids, John Wiley & Sons Ltd.

Johnson, B. and L. Christensen (2008). Educational research : quantitative, qualitative, and mixed approaches. Thousand Oaks, Calif., Sage Publications.

Kelly, G. (1955). The Psychology of Personal Constructs New York, Norton.

Kervyn, N., S. T. Fiske and V. Y. Yzerbyt (2013). "Integrating the stereotype content model (warmth and competence) and the Osgood semantic differential (evaluation, potency, and activity)." European Journal of Social Psychology **43**(7): 673-681.

Leach, J. (2003). "Improving user security behaviour." Computers & Security **22**(8): 685-692.

Myers, B., J. Hollan, I. Cruz, S. Bryson, D. Bulterman, T. Catarci, W. Citrin, E. Glinert, J. Grudin and Y. Ioannidis (1996). "Strategic directions in human-computer interaction." ACM Computing Surveys (CSUR) **28**(4): 794-809.

Olson, G. and J. Olson (2003). "Human-Computer Interaction: Psychological Aspects of the Human Use of Computing." Annual Review of Psychology **54**(1): 491.

Osgood, C., G. Suci and P. Tannenbaum (1957). The Measurement of Meaning, University of Illinois Press.

Parsons, K., A. McCormac, M. Butavicius, M. Pattinson and C. Jerram (2014). "Determining employee awareness using the Human Aspects of Information Security Questionnaire (HAIS-Q)." Computers & Security **42**: 165-176.

Pattinson, M. and G. Anderson (2007). "How well are information risks being communicated to your computer end-users?" Information Management & Computer Security **15**(5): 362-371.

Plano Clark, V. L. and M. Badiee (2010). "Research questions in mixed methods research." Mixed Methods in Social and Behavioral Research: 275-304.

Schneier, B. (2004). "The People Paradigm." CSO Security and Risk Newsletter Retrieved June 23, 2011, from http://www.csoonline.com/article/219787/bruce-schneier-the-people-paradigm.

Schrader, P. and K. A. Lawless (2004). "The knowledge, attitudes, & behaviors approach how to evaluate performance and learning in complex environments." Performance Improvement **43**(9): 8-15.

Stanton, J., K. Stam, P. Mastrangelo and J. Jolton (2005). "Analysis of end user security behaviors." Computers & Security **24**(2): 124-133.

Stewart, V., A. Stewart and N. Fonda (1981). Business Applications of Repertory Grid, McGraw-Hill Companies.

Tan, F. (1999). Exploring Business-IT Alignment Using the Repertory Grid, Citeseer.

Tan, F. and M. Hunter (2002). "The Repertory Grid Technique: A Method for the Study of Cognition in Information Systems." MIS Quarterly **26**(1): 39-57.

Thomson, M. and R. von Solms (1998). "Information security awareness: educating your users effectively." Information Management & Computer Security **6**(4): 167-173.

Trček, D., R. Trobec, N. Pavešsić and J. Tasič (2007). "Information systems security and human behaviour." Behaviour & Information Technology **26**(2): 113-118.

Vroom, C. and R. von Solms (2004). "Towards information security behavioural compliance." Computers & Security **23**(3): 191-198.

Whyte, G. and A. Bytheway (1996). "Factors affecting information systems' success." International Journal of Service Industry Management **7**(1): 74-93.

Wilde, G. (1994). Target risk, PDE Publications Toronto.

Wilde, G. J. (1998). "Risk homeostasis theory: an overview." Injury Prevention **4**(2): 89-91.

Zhang, P., I. Benbasat, J. Carey, F. Davis, D. Galletta and D. Strong (2002). "Human-computer interaction research in the MIS discipline." Communications of the AIS **9**(20): 334-355.

Inter-Organisational Information Sharing – Between a Rock and a Hard Place

F. Karlsson, E. Kolkowska, K. Hedström, and M. Frostenson

Örebro University School of Business, SE-701 82 Örebro, Sweden
e-mail: {fredrik.karlsson; ella.kolkowska; karin.hedstrom;
magnus.frostenson}@oru.se

Abstract

Although inter-organisational collaboration is common, most information security (IS) research has focused on IS issues within organisations. Confidentiality, integrity of data and availability (CIA) and responsibility, integrity of role, trust, and ethicality (RITE) are two sets of principles for managing IS that have been developed from an intra-organisational, rather static, perspective. The aim of this paper is thus to investigate the relation between the CIA and RITE principles in the context of an inter-organisational collaboration, i.e., collaboration between organisations. To this end we investigated inter-organisational collaboration and information sharing concerning Swedish cooper corrosion research in the field a long-term nuclear waste disposal. We found that in an inter-organisational context, responsibility, integrity of role and ethicality affected the CIA-principles, which in turn affected the collaborating actors' trust in each other over time.

Keywords

Information security, inter-organisational, CIA, RITE

1. Introduction

Although in today's global world, collaboration between different organisations is common and necessary, most of the research within the information security (IS) field focuses on IS issues within an organisation. A missing focus is thus IS in an inter-organisational setting (McLaughlin and Gogan, 2014). An inter-organisational collaboration entails integrated business processes and sharing of information that in an intra-organisational setting is considered an organisation's own property. Such changes raise new IS challenges related to the common technical infrastructure (technical aspects), common policies and procedures (formal aspects), as well as to goals, beliefs and values about how things should be done in relation to IS (informal aspects) (Dhillon et al., 2014).

While the international standard ISO 27002 (ISO, 2013) provides some practical guidelines how to maintain confidentiality, integrity and availability (CIA) of information by establishing technical and formal security safeguards in inter-organisational collaborations, the informal aspects are not considered. In response to CIA, Dhillon and Backhouse (2000) offered RITE (Responsibility, Integrity, Trust, and Ethicality), which can be seen as alternative, or complementing, principles. Both CIA and RITE are developed from an intra-organisational, rather static, perspective, and while CIA focuses the objectives of IS, RITE offers a way of managing IS. The aim of this paper is thus to investigate the relation between the CIA and RITE principles in the context of an inter-organisational collaboration. To this end we investigated inter-organisational collaboration and information sharing concerning Swedish cooper corrosion research in the field a long-term nuclear waste disposal.

The paper is structured as follows. Section 2 contains a discussion about existing research. First we address inter-organisational IS research, and second we look into the CIA and RITE principles. In section 3, we present our research design. Section 4 reports on our analysis of the case study. Finally, the paper ends with a discussion in Section 5 and a short conclusion in Section 6.

2. Related research

2.1. Inter-organisational research

Research focusing IS in the context of inter-organisational collaboration is scant (McLaughlin and Gogan, 2014). Most of the existing papers seem to target technical and formal aspects of IS, and we have only come across a few papers that deal with informal aspects. Technical aspects of IS in the context of inter-organisational collaboration are mostly studied in relation to access controls (e.g. Chen et al., 2007, Kayem et al., 2011) and architectural framework (e.g. Djordjevic et al., 2007, Yuan et al., 2009, Mao et al., 2008). When it comes to formal aspects a lot of effort has been put into researching the area of outsourcing (e.g. Pemble, 2004, Dommun, 2008, Berghmans and van Roy, 2011).

The few studies focusing informal aspects of IS in the context of inter-organisational collaboration are related to outsourcing (Tsohou et al., 2007, Robertson et al., 2010, Bahl et al., 2011). Bahl et al. (2011) identified cultural challenges in outsourcing to India and Tsohou et al. (2007) presented a conceptual framework in order to track down and manage cultural differences between organisations in outsourcing ventures. In the third study, Robertsson et al. (2010) investigated moral reasoning related to outsourcing decisions and concluded that from this perspective IS issues are more important than quality issues for the stakeholders. Against this backdrop we can conclude that to the best of our knowledge, principles of IS with regard to inter-organisational collaboration has not been researched at all and thus there is a need for more studies within this area. Our study contributes to this research by investigating the relation between the CIA and RITE principles in the context of an inter-organisational collaboration.

2.2. Principles of information security

Previous research and practice has identified a number of principles for managing IS in an organisation (Dhillon, 2007). Although it is important to understand the meaning and origin of these principles, such a discussion is beyond the scope of this paper. The principles of CIA are the most known and most frequently used within IS (Dhillon, 2007). According to ISO 27 001 (ISO, 2005) confidentiality states that information is not made available or disclosed to unauthorised individuals, entities or processes. Integrity of data means the of safeguarding the accuracy and completeness of assets. Availability is defined as information that is accessible and usable upon demand by an authorised entity (ISO, 2005). Dhillon and Backhouse (2000) argued that the CIA-principles are useful and important primarily in relation to formal and technical parts of IS management in an organisation, while they are insufficient when dealing with informal aspects of IS management. Therefore they offered additional principles, known as Responsibility, Integrity of role, Trust, and Ethicality (RITE). Responsibility means that members of an organisation, or in our case members of an inter-organisational collaboration, know and understand the existing rules and responsibilities. Based on that knowledge, these members are able to develop their own security practices in unexpected situations; practices that are in line with organisational rules and responsibilities. Integrity means having feelings of integrity as a member of an organisation and feeling loyalty to that organisation. Trust means that members in an organisation are not controlled but instead are trusted to act according to the organisation's norms and accepted patterns of behaviour. Ethicality means that members of an organisation should act according to ethical principles.

3. Research method

3.1. Case description

The relation between CIA and RITE was studied in the context of a reference group on copper corrosion research with regard to long-term nuclear waste disposal in Sweden. The reference group was established 2010, after researchers at the Royal Institute of Technology (KTH) in Stockholm found that copper can corrode in oxygen-free water indicating that the method for nuclear waste disposal advocated by the Swedish Nuclear Fuel and Waste Management Company (SKB) may be flawed. SKB was sceptical to the results and wanted to investigate them further. Two research projects were planned. The first at SP Technical Research Institute of Sweden on copper wires that had been in a test tube for 20 years and the other research project was planned at Uppsala University with the aim to repeat the experiments of the KTH researchers. The reference group, which was established on an initiative of SKB, was supposed to have full insight in the design and accomplishments of these experiments and also a possibility to review SKB's reports regarding these experiments before being published. SKB promised full transparency and openness regarding the experiments. The reference group consisted of researchers (KTH), SKB representatives, environmental groups, and representatives of public interests, such as politicians and civil servants of the local municipalities and regions affected by the nuclear waste deposit. In October 2012, an environmental group, the Swedish NGO Office for Nuclear Waste Review (MKG) officially left the group motivating this with SKB's unwillingness to improve public transparency into SKB's entire work with copper corrosion. MKG claimed that the transparency that SKB offered was far from what they promised when the reference group was established. In 2013, the KTH researchers decided to leave the group because of a conflict regarding the process of reviewing a preliminary report from the experiments. The KTH researchers claimed that they had been instructed by SKB to neglect some research findings that would influence the review of the report. They argued that such a review was unacceptable within established scientific practice. We can see that the different views on how the information should be handled and who should be trusted with sensitive information prevented the reference group from achieving its aim. Therefore, we found this case suitable for studying the relation between CIA and RITE in the context of inter-organisational collaboration. A detailed description of the case background can be found in Andersson (2014).

3.2. Data collection and data analysis

Given that several different views on the collaboration and its outcome exist, our study focused on perceived IS (Oscarson, 2007). The empirical data consists of interviews with key members of the reference group on copper corrosion and protocols from this group. The interviews took about one hour each, and were conducted by phone, tape-recorded, and subsequently transcribed. We chose interviews as data collection method as we were "interested in gaining a rich and inclusive account of the participant's experience" (Polkinghorne, 2005). In our case, reference group members' experiences about information sharing about copper corrosion differ. In order to deepen our understanding, as well as allow for multiple perspectives, we chose to include members with different and contrasting views on their role in the reference group. In order to validate the interviews, we also analysed 17 protocols from reference group meetings between 2010 and 2014.

The analysis was conducted in four steps. First, we searched for respondents' statements about information sharing in the collected empirical data (interviews and protocols). Second, these statements were subsequently classified according to the principles of CIA or RITE. Third, we sorted these statements with regard to time. Fourth, we searched for differences in the respondents' views on the collaboration and in relation to CIA or RITE. The statements reported in the paper were chosen for illustrative purposes. In order to capture multiple perspectives, we have chosen statements from different respondents.

4. Analysis

In this section we take a closer look at how the three actors perceived the collaboration with regard to IS. We do so by structuring the analysis according to the RITE and CIA-principles, and provide illustrative empirical examples related to these principles. An overview of the analysis is shown in Table 1. The table is structured into four columns. The leftmost column contains the principles we address, the second to fourth columns contain the different actors' views on each of the principles. Starting from the left we find SKB, in the middle column MKG, and finally KTH. In addition, we analyse the case based on two snapshots in time to capture the dynamics of the case; (T_1) when the reference group was initiated and (T_2) when the reference group was dissolved.

Responsibility: The three actors had different responsibilities in the collaboration. Throughout the reference group (T_1-T_2) SKB was the process owner. They had responsibility to investigate whether or not copper corroded in oxygen-free environments, and to "assess that the process did not affect safety of the long-term disposal of nuclear waste" (Protocol May 19, 2010). MKG joined the reference group (T_1) with the intention to safeguard quality of the process of selecting a technical solution for disposal of nuclear waste. Hence, they viewed themselves as process reviewers. KTH played the role as scientific reviewer and advisor to the projects that were to be executed. "We realised that we were the only ones who could comment on them [the results] scientifically" (KTH-researcher). These responsibilities were reinforced further as we approach T_2 where MKG and KTH opted-out as a result of how the work in the reference group unfolded.

Principle	SKB	MKG	KTH
Responsibility	Process owner	Process reviewer	Scientific reviewer and advisor
Integrity of role	Reference group concerning specific topics	The general public concerning all topics	Reference group
Trust	T_1: Moderate for KTH and MKG T_2: Moderate for KTH, low for MKG	T_1: High for KTH, low for SKB T_2: High for KTH, low for SKB	T_1: Moderate for SKB, and MKG T_2: Low for SKB, moderate for MKG
Ethicality	Only publish information that SKB has reviewed	No information may be withheld	No information relevant for scientific review may be withheld
Confidentia-lity	T_1: No project information is held confidential to the reference group T_2: Intermediate results are made confidential	T_1: No information about SKB's research should be confidential to the general public T_2: No information about SKB's research should be confidential to the general public	T_1: No project information should be held confidential to the reference group T_2: No project information should be held confidential to the reference group
Integrity of data	T_1: Integrity of data exists T_2: Integrity of data exists	T_1: Integrity of data exists T_2: Integrity of data does not exists	T_1: Integrity of data exists T_2: Integrity of data does not exists
Availability	T_1: All project information is available to the reference group T_2: Intermediate results are not made available	T_1: All information about SKB's research should be available to the general public T_2: All information about SKB's research should be available to the general public	T_1: All project information should be available to the reference group T_2: All project information should be available to the reference group

Table 1: Overview of analysis

Integrity of role: SKB used the reference group to discuss "corrosion of copper in an oxygen-free environment" (Protocol March 24, 2011). It meant that they did not view the reference group as a legitimate area to discuss all the research that they conducted. As process owner they felt able to choose projects, project results or parts thereof that were to be discussed in the reference group. In addition, they clearly stated that information to the public should only be provided when information where conclusive. MKG on the other hand demanded that information about all SKB's research activities should be available to the public. Hence, they saw no restriction in whom to include in the dissemination of research results. They based this view on the self-imposed role as process reviewer. KTH saw the members of the reference group as the group that should be trusted with disseminated research results. However, they experienced (T_1-T_2) that SKB viewed them "in the same way as the general public instead of having some kind of exclusive position because we were part of the reference group" (KTH-researcher).

Trust: When the reference group started (T_1) we saw that SKB trusted both KTH and MKG. However, there was a difference in the amount of trust for these organisations. SKB had high confidence in KTH as scientific reviewers in the reference group; at the same time SKB's confidence in MKG was a bit lower, mostly for historical reasons that MKG belongs to the environmental community. MKG on the other hand expressed a low confidence in SKB when they entered the reference group, much for the same reasons. MKG welcomed KTH's presence in the reference group because they would act as scientific reviewers; hence MKG had high confidence in them. Finally, KTH trusted both SKB and MKG when the reference group started.

The actors' trust in each other changed as the work in the reference group proceeded towards T_2. MKG and KTH started to distrust SKB. MKG expressed that "we are not impressed with how they [SKB] handled knowledge within the company" (MKG representative). This was mainly a result of how SKB made information available to the members of the reference group, and how they dealt with integrity of data which is discussed further below. KTH's loss of trust is evident in following statement: "it [transparency] was nice words in the beginning, but as time went by we understood that we did not get the transparency to the experiments. What we saw and commented on was what they [SKB] had decided from the start" (KTH-researcher).

SKB's trust in MKG was at the same time reduced because MKG disseminated information before official versions of the minutes were made available from the reference group. SKB claimed that MKG "was the one that each time after a meeting wrote on MKG's website ... we still had agreed that in order to get decent reports all minutes should be public and that all members of the reference group should be given the opportunity to give their opinion on the content before the minutes were made public" (SKB-representative). SKB's confidence in KTH partly remained intact during and after the reference group's lifetime, even though they left the reference group. It is shown by the following statement: "after the opt-out SKB wanted to associate KTH yet again to another group, where [person name] would be included" (KTH-researcher).

Ethicality: The three actors anchored their actions in different ethical principles that aligned with their responsibilities. SKB viewed it as ethical to review all research results before publishing them in order to only publish information that had their quality approval. MKG argued that "it [information] should be transparent" (MKG-representative) and made available as soon as possible. They meant it is the only way to guarantee well-informed choices with regard to nuclear waste disposal. KTH argued that information should be provided according to well-recognised scientific principles where all raw data from the research is made available to the reference group. Consequently, "to remove [research] results is a serious matter" (KTH-researcher).

Confidentiality: SKB claimed that when the reference group started (T_1) they had an IS policy not to keep any information concerning copper corrosion confidential. The SKB-representative claimed that "every actor in this context [the reference group] would have access to the results as they were produced". As the work proceeded, MKG, as process reviewer, requested that "SKB creates a reference group to follow the entire company's research on the KBS-method's barrier system, not only experiments on cooper corrosion in in deoxygenated water" (Protocol, March 23, 2011), and they requested to see unpublished reports. Consequently, they argued in line with the ethical principle of transparency. SKB "tried to oblige as much as possible. In the end, however, we had only agreed that the experiments in Uppsala were to be dealt with in the reference group" (SKB-representative).

As a consequence, SKB decided to change their IS policy (before T_2). "This reference group had great impact on SKB's policy for reporting" (SKB-representative). They started to divided research material into work-in-progress documents and final reports: "if we have the materials, which of course we have, which is work-in-progress material, it is never classified as a report or finished product. Instead it is a document" (SKB-representative). Work-in-progress documents were treated as confidential information and not released outside SKB. "It [the new policy] included the whole organisation, just not only research" (SKB-representative).

Integrity of data: As process owner SKB argued that they had to guarantee the quality of published research information. In one of the protocols we found: "SKB's policy is to only report data that we understand and trust" (Protocol November 15, 2010). This statement was anchored in SKB's ethical principle. They viewed it as their duty to remove research information that was uncertain, and that action did not affect the data integrity. MKG and KTH were of a different opinion. Both these actors argued that this process meant violating data integrity, that important data from the research projects were not included in the published information. For example, one disagreement concerned one of the reports. KTH described how "they [SKB] told us at a reference group meeting that all of the results were inaccurate because deficiencies in [test] equipment. Though they did not tell it in that report, where attempts were made to adapt the results to their own reality" (KTH-researcher). This view was also provided by MKG: "I think this is remarkable, scientifically, that these SKB-reports do not completely address the deficiency analysis of what is reported" (MKG representative).

Availability: As a consequence of not keeping any information concerning copper corrosion confidential to the reference group, SKB argued that they initially made all such information available (T_1). Information about some of the related projects were also made available on MKG's requests. However, MKG still argued that "the actual problem is that the transparency is not good enough" (MKG representative). Later on SKB changed their policy and work-in-progress documents were no longer available to MKG and KTH (before T_2). Both MKG and KTH argued that this made it impossible for them to fulfil their responsibilities as process reviewers and as scientific reviewers and advisors.

5. Discussion

Several principles exist for managing IS, such as CIA (ISO, 2013) and RITE (Dhillon and Backhouse, 2000). However, research on IS management has mainly had an intra-organisational focus (McLaughlin and Gogan, 2014), while inter-organisational collaboration is common today. Therefore, we have analysed the relation between the CIA and RITE principles in an inter-organisational collaboration.

Our findings show that differences in responsibility and integrity of role affected the collaborating actors' views on the implementation of confidentiality and availability. SKB, as process owner, shared information on specific topics with the reference group. Hence, they kept more information confidential than MKG and KTH expected from the start. In addition, in this case we also found a difference in the ethical principle; a difference related to the differences in responsibility and integrity of role. SKB saw it as their responsibility to only publish information that had passed their review process. This view differed from the views of their collaborating actors; they expressed a more liberate view on transparency of information and the process on how this information had been brought about. In the end this made the three actors disagree on the integrity of data that was made available to the reference group. The actors' different views on how the CIA-principles were implemented changed their trust in each other over time. In this specific case, MKG and KTH lost trust in SKB, mainly because they did not perceive that integrity of data was kept in SKB's reports to the reference group.

Hence, we have been able to show that the RITE and CIA principles are important to consider in inter-organisational collaboration. From a practitioner's point of view, it is important that collaborating actors are aware of their responsibilities and expectations, and that these are made explicit from the start. Furthermore, it is equally important that they have a shared view of the integrity of roles and ethicality because these views affect how they perceive the implementation of the CIA-principles. In the end it seems like the perceived implementation of the CIA-principles is crucial for building trust in inter-organisational collaboration. From a research point of view we contribute by showing the relation between these two sets of principles and how they affect each other over time in an inter-organisational setting. Moreover, earlier research on RITE principles (e.g. Dhillon and Backhouse, 2000) has focused on employees within organisations, i.e. on individuals in relation to an organisation. We have shown that it is fruitful to analyse IS management on an organisational level using these principles, i.e. an organisation in relation to one or more organisations.

6. Conclusion

Inter-organisational collaboration is important in today's society, but the knowledge on how to manage information security (IS) in such settings is limited. Against this backdrop the aim of this paper was to investigate the relation between the CIA (Confidentiality, Integrity of data, Availability) and RITE (Responsibility, Integrity of role, Trust, Ethicality) principles in the context of an inter-organisational collaboration. We conclude that there is a dynamic relation between these principles, which is important for organisations to be aware of when entering collaborations. Based on our investigated case we found that responsibility, integrity of role, and ethicality affected the perceived implementation of CIA. Differences in responsibility, integrity of role, and ethicality that the organisations are unaware of can create false expectations that can undermine collaboration, because the perceived implementation of CIA affects how (dis)trust is developed between the collaborating organisations over time.

Our findings are based on one single study of inter-organisational collaboration. Consequently, it is an obvious limitation of this study. However, our findings have shown an interesting opportunity for future research; more research is needed on IS principles in inter-organisational settings.

7. References

Andersson, K. 2014. Copper Corrosion in Nuclear Waste Disposal: A Swedish Case Study on Stakeholder Insight. *Bulletin of Science, Technology & Society,* 33, pp. 85-95.

Bahl, S., Wali, O. P. and Kumaraguru, P. Information Security Practices Followed in the Indian Software Services Industry: An Exploratory Study. *Second Worldwide Cybersecurity Summit (WCS 2011)* 2011 London, UK. IEEE, 1-2 June, 2011.

Berghmans, P. and Van Roy, K. 2011. Information Security Risks in Enabling e-Government: The Impact of IT Vendors. *Information Systems Management,* 28, pp. 284-293.

Chen, T.-Y., Chen, Y.-M., Wang, C.-B., Chu, H.-C. and Yang, H. 2007. Secure resource sharing on cross-organization collaboration using a novel trust method. *Robotics and Computer-Integrated Manufacturing,* 23, pp. 421-435.

Dhillon, G. 2007. *Principles of information systems security: text and cases,* Hoboken, NJ, Wiley Inc.

Dhillon, G. and Backhouse, J. 2000. Information security management in the new millenium. *Communication of the ACM,* 43, pp.

Dhillon, G., Chowdhuri, R. and Pedron, C. 2014. Organizational Transformation and Information Security Culture: A Telecom Case Study. *In:* Cuppens-Boulahia, N., Cuppens, F., Jajodia, S., Abou El Kalam, A. and Sans, T. (eds.) *ICT Systems Security and Privacy Protection - Proceedings 29th IFIP TC 11 International Conference, SEC 2014, Marrakech, Morocco, June 2-4, 2014.* Berlin: Springer

Djordjevic, I., Dimitrakos, T., Romano, N., Mac Randal, D. and Ritrovato, P. 2007. Dynamic security perimeters for inter-enterprise service integration. *Future Generation Computer Systems,* 23, pp. 633-657.

Dommun, M. R. 2008. Multi-level information system security in outsourcing domain. *Business Process Management Journal,* 14, pp. 849-857.

Iso 2005. ISO/IEC 27001:2005, Information Technology - Security Techniques - Information Security Management Systems - Requirements. International Organization for Standardization (ISO).

Iso 2013. ISO/IEC 27002:2013 Information technology — Security techniques — Code of practice for information security controls. International Organization for Standardization (ISO).

Kayem, A. V. D. M., Martin, P. and Akl, S. G. Efficient Enforcement of Dynamic Cryptographic Access Control Policies for Outsourced Data. *Information Security South Africa (ISSA), 2011,* 15-17 August, 2011 2011 Johannesburg, South Africa. IEEE Xplore, 1-8.

Mao, T., Williams, J. and Sanchez, A. Interoperable Internet Scale Security Framework for RFID Networks. *24th International Conference on Conference: Data Engineering Workshop,* 2008. IEEE Xplore, 94-99.

Mclaughlin, M.-D. and Gogan, J. INFOSEC in a Basket, 2004-2013. *The 20th Americas Conference on Information Systems (AMCIS 2014),* 2014 Savannah, Georgia, USA. AIS Electronic Library (AISeL), ISSecutity paper 6.

Oscarson, P. 2007. *Actual and perceived information systems security.* Linköping University.

Pemble, M. 2004. Transferring business and support functions: the information security risks of outsourcing and off-shoring. *Computer Fraud & Security,* 2004, pp. 5-9.

Polkinghorne, D. E. 2005. Language and Meaning: Data Collection in Qualitative Research. *Journal of Counseling Psychology,* 52, pp. 137-145.

Robertson, C. J., Lamin, A. and Livanis, G. 2010. Stakeholder Perceptions of Offshoring and Outsourcing: The Role of Embedded Issues. *Journal of Business Ethics,* 95, pp. 167-189.

Tsohou, A., Theoharidou, M., Kokolakis, S. and Gritzalis, D. 2007. Addressing Cultural Dissimilarity in the Information Security Management Outsourcing Relationship. *In:* Lambrinoudakis, C., Pernul, G. and Tjoa, A. M. (eds.) *Trust, Privacy and Security in Digital Business.* Springer.

Yuan, H., Chen, G., Wu, J. and Xiong, H. 2009. Towards controlling virus propagation in information systems with point-to-group information sharing. *Decision Support Systems,* **48,** pp. 57-68.

Exploring the Link Between Behavioural Information Security Governance and Employee Information Security Awareness

W. Flores and M. Ekstedt

Industrial Information and Control Systems, Royal Institute of Technology
e-mail: waldorf@kth.se; mathias.ekstedt@ics.kth.se

Abstract

This paper explores the relation between a set of behavioural information security governance factors and employees' information security awareness. To enable statistical analysis between proposed relations, data was collected from two different samples in 24 organisations: 24 information security executives and 240 employees. The results reveal that having a formal unit with explicit responsibility for information security, utilizing coordinating committees, and sharing security knowledge through an intranet site significantly correlates with dimensions of employees' information security awareness. However, regular identification of vulnerabilities in information systems and related processes is significantly negatively correlated with employees' information security awareness, in particular managing passwords. The effect of behavioural information security governance on employee information security awareness is an understudied topic. Therefore, this study is explorative in nature and the results are preliminary. Nevertheless, the paper provides implications for both research and practice.

Keywords

Information security, behavioural information security governance, information security awareness

1. Introduction

The presence of new ways to compromise information security has moved the attention from an security approach with a technological focus to a more holistic approach to information security management (Kayworth and Whitten, 2010). Several approaches focusing on the "human" side of holistic information security management have, therefore, been proposed by researchers. These approaches can roughly be divided in two categories: (1) approaches focusing on the 'individual' level of information security to understand behaviours of individuals (goes under the name of behavioural information security research (Fagnot, 2008; Crossler et al., 2013)); (2) approaches focusing on the managerial level to understand which factors determine effective holistic information security governance and management (in this paper referred to as behavioural information security governance in line with the terminology used by Mishra and Dhillon (2006)). A dominant part of the studies have focused on the first category (Warkentin and Willison, 2009). These studies have increased the understanding of factors explaining information system misuse on an end-user level. However, there are limited studies investigating the effect of behavioural information security governance, e.g., the establishment of organisational structures, processes and the implementation of security awareness programs on end-users perceptions of information security.

Although there are studies investigating the topic of behavioural information security governance, many of these studies have largely remained anecdotal (Puhakainen and Siponen, 2010). Existing work have proposed conceptual and practical principles that neither are theoretical grounded nor offer empirical evidence (e.g., Da Veiga and Eloff, 2007; Brotby, 2009; Sobh and Elleithy, 2013). Other works have based their empirical studies on best practice frameworks such as ISO/IEC 27002 (e.g., Chang and Ho, 2006; Dzazali and Zolait, 2012). Qualitative conclusions have also been drawn based on case studies or semi-structured interviews. Warkentin and Johnston (2007) attempted to understand the implications of two types of information security governance – centralized and decentralized governance. This comparative case study identified that organisations with a decentralized governance structure employees are responsible for their awareness training, while in organisations with a centralized governance structure formal awareness training were exclusively carried out by centralized IT personnel. Kayworth and Whitten (2010) developed a framework to support the attainment of information security strategy objectives. The components of the framework included nine organisational integration mechanisms (e.g., formal security unit, steering committee, information security embedded within key organisational processes) and four social alignment mechanisms (e.g., security awareness programs, executive commitment). All these aforementioned studies have increased the understanding of behavioural information security governance, and provided theoretical insights into the potential effects of an organisation's level of information security. However, none of them have empirically tested this effect, in particular, its effect of employees' information security awareness.

The purpose of this paper is to empirically examine the link between a set of behavioural information security governance factors and employees' information security awareness. This purpose is fulfilled by formulating the following research question:

RQ1: Which behavioural information security governance factors have a significant influence on employee information security awareness?

The rest of the paper is structured as follows. In section 2, the theoretical foundation related to behavioural information security governance and information security awareness is presented. In section 3, the methodology of the study is described. The section that follows presents the results from the empirical study employed in order to answer the study's research question. The final section discusses the results and concludes the paper.

2. Establishing a theoretical foundation

The theoretical foundation of this paper is based on findings from an explorative research stage. This stage led to the development of a theory proposing how behavioural information security governance might have an effect on employees' information security awareness. During this stage qualitative data was collected through interviews with six experts working with information security on a regular basis for 5 to 20 years. Of the six experts, three worked as senior information security consultants at two different information security consultancy firms; one worked as head of information security at a software application development firm; and the final two respondents were currently academics but with many years of practical experience as information security consultants (Rocha Flores and Ekstedt, 2013). The findings from the interviews were combined with searching literature to aid logical reasoning when establishing the theoretical foundation. In order to assure that we included relevant dimensions of behavioral information security governance and information security awareness, the comprehensiveness of the included factors was evaluated. This was done by collecting data through a survey completed by 18 content experts. For a more in-depth description of the underlying theory, the interested reader is recommended to turn to the following sources: Rocha Flores and Ekstedt (2012); Rocha Flores and Korman (2012); Rocha Flores and Antonsen (2013); Rocha Flores et al., (2014a). In sum, three factors were included to test the effects of behavioural information security governance on information security awareness: organisational structures, coordinating information security processes, and security knowledge sharing. In the following, these are described together with the information security awareness factor.

2.1. Organisational structures

Proper organisational structures facilitate the deployment of security efforts, and communication between executives, security personnel, and business representatives. This can help end-users to understand the importance of information security and how it can be used to support the business and not hinder it. Furthermore, structures ensure that the security function maintains alignment with business strategy, enable effective organisation of information security and contribute to the successful implementation and coordination of information security plans (Kayworth and Whitten, 2010). In this study, organisational structure is manifested through the two following forms of structures: formal structure (also referred to as a centralized information security structure) and coordinating structure such as the utilization of a diversity of coordinating information security committees.

2.2. Coordinating information security processes

Processes to coordinate information security efforts support the integration of information security in key organisational business processes (Kayworth and Whitten, 2010). This enables security to be a core element in the business environment and strengthen the link between high-level business requirements and operational security procedures. In our study, two key dimensions of coordinating processes were derived: risk management and performance monitoring. In order to coordinate any information security activities, the need for security should first be assessed by identifying vulnerabilities that can negatively affect business operations (Calder and Watkins, 2008). To support the coordination of information security, controls need to be checked for their effectiveness in practice. They also need to be adapted to users' perceived level of obtrusiveness, and any changes in the business environment that might pose an IT-risk or negatively affect business operations.

2.1 Security knowledge sharing

Security knowledge sharing enable management of employee information security behaviour (Belsis et al., 2005; Zakaria, 2006). In the field of knowledge sharing, knowledge is considered as information processed by individuals including ideas, facts, expertise, and judgments relevant for the individual, team, and organisational performance (Wang and Noe, 2010). Knowledge sharing refers to the provision of task information and know-how to help others and to collaborate with others to solve problems, develop new ideas, or implement policies or procedures. The objective with security knowledge sharing is to increase or maintain information security knowledge among individuals in an organisation. In organisations, security knowledge sharing is manifested trough both formal means (e.g., security education and awareness training, policy communication), and informal means (e.g., informal consulting and advisory services). The sharing of knowledge is facilitated by the use of technology (e.g., intranet-based knowledge management systems) (Cummings, 2004; Rhodes et al., 2008).

2.3. Information security awareness

Achieving employee information security awareness has been recognized as a critical outcome of information security management programs (Werlinger et al., 2009; Kayworth and Whitten, 2010). Therefore, studies have focused on assessing information security awareness in order to identify strategies to increase employees' awareness (Karakasiliotis et al., 2006; Dodge et al. 2007; Rocha Flores et al., 2014c). In this study information security awareness is defined as an employee's general knowledge about information security threats, and his or her knowledge of specific information security policies related to information security. This means that an employee can be aware of threats related to information security based on past experience or interest. The employee can also be aware of the organisations specific information security policies regulating proper security behaviour. This is a result of specific training on policies that the organisation has provided their employees. Hence, information security awareness can be shaped by the individual's own interest and experiences or by interventions carried out by the organisation's information security management group.

3. Methodology

To test the effect of behavioural information security governance on information security awareness, empirical studies were conducted at 24 organisations. We aimed to examine all relationships between dimensions of behavioural information security governance and information security awareness. Figure 1 shows which relationships that were examined on a high abstraction level. Figure 2 shows how the empirical study was carried out.

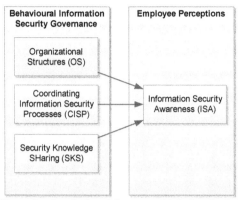

Figure 1: Examined relationships on a high level of abstraction

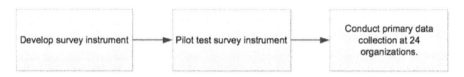

Figure 2: Research process

3.1. Development of survey questions

In the present study we correlated all survey questions related to the dimensions of behavioural information security governance and information security awareness. All survey questions were inspired on existing scales, but adapted and rewritten for the context of our study. Questions related behavioural information security governance were developed based on our understand of the factors through previous research (Rocha Flores and Ekstedt, 2012; Rocha Flores and Korman, 2012; Rocha Flores and Antonsen, 2013; Rocha Flores et al., 2014a). Questions related to the general information security awareness were based on Bulgurcu et al. (2010) and adapted to this study. Questions related to information security policy awareness were based on interviews with the six information security experts during the first stage of the research.

3.2. Assess content validity of survey questions

When developing new survey questions, MacKenzie et al. (2011) recommends to assess the content validity of the questions before colleting primary data. We quantitatively assessed the content validity using the item-sorting method (Anderson and Gerbing, 1991). The survey questions were tested for their content validity by collecting data using an email survey distributed to 452 content domain experts, of which 51 completed the survey. We also asked for comments on wording and if the survey questions were clearly understood. For more information on specific changes, the interested reader is referred to Rocha Flores and Antonsen (2013).

3.1 Pilot test and finalizing the survey questions

A pilot test was conducted by distributing the survey to 200 IT users known to the research department and working in different organisations and industries. After one reminder 47 employees had completed the survey. The survey asked for comments on wording, if the survey items were clearly understood and if the survey could be improved. Based on this pilot test minor corrections were made to the wording of the survey questions. All questions in the final survey measured on an 11-point Likert scale from 0 to 10, where 10 was strongly agree and 0 was strongly disagree. The final survey questions are outlined in Table 1.

Organisational structures (OS)
OS1: We have an organisational unit with explicit responsibility for organizing and coordinating information security efforts as well as handling incidents.
Coordinating organisational structures (COS)
OS2: There is a committee, comprised of representatives from various business units, which coordinates corporate security initiatives.
OS3: There is a committee, which deals with matters of strategic information security and related decision-making.
OS4: Tactical and operative managers are involved in information security decision-making, which is related to their unit, responsibilities and/or subordinates.
OS5: In our organisation, people responsible for security and representatives from various business units meet to discuss important security issues, both formally and informally.
Coordinating information security processes (CISP)
CISP1: Information about risks across business processes is considered.
CISP2: Vulnerabilities in the information systems and related processes are identified regularly.
CISP3: Threats that could harm and adversely affect critical operations are identified regularly.
CISP4: Performance of information security controls is measured, for example with regards to the amount of protection they provide as well as the obtrusiveness and performance limitations they pose to personnel, systems and business activities.
Security knowledge sharing
SKS1: Formal information security exercises take place in our organisation (e.g., training of backup procedures or reaction on security incidents).

SKS2: In our organisation, there is a formal program for information security awareness, training and education.
SKS3: Our organisation provides informal/voluntary consulting and advisory services in information security for our employees.
SKS4: There is an intranet site dedicated to information security (e.g., general threats and howtos, policy and guidelines).
SKS5: There is an intranet site, a quality control system or another information system or portal, which contains work- and task-related information security information such as cues, reminders or warnings bound to an action, process or a situation.
SKS6: Information technology is actively used to share knowledge and experience regarding information security within our organisation.
SKS7: Our organisation saves and renews important knowledge on both general information security and threats related to information security onto the computer for easy browsing.
Information security awareness
ISA1: I am aware of the potential threats and negative consequences that inadequate information security in my work can cause.
ISA2: I understand the risks posed by inadequate information security in general.
ISA3: I am aware of how acceptable use of IT products and services (e.g. computers, the Internet, e-mail, etc.) are described in our policy.
ISA4: I am aware of how acceptable installation of software is described in our policy.
ISA5: I know how our policy governs management of sensitive and confidential information.
ISA6: I am aware of my obligations under our policy regarding the use and management of passwords for my work computer.

Table 1: Survey items

3.3. Primary data collection

To statistically test the proposed relationships, we attempted to collect data from as many organisations as possible. To identify potential respondents the key informant methodology was used. The key informant methodology advocates that respondents should be identified based on their position, experience, and professional knowledge rather than by the traditional random sampling procedure (Segars and Grover, 1999). In this study, we decided to include two key informants. The first group of respondents was each organisation's high-level executives such as CISOs, Security Officers, CEOs, CIOs, and IT managers. This group was given the survey on behavioural information security governance factors. The second group was employees of each organisation, and these employees were given the survey including the information security awareness construct.

To identify potential respondents, security executives from organisations that were both known and unknown to the research department were contacted and invited to participate in the research study. In total, executives from 50 organisations were contacted trough telephone or email. They received a letter explaining the purpose of the study and were asked about their organisations' willingness to participate in the research study. Each information security executive was instructed to select and ensure that at least a sample of 10 employees from their organisations would complete the survey. In total, 24 companies participated in the study. The data collection procedure was identical for each of the participant organisations. To facilitate the data collection the researchers worked in close cooperation with the executives from participating organisations. The survey was hosted by a widely used internet-based application (SurveyMonkey 2014). After two reminders, 1420 employees from the 24 organisations had completed the survey. Of the organisations five are in energy; seven in manufacturing; four in IT industries; three wastewater treatment services; two in the government and academic sector; and one each in financial services, healthcare, and retail/wholesale. Three of the participant organisations had more than 5000 employees; three of the participant organisations had between 1000-5000 employees; three of the participant organisations had between 500-999 employees; five of the participant organisations had between 100-499 employees; and ten had less than 100 employees. Among the respondents, 63 percent where male and 37 percent female; 53 percent were older than 45 years, and 47 percent younger than 45 years.

As previously described, each information security executive was instructed to ensure that at least a sample of 10 employees from their organisations would complete the survey. In 11 organisations the sample was exactly 10 employees, and in the remaining 13 the sample was large than 10. As this was something that the researchers could not control, and a statistical analysis of data was to be conducted, 10 respondents were randomly selected per organisation with a sample larger than 10. Hence, the total sample comprised 240 employees from 24 different organisations.

4. Analysis and results

In order to analyse the relationship between investigated variables, Pearson correlation was used (Cohen and Cohen 1983). To enable correlation tests, the mean value of the responses to each survey question from the 10 selected respondents were calculated. This yielded a unique score per survey question for each organisation. The results from testing the relationships are shown in Table 2.

	ISA1	ISA2	ISA3	ISA4	ISA5	ISA6
OS1	.251	.480**	.347*	.488**	.248	.121
OS2	-.164	.002	-.099	.041	-.076	-.202
OS3	-.122	.065	-.072	.031	-.009	-.178
OS4	.063	.233	.163	.177	.189	.031
OS5	.123	.371*	.235	.434*	.159	.016
CISP1	-.068	.083	-.118	.002	-.029	-.270
CISP2	-.228	-.081	-.177	-.124	-.159	-.401*
CISP3	.041	.078	.114	.118	.228	.083
CISP4	.114	.118	.228	.041	.083	.078
SKS1	.010	-.034	-.078	-.079	.037	-.156
SKS2	-.144	.063	.154	.287	.000	.109
SKS3	-.001	.048	.082	.057	.152	-.102
SKS4	.215	.382*	.390*	.488**	.257	.167
SKS5	.221	.138	.144	.163	.120	.047
SKS6	.205	.302	.158	.162	.148	.011
SKS7	.200	.258	.158	.080	.184	-.011

Table 2: Overall results from correlation analysis
Notes: * indicates statistical significance at $p < 0.05$; ** at $p < 0.01$.

As the results display our empirical analysis reveal that there are 9 significant relationships between the investigated behavioural information security governance variables and information security awareness. Specifically, formal information security structure has a significant correlation with employees understanding of the risks posed by inadequate information security in general ($r = 0.347**$), employees awareness of how the policy describe acceptable use of IT products and services ($r = 0.480**$), and how acceptable installation of software is described in the policy ($r = 0.488**$). Furthermore, establishing routines that people responsible for security and representatives from various business units meet to discuss important security issues correlates with both employees understanding of the risks posed by inadequate information security in general ($r = 0.371**$) and awareness of how acceptable installation of software is described in the policy ($r = 0.434**$). A positive significant correlation was identified between the establishment of an intranet site dedicated to information security and employees understanding of the risks posed by inadequate information security in general ($r = 0.382**$), employees awareness of how the policy describe acceptable use of IT products and services ($r = 0.390**$), and how acceptable installation of software is described in the policy ($r = 0.488**$). Finally, regular identification of vulnerabilities in information systems and related processes is significantly negatively correlated with employees' awareness of policy regulating obligations regarding the use and management of passwords for work computers ($r = -0.401**$).

5. Discussion and conclusions

Our study has empirically investigated the effect of behavioural information security governance on employee information security awareness. To the best of our knowledge this is the first empirical study investigating this link. The study can therefore be seen as exploratory, which limits the generalizability of our findings. Our results points to the usefulness of having a specific unit with explicit responsibility for organizing and coordinating information security, and routines that people responsible for security and representatives from various business units meet to discuss important security issues both formally and informally. One explanation could be that information security is highly prioritised in organisations that have these structures in place. This might be manifested by leaders promoting information security and communicating the role and responsibility of the information security department of the organisation. This could then serve as the foundation to shape an information security culture, which in turn directly influences employees' awareness of information security threats. As there is a relative hierarchical distance between the structural mechanisms and employee perceptions, future studies should attempt to disentangle the interrelated influences of formal structures and employees perceptions of information security.

Support for security knowledge transfer by using technology such as intranet site dedicated to information security (e.g., general threats and howtos, policy and guidelines), seem beneficial as it influence employees' perception of information security. Apparently, employees are keen to use technology to learn about information security and making them aware of common threats. This is beneficial, as using different tools (e.g. e-learning tools) to share knowledge about information and educate employees is a cheap investment and can easily reach all members of an organisation.

Finally, regular identification of vulnerabilities in information systems and related processes is significantly negatively correlated with employees' awareness of policy regulating obligations regarding the use and management of passwords for work computers. At this point we do not have a strong explanation why this relationship is negative. One might believe that vulnerability analysis would increase information security. However, one explanation could be that vulnerability analysis, as posed by the question, is regarded as a technical measure to identify weaknesses in the information system, and not in humans accessing these information systems. Could it be that companies investing in technical vulnerability analyses lack in providing 'social' controls to their employees? Consequently, companies might be overinvesting in technical countermeasure leading to less focus on countermeasures related to employees'' information security awareness. Naturally, future research should investigate this question further.

There exist several limitations which should be taken into account when interpreting the results. First, out of 114 relationships that were statistically tested, only 9 showed significant correlation. Hence, this questions the effect of the dimensions of behavioural information security governance that we identified through the explorative stage of the research. Consequently, future research should include other governance variables that could potentially have a stronger link to employee information security awareness.

Second, although our study identified significant correlation between dimensions of behavioural information security governance and information security awareness, the sample is still small. Therefore, conclusions based on the results from our correlation analysis should be drawn cautiously. However, the study sheds a light on the effect of behavioural information security governance on employee information security awareness, which is an understudied topic. Therefore, this study contributes by providing results that researcher can use in their future studies.

6. References

Anderson, J.C. & Gerbing, D.W., 1991. Predicting the performance of measures in a confirmatory factor analysis with a pretest assessment of their substantive validities. *Journal of Applied Psychology*, 76(5), pp.732–740.

Brotby, K., 2009. *Information Security Governance*, John Wiley & Sons, Inc.

Calder, A. & Watkins, S., 2008. *IT governance A manager's guide to Data Security and ISO 27001/ISO 27002* 4th ed., Kogan Page.

Chang, S. & Ho, C., 2006. Organizational factors to the effectiveness of implementing information security management. *Industrial Management & Data Systems*, 106(3), pp.345 – 361.

Cohen, J. & Cohen, P., 1983. *Applied multiple regression/correlation analysis for the behavioral sciences*, NJ: Erlbaum: Hillsdale.

Crossler, R.E. et al., 2013. Future directions for behavioral information security research. *Computers & Security*, 32(null), pp.90–101.

Cummings, J.N., 2004. Work Groups, Structural Diversity, and Knowledge Sharing in a Global Organization. *Management Science*, 50(3), pp.352–364.

Dodge, R., Carver, C. & Ferguson, A., 2007. Phishing for user security awareness. *Computers & Security*, 26(1), pp.73–80.

Dzazali, S. & Zolait, A.H., 2012. Assessment of information security maturity: An exploration study of Malaysian public service organizations. *Journal of Systems and Information Technology*, 14(1), pp.23–57.

Fagnot, I.J., 2008. Behavioral information security. In L. Janczewski & A. Colarik, eds. *Encyclopedia of cyber warfare and cyber terrorism*. PA: USA: Hershey, pp. 199–205.

Karakasiliotis, A., Furnell, S. & Papadaki, M., 2006. Assessing end-user awareness of social engineering and phishing. In *Australian Information Warfare and Security Conference*. Citeseer, p. 60.

Kayworth, T. & Whitten, D., 2010. Effective Information Security Requires a Balance of Social and Technology Factors. *MIS Quartely Executive*, 9(3), pp.303–315.

MacKenzie, S.B., Podsakoff, P.M. & Podsakoff, N.P., 2011. Construct measurement and validation procedures in MIS and behavioral research: integrating new and existing techniques. *MIS Quarterly*, 35(2), pp.293–334.

Mishra, S. & Dhillon, G., 2006. Information Systems Security Governance Research: A Behavioral Perspective. In *2nd Annual Symposium on Information Assurance.* New York State.

Puhakainen, P. & Siponen, M., 2010. Improving employees' compliance through information systems security training: an action research study. *MIS Quarterly*, 34(4), pp.757–778.

Rhodes, J. et al., 2008. Factors influencing organizational knowledge transfer: implication for corporate performance. *Journal of Knowledge Management*, 12(3), pp.84–100.

Rocha Flores, W. et al., 2014. Using Phishing Experiments and Scenario-based Surveys to Understand Security Behaviours in Practice. *Information Management & Computer Security*, 22(4).

Rocha Flores, W. & Antonsen, E., 2013. The development of an instrument for assessing information security in organizations: Examining the content validity using quantitative methods. In *Proceedings of the 2013 International Conference on Information Resources Management.* Natal, Brazil, May 22-24.

Rocha Flores, W., Antonsen, E. & Ekstedt, M., 2014. Information security knowledge sharing in organizations: Investigating the effect of behavioral information security governance and national culture. *Computers & Security*, 43(June), pp.90–110.

Rocha Flores, W. & Ekstedt, M., 2012. A Model for Investigation Organizational Impact on Information Security Behavior. In *Seventh Annual Workshop on Information Security and Privacy (WISP) 2012.*

Rocha Flores, W. & Ekstedt, M., 2013. Countermeasures for Social Engineering-based Malware Installation Attacks. In *Proceedings of the 2013 International Conference on Information Resources Management.* Natal, Brazil, May 22-24.

Rocha Flores, W. & Korman, M., 2012. Conceptualization of Constructs for Shaping Information Security Behavior: Towards a Measurement Instrument. In *Proceedings of th 7th Annual Workshop on Information Security and Privacy.* Orlando, Florida, USA, December 16.

Segars, A.H. & Grover, V., 1999. Profiles of Strategic Information Systems Planning. *Information Systems Research*, 10(3), pp.199–232.

Sobh, T. & Elleithy, K. eds., 2013. Information Management for Holistic, Collaborative Information Security Management. In *Emerging Trends in Computing, Informatics, Systems Sciences, and Engineering.* Lecture Notes in Electrical Engineering. New York, NY: Springer New York, pp. 211–224.

SurveyMonkey, 2014. SurveyMonkey: Free online survey software & questionnaire tool. Available at: https://www.surveymonkey.com/.

Da Veiga, A. & Eloff, J.H.P., 2007. An Information Security Governance Framework. *Information Systems Management*, 24(4), pp.361–372.

Wang, S. & Noe, R.A., 2010. Knowledge sharing: A review and directions for future research. *Human Resource Management Review*, 20(2), pp.115–131.

Warkentin, M. & Johnston, A.C., 2007. It Governance and Organizational Design for Security Management. In D. W. Straub, S. Goodman, & R. L. Baskerville, eds. *Information Security: Policy, Processes, and Practices.* pp. 46 – 68.

Warkentin, M. & Willison, R., 2009. Behavioral and policy issues in information systems security: the insider threat. *European Journal of Information Systems*, 18(2), pp.101–105.

Werlinger, R., Hawkey, K. & Beznosov, K., 2009. An integrated view of human, organizational, and technological challenges of IT security management. *Information Management & Computer Security*, 17(1), pp.4–19.

Zakaria, O., 2006. Internalisation of Information Security Culture amongst Employees through Basic Security Knowledge. In S. Fischer-Hübner et al., eds. *Security and Privacy in Dynamic Environments*. IFIP International Federation for Information Processing. Boston: Kluwer Academic Publishers, pp. 437–441.

An Information Security Training and Awareness Approach (ISTAAP) to Instil an Information Security-Positive Culture

A. Da Veiga

College of Science, Engineering and Technology, School of Computing, University of South Africa, P.O. Box 392, UNISA 0003, South Africa
e-mail: dveiga@unisa.ac.za

Abstract

This paper proposes a unique information security training and awareness approach (ISTAAP) that can be used to instil an information security-positive culture which will assist in addressing the risk that human behaviour poses to the protection of information. An information security culture assessment tool is used as the critical diagnostic instrument to assess the information security culture within the context of ISTAAP. A case study is discussed where the ISTAAP was deployed. This provided empirical data to illustrate the value of ISTAAP to direct employee behaviour through focused training and awareness based on the outcome of the information security culture assessment data.

Keywords

Information security culture, awareness, training, approach, survey, measure, human, people, behaviour

1. Introduction

Information security training and awareness are two of the most effective offsets to mitigate the human risk posed to information security (Parsons *et al.*, 2014). Current and former employees in organisations are still regarded as a risk to the protection of information and are often the cause of information security incidents (Schlienger and Teufel, 2005, Ashenden, 2008, Thomson *et al.*, 2006, Herath and Rao, 2009, Kraemer *et al.*, 2009, Herold, 2011, Furnell and Clarke, 2012, Furnell and Rajendran, 2012, Padayachee, 2012, Crossler *et al.*, 2013, Flores *et al.*, 2014, PwC, 2014). Research indicates that up to a third of incidents are caused by employees (Ponemon, 2013). This could be as a result of deliberate attacks, error or negligence of employees. Consequently, organisations need to prioritise employee information security training and awareness to close the gap from an employee perspective.

However, information security training and awareness are regarded as a challenge for many organisations (PwC, 2014) for a number of reasons. Some of the reasons relate to the constant change in information technology, the numerous devices in which information is processed, the wide distribution of locations where information is accessed and stored and the heightened regulatory environment for handling and processing information (Herold, 2011). These aspects result in organisational policy changes that employees need to constantly be made aware of and trained in to ensure compliance and to minimise the risk to information. In addition, the general awareness of employees, their computer literacy levels and the organisational budget could be a hindrance to the effectiveness of information security awareness programmes (Shaw *et al.*, 2009).

Information security training is essential in organisations to embed compliance behaviour in line with the information security policy requirements and to yield lasting behaviour changes (ISF, 2000). Whilst training is deployed in organisations to increase knowledge on a certain subject or trait or to change behaviour, it also improves skill and can change employee attitude (Berry & Houston, 1993). Effective training and awareness both result in behavioural change in organisations and are critical in embedding information security principles at employee level. Information security awareness initiatives are often conducted in conjunction with information security training to build and sustain an information security-positive culture (ISF, 2002). Cobit for Information Security (2012) emphasises the importance of creating information security awareness at organisational and individual level. By stimulating effective information security training and awareness at all levels in an organisation, a positive information security culture can be promoted to enhance protection of information, minimise risk and contribute to compliance (Hassan and Ismaila, 2012, Da Veiga and Martins, 2015).

The aim of this research study is to define an approach that can be deployed to focus information security training and awareness efforts. This, in turn, contributes to instil an information security-positive culture. In order to achieve the research aims, the information security training and awareness approach (ISTAAP) is proposed and was deployed in an international organisation to establish whether it yielded positive results as part of an empirical study. This research study aimed at complementing the body of literature on information security training and awareness by empirically testing the theoretical, proposed ISTAAP model to establish its impact on information security culture.

2. Background

2.1. Reasons for stimulating information security training and awareness

Information security training help to minimise the risk of employee behaviour by deliberately focusing on a set of learning experiences to increase information security knowledge (Berry & Houston, 1993), such as what confidential information is, what the risks are to information and what employees should do to protect information. The information security training can further help improve employee skills when, for instance, using encryption, selecting a strong password or including information security controls in system design. The attitude of employees towards the implementation of information security controls can also be influenced positively. In time, this becomes the way things are done and inculcates a positive information security culture (Da Veiga and Eloff, 2010).

Information security training and awareness can be used to ensure that information security policy requirements become part of the knowledge base of employees, enabling them to meet policy requirements (Thomson *et al.*, 2006). Information security training is also deployed to orientate new employees through induction training, which includes an overview of policies and procedures of the organisation (Byars and Rue, 1997).

The Organisation for Economic Co-operation and Development (OECD, 2002) emphasises the need to develop a strong information security culture through various factors, two of which are training and awareness. The ISO/IEC 27002 (2013) also emphasises the importance of information security training and awareness. The objective of this training and awareness should be to move from an information security-negative or neutral culture to an information security-positive culture. This will contribute to sustainable change in employee attitude as well as their behaviour towards information security. Attitudes and beliefs together with basic assumptions are the core substances of corporate culture and as such also of an information security culture (Schein, 1985). It is therefore critical that the approach to information security training and awareness integrate the concept of information security culture.

2.2. Existing approaches for implementing information security training and awareness

Information security training and awareness have to be managed as part of the information security programme in a structured and organised manner. In many instances information security awareness campaigns are conducted on an ad hoc basis, for instance communication e-mails are sent out and posters are placed in key locations. Organisations also use computer-based training modules and newsletters, include information security sessions in induction training and hand out promotional items, such as mouse pads with information security information on them (Albrechtsen & Hofden, 2010). Engaging in these activities could create the perception that "all is well" and that management can tick the box. This creates the expectation that employees are aware of the information security policy requirements and will exhibit compliance behaviour.

Organisations cannot illustrate due diligence by merely indicating that they have conducted training and awareness without evaluating the effectiveness of the actions implemented. The effectiveness of training and awareness is often evident in the culture of the organisation when certain behaviour becomes the accepted norm. Employees might use unprotected memory sticks for back up or save confidential client information in an unprotected cloud environment. These behaviours could result in potential information security incidents and data breaches if the information is accidently lost, exposed, accessed or changed without authorisation or used inappropriately.

The effectiveness of awareness and training is also evident in the number of existing metrics in an organisation, such as the number of information security and privacy incidents, network downtime as a result of malicious code, customer complaints, findings in audit and risk reports, inappropriate authorisations for transactions, regulatory fines or the number of lost information assets such as laptops and portable storage devices (Herold, 2011).

Organisations need to utilise a method to evaluate the effectiveness of information security awareness and training programmes. Parsons *et al.* (2014) developed the human aspects of information security questionnaire (HAIS-Q) to evaluate the information security health of an organisation by assessing employee knowledge, attitude and behaviour in relation to information security. It does not, however, use a validated information security culture questionnaire based on information security culture constructs to direct and target employee behaviour of certain stakeholder groups. Herold (2011) introduced a comprehensive approach to identify current awareness and training needs, create a roadmap and develop, deliver and evaluate the training. Various evaluation methods are included ranging from checklists and surveys to computer-based training assessments, the output of which is used to tailor future awareness and training topics and delivery methods. This method does not incorporate a validated and reliable questionnaire to assess the impact of awareness on the information security culture, nor to assess whether the efforts contributed to a security-positive culture, but rather focuses on improving the awareness levels in the organisation.

Other researchers have also defined approaches to implementing information security awareness and training (ISF, 2002, Zakaria and Gani, 2003, Schlienger and Teufel, 2005, Thompson *et al.*, 2006, Power and Forte, 2006, Kruger and Kearney, 2006, Kritzinger and Smith 2008, Albrechtsen and Hovden, 2010). None of the current approaches propose an information security awareness and training approach that is holistic comprising formal phases that extend to assessing the effectiveness of the awareness and training within the context of an information security culture using a validated assessment instrument. Such an approach would allow the impact of training and awareness on the information security culture to be determined through valid and reliable results, and would also enable continuous monitoring of changes and the implementation of corrective actions to ensure that an information security-positive culture is sustained.

As such, the following research questions were defined:

- Does the ISTAAP serve as an effective approach to implement information security training and awareness initiatives whereby success can be measured in the context of an information security culture?
- Is the ISTAAP effective to focus information security training and awareness initiatives?

3. Information security training and awareness approach (ISTAAP)

The ISTAAP is proposed in Figure 1. It is a holistic approach focusing on inculcating an information security-positive culture in an organisation to aid in mitigating the risk of the human element in the protection of information. ISTAAP is a unique approach in the sense that it incorporates an information security culture assessment as a core element to direct training and awareness. ISTAAP consists of four distinct phases which are implemented on a cyclical basis. Each phase comprises of a number activities that are conducted in response to the ISCA that is conducted in the evaluate effectiveness phase.

Evaluate Effectiveness (EE): Prior to developing training and awareness, it is essential to conduct a needs analysis (Berry and Houston, 1993, Byars and Rue, 1997, Herold, 2011). During this phase the information security culture level is assessed using the information security culture assessment (ISCA) (Da Veiga and Martins, 2015) as an initial needs assessment and to benchmark future assessments. The ISCA questionnaire comprises of nine constructs, each with items that have to be answered on a Likert scale.

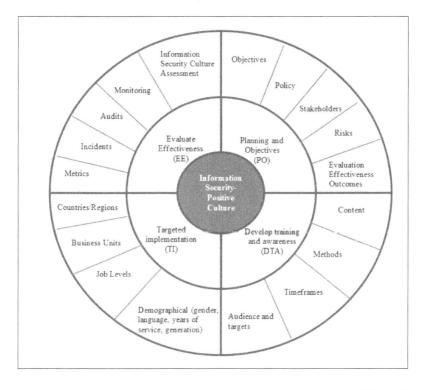

Figure 1: Information security awareness and culture model (ISTAAP)

The ISCA assessment is conducted in the form of an electronic survey, which is distributed to all employees in the organisation to complete. Focus groups are also used to confirm the results of the ISCA. Empirical data is derived from the ISCA to understand the level of information security culture in the organisation, the required content of training and awareness and the stakeholders to prioritise based on their information security-negative (or low) culture.

The overall information security culture rating or score is determined (i.e. the average of all the items across the constructs) for the organisation as a whole and for the biographical groups such as the countries, departments, job levels, generation groups or ethnic groups. The lowest and highest items are identified per biographical group to identify focus areas for training and awareness activities. Further statistical analysis is conducted to identify recommendations for improvement which is discussed under the case study findings.

As ISCA has been validated through statistical methods, it provides valid and reliable results over time to facilitate employee attitude and related behaviour change to inculcate an information security-positive culture (Da Veiga and Martins 2015).

To supplement the ISCA results and draw correlations, other metrics can be used to obtain a holistic view of the information security posture in the organisation, such as monitoring, compliance audits, internal and/or external audits, incident management data, risk assessment outcomes, and so on.

Planning and Objectives (PO): The information security training and awareness objectives are derived from the business and information security strategy, but also based on the information security policy and regulatory requirements. The impact and value of ISTAAP are derived by tailoring the objectives and planning according to the outcomes of the evaluation of the effectiveness of the information security training and awareness as derived from ISCA.

Develop Training and Awareness (DTO): There are many techniques or methods that can be used to deliver information security training. The content, delivery method and audience need to be considered. This will depend on the effectiveness evaluation outcomes, budget available and resources to develop and deliver material. A number of methods are often used in organisations for information security training, such as web-based training, discussion groups, brown bag sessions and hands-on training (ISF, 2002, Herold, 2011). Posters, desk drops, text messages, e-mails and newsletters are categorised as awareness methods to communicate information to employees (Herold, 2011). These methods are often employed as part of an awareness programme with specific activities per month.

The outcome of the ISCA is used to define what training and awareness material and content to develop. It has been found that the ISCA results often vary between the biographical groups necessitating customised training for each group pertaining to the contents. Questions regarding to the most preferred methods of communication are included in the ISCA to identify which method to consider for each biographical group.

Targeted Implementation (TI): The ISCA results provide empirical data with the most preferred and effective training and awareness methods per stakeholder group in the organisation. Targeted training and awareness are implemented for each group, focusing on the key concepts and preferred delivery method per group based on the ISCA data. Implementation can be conducted in order of priority, starting with the most negative biographical areas in the organisation. Implementation usually spans over a few months and even up to a year.

Once the implementation phase has been rolled out a follow up ISCA is conducted, moving on to the EE phase, to establish whether the implemented actions have had a positive impact on the information security culture. A follow up ISCA also provides insight to determine whether the identified activities were successful and whether other developmental areas arose over time. Data from more than one ISCA for a specific organisation serves as successful monitoring of the culture change over a period of time.

4. Research methodology

The research methodology in this study was a quantitative research design. The ISTAAP was deployed in an international organisation to monitor the success of the information security programme, identify where to focus training and awareness initiatives and determine what to change in order to instil an information security-positive culture. The ISTAAP cycle was repeated four times from 2006 up to 2013 by deploying the ISCA on four occasions in the organisation, see Figure 2. For the purpose of this research paper the application of the ISCA in the context of ISTAAP will be the focus in the research methodology discussion.

4.1. Sample

A period of four to five weeks was defined for employees to respond to the ISCA survey for each of the EE phases. The first ISCA was conducted in 2006 with a sample of 1 941 employees, see figure 2. A year later the second ISCA was conducted with a sample of 1 571 employees.

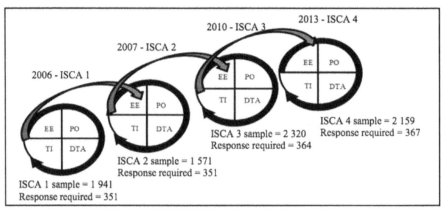

Figure 2: ISTAAP implementation cycles

The 2010 ISCA included a sample of 2 320 employees and the ISCA in 2013, a sample of 2 159 employees. The required sample was calculated for each ISCA occasion based on a marginal error of 5% and a confidence level of 95% to ascertain the findings across the organisation (Krejcie and Morgan, 1970). This is critical to ensure that the information security culture scores derived are valid for the population (i.e. organisation) and should be calculated for each implementation of ISTAAP. For each of the ISCA occasions an adequate number of responses were obtained. Corrective actions as identified in ISCA were implemented for each ISTAAP cycle.

4.2. Case study findings

The statistical analysis for each year was conducted using Survey Tracker (2015) and IBM SPSS Statistics 22 (2011). The data were analysed and the means, frequencies and frequency distribution were determined for the overall data and biographical segmentation. Anova and t-tests were used to determine the significant differences between the biographical groups in order to prioritise training and awareness initiatives. Regression analysis was further used to determine the most important focuses of each year which were used to direct the PO phase. Biographical groups with less than five responses were not included in the analysis in order to protect the respondent's confidentiality and to meet the sampling requirements. When deploying ISTAAP it is critical to conduct these statistical analyses in order to ensure that the data is interpreted correctly for management decisions.

The overall average information security culture scores improved from one assessment to the next with the most positive results in 2013. The overall mean in 2006 was 3.89, which improved to 4.10 in 2013. This data indicates that the information security culture became more positive over time. One of the reasons is related to the implementation of ISTAAP where the Group ISO implemented the recommended developmental actions as identified in each ISCA.

Figure 3 portrays the information security culture scores (% agree) for the group of employees that had received prior training and awareness compared with those that had not, as well as the overall information security culture scores. The data illustrates that the overall information security culture level improved, and thus a more positive information security culture was inculcated over time. There was a significant improvement from 2010 to 2013. The ISCA corrective actions that were implemented as part of ISTAAP contributed to this improvement.

The organisation restructured before the 2010 survey, which could be a reason for the decline in the information security culture. This illustrates that information security should also be addressed when change is instituted in the organisation to maintain the information security culture level. The improvement from the 2010 to the 2013 ISCA illustrates the positive impact of ISTAAP and the use of ISCA as the key assessment component to direct training and awareness methods to positively influence the information security culture.

Employees that had been exposed to prior training and awareness were more positive than those that had not. This illustrates the value and impact of the corrective actions as deployed in ISTAAP based on the outcomes of ISCA. It is interesting to note that the information security culture gap (level) between employees that had received prior training compared with those that did not became smaller between 2006 and 2013, see figure 3. This indicates that the information security culture level also improved for the group of employees that had not been exposed to prior training and awareness. One explanation could be that their behaviour was influenced by the group of employees that had been exposed to training and awareness and that there was overall a more positive perception of information security in the organisation.

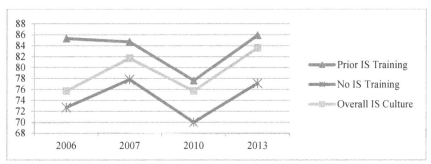

Figure 3: ISCA average scores for the four ISCAs

The statistical reports with conclusions and recommendations of ISCA were used as part of the PO phase to define the training and awareness objectives. The training and awareness content that was developed was based on the top ten most negative concepts derived from the ISCA for each biographical group.

ISCA includes a statement relating to the training and awareness preference of employees. In all four ISCAs it was found that e-mail was the most preferred method, followed by presentations and web-based training. These ISCA findings provided input to the DTO phase in which a combined method was used to conduct training and awareness. As such, e-mails were sent on a monthly basis to all employees and group presentations were conducted in each country facilitated by the Group ISO in each instance. It is important to note that the preferred methods of communication by employees could vary between organisations.

5. Discussion and conclusion

In this research the ISTAAP is proposed as a flexible approach to tailor and focus training and awareness initiatives with the objective of inculcating an information security-positive culture. The ISCA is used as the central assessment tool in ISTAAP to determine the information security culture level. At the same time, it provides data that can be used to determine the effectiveness of training and awareness initiatives that can be leveraged off to influence the information security culture. The ISTAAP contributes to minimise the risk posed by employee behaviour as specific actions can be derived to change employee perception and ultimately employee behaviour when interacting with organisational information. The information security culture in the case study organisation became more positive over time as is evident in the data of the ISCA used within the context of ISTAAP. A more positive information security culture will result in employees displaying risk-averse behaviour, introducing less incidents, complying with policies and ultimately assisting in protecting information. ISTAAP therefore helps counter the risk posed by human behaviour by providing empirical data through ISCA to address critical constructs and biographical groups in order to positively influence the information security culture.

The first research question has been answered in that the effectiveness of ISTAAP and the success of the training and awareness is evident in the improvement of the average information security culture scores from the first assessment to the most recent one. In addition, the group of employees that had been exposed to prior information security training and awareness had a more positive information security culture compared with those that had not.

In answering the second research question, the ISTAAP was found to be effective in focusing information security training and awareness initiatives, as the empirical data can be used to identify biographical groups that are more negative compared with other groups. The data can also be used to identify the most preferred methods of communication and the critical messages to relay to each biographical group and finally the improvement can be monitored by benchmarking the data with the follow-up ISCAs.

A limitation of the research is that only the data of ISCA was considered and monitored throughout the case study. The ISTAAP can further be improved by incorporating other assessment methods and data with the ISCA data to verify the change in employee behaviour and to identify any correlations. Further research will also focus on conducting reliability and validity tests, to determine the factorial invariance across countries for the ISCA questionnaire and to establish how the impact of national culture can be incorporated in ISTAAP.

6. References

Albrechtsen, E. and Hovden, J. (2010), "Improving information security awareness and behaviour through dialogue, participation and collective reflection. An intervention study", *Computers & Security*, Vol. 29, pp432–445.

Ashenden, D. (2008), "Information security management: A human challenge?", *Information Security Technical Report*, Vol. 13, No. 4, pp95–201.

Berry, M.L. and Houston, J.P. (1993), Psychology at work, Brown and Benchmark, Wisconsin, ISBN: 9780697246134.

Byars, L.L. and Rue, L.W. (1997), *Human resource management*, 5th edition, Irwin McGraw-Hill, Boston, ISBN: 9780256201932.

Cobit for Information Security. (2012), "ISACA", www.isaca.org, (Accessed 5 November 2014).

Crossler, R.E., Johnston, A.C., Lowry, P.B., Hu, Q., Warkentin, M. and Baskerville, R. (2013), "Future directions for behavioral information security research", *Computers & Security*, Vol. 32, pp90-101.

Da Veiga, A. and Eloff, J.H.P. (2010), "A framework and assessment instrument for information security culture", *Computers & Security*, Vol. 29, pp196–207.

Da Veiga, A. and Martins, N. (2015), "Improving the information security culture through monitoring and implementation actions illustrated through a case study", *Computers & Security*, Vol. 49, pp162-176,

Flores, W.R., Antonsen, E. and Ekstedt, M. (2014), "Information security knowledge sharing in organizations: Investigating the effect of behavioral information security governance and national culture", *Computers & Security*, Vol. 43, pp90–110.

Furnell, S. and Clarke, N. (2012), "Power to the people? The evolving recognition of human aspects of security", *Computers & Security*, Vol. 31, pp983–988.

Furnell, S. and Rajendran, A. (2012), "Understanding the influences on information security behavior", *Computer Fraud and Security*, Vol. 2012, pp12–15.

Hassan, N.H. and Ismail, Z. (2012), "A conceptual model for investigating factors influencing information security culture in healthcare environment", (ICIBSoS 2012), *Procedia - Social and Behavioral Sciences*, Vol. 65, pp1007 – 1012.

Herath, T. and Rao, H.R. (2009), "Encouraging information security behaviors in organizations: Role of penalties, pressures and perceived effectiveness", *Decision Support Systems*, Vol. 47, pp154–165.

Herold, R. (2011), *Managing an information security and privacy awareness and training program*, 2nd edition, CRC Press, Boca Rotan, ISBN: 9781439815458.

IBM SPSS Statistics (2011) (Version 21.0 for Microsoft Windows platform)[Computer Software]. Chicago, IL: SPSS Inc

Information Security Forum (ISF). (200), Information Security Culture – A preliminary investigation", November 2000, https://www.securityforum.org, (Accessed Feb 2009).

Information Security Forum (ISF). (2002), "Effective security awareness workshop report, April 2002", https://www.securityforum.org, (Accessed Feb 2009).

ISO/IEC 27002:2013. (2013), *Information technology – Security techniques – Code of practice for information security management*, New York.

Kraemer, S., Carayon, P. and Clem, J. (2009), "Human and organizational factors in computer and information security: Pathways to vulnerabilities", *Computers & Security*, Vol. 28, pp509–520.

Krejcie, R.V. and Morgan, D.W. (1970), "Determining sample size for research activities", *Educational and Psychological Measurement*, Vol. 30, pp607–610.

Kritzinger, E. and Smith, E. (2008)," Information security management: An information

security retrieval and awareness model for industry", Computers and Security, Vol. 27, pp124–231.

Kruger, H.A. and Kearney, W.D. (2006), "A prototype for assessing information security awareness", *Computers & Security*, Vol. 25, pp289-296.

OECD. (2002), "Guidelines for the Security of Information Systems and Networks, Towards a Culture of Security", www.oecd.org/dataoecd/16/22/15582260.pdf, (Accessed 10 June 2014).

Padayachee, K. (2012), "Taxonomy of compliant information security behavior", *Computers & Security*, Vol. 31, pp673–680.

Parsons, K., McCormac, A., Butavicius, M., Pattinson, M. and Jerram, C. (2014), "Determining employee awareness using the Human Aspects of Information Security Questionnaire (HAIS-Q)", *Computers & Security*, Vol. 42, pp165-176.

Ponemon Institute. (2013), "Cost of data breach study: Global analysis benchmark research sponsored by Symantec", http://www.symantec.com, (Accessed 10 June 2014).

Power, R. and Forte, D. (2006), "Case study: A bold new approach to awareness and education, and how it met an ignoble fate", *Computer Fraud and Security*, Vol. 2006, pp7-10.

PricewaterhouseCoopers (PwC), (2014), "The global state of information security survey", http://www.pwc.com/gx/en/consulting-services/information-security-survey/download.jhtml, (Accessed 10 June 2014).

Schein E.H. (1985), *Organizational culture and leadership*, Jossey-Bass, San Francisco, ISBN: 0875896391.

Schlienger, T. and Teufel, S. (2005), "Tool supported management of information security culture: An application to a private bank", in Sasaki, R., Okamoto, E. and Yoshiura, H., (eds) *Security and privacy in the age of ubiquitous computing*, Kluwer, Japan.

Shaw, R.S., Chen, C.C., Harris, A.L. and Huang, H., "The impact of information richness on information security awareness, training effectiveness", *Computers & Education*, Vol. 52, pp92–100.

Survey Tracker. Training Technologies Inc; (2015), https://www.surveytracker.com/. (Accessed 30 April 2015).

Thomson, K., Van Solms, R. and Louw, L. (2006), "Cultivating an organisational information security culture", *Computer Fraud and Security*, October, pp7–11.

Zakaria, O. and Gani, A. (2003), "A conceptual checklist of information security culture", in Hutchinson, B. (Ed.) *Proceedings of the 2nd European Conference on Information Warfare and Security*, MCIL, Reading, pp365-372.

Effect of Motivation and Physical Fitness on Cyber Tasks

K. Helkala, S. Knox and M. Lund

Norwegian Defence Cyber Academy
e-mail: {khelkala; sknox; maslund}@mil.no

Abstract

Today, and especially in the future, soldiers have to be able to operate and maintain a large variety of devices connected to the cyber domain in whatever environment they are operating in. This places a high demand on soldiers' cognitive abilities and mechanisms that humans use to process and store information. In this paper we study how motivation, gained by understanding the purpose of tasks connected to the cyber domain and level of physical conditioning affect cognitive abilities. A cognitive test designed for this study contains tasks that are similar to real cyber operations or incidents. The test was conducted three times during a two-week long military exercise where sleep and nutrition were highly reduced and physical activity significantly increased. We show that both motivation (given by task explanations) and high physical fitness has a positive effect on performance in cyber tasks.

Keywords

Motivation, physical fitness, cognitive abilities, cyber solder, military exercise

1. Introduction

The threats in the cyber domain do not only apply to civil society, they also apply to the military (Lynn III 2010, Gertz 2014). Military ICT services are to be secure and functioning in times of peace as well as in times of conflict. In addition, the services have to be operational from the combat edge to headquarters, not just from headquarters to home. Therefore, today's soldiers have to be capable of handling large amounts of information received and sent via the cyber domain. They also need skills and knowledge to operate and maintain a large variety of devices connected to the cyber domain in whatever environment (inside, outside, conflict or peace) they find themselves. This requires that the soldiers have high levels of cognitive ability.

Our academy delivers a four-year cyber warrior education program: sergeants with a bachelor degree in computer science and telematics combined with good physical fitness. Good physical fitness is an issue under discussion; Andress and Winterfeld (2011) see it as not a necessary skill for a cyber-warrior.

Existing research results have shown that physical activity and positive motivation have positive effect on cognitive abilities. In this paper, we want to verify if the existing research results also apply to our adult students – who, generally, have better condition than an average citizen - in a military exercise, where the amount of food and sleep are significantly limited and physical activity is heavily increased. This paper reports the results of cognitive tasks related to the cyber domain during a two-week military exercise called Exercise Cyber Endurance. Military exercises are an appropriate environment to study human performance and physiology as was shown by Leiberman et. al (2006) who studied soldiers' cognition, mood and physical performance during a 96-hour sustained operation. The rest of the paper contains the following section: State of Art, Experiment setup, Results, Discussion, Conclusion, and Future Work.

2. State of Art

Humans make errors. The nature of an error defines the damage a wrong decision or an action based on the error causes. In a critical situation a human error might have fatal consequences. Psychological factors divide human errors as intentional or unintentional. Unintended actions can cause errors as slips; attentional failures, or lapses; memory failures. Intended action can cause mistakes; rule-based and knowledge-based mistakes, or violations; routine violations, exceptional violations and acts of sabotage (Angles, 2004).

Education and training reduce knowledge-based mistakes and rule-based mistakes as well as violations. However, avoiding unintended actions, especially occurring with environmental stresses, anthropometric factors and human sensory factors (size, shape, strength, and senses (Angles, 2004)) cannot be achieved with pure academic education. Unintended actions are a declination of cognitive abilities. Cognitive abilities such as perception, attention, memory, motor, language, visual-spatial processing and executive functions are mechanisms used to process and store information (Pascale 2006). Our actions are then based on the processed information.

Cognitive incapability is often thought to be a problem for a person with old age. Even if there exists clear generalities on age-related changes, the individual variance is large (Glisky, 2007), and the age is definitely not the only attribute that changes human's cognitive abilities. For example; fatigue (Hartzler, 2014), hunger (Gailliot, 2013) and stress (Harris, 2007), have a negative effect.

Physical activity, on the other hand, has a positive effect (Fisher et al. 2011, Gregory et.al 2012, and Reed ct.al 2013). Also environmental attributes (Dahlman et. al, 2012) and motivation (Gaillard, 2007) have shown to affect cognition. Some studies such as Lees and Hopkins, (2013) and Koch and Hasbrouck (2013) imply that good physical condition has a positive effect on academic achievement.

Emotional arousal has also shown to have a positive effect on cognitive abilities and especially memorability. Positive or negative emotional arousal helps maintain a readiness to respond (McPherson, 2011) which helps them notice and recall incidents or details. For example Lee and Sternthal (1999) showed that a positive mood enhanced learning in relation to a neutral mood, when participants learned names of different brands and Dietrich et al. (2001) outlined the influence of emotional contents on recognition performance. Also positive password sentences seemed to have a higher recall rate than sentences with a negative content (Helkala, 2014).

3. Experiment context and setup

The experiment took place in Exercise Cyber Endurance (a two week long military exercise containing three simulated military field operations), in the 4th semester. During the exercise students lived in an outdoor military base, their nutrition and sleep were reduced and physical exhaustion was increased from the normal level. Each day the students either practiced previously taught military and engineering skills or learned new skills. The students were tasked to integrate military and civilian based ICT systems to solve varying operational needs. For example; they were instructed to build, and program, a static intrusion alarm system for their base that was networked to a their deployable Battle Management System (BMS).

3.1. Study design

40 students took voluntarily part to the study (4 women and 36 men, 21-27 years). The cognitive test set was combined with combat conditioning training in the following-way: the participants conducted 2 x 14 minute long training sessions with 2 minutes pauses; after which they commenced the individual cognitive test. The test was conducted three times. The first test was two days before the actual start of the exercise. The participants had slept normally, received normal nutrition and were still living indoors. The second test was on the 3rd day of the exercise. The third and final test run was on the 10th day of the exercise. The second and third tests took place between 9pm and midnight. Between the first and second tests, the sleeping hours had been limited to maximum five hours per night and the feeding had been reduced slightly. Between the second and third test, the sleeping hours were reduced to a couple of hours per night due to the operational scenario. Three days before the third test the feeding was reduced to max 1400 kcal per student per day. The day of the third test, the students were not provided with any food. The students had unlimited access to water during the entire exercise period.

3.2. Test groups

Motivation has earlier been shown to strengthen the ability to remain concentrated (Gaillard, 2007). In order to see if the students gained motivation based on the importance of a task, they were divided into two groups and conducted tests with different instructions. The control group (CG) did the test with the neutral instructions. The explanation group (EG) conducted the same tasks, but this time also the purpose of each task was explained as an act or incident in the cyber domain.

In the analysis phase, both control and explanation groups were further divided into two smaller groups. This division was based on students' physical fitness level. Their physical fitness level was determined based on their overall progression in physical performance during pre-exercise tests; combination of upper body strength and speed in running a distance of 3000 meters. The students with the character B or above in physical tests formed the high physical level groups (CHL and EHL). The lower physical level groups (CLL and ELL) contained student with characters C or lower.

(The requirements to receive B for men (women) in tests are: 3000 m: 10 min 55 sec (12:05), sit-ups: 53 (53), push-ups: 34 (20), and hang-ups: 10(15).)

3.3. Cognitive test

The cognitive test followed the general lines of the Montreal Cognitive Assessment test (Moca) and the test-set used in the study of Leiberman et. al (2006). However, the tasks were modified so that they reflected cyber operations or incidents. No knowledge of cyber operations is needed to conduct the tasks. The test consisted of five tasks and takes 30-40 minutes to complete.

1st task measured attention by visual vigilance test and is similar to the study of Leiberman et. al (2006). The test demanded that students detect bars taller or equal to 3000 in a continuously moving diagram, see Fig. 1. The bars appeared for 7,5 seconds with 0,25 second intervals with random heights. The explanation group were told to monitor network traffic data and raise an alarm when a traffic peak was taller or equal to 3000. The task lasted 20 minutes and the amount of "alarm" bars varied between 115 and 120. Detection was correct if the bar was visible on the screen.

2nd task measured attention and short-term spatial memory. In this task we combined two tasks from the study of Leiberman et. al (2006): four-choice reaction time and matching-to-sample tasks. In our task, see Fig. 2, a single-colour or two-colour basic geometric figure was presented for one second. After that, a 2 x 2 matrix appeared and the students had to identify and locate the figure in the matrix. The matrix was visible of 3 seconds. In total, 75 single figure and corresponding matrix pairs were presented. The task lasted 5 minutes. The explanation group was told that the purpose of the task was to detect different states of different network devices in a very unstable environment.

3rd task measured short-term memory and the ability to learn by trial-and-error. The task was a variation of the task used in the study of Leiberman et. al (2006). In our task, a student had to memorize a random 12 digit long sequence, see Fig. 3. The digits from one to five were used to form the sequence. An empty 1 x 12 matrix was shown to the students. A digit was entered into the first square and "enter" was pressed. If the digit was correct it stayed visible, and the cursor moved to the next square. If not, the digit vanished. Using the trial-and-error method, the student filled the whole 1 x 12 matrix. When the last digit was correct and "enter"-key pressed, an empty 1 x 12 matrix appeared again. The same sequence was to complete again.

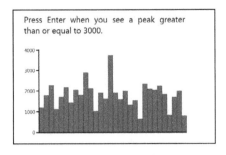

Figure 1: Visual vigilance task (1)

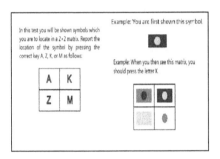

Figure 2: Matching-to-sample task (2)

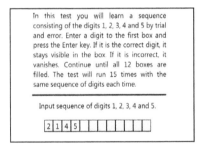

Figure 3: Trial-and-error method (3)

Figure 4: Example of memory task (5)

This was repeated 15 times. The explanation group was told to memorize an encryption key. In each of the three test runs, the student had a different sequence to learn. We recorded the amount of incorrect digits for each 1 x 12 matrix.

4th task confirmed if the 12 digit long sequence really had been memorised. The students only had one chance to type the sequence. We recorded if the sequence was correct or not.

5th task measured visual-spatial, executive memory and language abilities. The students memorized three Norwegian (students' mother tongue) sentences with a total of 13-14 words and a picture of five single-colour basic geometric figures in one minute, see Fig. 4. Subsequently, they had to write down the sentences and draw the figures with coloured pencils. The sentences and the figures were different in each test run. The correct words, forms and colours were counted. The word was correct if placed in the correct place in the correct sentence. The form was correct, if it had the correct shape and was positioned in the correct place on the figure. For the colour to be correct it had to be in the correct place in the figure. The explanation group were instructed to memorize coded messages sent from a terrorist grouping.

4. Results

A comparison of performance rates was conducted between control group (CG) and explanation group (EG). Additionally, comparison between high physical and low physical level subgroups in both control group (CG) and explanation group (EG) was conducted.

Performance was shown as average success rates for each group for each test run. When studying cognitive abilities, behavioural statistics analysis is recommended. Therefore, Cohen's effect size is used for comparison between different groups (Cohen, 1988). If *Cohen's d* is 0.8 or above, the effect size is large. Effect size is medium if *d* is 0.5 or above and small if *d* is 0.2 or above. The results, when appropriate, were also roughly compared to the findings in the study of Leiberman et. al (2006). The participants in both our and Leiberman et. al's study were the same age and had completed their first year of military service. However, our sample size was larger (40 vs. 13 soldiers) and the duration of our exercise was 3.5 times longer.

Test	Nr	Control (%)	Explanation (%)	Cohen's Effect size
Task 1	1	97	98	Small: 0,43
	2	96	98	Small: 0,37
	3	87	93	Small: 0,37
Task 2	1	90	90	-0,03
	2	95	97	Small: 0,35
	3	85	89	Small: 0,26
Task 4	1	68	95	Medium:0,7
	2	95	85	-0,33
	3	85	80	-0,13
Task 5	1	83	86	Small: 0,26
	2	84	89	Small: 0,32
	3	82	84	0,09

Table 1: Performance rates and Cohen's effect size for the tasks

4.1. Effect of motivation: control group vs. explanation group

Task 1: Visual vigilance. Cohen's effect size in all test runs shows that explanation has a small positive effect on the amount of correctly raised alarms, see Table 1.

Task 2: Matching-to-sample. The first performance rate (test run 1) for both groups is slightly biased, because three control group and four explanation group students did not stop to read the given example and therefore ended up pushing wrong keys in the beginning of the task. For test runs 2 and 3 Cohen's effect size shows that explanation has a small positive effect, see Table 1.

Task 3: Motor learning. Error-curves for the control and explanation groups in each of the test runs are shown in Fig. 5. The error-curves show the amount of errors the students made when guessing digits for each 15 matrices. It was expected that the students would make plenty of errors the first matrix as they learnt the sequence. Ideally, the amount of errors should decrease for each new matrix, ending in zero errors. As it can be seen from Fig. 5, there is a difference in error-curves in the first test. Cohen's effect size shows that explanation has a medium positive effect (0,55) in the first test run, however it does not have an effect later on.

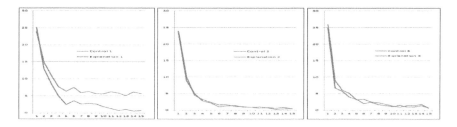

Figure 5: Error-curves of motor learning (task 3)

Task 4: Sequence control. The purpose of this task was to control if the students had really learnt the correct sequence from Task 3. This type of learning was unfamiliar to students and two students from the control group did not understand that the sequence asked in Task 4 was the sequence they have tried to learn in Task 3. That lowered the recall rates in the first test run. Cohen's effect size can now be misleading due to the misunderstanding in the first test run. It shows that explanation has medium positive effect on remembering the sentence. However, the results support the finding in Task 3 in the first test run. In second and third test runs, the explanation did not have an effect anymore, see Table 1.

Task 5: Visual-spatial and executive memory and language ability: Cohen's effect size shows that explanation has a small positive effect on memorizing three sentences and a coloured figure in the first two test runs. In the last run, when students were most tired, the explanation did not have an effect.

4.2. Effect of physical fitness level

Here we analyse the effect on physical fitness. The analysis is done separately for both control and explanation groups due to the different explanations. Our hypothesis is that the students having higher physical fitness level would perform better in the last test run as they would be more robust against physical exhaustion than lower physical fitness level students. Therefore we focus the results of the last test run.

Performance rates for high physical level (HL) and lower physical level (LL) together with Cohen's effect size are shown in Table 2. Error-rate curves are not included to this paper as they are similar to curves in Fig. 5 showing no differences between physical fitness groups in the two last test runs. However, in the first test run, high physical level students in control group performed worse.

The results in Table 2 show that physical fitness has a higher effect in the control group than in the explanation group in the last test run. In the control group, high physical level had a large positive effect for the performance rates in Task 1 (visual vigilance), small positive effect in Task 4 (sequence control), and medium positive effect in Task 5 (visual-spatial, executive memory and language ability). Physical fitness did not have effect in Task 2 (matching-to-sample). In the explanation group only small positive effect can be found in the third test run in Task 1 and Task 5.

Similar tests were conducted in a 96-hour sustained operation study in the USA in 2006 by Leiberman et. al (2006). A 96-hour operation is shorter than our exercise and therefore only first and second test run results are somewhat comparable. The results of Leiberman et. al's visual vigilance test (Task 1) were similar to ours. The performance level did not drop between first and second test runs. In matching-to-sample task (task 2) Leiberman et. al found significant declination already on the 3rd day of SUSOPS. This was not the case with our students. Leiberman et. al did not find statistically significant difference between their participants baseline results and results on 4th SUSOPS day in motor learning task (task 3). Our finding is the same. Task 4 and 5 were not included in Leiberman's et. al's study.

	Nr	Control Group			Explan. Group		
		HL %	LL %	Cohen	HL %	LL%	Cohen
Task 1	1	98	96	0,60	98	99	-1,26
	2	97	95	0,63	97	99	-0,86
	3	96	72	Large: 1,11	96	90	Small: 0,49
Task 2	1	88	93	-0,22	95	81	0,74
	2	96	93	0,23	98	96	0,6
	3	86	83	0,19	88	90	-0,11
Task 4	1	58	86	-0,64	100	88	0,53
	2	92	100	-0,43	100	67	1,00
	3	92	75	Small: 0,46	82	78	0,10
Task 5	1	84	70	0,56	88	84	0,38
	2	83	87	-0,24	89	89	0,04
	3	87	75	Medium:0,57	86	82	Small: 0,27

Table 2: Performance rates of physical fitness groups with Cohen's effect size

5. Discussion

The results indicate that motivation given by explaining the goal and importance of a task has a positive effect on the execution of cyber tasks. This is in line with a finding that information awareness education will be more effective if reasons behind each security action are explained (Parsons et. al, 2014). According to motivation theories a new task can act as motivation alone, as it gives a feeling of personal growth and learning (Ramlall, 2004). When a task is connected to a real work situation, responsibility becomes a motivation factor. Also, emotions towards content of tasks might have an effect (McPherson, 2011).

The results also show that high physical fitness levels have a positive effect on cognitive abilities in neutrally explained tasks when a person is under sleep deprivation, lacks nutrition and is not under (heavy) time pressure. The result supports earlier research (Fisher et al. 2011, Gregory et.al 2012, Reed et.al 2013). It was also noticed that high physical fitness levels did not affect the explanation group. This might indicate that motivation has a stronger effect than pure physical fitness.

6. Conclusion

In this study we designed a cognitive test set to measure students' cognitive abilities. Attention, short-term memory, visual-spatial memory, execution of language skills and ability to learn were all tested at three separate occasions during a two-week exercise. The exercise was physically demanding due to sleep and nutrition being heavily reduced and physical activity being heavily increased.

We found that motivation gained by the explanation of tasks and their importance, helps performance in cyber tasks. We also found that good physical condition has a positive effect when conducting cyber task. This is particularly noticeable in cases where a person has been in a physically demanding environment for an extended period of time. The study encourages us to build on the integration of cognitive engineering tasks with structured military physical training at our academy. Maintaining, operating and defending networks are not only tasks for military personnel. Civil networks are also maintained, operated and defended in similar ways. Based on the results of this study, physical training should not be forgotten in civilian Computer Emergency Response Teams, CERTs. Good physical condition could support analysts' ability to perform when operating under stress.

7. Future Work

In spring 2015 similar cognitive test were conducted for the new second year students. The results will be compared. We also plan to study how to strengthen mental robustness and capacities to carry out effective teamwork under demanding conditions.

8. References

Angeles, Rolly. 2004. "Rootcause Failure Analysis Module 3:Why humans commit errors?" RSA. www.rootcauselive.com/PowerPointPresentations/Angeles-What%20is%20RCA/Rootcause%20Failure%20Analysis3.pdf, Accessed 30th May 2014.

Andress, Jason and Steve Winterfeld. 2011. "Cyber Warriors." Chap. 4 in *Cyber warfare: techniques, tactics and tools for security practitioners* 61-81. Elsevier.

Cohen, Jakob. 1988. "The Analysis of Variance" Chap. 8 in *Statistical Power Analysis for the Behavioral Sciences* 2nd edition. Lawrence Erlbaum associates.

Dahlman, Sofie, Per Bäckström, Gunilla Bohlin, and Örjan Frans. 2012. "Cognitive abilities of street children: Low-SES Bolivian boys with and without experience of living in the street." *Child Neuropsychology: A Journal on Normal and Abnormal Development in Childhood and Adolescence* 19(5):540-556.

Dietrich, Detlef, Christiane Waller, Johannes Sönke, Bernardina Wieringa, Hinderk Emrich, and Thomas Münte. 2001. "Differential effects of emotional content on event-related potentials in word recognition memory." *Neuropsychobiology*, 43:96-101.

Fisher, Abigail, Jame Boyle, James Patron, Phillip Tomporowski, Christine Watson, John McColl, and John Reilly. 2011. "Effects of a physical education intervention on cognitive function in young children: randomized controlled pilot study." *BMC Pediatrics* 11:97.

Gaillard, Anthony. 2007. "Concentration, Stress and Performance." Chapter in *Performance Under Stress:* 59-76, Ashgate Publishing, 2007

Galliot, Matthew. 2013. "Hunger and Reduced Self-Control in the Laboratory and across the World: Reducing Hunger as a Self-Control Panacea." *Psychology(2152-7180)* 4(1):59-66.

Gertz, Bill. 2014. "U.S. military not prepared for cyber warfare, commander warns." www.washingtontimes.com/news/2014/feb/28/us-military-not-prepared-cyber-warfare-commander-w/?page=all Accessed 13th June 2014

Glisky, Elizabeth. 2007. "Changes in Cognitive Function in Human Aging." Chapter 1 in *Brain Aging: Models, Methods, and Mechanisms*. Baca Ranton. CRC press.

Gregory, Sara, Beth Parker, and Paul Thompson. 2012. "Physical Activity, Cognitive Function, and Brain Health: What Is the Role of Exercise Training in the Prevention of Dementia?" *Brain Sciences* 2: 684-708.

Harris, Wayne, Karol Ross, and P.A. Hancock. 2007. "Changes in Soldier's Information Processing Capability under Stress." Chapter in *Performance Under Stress:* 101-114, Ashgate Publishing, 2007.

Hartzler, Beth. 2014. "Fatigue on the flight deck: The consequences of sleep loss and the benefits of napping." *Accident Analysis & Prevention* 62: 309-318.

Helkala, Kirsi. 2014. "Effect of password sentences with emotional content." In proceedings of the Norwegian Information Security Conference.

Koch, Christopher, and LaMar Hasbrouck. 2013. "Exploring the Link between Physical Activity, Fitness and Cognitive Function." http://www.isbe.net/EPE/pdf/reports-webinars/iphi-epetf-rpt0313.pdf. Accessed 9th April 2014.

Lee, Angela and Brian Sternthal. The effects of positive mood on memory. 1999. *Journal of Consumer Research*, 26(2):115-127.

Leiberman, Harris, Philip Niro, William Tharion, Bradley Nindl, John Castellani, and Scott Montain. 2006. "Cognition During Sustained Operations: Comparison of a Laboratory Simulation to Field Studies." *Aviation, Space, and Environmental Medicine* 10(9): 929-935.

Lees, Caitlin, and Jessica Hopkins. 2013. "Effect of Aerobic Exercise on Cognition, Academic Achievement, and Psychosocial Function in Children: A Systematic Review of Randomized Control Trials." *Preventing Chronic Disease* 10.

Lynn III, Willam. 2010. "Defending a new domain." www.foreignaffairs.com/articles/66552/william-j-lynn-iii/defending-a-new-domain Accessed 13th June 2014.

McPherson, Fiona. 2011. "The role of emotion in memory." www.memory-key.com/memory/emotion. Accessed 30th May 2014.

Michelon Pascale . 2006. "What are cognitive abilities and skills, and how to boost them?" sharpbrains.com/blog/2006/12/18/what-are-cognitive-abilities/ Accessed 29th May 2014.

Montreal Cognitive Assessment (MOCA). www.mocatest.org. Accessed 27th April 2014.

Parsons, Kathryn, Agata McCormac, Marcus Butavicius, Malcolm Pattison, and Cate Jerram. 2014. "Determining employee awareness using Human Aspects of Information Security Questionnaire (HAIS-Q)", Computers & Security 42:165-176.

Ramlall, Sunil. 2004. "A review of employee motivation theories and their implications for employee retention within organizations." *Journal of American Academy of Business, Cambridge:* 52-63.

Reed, Julian, Andrea Maslow, Savannah Long, and Morgan Hughey. 2013. "Examining the impact of 45 minutes of daily physical education on cognitive ability, fitness performance, and body composition of African American youth." *Journal of Physical Activity & Health* 10:185-197.

Studying Safe Online Banking Behaviour: A Protection Motivation Theory Approach

J. Jansen[1,2]

[1]Faculty of Humanities and Law, Open University of the Netherlands
[2]Cybersafety Research Group, NHL University of Applied Sciences
e-mail: j.jansen@nhl.nl

Abstract

In this paper, a conceptual research model is proposed to study safe online banking behaviour. The Protection Motivation Theory functions as the core of the model. The model is extended with additional variables, making it suitable for the online banking context. The coping perspective, which is central to the Protection Motivation Theory, seems to be valuable to study behaviour in information systems. By taking a cognitive behavioural perspective, it can be examined how individuals cope with threats, which may contribute to the development of effective intervention programs aimed at safe online banking.

Keywords

Protection Motivation Theory, Online Banking, Customer Behaviour, Risk, Coping

1. Introduction

This study concentrates on online banking, a means by which customers can access different kinds of banking services via the internet. By 2014, more than eighty percent of Dutch citizens aged sixteen and over had adopted this service (Eurostat, 2014). Online banking is not without risk, it also attracts criminals. The rise of online banking has changed the nature of attacks on the flow of payments. Attacks are now more targeted at customers instead of banks (NVB, 2011).

The Dutch Banking Association (NVB) annually reports figures concerning online banking fraud. The financial damage in 2013 caused by fraudulent transfers was estimated to be 9.6 million euros. Online banking fraud is mainly caused by phishing and malware attacks. The financial damages in 2011 and 2012 were respectively 35.0 and 34.8 million euros (NVB, 2013). Although the numbers tend to decline, it is still a considerable problem that banks and users of online banking need to deal with.

A trend regarding online banking is that customers are attributed with more responsibility (Anderson, 2007; Davinson and Sillence, 2014). This is not surprising because the safety and security of online banking cannot be addressed by one party; it is a joint responsibility of multiple parties. Thus, customers also have certain responsibilities considering the safety and security of online banking. Consequently, customers should be able to cope with threats aimed at online banking.

The definition of coping used in this study is that customers are aware of the threats of online banking, (try to) prevent them, recognize them and act accordingly. First, someone must be aware of a specific threat, such as fraud. If the threat, despite all actions, could not be avoided, it is important to recognize or detect it as soon as possible. If a threat is quickly noticed, its impact might be reduced or possibly mitigated entirely. In other words, coping is not only about eliminating threats, but also about managing them. This study focuses on two specific parts of coping, namely the identification and prevention of threats. The coping approach is supported by various scientific disciplines, such as health and consumer psychology, but is relatively new in the field of information systems (Lai *et al.* 2012).

As of January 1st 2014, Dutch private customers who use online banking need to adhere to the so-called unified safety rules for online banking, which are defined in the General Terms & Conditions of all banks in the Netherlands. This effort is made under the supervision of the Dutch Banking Association and the Dutch Consumer Association, to create more uniformity in the policies of banks. The safety rules are: keep your security codes secret, make sure that your debit card is not used by other persons, secure the devices you use for online banking properly, check your bank account regularly, and report incidents directly to your bank.

The purpose of this study is to gain insight into the factors that affect customers to take protective measures against online banking fraud, i.e. to comply with the unified safety rules. The main research question is: What factors affect customers to take safety measures to protect themselves against online banking fraud? The outcome of this study is a conceptual research model to study safe online banking behaviour. The Protection Motivation Theory is used as a theoretical lens to study this problem.

This study is part of a PhD research program on the safety and security of online banking. This program is funded by the Dutch banking sector (represented by the Dutch Banking Association), the Police Academy, and the Dutch National Police.

2. Conceptual Research Model for Safe Online Banking

In this section, a brief overview is given of the Protection Motivation Theory (PMT), its constructs and the reasons why this specific theory is chosen. The constructs are divided in four levels: threat appraisal, coping appraisal, protection motivation, and control variables. Additional constructs which seem valuable for the online banking context are presented within these categories. These are: trust in online banking, locus of control, injunctive norms, descriptive norms and attitude. Conclusively, the conceptual research model is presented and explained.

2.1. Selecting the Protection Motivation Theory

There are several theories that try to explain and predict behaviour (Floyd *et al.* 2000). For example, in information systems research already much is known about the adoption of technology. Technologies that have been studied are often *beneficial technologies* (Chenoweth *et al.* 2009), of which online banking is an example.

Regarding the use of *protective technologies*, which are focused on preventing negative outcomes, less is known (Chenoweth *et al.* 2009). Few studies have been conducted on security behaviour of end users and on how such behaviour can be changed (Ng *et al.* 2009). Research has shown that there are significant differences between the use of beneficial and protective technologies (Dinev and Hu, 2005). Therefore, other theories than adoption theories may be more appropriate.

After evaluating several psychological theories, the PMT (Rogers, 1975) is chosen as the basis for this study, a social cognitive theory that predicts behaviour (Milne *et al.* 2000). The main reasons for this choice are as follows. The PMT has been successfully applied to understand and predict the use of various protective measures (Milne *et al.* 2000) and is considered one of the most powerful explanatory theories for safe behaviour (Floyd *et al.* 2000). The theory is applied, sometimes in an adjusted form, to the field of information systems and has been found useful in predicting individual computer security behaviour in both home (Anderson and Agarwal, 2010; Chenoweth *et al.* 2009; Crossler, 2010; Johnston and Warkentin, 2010; Lai *et al.* 2012; Liang and Xue, 2010) and working situations (Herath and Rao, 2009; Ifinedo, 2012; Lee, 2011; Lee and Larsen, 2009; Pahnila *et al.* 2007; Vance *et al.* 2012; Workman *et al.* 2008; Workman *et al.* 2009), making it a useful theory for studying safe online banking behaviour. Strength of the PMT is that it includes the concept of risk, which is neglected in adoption theories (Johnston and Warkentin, 2010). Furthermore, attention is not only paid to the predicting variables, but also to how these variables are related. Finally, the theory is useful for the development of interventions (Floyd *et al.* 2000).

2.2. The Protection Motivation Theory and Its constructs

Central to the PMT are two cognitive processes, namely threat appraisal and coping appraisal. In the threat appraisal process, individuals evaluate the likelihood and impact of a threat. This is followed by the coping appraisal process in which individuals evaluate possible coping strategies against the threat. This process is driven by the effectiveness of a strategy or measure, the degree to which the individual is able to perform the required action and the costs involved. The cognitive processes are initiated by receiving information, which is called sources of information, and includes environmental and interpersonal sources. Both processes in their turn affect the protection motivation, i.e. the intention to perform certain behaviour. For more information about the PMT, see Milne *et al.* (2000) and Norman *et al.* (2005).

2.2.1. Threat appraisal

In the threat appraisal process, an estimate is made of the threat. This is performed initially, because a threat must be observed first before one can assess coping strategies (Floyd *et al.* 2000; Liang and Xue, 2009). Crossler (2010 p.2) defines this process as "an individual's assessment about the level of danger posed by a security event". Threat appraisal consists of the constructs *perceived vulnerability* and *perceived severity*, which both make up *perceived risk*. The *rewards* construct is also part of the threat appraisal process. However, rewards are barely operationalized in PMT studies (Milne *et al.* 2000). This is mainly because the conceptual difference between the value of a reward for risky behaviour and the response costs for a security measure (see coping appraisal) is not always clear (Abraham *et al.* 1994). Therefore, this construct is dropped. For threat appraisal one additional construct is added, namely *trust in online banking*.

In the context of online banking, perceived risk is defined as "the potential of loss in the pursuit of a desired outcome from using electronic banking services" (Yousafzai *et al.* 2003 p.851). When a risk is perceived, individuals will change their behaviour based on how much risk they are willing to accept for the particular threat (Workman *et al.* 2008). Based on this notion, it is expected that the higher the perceived risk, the more likely a customer will be inclined to take protective measures.

Perceived vulnerability is "an individual's assessment of the probability of a threatening security event occurring" (Crossler, 2010 p.2). This involves an individual's believe on how likely it is to be victimized by online banking fraud. It is expected that perceived vulnerability has a positive influence on perceived risk. The perceived impact of a threat is "an individual's assessment of the severity of the consequences resulting from a threatening security event" (Crossler, 2010 p.2). This involves how serious the consequences of online banking fraud are perceived. It is expected that perceived severity of a threat has a positive influence on perceived risk. Liang and Xue (2010) argue that perceived vulnerability and perceived severity have an interaction effect on the formation of perceived risk. They state that perceived risk is a calculation of probability times impact and that when one of the two is zero, the perceived risk disappears. This effect will be included in the model.

Literature on online banking adoption has repeatedly shown that a high level of trust reduces the perception of risk (e.g. Yousafzai *et al.* 2009). This study adopts the definition of Yousafzai *et al.* (2003 p.849) who define trust in online banking as "a psychological state which leads to the willingness of customer to perform banking transactions on the Internet, expecting that the bank will fulfil its obligations, irrespective of customer's ability to monitor or control bank's actions". Trust is not often integrated in PMT studies. However, it is an important construct in risk literature. Therefore, a logical place for trust in the conceptual model is within the treat appraisal process. It is hypothesised that trust in online banking has a negative influence on risk perception.

2.2.2. Coping appraisal

Assessing threats is not enough. When individuals feel vulnerable and think that the potential severity of a threat is high, that does not change their behaviour immediately. There are additional barriers that must be overcome (Furnell *et al.* 2006). The coping appraisal process includes an evaluation of the estimated coping strategies to avoid or minimize the threat. Crossler (2010 p.2) defines this process as "an individual's assessment of his ability to perform a given behaviour and his confidence that a given behaviour will be successful in mitigating or averting the potential loss or damage resulting from a threatening security event, at a perceived cost that is not too high". Threat appraisal consists of the constructs *response efficacy, self-efficacy* and *response costs*. Four additional constructs are added, namely *locus of control, injunctive norms, descriptive norms* and *attitude*.

Response efficacy "concerns beliefs about whether the recommended coping response will be effective in reducing threat to the individual" (Milne *et al.* 2000 p.109). If the individual is sufficiently satisfied that the protective measure will actually work, then that is an incentive to apply it. Liang and Xue (2010) argue that it is possible that response efficacy, what they call safeguard effectiveness, interacts with perceived risk. This interaction effect is included in the model.

Self-efficacy "concerns an individual's beliefs about whether he or she is able to perform the recommended coping response" (Milne *et al.* 2000 p.109). Rhee *et al.* (2009) studied self-efficacy and its impact on safe behaviour by end users. In their article, it is explained that it is important to assign a domain-specific framework to self-efficacy, which increases its predictive value. Rhee *et al.* (2009 p.818) speak of self-efficacy in information security, which they define as "a belief in one's capability to protect information and information systems from unauthorized disclosure, modification, loss, destruction, and lack of availability". The assumption is that the higher the self-efficacy in terms of taking safety measures, the more an individual will be inclined to take such measures.

Response costs "concern beliefs about how costly performing the recommended response will be to the individual" (Milne *et al.* 2000 p.109). This involves both tangible and intangible costs. When the costs of applying safety measures exceed the costs of a potential threat, then the response costs have a negative influence on protection motivation.

In line with the work of Workman *et al.* (2008), locus of control is considered to be part of the coping appraisal process. This concept is concerned with the conviction of individuals whether they have the outcome of a given situation under control (internal locus of control), or that it is controlled by others (external locus of control). In the case of online banking, it is possible that customers push off responsibility for its safety to the supplier, i.e. the bank. In addition, customers might feel that they have no control over the safety and security of online banking. Consequently, locus of control has impact on the behaviour of individuals. It determines whether the behaviour is proactive (taking responsibility) or reactive (leaving it to others) (Workman *et al.* 2008). The assumption is that when a customer feels in control of the situation, he or she will be motivated to take action.

According to Anderson and Agarwal (2010 p.616) there is lack of attention for social variables in information systems research "even though the information systems adoption literature and the underlying theories they draw upon suggests [...] that norms can be influential in the formation of behavior". Therefore, the constructs injunctive and descriptive norms are added to the model. Ifinedo (2012) placed norms within the coping appraisal process, which is also done in this study.

"Injunctive norms refer to perceptions concerning what should or ought to be done with respect to performing a given behaviour, whereas descriptive norms refer to perceptions that others are or are not performing the behavior in question" (Fishbein and Ajzen, 2010 p.131). Both injunctive and descriptive norms have a positive influence on protection motivation.

Finally, attitude is added to the model, which is defined as "an individual's positive or negative feelings (evaluative effect) about performing the target behavior" (Fishbein and Ajzen, 1975 p.216). The relation between attitude and intentional behaviour is extensively tested in information systems research (Venkatesh *et al.* 2003). It is assumed that a positive attitude towards protective measures will have a positive influence on taking such measures.

2.2.3. Protection motivation

The protection motivation is the decision or intention to proceed to, continuation of, or the avoidance of the studied behaviour (Floyd *et al.* 2000). "Protection motivation is an intervening variable that has the typical characteristics of a motive: it arouses, sustains, and directs activity" (Rogers, 1975 p.98). The protection motivation can manifest itself in an adaptive or maladaptive coping response. An adaptive response implies that customers protect themselves. A maladaptive response is the opposite, namely that customers do not protect themselves. This response suggests that an individual is at risk.

In this study, the PMT is applied to explain why online banking customers adopt the desired behaviour, i.e. an adaptive coping response. The desired behaviour is compliance with the unified rules for safe online banking, the outcome variable of the conceptual model. Thus, the independent variable consists of multiple actions. This is, however, not an issue considering that securing online banking, as is the case with securing a computer, "is about performing a number of different practices, not one in particular" (Crossler and Bélanger, 2014 p.54). These authors furthermore state that a more holistic view on safe behaviour is acquired when measuring multiple behaviours instead of one.

In information systems research, it is preferred to measure actual behaviour instead of intentional behaviour (Anderson and Agarwal, 2010; Workman *et al.* 2009). However, this will be difficult to achieve. Therefore, it is chosen to measure intentional behaviour. Anderson and Agarwal (2010 p.614) who also studied intentional behaviour instead of actual behaviour justified their choice by findings from earlier studies which indicated that the relationship between intentional and actual behaviour is strong, consistent and theoretically grounded.

2.2.4. Control variables

For this study, four control variables are included. These are *internet experience, habit, victimization of online banking fraud* and *demographic variables*. The first three are considered prior experience, an aspect of the PMT which is often neglected

(Vance *et al.* 2012), but is deemed a strong predictor of future behaviour (Norman *et al.* 2005). In order to keep the model as parsimonious as possible, personality variables like risk propensity and trust propensity are omitted.

While online banking is not a new phenomenon, it is a relatively new online service. According to Mannan and Van Oorschot (2008) people who adopt online banking at later times are less technical savvy. Prior experience with a website or other internet activities can have an impact on current behaviour of customers in terms of security choices (Chen and Bansal, 2010). In this study, it is assumed that more experienced internet users better understand security issues regarding online banking and therefore are more inclined to protect themselves against the possible threats.

A study that included prior experiences, in the form of habit, is that of Vance *et al.* (2012). Habit theory assumes that many actions are taken without thinking about it deeply, and that actions are performed because individuals are accustomed to them (Vance *et al.* 2012). Habits are thus acts performed unconsciously or automatically. Consequently, it is proposed that habits related to information security have a positive impact on complying with the safety rules for online banking.

Prior experience as an online banking fraud victim can also influence the protection motivation. People who once were victimized might easily regard themselves as victims again (Workman *et al.* 2008). In this study, it is expected that earlier victimization motivates a customer to take measures to prevent fraud in the future.

Finally, demographic variables are included in the model. The demographic variables that will be included are gender, age, educational level and work situation. It is not only important to determine which variables matter in terms of taking measures to keep online banking as safe as possible. It is also important to identify whether there are differences between specific groups of customers. By including such variables, it will be possible to make targeted recommendations for intervention strategies.

2.3. The model

The protection motivation, in this case compliance with the rules for safe online banking, results from the threat and coping appraisal processes (Figure 1). The arrows in this model indicate which variables have an impact on what other variables. A minus-sign means that a negative relationship is expected. In other cases, the expected relationship is positive. The circles represent interaction effects.

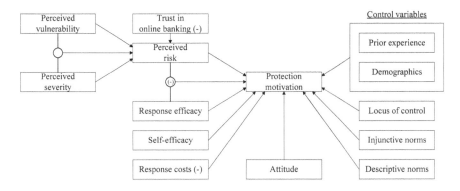

Figure 1: Conceptual research model

The protection motivation is a positive function of risk perception, response efficacy, self-efficacy, locus of control, injunctive norms, descriptive norms and attitude, and a negative function of response costs. In the model, protection motivation is controlled for by prior experience and demographic variables. Risk perception in its turn is positively influenced by perceived vulnerability and perceived severity, and negatively by trust in online banking.

3. Conclusions and future research

Research shows that technical security cannot guarantee the safety of online banking; the behaviour of end users is also vital (Davinson and Sillence, 2014; Furnell *et al.* 2006; Liang and Xue, 2010; Ng *et al.* 2009; Rhee *et al.* 2009). It is recognized that research is scarce in the domain of individual security related behaviour (Liang and Xue, 2010). Anderson and Agarwal (2010 p.613) state for example: "there is limited understanding of what drives home computer users to behave in a secure manner online, and even less insight into how to influence their behaviour".

Based on the above, it is concluded that the PMT is a suitable theory to take as a starting point for further study. In literature, no studies were found that applied the PMT to online banking. By applying the PMT to a new territory, it can be assessed whether the PMT, extended with additional variables, maintains its value. The proposed model will be evaluated in a later study on a representative sample of Dutch online banking customers. In addition, the PMT approach seems applicable to more fields other than online banking.

4. References

Abraham, C.S., Sheeran, P., Abrams, D. and Spears, R. (1994), "Exploring teenagers' adaptive and maladaptive thinking in relation to the threat of HIV infection", *Psychology & Health*, Vol. 9, No. 4, pp253–272.

Anderson, C.L. and Agarwal, R. (2010), "Practicing safe computing: A multimethod empirical examination of home computer user security behavioral intentions", *MIS Quarterly*, Vol. 34, No. 3, pp613–643.

Anderson, R. (2007), "Closing the phishing hole: Fraud, risk and nonbanks", *Proceedings of the Payments System Research Conferences*, pp1–16.

Chen, L.-C. and Bansal, G. (2010), "An integrated model of individual web security behavior", *Proceedings of the 16th Americas Conference on Information Systems*, pp485–492.

Chenoweth, T., Minch, R. and Gattiker, T. (2009), "Application of protection motivation theory to adoption of protective technologies", *Proceedings of the 42nd Hawaii International Conference on System Sciences*, pp1–10.

Crossler, R. and Bélanger, F. (2014), "An extended perspective on individual security behaviors: Protection motivation theory and a unified security practices (USP) instrument", *ACM SIGMIS Database*, Vol. 45, No. 4, pp51–71.

Crossler, R.E. (2010), "Protection motivation theory: Understanding determinants to backing up personal data", *Proceedings of the 43rd Hawaii International Conference on System Sciences*, pp1–10.

Davinson, N. and Sillence, E. (2014), "Using the health belief model to explore users' perceptions of "being safe and secure" in the world of technology mediated financial transactions", *International Journal of Human-Computer Studies,* Vol. 72, No. 2, pp154–168.

Dinev, T. and Hu, Q. (2005), "The centrality of awareness in the formation of user behavioral intention toward preventive technologies in the context of voluntary use", *Proceedings of the International Conference of Information Systems,* pp1–5.

Eurostat (2014), "Individuals using the internet for internet banking", http://ec.europa.eu/euro stat/tgm/refreshTableAction.do;?pcode=tin00099&language=en, (Accessed 2 March 2015).

Fishbein, M. and Ajzen, I. (1975), *Belief, attitude, intention and behavior: An introduction to theory and research*, Addison-Wesley, MA, ISBN: 978-0-2010-2089-2.

Fishbein, M. and Ajzen, I. (2010), *Predicting and changing behavior: The reasoned action approach*, Taylor & Francis, New York, ISBN: 978-0-8058-5924-9.

Floyd, D.L., Prentice-Dunn, S. and Rogers, R.W. (2000), "A meta-analysis of research on protection motivation theory", *Journal of Applied Social Psychology*, Vol. 30, No. 2, pp407–429.

Furnell, S.M., Jusoh, A. and Katsabas, D. (2006), "The challenges of understanding and using security: A survey of end-users" *Computers & Security*, Vol. 25, No.1, pp27–35.

Herath, T. and Rao, H.R. (2009), "Protection motivation and deterrence: A framework for security policy compliance in organisations", *European Journal of Information Systems*, Vol. 18, No. 2, pp106–125.

Ifinedo, P. (2012), "Understanding information systems security policy compliance: An integration of the theory of planned behavior and the protection motivation theory", *Computers & Security*, Vol. 31, No. 1, pp83–95.

Johnston, A.C. and Warkentin, M. (2010), "Fear appeals and information security behaviors: An empirical study", *MIS Quarterly*, Vol. 34, No. 3, pp549–566.

Lai, F., Li, D. and Hsieh, C.-T. (2012), "Fighting identity theft: The coping perspective", *Decision Support Systems*, Vol. 52, No. 2, pp353–363.

Lee, Y. (2011), "Understanding anti-plagiarism software adoption: An extended protection motivation theory perspective", *Decision Support Systems*, Vol. 50, No. 2, pp361–369.

Lee, Y. and Larsen, K.R. (2009), "Threat or coping appraisal: Determinants of SMB executives' decision to adopt anti-malware software", *European Journal of Information Systems*, Vol. 18, No. 2, pp177–187.

Liang, H. and Xue, Y. (2009), "Avoidance of information technology threats: A theoretical perspective", *MIS Quarterly*, Vol. 33, No. 1, pp71–90.

Liang, H. and Xue, Y. (2010), "Understanding security behaviors in personal computer usage: A threat avoidance perspective", *Journal of the Association for Information Systems*, Vol. 11, No. 7, pp394–413.

Mannan, M. and Van Oorschot, P.C. (2008), "Security and usability: The gap in real-world online banking", Proceedings of the 2007 Workshop on New Security Paradigms, pp1–14.

Milne, S., Sheeran, P. and Orbell, S. (2000), "Prediction and intervention in health-related behavior: A meta-analytic review of protection motivation theory", Journal of Applied Social Psychology, Vol. 30, No. 1, pp106–143.

Ng, B.-Y., Kankanhalli, A. and Xu, Y.C. (2009), "Studying users' computer security behavior: A health belief perspective", *Decision Support Systems*, Vol. 46, No. 4, pp815–825.

Norman, P., Boer, H. and Seydel, E.R. (2005), *Protection motivation theory*, In: Predicting health behaviour: Research and practice with social cognition models, Open University Press, Maidenhead, pp81–126.

NVB (2011), *"Annual report 2011"*, Dutch Banking Association, Amsterdam, pp.1–52.

NVB (2013), *"Position paper online payments: May 30th 2013"*, Dutch Banking Association, Amsterdam, pp1–5.

Pahnila, S., Siponen, M. and Mahmood, A. (2007), "Employees' behavior towards IS security policy compliance", *Proceedings of the 40th Annual Hawaii International Conference on System Sciences*. pp156–165.

Rhee, H.-S., Kim, C. and Ryu, Y.U. (2009), "Self-efficacy in information security: Its influence on end users' information security practice behavior", *Computers & Security*, Vol. 28, No. 8, pp816–826.

Rogers, R.W. (1975), "A protection motivation theory of fear appeals and attitude change", *The Journal of Psychology*, Vol. 91, No. 1, pp93–114.

Vance, A., Siponen, M. and Pahnila, S. (2012), "Motivating IS security compliance: Insights from habit and protection motivation theory", *Information & Management*, 49, pp190–198.

Venkatesh, V., Morris, M.G., Davis, G.B. and Davis, F.D. (2003), "User acceptance of information technology: Toward a unified view", *MIS Quarterly*, Vol. 27, No. 3, pp425–478.

Workman, M., Bommer, W.H. and Straub, D. (2008), "Security lapses and the omission of information security measures: A threat control model and empirical test", *Computers in Human Behavior*, Vol. 24, No. 6, pp2799–2816.

Workman, M., Bommer, W.H. and Straub, D. (2009), "The amplification effects of procedural justice on a threat control model of information systems security behaviours", *Behaviour & Information Technology*, Vol. 28, No. 6, pp563–575.

Yousafzai, S., Pallister, J. and Foxall, G. (2009), "Multi-dimensional role of trust in Internet banking adoption", *The Service Industries Journal*, Vol. 29, No. 5, pp591–605.

Yousafzai, S.Y., Pallister, J.G. and Foxall, G.R. (2003), "A proposed model of e-trust for electronic banking", *Technovation*, Vol. 23, No. 11, pp847–860.

New Insights Into Understanding Manager's Intentions to Overlook ISP Violation in Organizations through Escalation of Commitment Factors

M. Kajtazi[1,2], E. Kolkowska[1] and B. Bulgurcu[3]

[1]Örebro University, Örebro, Sweden
[2]Linnaeus University, Växjö, Sweden
[3]Boston College, Boston, Massachusetts
e-mail: {miranda.kajtazi; ella.kolkowska}@oru.se; burcu.bulgurcu@bc.edu

Abstract

This paper addresses managers' intentions to overlook their employees' Information Security Policy (ISP) violation, in circumstances when on-going projects have to be completed and delivered even if ISP violation must take place to do so. The motivation is based on the concern that ISP violation can be influenced by escalation of commitment factors. Escalation is a phenomenon that explains how employees in organizations often get involved in *nonperforming* projects, commonly reflecting the tendency of persistence, when investments of resources have been initiated. We develop a theoretical understanding based on Escalation of Commitment theory that centres on two main factors of noncompliance, namely completion effect and sunk costs. We tested our theoretical concepts in a pilot study, based on qualitative and quantitative data received from 16 respondents from the IT – industry, each representing one respondent from the management level. The results show that while some managers are very strict about not accepting any form of ISP violation in their organization, their beliefs start to change when they realize that such form of violation may occur when their employees are closer to completion of a project. Our in-depth interviews with 3 respondents in the follow-up study, confirm the tension created between compliance with the ISP and the completion of the project. The results indicate that the larger the investments of time, efforts and money in a project, the more the managers consider that violation is acceptable.

Keywords

Escalation of commitment, ISP violation, IT-industry, completion effect, sunk costs.

1. Introduction

For all the benefits of information technology (IT), particularly the revolution in how organizations operate, information security is still a concern for management (Bulgurcu et al., 2010; Vance & Siponen, 2012). As a result, reserving the right budget for information security (IS) is one of the most difficult management tasks (Cavusoglu et al., 2004; Hsu et al., 2012). Organizations find it very challenging to define the value of their IS investments, mainly because an IS investment is expected to return a tangible benefit (Sonnenreich et al., 2006).

Prior research suggests that the focus of IS should be strengthened from the socio-organizational perspective (Boss et al., 2009; Bulgurcu et al., 2010; Dhillon and

131

Backhouse, 2001; Warkentin et al., 2011; Willison and Warkentin 2013). Highlighting the significance of the insiders is key, as employees are considered the weakest link in IS (Mitnick and William, 2003), since the challenge to keep information safe is not much of a technical challenge, but the challenge is how to make people use the technological services correctly, e.g. the use of passwords in a correct way (Furnell, 2014). Although research in this area has developed extensively (Bulgurcu et al., 2010; D'Arcy et al., 2009; Dhillon and Backhouse, 2001; Herath and Rao, 2009b; Johnston and Warkentin, 2010; Siponen and Vance, 2010), little is understood about business managers' influence on employees' compliance with ISP. Boss at al (2009) argue that business managers are an important part of IS management and play a significant role in affecting the employees' willingness to comply with the existing ISP. Thus it would be problematic if business managers tend to overlook the violation of the ISP.

Drawing on this motivation, the objective of this paper is to explain whether the management level in the organization tends to overlook the ISP violation, especially when they consider that some violation may be positive in certain situations, such as when a project needs to be completed, hence violation is for the benefit of the organization. We utilize the escalation of commitment theory to tackle managers' intention to justify violation with the organization's ISP. We do so by understanding which escalation factors influence managers' intentions to overlook and even accept ISP violation. Escalation of commitment is a phenomenon that explains how employees in organizations often get involved in a failing course of action, and reflect the tendency of not knowing whether persistence or withdrawal from that action is the best solution (Staw and Ross, 1989). For instance, employees must decide whether to withdraw or persist continuing on a nonperforming project, in which they should stop their investment of time, efforts and other resources, such as money. Empirically, we do not test if a project is failing or not, but we investigate the impact that escalation of commitment factors of sunk cost and completion effect may have on ISP violation in organizations by understanding managers' intentions to overlook ISP violation and even view it positively.

The rest of the paper is structured as follows. We continue to present our motivation and theoretical background. We then present our methodological approach followed by data analyses and results. Finally, we present the conclusions and some prospects to continue this research in the future.

2. Theoretical Framework

Among the many troubling phenomena that follow organizations, the escalation of commitment tops the list (Sleesman et al., 2012). Even during their phase of peaking with innovation and success, organizations commit costly decision errors, because of the tendency of decision-makers to maintain their commitment to a losing course of action, albeit that negative feedback on that action has occurred (Staw and Ross, 1989). Designing a behavioural model of rational choice, Simon (1955) assumed that employees behave rationally by having a well-organized and stable system of preferences. In fact, the employees are programmed to find rational adjustments that are good enough for practical circumstances. However, escalation of commitment theory focuses on understanding the commitment of an individual to make risky decisions in a given context, especially when the act is deliberate (Staw and Ross, 1989). Central to it is the understanding of the behaviour of an escalation of commitment. In practice, escalation of commitment is a characteristic of employees who often become committed to a losing course of action, throwing good money or effort after bad (Ross and Staw, 1993; Staw and Ross, 1989), when an employee exhibits high risk-taking behaviour as a result of a deliberate decision (Keil et al., 2000).

Accordingly, this paper presents escalation of commitment as a theoretical framework to account for an understanding of its effects that triggers managers at various organizations to overlook ISP violation, which in return may motivate employees even more to engage with the ISP violation. Such an account can possibly inform the development of future IS strategies to improve the protection of vulnerable information in organizations. Therefore we propose that a detailed understanding of the effects of escalation on managers' intentions to accept their employees' violation of the ISP of their organizations can possibly bring a significant theoretical redirection to increase our understanding of employees' intentions to violate ISPs in the IS domain.

2.1. Two Factors in Action

Completion effect is a type of motivation for an individual to achieve a goal, as the individual gets closer to that goal (Conlon and Garland, 1993). In the context of violation, the completion effect suggests that when projects are near completion, a manager's intention to overlook ISP violation may increase.

The completion effect is a psychological effect suggesting that the desire to achieve the completion of a project can have a significant influence on behaviour (Katz and Kahn, 1966). Similarly, Brockner et al. (1986) stated that an individual's motivation for pursuing a course of action may shift over time due in part to the presumed increased proximity to the goal. Results from a series of experiments appear to provide support for these assertions about the completion effect (Keil et al., 2000; Park et al., 2012).

Despite the fact that the completion effect has served as an important indicator of project management failures, Keil et al. (2000) have indicated that measuring the completion level for a particular action, e.g. the completion effect of a task in a project, may be extremely difficult. In practice this is extremely difficult because employees who depend on due dates for submitting their tasks believe that the closer the due date the closer they are to the completion of the project.

In our theoretical framework, the completion effect plays an important role. It acts as an independent factor to explain noncompliance with an ISP. Theoretically, however, we do not intend to utilize the completion effect for the purpose of measuring the level of project completion. We utilize the completion effect for measuring its influence on manager's intention to overlook ISP violation. More specifically, the completion effect is intended to explain if ISP violation is seen as a positive behaviour when projects are near completion or vice versa.

Linked to completion effect, we also consider the role of sunk cost effect on manager's intention to overlook ISP violation. Invested resources on a project explain that a manager's intention to get locked into considering that ISP violation may be positive for the project depends on the effect of the sunk costs. This phenomenon is commonly referred to as the sunk cost effect, which relates to at least three types of investments in the project: *time, efforts and money* (Staw and Ross, 1989). To better understand the interaction between completion effect and sunk cost in affecting manager's intentions, Figure 1 gives a visual representation of that interaction.

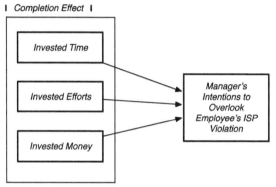

Figure 1: Research model – the escalation of commitment factors of completion effect and sunk cost towards understanding manager's intention to overlook employee's ISP violation

We posit that in terms of overlooking ISP violation, employees would exhibit a willingness to engage in ISP violation when they realize that they have already invested a large amount of time, efforts and money in trying to complete their project. Engaging in such behaviour when the project is nearly completed, allows the managers to believe that some ISP violation may even turn out to be positive for the organization.

The completion effect and sunk cost factors present two basic arguments why ISP violation as a result of escalation of commitment may take place, often in a large scale. While our intention is not to understand whether a project is actually failing, we consider that understanding the role of such escalation of commitment factors in ISP violation may bring a theoretical redirection in the ISP compliance and noncompliance literature. We continue to highlight the methodological approach and thereafter the results of our pilot study.

3. Methodological Approach

The purpose of this pilot study is to strengthen the view on the problem initially introduced, namely the managers' intentions to overlook their employees' ISP violation as a need to avoid project failure. The empirical investigation was driven by data collected from a mixed approach via an on-line questionnaire that featured a scenario in the beginning. We received qualitative and quantitative feedback from 16 respondents of 16 different organizations, which led us to extend the study with 3 more in depth interviews with the participating managers. The aim of these interviews was to follow-up the results from the questionnaire and to further discuss the problem of managers' intention to overlook employees' violation of ISP. The scenario and the questions for our respondents were based on theory that we effectively used to study how the managers' intentions to overlook ISP violation led us to better understand ISP violation among employees.

As described in Table 1, each participant was subject to the same context-specific scenario. The scenario was intended to inform the respondents that during the process of completion of their employees' specific tasks, their employees might become involved with the ISP violation in that process. The participants were then questioned whether they would find such a scenario to occur in their organization and whether they would accept such behaviour. A set of questions based on the adapted completion effect construct from Keil et al. (2000) and Ross and Staw (1993) were then asked[1]. Two questions were designed to be open-ended, one for the purpose of encouraging the managers to present their own perspectives on the reasons they would find for accepting such a violation of the ISP, the other for the purpose of receiving any other feedback they might have had.

Scenario
Assume that an employee that you supervise in your organization has been working on a certain project which needs to be finished by a deadline. The deadline is approaching and the employee has almost finished the project except a particular task which the employee does not know how to accomplish. In order to complete the project, that particular task has to be completed. The employee knows an expert who can help him/her to complete that task. But, some confidential customer information will be exposed to the expert while getting help from him/her. You know that your organization has an explicit information security policy stating that no customer information shall be exposed (disclosed, divulged, given away, or given access) to anyone outside the area of responsibility.
Think about this situation, and indicate your agreement/disagreement with the following questions.

Table 1: Pilot Study Scenario

---

[1] Due to limited space, we only introduce the scenario.

Although the number of respondents is relatively low, we consider that data collected from a qualitative and quantitative perspective with 16 respondents, as well as follow-up in-depth interviews with 3 of the respondents is sufficient to understand and start theorizing whether managers have intentions to overlook ISP violation in specific contexts, such as when projects are near completion. We also consider the number is sufficient to derive such an understanding considering that 16 organizations participated, and that one manager represents one company.

4. Data Analyses and Results

The data collected were analysed in two forms. We first used descriptive statistics for the scale questions, followed by text analyses for the open-ended answers. The analyses present the understanding of the IT industry manager's intentions on overlooking their employee's ISP violation. The total number of respondents to the survey was 16 participants from the management level of 16 IT-companies. Around 50% of these managers believe that it is very likely that ISP violation can be caused as a result of escalation of commitment behaviour, while 31% of the managers strongly believe that such misbehaviour is likely to occur. The remaining 19% of the respondents have vague beliefs that such behaviour occurs. The other half, 50% believe it is unlikely that ISP violation in organizations occurs as a result of escalation of commitment behaviour. Furthermore, 87% believe it is not acceptable if an employee of their organization violates information management rules and regulations of their organization by ISP violation, while 13% believe that this is not a serious issue. Following these responses, the same 87% of managers would never accept such violation, while the same 13% of managers would accept such violation.

Around 42% of these managers who think they would never accept ISP violation, realize that such violation may be out of their control. In this regard, one manager who believes that it is likely that ISP violation occurs, but would not accept violation, states that "*depending on the importance of the information given and to whom, I might be indulged with that kind of behaviour*". Similar to those beliefs, another manager thinks that if there is "*acceptance from the customer*" or by signing a "*non-disclosure agreement with the expert*", he might accept such violation. Three other managers consider that trusting their employees is an important factor to accepting such violation. One manager expects that their employees should let him know if such violation is necessary, therefore he would accept the violation. The other two managers believe that a non-disclosure agreement would keep information confidential. One manager would trust his employee that the violation is in the "*employee's best intention*", and that the violation would be acceptable, while the other believes that such "*violation would not matter as much*", when the non-disclosure agreement is signed. Another manager thinks that an "*ad hoc approval by higher management can be made possible, however employees own decision to talk cannot be acceptable*". Consequently even if the managers state that they would not accept the employees ISP violation, their answers to the open-ended questions indicate that they tend to explain and justify employees ISP violation.

The managers, seem to be influenced to change their beliefs about accepting the violation of their employees when very specific escalation of commitment related questions were asked. They seem to be influenced when their employees' escalation of commitment in terms of their invested time, efforts and money are considered important factors the closer their employee would get to the project completion.

If a project is 10% completed, then the majority of managers (75%), would not at all be influenced to accept violation because of time, efforts or money. Few managers, 25%, would be very little or somewhat influenced by the time spent on the project to accept such violation. Out of 25%, 18% indicate they would be very little influenced to accept such violation because of efforts and money spent on the project, while 7% indicate they would be moderately influenced to accept violation.

If a project is 50% completed, then around 68% of managers would not at all be influenced to accept violation because of time, efforts or money. Only 32% of managers indicate that they are somewhat influenced by the time spent on the project to accept such violation. Out of 32%, 25% indicate they would be somewhat influenced by the efforts and money spent on the project to accept such violation, while 7% indicate they would be frequently influenced by the efforts and money spent on the project to accept such violation.

If a project is 95% completed, then more than half of the managers, 62.5%, would not be influenced to accept violation because of the three reasons. 12.5% would be very little influenced to accept violation because of the three reasons. 12.5% would be moderately influenced to accept violation because of time. Approximately, 12.5%, would be very much influenced to accept violation because of time, efforts and money invested.

The results show that even if the majority of managers would never accept ISP violation, their beliefs about refusing to accept such violation seem to change. Their beliefs change when they realize that their employees are closer to completing their projects. In this regard, some managers indicated that they would indeed consider to accept ISP violation, only when they understand that a lot of time, efforts and money have been spent on their project.

Of the 16 managers, 3 managers were interviewed to further discuss if their intentions were to overlook violation when there is a need to complete a project. When asked how often do they face project deadlines that were facing obstacles, one of the three managers responded as *"there are many such projects in our organization, every month we get into difficult situations for the delivery process"*, the other said *"just last week, we had a situation when a task in the project was delaying the project delivery, and we wanted to do anything just to complete it and submit the project"*, the third displayed a worrisome voice saying that *"these situations happen all the time and the problem is that our employees do not notify me on time about the problems, that is why we need to react fast and make sure we deliver the project, it is the customer who is waiting"*.

When the three managers were asked again to discuss in more details whether they would or would not accept their employees violation of the ISP in order to make a successfully delivery of the project, their reactions were different, yet had the same intentions. The first manager discussed how the importance of the ISP in the organization and the rules described in it are often blurred, leaving the manager and the employees believe that violation to complete the project would not be as damaging. The second manager mentioned that despite he would never allow his employees to engage in violation for any reason, if violation would involve some insider with whom the violation is done, he would find this reasonable not to loose a project delivery, which may cost thousands to the organization if delayed. The third manager mentioned that his organization's ISP is so out-dated that any project-related violation would not even be considered as a violation, due to the ISP not covering such forms of violation.

These critical points raised, showed us that these managers were willing to accept and even encourage violation for the sake of a project. As previous literature has not considered these aspects of violation, we think that this is an issue that needs in-depth understanding of the violation of the ISP, which may shed new light on why employees are often noncompliant with the security rules and regulations of their organization.

5. Conclusion and Future Research

For organizations, controlling IS has become a daunting task. Insider attacks, i.e. employees in organizations, and outsider attacks, i.e. hackers, are increasing more than ever, generating far-reaching consequences, most often with millions of online personal data compromised, and billions of dollars registered in losses.

Our theoretical approach tackled a practical organizational problem by intending to understand how managers' intentions to overlook ISP violation among their employees increases, when they consider that enough spent resources of time, efforts and money on a project can be used as an argument to go against the ISP and make sure that they can deliver the project on-time, rather than look like a failure in front of the others in the organization, if the project has to be abandoned due to ISP. The empirical study based on 16 responses from the management level showed that the closer the employees are to completing their projects, the more their managers tend to overlook their ISP violation, if such a wrongdoing would save the project from failing. Time, efforts and money have been seen as three important resources that would identify the resources spent towards the completion of a project. We therefore suggest that organizations should focus on decreasing ISP violation not only by targeting employees at the front desks, but also by carefully targeting managers at any level, who can be considered as the source of allowing ISP violation to increase. While many well-established organizations are very careful about designing security rules and regulations, organizations that tend to overlook security issues, hence do not specify rules in this regard are the most vulnerable. Examining the factors that influence ISP violation as a result of escalation of commitment, such are the completion effect and sunk costs, can guide security managers in ensuring compliance in the future. For instance, organizations can effectively design new ISPs or re-design their existing ISPs by carefully focusing on informing the employees that the escalation of commitment is discouraged, whereas, the benefit of reporting project problems would allow organizations to find assistance for their employees, reducing the need for ISP violation.

There are several limitations of this study. First, we did not test if a project would actually be in the process of escalation of commitment or not. We only asked our respondents to hypothetically consider that a project would not be delivered if their employees would not violate the ISP. Tests in a real setting where a project may be in the escalation of commitment process can bring very important feedback to better understand if violation may be a result of escalation of commitment. Second, because of the limited number of respondents participating in this pilot study we cannot generalize our results, however findings form this study give us a valuable input to future research aiming to further explore the problem of managers' intention to overlook the ISP violation, especially when they consider that violation would save an on-going project from failing. Third, we consider that this study did not give us a detailed feedback to validate the scenario, which we believe should be tackled deeply in the future. As a result and in reference to this study, we aim to develop our theoretical framework and the survey instrument to be able to empirically test our theoretical assumptions.

6. References

Boss, S.R., Kirsch, L.J., Angermeier, I., Shingler, R.A. and Boss, R.W. (2009), "If someone is watching, I'll do what I'm asked: mandatoriness, control, and information security", European Journal of Information Systems, Volume 18, Number 2, 2009, pp151-164.

Brockner, J., Houser, R., Birnbaum, G., Lloyd, K., Deitcher, J., Nathanson, S. and Rubin, J.Z. (1986), "Escalation of Commitment to an Ineffective Course of Action: The Effect of Feedback Having Negative Implications for Self-Identity", Administrative Science Quarterly, Volume 31, Number 1, pp109-126.

Bulgurcu, B., Cavusoglu, H. and Benbasat, I. (2010), "Information Security Policy Compliance: An Empiricael Study of Rationality-Based Beliefs and Information Security Awareness", MIS Quarterly, Volume 34, Number 3, pp523-548.

Cavusoglu, H., Mishra, B. and Raghunathan, S. (2004), "A Model for Evaluating IT Security Investments", Communications of the ACM, Volume 47, Number 7, pp87-92.

Conlon, D.E. and Garland, H. (1993), "The Role of Project Completion Information in Resource Allocation Decisions", Academy of Management Journal, Volume 36, Number 2, pp402-413.

Dhillon, G. and Backhouse, J. (2001), "Current directions in IS security research: towards socio-organizational perspectives", Information Systems Journal, Volume 11, Number 2, pp127-153.

Eisenhardt, K.M. and Brown, S.L. (1998), "Competing on the Edge: Strategy as Structured Chaos", Long Range Planning, Volume 31, Number 5, pp786-789.

Furnell, S. (2014), "Password Practices on leading websites-revisited", Computer Fraud and Security, Volume 12, Issue 2014, pp5-11.

Hsu, C., Lee, J.N. and Straub, D. W. (2012), "Institutional Influences on Information Systems Security Innovations", Information Systems Research, Volume 23, Number 3, pp918-939.

Katz, D. and Kahn, R.L. (1966), "The Social Psychology of Organizations", New York: John Wiley & Sons.

Keil, M., Mann, J. and Rai, A. (2000), "Why Software Projects Escalate: An Empirical Analysis and Test of Four Theoretical Models", MIS Quarterly, Volume 24, Number 4, pp631-664.

Mitnick, K.D. and William, S.L. (2003), "The Art of Deception: Controlling the Human Element of Security", New York: John Wiley & Sons.

Njenga, K. and Brown, I. (2012), "Conceptualising Improvisation in Information Systems Security", European Journal of Information Systems, Volume 21, Number 6, pp592–607.

Park, S.C., Keil, M., Kim, J.U. and Bock, G.W. (2012), "Understanding Overbidding Behavior in C2C Auctions: An Escalation Theory Perspective", European Journal of Information Systems, Volume 21, Number 6, pp643-663.

Ross, J. and Staw, B. (1993), "Organizational Escalation and Exit: Lessons from the Shoreham Nuclear Power Plant", Academy of Management Journal, Volume 36, Number 4, pp701-732.

Simon, H.A. (1955), "A Behavioral Model of Rational Choice", The Quarterly Journal of Economics, Volume 69, Number 1, pp99-118.

Sleesman, D.J., Conlon, D.E., Gerry, M. and Miles, J.E. (2012), "Cleaning up the Big Muddy: A Meta-Analytic Review of the Determinants of Escalation of Commitment", Academy of Management Journal, Volume 55, Number 3, pp541-562.

Sonnenreich, W., Albanese, J. and Stout, B. (2006), "Return On Security Investment (ROSI) - A Practical Quantitative Model", Journal of Research and Practice in Information Technology, Volume 38, Number 1, pp55-66.

Staw, B.M. and Ross, J. (1989), "Understanding Behavior in Escalation Situations", Science, Volume 246, Number 4927, pp216-220.

Straub, D.W. and Welke, R.J. (1998), "Coping with systems risk: security planning models for management decision making", MIS Quarterly, Volume 22, Number 4, pp441-469.

Vance, A. and Siponen, M. (2012), "IS Security Policy Violations: A Rational Choice Perspective", Journal of Organizational and End User Computing, Volume 24, Number 1, pp21-41.

Warkentin, M., Johnston, A.C. and Shropshire, J. (2011), "The influence of the informal social learning environment on information privacy policy compliance efficacy and intention", European Journal of Information Systems, Volume 20, Number 3, pp267-284.

Willison, R., and Warkentin, M. (2013), "Beyond Deterrence: An Expanded View of Employee Computer Abuse", MIS Quarterly, Volume 37, Number 1, pp1-20.

Arguments For Anonymity

H. Webb, N. Savage and P. Millard

School of Computing, University of Portsmouth, Portsmouth, United Kingdom
e-mail: hazel.webb@myport.ac.uk

Abstract

This research identifies the balance of arguments relating *for* and *against* the use of online anonymity in society in the context of linking users to their true identity via real name policies. Survey results were extracted based on occupational status, focussing on both technology students and those in full time employment, which primarily consisted of staff at a High School. This provided a range of awareness and information (for instance with regard to online risk) of which is believed to influence the participants opinions and attitudes.

In summary, results suggest students are less inclined to sacrifice the element of freedom and privacy associated with anonymity in comparison to those in full time employment. Students appear more aware and concerned with the barrier and difference between reality and virtual reality and, should they be identifiable, are likely to change their behaviours as a result. However, this measured as less of a concern for those in full time employment, who seemed more inclined than students towards the introduction of real name policies.

Keywords

Cyber-disinhibition, Anonymity, Real name policy, Privacy

1. Introduction

With the volume of daily Internet users and the availability of the Internet in UK households steadily increasing (Office for National Statistics, 2014), it is of little surprise that cybercrime is "the fastest growing form of crime" (Hodges, 2007). Goleman (n.d.) suggests use of the Internet hinders the function of the brains inhibitory circuits that are responsible for keeping unruly urges in check, known as cyber-disinhibition. Whilst Goleman goes into little detail as to *how* this cyber-disinhibition is instigated, links can be identified from Sulers' theory of The Online Disinhibition Effect (2004) to assist in identifying its causes. Suler defines six factors which primarily construct this effect; dissociative anonymity, invisibility, asynchronicity, solipsistic introjection, dissociative imagination and minimization of status and authority. However, "most approaches to understanding the phenomenon confine themselves to considering the impact of a single factor – anonymity" (Gackenbach, 2011, p. 89). Having the understanding of anonymity as a main influence of cyber-disinhibition, it seems logical that linking users to their true identity will control the propensity for cybercrime and deviant behaviour online, known also as toxic disinhibition (Suler, 2004).

The effects of disinhibition will apply to both the computer-assisted and computer-focussed categories of cybercrime, particular focus in the context of this research is that of computer-assisted cybercrimes. These consists of traditional crimes which are able to be committed without the use of a computer (Furnell, n.d.) and are subsequently increased in scale and reach as a result, for instance cyberbullying.

With regards to social media in particular, a popular platform for cyberbullying, the Select Committee on Communications (2014, p. 20) state "the law is rarely the most effective tool for changing behaviour: effective law tends to reinforce, rather than in itself change, social attitudes". As a result, it is suggested a suitable method of changing a user's behaviour is by means of policy interventions, such as Real Name Policies. However, there are a number of arguments *for* and *against* the introduction of such policies, as identified by Reusch & Märker (2012) which can be supported by other authors, these include:

For:
- The Self-Control Argument

  Increasing the linkability to one's true identity will provide increased self-regulation based on users being held accountable for their online activities. Research into the impact of the South Korean Real Name Verification Law (temporarily introduced in 2007, which involved linking users accounts to their resident registration numbers for websites with a daily viewership over 100,000) displayed an overall reduction in uninhibited behaviours, thus proving the validity and significance of this argument (Cho, 2011; Reusch & Märker, 2012).

- The Legal Argument

  Holding users legally accountable for their actions by generating identifiable profiles will prove beneficial for law enforcement when dealing with criminal acts. As stated by the Select Committee on Communications, "there is little point in criminalising certain behaviour and at the same time legitimately making that same behaviour impossible to detect" (Select Committee on Communications, 2014, p. 16; Reusch & Märker, 2012).

- Offline = Online Argument

  If we are accountable with our own names offline, it should not be any different online. This is based on the concept of real names being "natural", where people are forced to communicate via their real name in the real world and this should therefore be emulated in the online world (Edwards & McAuley, 2013, p. 2; Reusch & Märker, 2012).

Against:
- The Open Participation Argument

  Forcing users to register with their real name may reduce their willingness to participate, particularly regarding vulnerable groups such as victims of crime or abuse, authoritarian regimes or political activists. However, previous research into the South Korea Real Name Verification Law revealed a decrease of participation on a short-term basis only, with little impact overall in the long-term (Reusch & Märker, 2012; Cho, 2011).

- The Freedom Argument

  It is maintained that "every user has the right to freedom of expression" (Select Committee on Communications, 2014, p. 5) and as a result, this could be infringed with the introduction of a real name policy. In addition, the Internet enables the opportunity for multiple identities of which can be creatively explored (Reusch & Märker, 2012).

- The Privacy Argument

  Section 1 (3) of the Human Rights Act 1998 states "Everyone has the right to respect for his private and family life, his home and his correspondence" (Human Rights Act 1998) where rights to privacy existing offline should also be applied online (UK Statement at the Panel on the Right to Privacy in the Digital Age, Human Rights Council, Geneva, 2014). In addition, this request for personal data also brings an increased risk of information leakage (Reusch & Märker, 2012) causing an increase in risk, for instance regarding harassment and identity theft.

It is suggested Western societies gravitate towards websites with lower levels of anonymity (Morio & Buchholz, 2009), however there are a number of other influences suggested to determine the extent of each argument on an individual user. For instance, an individual's ability to make privacy-sensitive decisions is believed to be influenced by; incomplete information (with regards to externalities, risk and uncertainties), bounded rationality (individual's ability to acquire, memorise and process all relevant information) and systematic psychological deviations (deviation from the rational strategy) (Acquisti & Grossklags, 2005). Therefore, these elements with regards to each individual should be considered when conducting primary research, as they may influence the responses that are collected.

2. Methodology

In order to determine the significance and extent of the proposed arguments for and against addressing anonymity, in particular identifying any primary source of controversy, an online survey was conducted. This questioned the participants' opinions and attitudes regarding the linkability between their offline and online identity in the context of real name policies. Questions were split into three main categories; anonymity, real name policies and demographics. Though consisting of mainly closed-ended questions, open-ended questions were asked in order for participants to justify particular responses should they wish to do so.

Whilst the focus of this research is aimed at identifying the significance of each argument in society, theories relating to the availability of information in decision making, such as risk, also proves significant in such an investigation. As a result, the distribution of the survey was mainly focussed on two main groups (where it is assumed the degree of information varied) of which could be compared;

- Computing students
- Staff at a High School

3. Results

When collating the responses from students (50), full time employment (52) part time employment (9) and unemployed (3), research demonstrated the extent of each argument and how greatly it varied. For instance as illustrated in Figure 1, when looking at the responses as a whole, it was found 54% of respondents either definitely or moderately agreed with the statement which debated the offline = online argument (Reusch & Märker, 2012). Should these be extracted by students responses and those in full time employment (referred to as FTE), it reveals that in fact only 40% of students either definitely or moderately agreed, a difference when compared to the 63% of those in FTE.

Figure 1: Differentiation Between Results

As a result, the responses to this survey, summarised in Table 1, have been extracted based on the participants occupational status, focussing on students and those in full time employment. Whilst all responses for each question should be considered, answer(s) which received a high number of responses in each group have been highlighted in order to determine on average which arguments are deemed of least and most significance.

Question	Response (%)					
	Group	**DA**	**MA**	**N**	**MD**	**DD**
People should have the ability to use the Internet anonymously for certain kinds of online activities.	Students	**66**	*22*	*4*	*8*	*0*
	FTE	*21*	**46**	*6*	*15*	*12*
We are accountable with our real names offline, so it shouldn't be any different online.	Students	*14*	*26*	*22*	*14*	*24*
	FTE	*21*	**42**	*12*	*17*	*8*
Introducing Real Name Policies would prevent me from visiting certain websites.	Students	**32**	*30*	*18*	*16*	*4*
	FTE	*6*	*33*	*11*	*29*	*21*
I would consider more carefully what I am posting online if I had to use my real name.	Students	**52**	*20*	*8*	*14*	*6*
	FTE	*21*	*21*	*23*	*18*	*17*
The introduction of Real Name Policies would make me feel safer online.	Students	*2*	*24*	*20*	*24*	*30*
	FTE	*23*	**35**	*21*	*15*	*6*
I think real name policies should be more widely used.	Students	*4*	*20*	*20*	*22*	*34*
	FTE	*17*	**35**	*27*	*13*	*8*
I would be willing to sacrifice my privacy for the purposes of a safer online experience.	Students	*0*	*20*	*16*	*26*	*38*
	FTE	*21*	**38**	*6*	*27*	*8*
-	Response (%)					
	Group	**Yes**		**No**		**Don't Know**
Have you ever decided not to use a website because they asked for your real name?	Students	42		48		10
	FTE	42		52		6
-	Response (Number of responses)**					
	Group	**A**	**B**	**C**	**D**	**E**	**F**
Why do you prefer to use an anonymous identity?	Students	*25*	*3*	*41*	*28*	*4*	*0*
	FTE	*10*	*0*	*35*	*15*	*9*	*1*

DA: Definitely Agree   **MA:** Moderately Agree **N:** Neutral **MD:** Moderately Disagree **DD:** Definitely Disagree

A.   *I can be more open and honest.*
B.   *I am able to make mean-spirited remarks without being identified.*
C.   *To protect my identity (for security purposes)*
D.   *To provide equality between users (e.g. free of gender, race or appearance).*
E.   *I do not user an anonymous identity as I prefer not to.*
F.   *Other*

Table 1: Survey Results - Quantitative Data

The participants also had the opportunity to expand on their responses given to two of the questions, some of which have been identified in Table 2, outlining areas of particular interest.

We are accountable with our real names offline, so it shouldn't be any different online.		
	Students	**Full Time employment**
Definitely or Moderately Agree	*"People who use the internet to 'troll' or target a group of people based on gender, sexual orientation or religion should be held accountable should anything happen to the targeted individual."*	*"I am me and therefore I shouldn't pretend to be anybody else except who I am"* *"Certain online activities are more meaningful if real names are used."*
Definitely or Moderately Disagree	*"Sometimes I can say and do things online that don't necessarily reflect me as a person. I like the anonymity that being online gives me so I don't face repercussions for absolutely everything I do."*	*"People feel more able to express themselves behind anonymity. Whilst this can sometimes lead to cyber-bullying & hate crime it also allows them to be who they feel they can't be in real life."*
I think Real Name Policies should be more widely used.		
	Students	**Full Time Employment**
Definitely or Moderately Agree	*"I would feel more secure and would find the person more trustworthy if they used their real name."*	*"I am naïve and assume that most people used their real names - clearly I do not live in the real world!"* *"To protect all innocent parties, particularly children"*
Definitely or Moderately Disagree	*"I do not want everyone to know my business. At times people benefit from being anonymous as they are not judged."* *"Real Name Policies do not make you any safer. The opposite is true. In addition, Real Name Policies are a way for governments to stifle free speech and activism on the internet. Anonymity is important."*	*"You need to protect yourself from fraud or identity theft, if you have a limited understanding of what your using online a fake name can give you reassurance"*

Table 2: Survey Results - Qualitative Data

Participants were asked to provide some basic details, of which can be seen in Table 3 in order to assist in the analysis of the results. This identified that, on average, the majority of students spent between 3-9 hours online with those in full time employment spending between 0-6 hours online. It was also identified that of the students asked, they were predominantly male.

Question	Response (%)				
		Male		**Female**	
Gender:	Students	82		18	
	FTE	44		56	
-	Response (%)				
On average, how often would you say you go online each day? (hours)		**Under 3**	**3-6**	**6-9**	**9-12**	**12 +**
	Students	4	34	36	14	12
	FTE	34	46	10	8	2

Table 3: Survey Results - Participant Demographics

4. Discussion

The results themselves demonstrated the diversity in attitudes and opinions associated linking a user's offline and online identity. It can be assumed this range in opinion is the main source of controversy when introducing such a policy, with such a diverse balance between the arguments for and against the introduction of a real name policy.

The overall consensus of the student results demonstrated an increased preference in anonymity online as opposed to being identifiable, however this was deemed less significant for those in full time employment. The majority of students felt they had the right to use the Internet anonymously should they wish to do so and whilst to a lesser degree, this also proved the case for those in full time employment. When looking at the purposes of anonymous identities, both groups showed similarities suggesting these identities are primarily used in order to protect their own identity, with a significant volume of students also stating that being anonymous enables them to be more open and honest and provides equality between users.

However, should a real name policy be introduced, results suggest one of the main areas of concern for students would be in relation to the privacy argument (Reusch & Märker, 2012), with the vast majority suggesting they would not be willing to sacrifice their privacy for the purposes of security. One student suggested that real name policies allow others to participate in more focussed and personal harassment. However, this proved less of a concern for those in full time employment, where it was stated such measures will "protect all innocent parties, particularly children" as criminals can be more easily identifiable. Whilst not applicable to all of the responses, this demonstrates the differing opinions between being identifiable for a matter of protection or viewing it as the enabler to target attacks.

In addition, results suggest that students' online behaviour would also be likely to change as a result, for instance they would be less willing to participate on certain websites, known as the open participation argument (Reusch & Märker, 2012). It is suggested that requiring the use of a user's real name has previously prevented users, both students and those in full time employment, from using a particular website, however only a third of those in full time employment agreed that the requirement to use their real name online would reduce the likelihood of their participation. Taking this into consideration, a previous study into the impact of the South Korea Real Name Verification Law showed a reduction participation on a short-term basis only (Cho, 2011), therefore it can be loosely suggested that on a long term basis, this may not be a significant issue, however this cannot be evidenced without repeating the study conducted by Cho (2011).

In addition, the majority of both students and those in full time employment suggest they would consider what they are posting online should it be linkable to their true identity, though proved to a significantly lesser degree for those in full time employment. Several of the open-ended responses from students demonstrated a differentiation and detachment between virtual life and reality, thus reducing the element of accountability associated with their online activities (all of which can be attributed to cyber-disinhibtion (Suler, 2004; Goleman, n.d.)). For instance, as stated in Table 3, a student added "sometimes I can say and do things online that don't necessarily reflect me as a person" later suggesting they do not have to face the repercussions of their actions in the real world. The prevalence of this and similar responses describe the *freedom* argument (Reusch & Märker, 2012) as an important factor for students. This also proves significant for some of those in full time employment, however not to the same extent as students. For instance as seen in Table 3, one participant in full time employment stated "I am me and therefore I shouldn't pretend to be anybody else except who I am" suggesting a greater acceptance and confidence with one's own identity.

Moreover, one participant in full time employment who agreed that real name policies should be implemented, stated "I am naïve and assume that most people used their real names - clearly I do not live in the real world!", whilst this may indeed be an isolated case, this may indicate the value of incomplete information in making decisions, where users are unaware and misinformed of the risks in cyberspace which influences the decision of which they ultimately make.

As indicated, one method of interpretation when conducting analysis was to look at these in terms of what a user would need to consider when responding to each question. For instance, amongst other factors it is suggested an individual's knowledge of the externalities, risk and uncertainties will influence their decision (Acquisti & Grossklags, 2005). As a result, the questionnaire was distributed to technology students of which it was believed may have a greater understanding of these and by contrast (though not explicitly), to staff at a High School. Whilst this approach was initially taken, it was noted that there appeared to be a distinct differentiation between the opinions reflected by these groups; students appear to value anonymity and the ability to create an online persona separate from reality, whereas those in full time employment seem more content and established within their own identities and are therefore happy to extend this into cyberspace. However, this cannot be directly attributed to occupational status, it could be inferred a result of age (where the average age was higher for those in full time employment) or time spent online (where students generally spent an increased amount of time online in comparison to those in full time employment).

5. Conclusion

This research highlights the key concerns in introducing anonymity reducing measures in the context of real name policies in relation to; the self-control argument, the legal argument, offline = online argument, the open participation argument, the freedom argument and the privacy argument (Reusch & Märker, 2012).

The results demonstrate the diversity in attitudes towards generating a linkability between users' offline and online identities if viewing all of the collated results. However, if differentiating between students results (of which were technology students) and those in full time employment (primarily staff at a High School), it identified several areas by which attitudes and opinions differed. Based on these results, students seem less inclined to sacrifice their privacy for the purposes of security, preferring to use (or at least having the ability to use) anonymous identities, with several students suggesting they prefer having the potential to differentiate their identities between the virtual and real world and the freedom this entails.

The results suggested those in full time employment seemed more inclined than students to embrace the introduction of a real name policy, however agree that this would cause them to consider more carefully what they were posting online and what websites they are visiting. Whilst this also proved a concern for students, those in full time employment seem more inclined to make this sacrifice.

It was initially suspected that the availability of information, for instance the participants' understanding of risk and uncertainties, was an influence the decision making process, such as when privacy-sensitive decisions (Acquisti & Grossklags, 2005). Whilst technical ability may have played a part in shaping the responses gathered, as previously discussed, this cannot be directly linked as a causation. Moreover, there appeared to be a distinct differentiation between the use of anonymity which may influence the way in which a participant is likely to respond; students appear to value anonymity and the ability to create an online persona separate from reality, whereas those in full time employment seem less concerned with this aspect of anonymity and prove more content with their true identity, therefore more willing to extend this into cyberspace. As a result, this may be influenced by age (where the average participant age was higher for those in full time employment) or time spent online (where students generally spent an increased amount of time online in comparison to those in full time employment).

6.   References

Acquisti, A., & Grossklags, J. (2005). Privacy and rationality in individual decision making. *IEEE Security & Privacy*, 26 - 33.

Cho, D. (2011). Real Name Verification Law on the Internet: A Poison or Cure for Privacy? Pittsburgh, Pennsylvania.

Edwards, L., & McAuley, D. (2013). *What's in a name? Real name policies and social networks.* Paris.

Furnell, S. M. (n.d.). *Categorising Cybercrime and Cybercriminals: The Problem And Potential Approaches.* Plymouth.

Gackenbach, J. (2011). *Psychology and the Internet: Intrapersonal, Interpersonal and Transpersonal Implications.* Burlington: Academic Press.

Goleman, D. (n.d.). Cyberdisinhibition. In n.d., *What is your dangerous idea?* (pp. 74-76).

Hodges, M. (2007). Review: Cybercrime: The Reality of the Threat. Retrieved January 14, 2015, from https://www.suffolk.edu/documents/jhtl_book_reviews/Hodges07.pdf

Human Rights Act 1998. (n.d.). Retrieved March 13, 2015, from Legislation Gov UK: http://www.legislation.gov.uk/ukpga/1998/42/schedule/1

Morio, H., & Buchholz, C. (2009). *How anonymous are you onliine? Examining online social behaviours from a cross-cultural perspective.* London: Springer-Verlag London Ltd.

Office for National Statistics. (2014). *Internet Access - Households and Individuals 2014.*

Pakes, F., & Pakes, S. (2009). *Criminal Psychology.* Cullompton: Willan Publishing.

Reusch, M. A., & Märker, O. (2012). CeDEM 12 Conference for E-Democracy and Open Government. *Conference for eDemocracy and open Government.* Austria: Danube-University Krems.

Select Committee on Communications. (2014). *Social Media and Criminal Offences.* London: House of Lords.

Suler, J. (2004). The Online Disinhibition Effect. *Cyberpsychology & behaviour*, 321-326.

Uk Statement at the Panel on the Right to Privacy in the Digital Age, Human Rights Council, Geneva. (2014, September 12). Retrieved March 13, 2015, from Gov UK: https://www.gov.uk/government/world-location-news/uk-statement-at-the-panel-on-the-right-to-privacy-in-the-digital-age-human-rights-council-geneva

Understanding Security Practices Deficiencies: A Contextual Analysis

M. Sadok[1] and P. Bednar[2, 3]

[1]Higher Institute of Technological Studies in Communications in Tunis, Tunisia
[2]School of Computing, University of Portsmouth, UK
[3]Department of Informatics, Lund University, Sweden
E-mails: Moufida.sadok@port.ac.uk, peter.bednar@port.ac.uk

Abstract

This paper seeks to provide an overview of how companies assess and manage security risks in practice. For this purpose we referred to data of security surveys to examine the scope of risk analysis and to identify involved entities in this process. Our analysis shows a continuous focus on data system security rather than on real world organizational context as well as a prevalent involvement of top management and security staff in risk analysis process and in security policy definition and implementation. We therefore suggest that three issues need to be further investigated in the field of information security risk management in order to bridge the gap between design and implementation of secure and usable systems. First, there is a need to broaden the horizon to consider information system as human activity system which is different from a data processing system. Second, the involvement of relevant stakeholders in context for risk analysis leads to better appreciation of security risks. Third, it is necessary to develop ad-hoc tools and techniques to facilitate discussions and dialogue between stakeholders in risk analysis context.

Keywords

Information security, Risk analysis, Security practices, Contextual analysis, Security surveys

1. Introduction

Security surveys published in many countries by professional bodies provide an overview of security practices of companies. The analysis of these surveys also provides opportunities to reflect on ways how companies deal with increasing security risks. This paper considers three security surveys published in USA, UK and France. Hence, the focus will be not just on describing security practices, but, rather, on the identification of gaps in such practices and alternative perspectives for better management of security risks. In fact, the trend towards social networking, BYOD and cloud computing technologies among other factors has increased security vulnerabilities and threats.

The key findings of several security surveys reveal that companies are struggling to keep up with security risks (e.g. The Global State of Information Security Survey, 2014; 2015; Symantec Internet Security Threat Report 2014; 2015). In particular, enterprises experience difficulties in assessing and managing their security risks, applying appropriate security controls, as well as preventing security threats. These findings also indicate that security controls and procedures deployed by enterprises cannot match the requirements of their real business processes.

We argue in this paper that two reasons could potentially explain the poor effectiveness of the implemented security solutions and procedures: the boundary problem of risk analysis scope and the background of involved actors in risk assessment and in security policy design. The drive for change is three-fold: first, we realized that security surveys are adopting a formal approach of security and are confusing information systems security with data systems security; second, we can draw a correlation between this perspective and security practices patterns; and third, we provide alternative perspectives on the process and practice of security risk management to handle an effective alignment of security controls with business requirements.

The remainder of the paper is organized in three sections. The first section introduces related literature in practice-based information systems security (ISS). The second section reports key findings of security surveys in USA, UK and France. The third section discusses identified gaps in security practices and proposes alternative perspectives to address deficiencies in security design and implementation. The conclusion sets up a research agenda for potential future works.

2. Background

In the ISS literature, a wealth of prior research sheds light on many ways that organizations can use to take into consideration contextual factors such as national culture as (Yildirima et al., 2011), organizational structure and culture, management support, training and awareness, users' participation in the formulation process, business objectives, legal and regulatory requirements (Karyda et al., 2005; Knapp et al., 2009). Another focus of attention of ISS researches has been the compliance of employees to security procedures and guidelines viewed from behavioral perspective and applying socio-cognitive theories (Herath and Rao, 2009; Ifinedo, 2012; Vance et al., 2012; Shropshire et al., 2015).

It is also acknowledged that security measures which are modeled outside of the real world organizational context are prone to antagonize effective organizational practices and the literature maintains a plethora of such real world cases. In the case study conducted by Kolkowska and Dhillon (2013), the workers noted that "The checks and balances that have been built into the system are not necessarily the way in which any of the case-workers operate". By failing to appreciate the complex relationships between use, usability and usefulness, security procedures imposed are not only subject to possible misuse but they are likely to be a core hindrance to everyday legitimate work. Albrechtsen (2007) has furthermore identified that an increased security workload might create difficulties for work functionality and efficiency. The author also noticed a trivial effect of documented requirements of expected information security behaviour and general awareness campaigns on user behaviour and awareness. The study of Parsons et al., (2014) has also noticed the lack of efficiency of generic courses based on a lecture on knowledge of security policy and procedure.

The weakest link is not necessarily in the (technical) system itself but the difference between the formal model of usage and real usage of system content (data) as such in a human activity system. Consequently, designers have to find a balance between security, performance and usability (Sommerville, 2011) and IT specialists should also continue to work on methods that minimize inconvenience and delays (Oz and Jones, 2008).

The implementation of a security policy is also expected to change organisational procedures and practices as well as to shape and monitor the behavior of employees, through education and training, to ensure compliance with security requirements. Bocij *et al.*, (2008) argued for the formulation of a comprehensive policy on security in order to ensure employees adhesion to policy guidelines. Albrechtsen and Hovden (2010) discussed ways in which security awareness and behaviour may be improved and changed through dialogue, participation and collective reflection. In addition, one line of solution is to enhance the situational awareness that involves an intelligence-driven process to systematically collect and analyse security risk data prior to decision-making (Webb *et al.*, 2014; Franke and Brynielsson, 2014).

To attempt to explain why deficiencies in the practice of information security risk assessment occur, a stream in ISS research has focused on the background of involved actors in risk analysis and security policy processes. For example, Samela (2008) pointed out that business process analysis is an understudied approach when it comes to assess ISS risks. In most of the companies, professionals with operational knowledge pertinent to risk analysis are not efficiently involved (Shedden et al., 2011). Therefore, there is a need to conduct risk analysis activities by business process owners (Coles and Moulton, 2003). Taking several researches recommendations that emphasize the centrality of human and social issues in information security, Reece and Stahl (2015) have discussed new areas of competences that can potentially be used to found a new claim of professional identity of information security practitioner. The authors recommend including particular skills and knowledge in undergraduate socialisation and training.

In order to demonstrate the importance and necessity of the contextual dimension in the design of a secure information system, the study of Spears and Barki (2010) provides a particular application of this view in the context of regulatory compliance and confirms the conclusion that the engagement of users in ISS risk management process contributes to more effective security measures and better alignment of security controls with business objectives. A systemic and value-focused view of security would result in a better understanding of organizational stakeholders of the role and application of security functions in situated practices and an achievement of contextually relevant risk analysis (Bednar and Katos, 2009; Dhillon and Torkzadeh, 2006). Therefore, a holistic security strategy needs to include human aspects as a core part of secure and usable systems (Furnell and Clarke, 2012).

3. Existing practices

While information security risks have evolved and financial costs of cybercrime have increased, security practices and strategies have not adequately kept up with dynamic and challenging attacks that are highly complex and difficult to detect.

According to the PwC-US (2014), CLUSIF (2014) and PwC-UK (2014) reports an important percentage of the interviewed enterprises have proceeded to the formalization of their security policies. However, the existence of a security policy by itself does not mean its efficient implementation or relevance. In the case of the UK businesses, only a quarter of respondents with a security policy believe their staff have a very good understanding of it. Moreover, 70% of companies where security policy was poorly understood had staff-related breaches versus 41% where the policy was well understood.

As to security risk analysis, although there is a wide consensus that security is a high priority PwC-US (2014) report shows that only 38% align their security spending with business strategy and most of the interviewed enterprises do not implement the tools and processes necessary for a comprehensive assessment. In PwC-UK (2014), 20% of the respondents have not carried out any form of security risk assessment and many organisations still struggle to evaluate the effectiveness of their deployed security controls. In addition, an organization needs to classify its information assets in accordance to their business value and sensitivity in order to ensure an effective protection. Information assets inventories and classification help organizations to perform security risk assessment and to delimit the required protection levels as well as to ensure cost effectiveness of implemented security measures. In the case of US businesses, only 17% classify the business value of data. PwC-UK (2014) report indicates that large organisations seem to struggle to clearly define responsibilities for owning critical data and for protecting it. Also 20% said the responsibilities are not clear and, none believe the responsibilities were very clear. Discussions with senior management and views of internal security experts remain the most popular other sources for evaluating cyber threats. Large organisations rely on external security consultants and alerts from government/intelligence services.

In France, Clusif (2014) provides an extensive overview of security practices of 350 companies and 150 hospitals. Table 1 illustrates that a relatively large (47%) percentage of enterprises and hospitals (41%) do not carry any risk analysis. This could be related in some extent to the lack of data classification which is a necessary input to risk analysis process.

	Data inventory		Risk analysis	
	Companies	Hospitals	Companies	Hospitals
Yes, totally	31%	17%	21%	19%
Partly, data system	14%	30%	22%	27%
Partly, data jobs	21%	25%	8%	13%
No	32%	25%	47%	41%

Table 1: Percentage of enterprises and hospitals carrying out data classification and risk analysis, adapted from Clusif (2014)

Another aspect comes out this table is when a data inventory is achieved, it is clearly focusing on data system as data related to particular activities or jobs are mostly overlooked.

Delving into the background or organizational position of involved entities in risk analysis and security policy formulation reveals some interesting findings. For companies, Clusif survey respondents report a significant influence of top management and IS directorate on security policy definition. In table 2, only 12% of respondents involve directors of business activities such as marketing or production in security policy design. Parsing further Clusif data, we noticed that the hierarchical reporting of ISS executive belongs to IS directorate in 46 % of the cases and to top management in 27 %.

	Security policy	Risk analysis
Top Management	50%	-
IS Directorate	54%	-
ISS Executive	39%	56%
Job Director	12%	12%

Table 2: Involved entities in risk analysis and security policy definition, adapted from Clusif (2014)

When it comes to areas of risk mitigation, most organizations are still focused on updating their technologies and providing more training and education for staff to guarantee more compliance to security policy guidelines as well as the formalization of the security organizational procedures to have more "standardized behavior" (PwC-UK, 2014; Clusif, 2014). This leads to the conclusion of the predominance of technical and formalized paradigm in the development and implementation of IS security policies and procedures.

4. Discussion

A comprehensive review of security surveys has highlighted a number of gaps in security practices. Essentially, we consider that the distinction between IS as a data processing system and IS as a human activity system provides a frame of reference to explain the reasons why the gaps in matching security practices to organizational and business needs continue to be relevant issues to explore in IS security research. Therefore, we first argue for broadening the scope of security risk analysis; Second, involving relevant stakeholders in context and third further investigating techniques and methods to allow discussion and develop understanding of security risks in uncertain and complex environment.

The data centric focus in ISS practices influences work practices and creates unintended consequences and changes in a human activity design instead of being a part of its design. The prevalence of centralized security controls and related top-down management are challenged by dynamic business and technological environments. Basing security risk analysis solely on data system, and ignoring human activity system, means that misleading assumptions about rational and irrational behaviour of users may explain many security measures failure. If security policy and procedures were developed as an add-on to the real world business practices it is quite possibly the case that breach of security policy may in some instances be necessary as in practice it might be the only way for an employee to do a good job. Filkins B. (2013) illustrates this misfit in the case of the help desk services which are not consider enough in risk analysis scope even though they could be a vulnerable entry point to conduct social engineering attacks or to disclosure sensitive data.

Taking a proactive approach to develop a holistic security strategy, systemic risk analysis requires attention be paid to the background of involved actors in this process. The challenge of introducing security in a sensible and useful manner can be addressed by considering the contextual perspectives. By considering the human activity systems as a point of reference rather than a variable IS development process as an ongoing contextual inquiry (Bednar, 2000; 2007; Bednar and Welch, 2014) is characterized as an emergent systemic change process conducted through sense making and negotiations among relevant stakeholders. From a socio-technical perspective, it is claimed that a viable system would be more user-centric by accommodating and balancing human processes rather than entertaining an expectation of a one sided change of behavior of the end user.

As noted in security surveys, the involvement of security experts has been a significant input in many of the ISS models (Feng and Li, 2011; Ryan *et al.*, 2012; Feng *et al.*, 2014). However, the judgment of security risks cannot be only based on the security expert experience and knowledge, as the risk is contextually situated (Katos and Bednar, 2008). In practice, the evaluation of risk under uncertainty and complexity requires the involvement of relevant stakeholders who make use of their own norms and values to set up the boundaries of a problem space. This leads to the generation of multi-perspectives and mutually inconsistent possible alternatives. Unique perspectives of individual stakeholders may be particularly important in highlighting aspects of a problem situation which may have become 'invisible' due to over-familiarity (Bednar and Welch, 2006). At a collective level, it is important to recognise and consider each individual's unique perspectives without temptation to unify or integrate the differences in a shared understanding of a problem space, to seek a premature consensus or to set up an artificial imposed scale of agreement.

To assist and facilitate assessment of risk with multi-value scales according to different stakeholders' point of view, a potential interdisciplinary research area emerges to develop techniques and modelling support for analysis aiming at inquiries into uncertain and complex problems spaces. In this setting, the SST framework (Bednar, 2000) incorporates para-consistent logic, techniques for structuring uncertainty from multiple systemic perspectives and techniques for modelling diversity networks. Sadok *et al.*, (2014) addressed the potential relevance of cognitive maps use in ISS context to support the exploration of individual understanding leading to richer elaboration of problem spaces.

Being aware of the merits of sharing information and knowledge about security threats, the PwC-US (2014) report points up that 82% of companies with high-performing security practices collaborate with others (e.g. third-party service providers and partners) to learn and to stimulate conversations about security risks and tactics. We argue in this paper that the exploration and understanding of security risks should equally involve internal stakeholders to better align security practices to business needs.

5. Conclusion

This paper aimed to shed light on key findings of security surveys in relation to risk analysis scope and involved actors. More fundamentally, deficiencies in security practices can be attributed to many reasons but it is relevant to include among them an exclusive technical focus and a top-down approach. Emphasising the centrality of human issues in information security, we highlight in this paper that the contextualization of security risk analysis as well as security policy design and implementation continue to be relevant and necessary research topics to explore. Questions about security failures in context could address the relevance of security policies and measures from professional stakeholders' perspective as in many cases they work around security compliance or bypass security measures to effectively do the work.

Rather than a dominant emphasis on technologies, for instance, it is essential to fund processes that fully bridge the gap between design and implementation of secure and usable systems through open discussion and dialogue between relevant stakeholders leading to better contextual appreciation of risks.

6. References

Albrechtsen, E. (2007), "A qualitative study of users' view on information security", *Computers & Security*, Vol. 26, pp 276-289.

Albrechtsen, E. and Hovden, J. (2010), "Improving information security awareness and behaviour through dialogue, participation and collective reflection. An intervention study", *Computers & Security*, Vol. 29, pp 432-445.

Bednar, P. (2000), "A Contextual Integration of Individual and Organizational Learning Perspectives as part of IS Analysis", *Informing Science Journal*, Vol. 3, No. 3, pp 145-156.

Bednar, P. and Welch, C. (2006), "Structuring uncertainty: sponsoring innovation and creativity", in Adam, F. et al. (Ed.) Creativity and Innovation in Decision Making and Decision Support, London, Decision Support Press, ISBN: 1-905800-00-2.

Bednar, P. (2007), "Individual emergence in contextual analysis", *Systemica*, Vol. 14, No. 1-6, pp 23-38.

Bednar, P. and Welch, C. (2014), "Contextual Inquiry and Socio-Technical Practice", *Kybernetes*, Vol. 4, No. 3, pp 9-10.

Bednar, P.M. and Katos, V. (2009), "Addressing the human factor in information systems security", In Poulymenakou, A., Pouloudi, N., Pramatari, K. (eds) 4th Mediterranean Conference on Information Systems, Athens, Greece, September 25-27.

Bocij, P., Chaffey, D., Greasley, A., & Hickie, S. (2008), *Business information systems – Technology, Development & management for the e-business*, Pearson Education Limited, ISBN: 978-0-273-71662-4.

Clusif, (2014) Menaces informatiques et pratiques de sécurité en France, www.clusif.asso.fr

Coles, R. S and Moulton R. (2003), "Operationalizing IT risk management", *Computers & Security*, Vol. 22, No. 6, pp 487-493.

Dhillon, G. and Torkzadeh, G. (2006) "Value-focused assessment of information system security in organizations", *Information Systems Journal*, Vol. 16, pp 293-314.

Feng, N. and Li, M. (2011), "An information systems security risk assessment model under uncertain environment", *Applied Soft Computing*, Vol. 11, pp4332–4340.

Feng, N., Wang, H. and Li, M. (2014), "A security risk analysis model for information systems: Causal relationships of risk factors and vulnerability propagation analysis", *Information Sciences*, Vol. 256, pp 57–73.

Filkins B. (2013) "The SANS 2013 Help Desk Security and Privacy Survey", www.sans.org

Franke, U. and Brynielsson, J. (2014), "Cyber situational awareness-A systematic review of the literature", *Computers & Security*, Vol. 46, pp 18-31.

Furnell, S. and Clarke, N. (2012), "Power to the people? The evolving recognition of human aspects of security", *Computers & Security*, Vol. 31, pp 983-988.

Herath, T., and Rao, H.R. (2009), "Encouraging information security behaviors in organizations: Role of penalties, pressures and perceived effectiveness", *Decision Support Systems*, Vol. 47, pp 154–165.

Ifinedo, P. (2012), "Understanding information systems security policy compliance: An integration of the theory of planned behavior and the protection motivation theory", *Computers & Security*, Vol. 31, pp 83-95.

Karyda, M., Kiountouzis, E., and Kokolakis, S. (2005), "Information systems security policies: a contextual perspective", *Computers & Security*, Vol. 24, pp 246-260.

Katos, V. and Bednar, P. (2008), "A cyber-crime investigation framework", *Computer Standards & Interfaces*, Vol. 30, pp 223–228.

Knapp, K. J., Morris, F., Marshall, T. E., and Byrd, T. A. (2009), "Information security policy: An organizational-level process model", *Computers & Security*, Vol. 28, pp 493–508.

Kolkowska, E., and Dhillon, G. (2013), "Organizational power and information security rule compliance", *Computers & Security*, Vol. 33, pp 3-11.

Oz, E., & Jones, A. (2008), *Management information systems*, Cengage Learning EMEA, London, ISBN: 978-1-84480-758-1.

Parsons K., McCormac, A., Butavicius, M., Pattinson, M., and Jerram, C. (2014), "Determining employee awareness using the Human Aspects of Information Security Questionnaire (HAIS-Q)", *Computers & Security*, Vol. 42, pp 165-176.

PwC-UK, 2014 UK information security breaches survey, www.pwc.co.uk

PwC-US, 2014 US State of Cybercrime Survey, www.pwc.com

Reece, R.P. and Stahl, B.C. (2015), "The professionalisation of information security: Perspectives of UK practitioners", *Computers & Security*, Vol. 48, pp 182-195.

Ryan, J.J.C.H., Mazzuchi, T.A., Ryan, D.J., Lopez de la Cruz, J. and Cooke, R. (2012), "Quantifying information security risks using expert judgment elicitation", Computers & Operations Research, Vol. 39, pp774–784.

Sadok, M., Katos, V. and Bednar P. (2014)) "Developing contextual understanding of information security risks", International Symposium on Human Aspects of Information Security & Assurance (HAISA 2014), Plymouth University, 8th - 10th July 2014.

Salmela, H. (2008), "Analysing business losses caused by information systems risk: a business process analysis approach", *Journal of Information Technology*, Vol. 23, pp 185–202.

Shedden P., Scheepers R., Smith W., Ahmad A. (2011), "Incorporating a knowledge perspective into security risk assessments", *VINE Journal Information Knowledge Management System*, Vol. 41, No. 2, pp 152-166.

Shropshire J., Warkentin M., and Sharma S. (2015), "Personality, attitudes, and intentions: Predicting initial adoption of information security behavior", *Computers & Security*, Vol. 49, pp 177–191.

Sommerville, I. (2011), *Software engineering*, Pearson Education Inc, ISBN: 978-0-13-705346-9.

Spears, J. L. and Barki, H. (2010) "User participation in information systems security risk management", *MIS Quarterly*, Vol. 34, No. 3, pp 503-522.

The Global State of Information Security Survey (2015) "Managing cyber risks in an interconnected world", www.pwc.com/gsiss2015

Vance, A., Siponen, M., and Pahnila, S. (2012), "Motivating IS security compliance: Insights from Habit and Protection Motivation Theory", *Information & Management*, Vol. 49, pp 190–198.

Webb J., Ahmad A., Sean B. Maynard S.B. and Shanks G. (2014), "A situation awareness model for information security risk management", *Computers & Security*, Vol. 44, pp 1-15.

Yildirima, E. Y., Akalpa, G., Aytacb, S. and Bayramb, N. (2011), "Factors influencing information security management in small-and medium-sized enterprises: A case study from Turkey", *International Journal of Information Management*, Vol. 31, pp 360-365.

Managing Social Engineering Attacks- Considering Human Factors and Security Investment

R. Alavi[1], S. Islam[1], H. Mouratidis[2] and S. Lee[1]

[1]School of Architecture, Engineering and Computing, University of East London,
[2]School of Computing, Engineering and Mathematics, University of Brighton
e-mail:{reza, shareeful, s.w.lee}@uel.ac.uk; H.Mouratidis@brighton.ac.uk

Abstract

Soliciting and managing the protection of information assets has become a objective of paramount importance in an organizational context. Information Security Management System (ISMS) has the unique role of ensuring that adequate and appropriate security tools are in place in order to protect information assets. Security is always seen in three dimensions of technology, organization, and people. Undoubtedly, the socio-technical challenges have proven to be the most difficult ones to tackle. Social Engineering Attacks (SEAs) are a socio-technical challenge and considerably increase security risks by seeking access to information assets by exploiting the vulnerabilities in organizations as they target human frailties. Dealing effectively and adequately with SEAs requires practical security benchmarking together with control mechanism tools, which in turn requires investment to support security and ultimately organizational goals. This paper contributes in this area. In particular, the paper proposes a language for managing SEAs using several concepts such as actor, risks, goals, security investment and vulnerabilities. The language supports in-depth investigation of human factors as one of the main causes of SEAs. It also assists in the selection of appropriate mechanisms considering security investment to mitigate risks. Finally, the paper uses a real incident in a financial institution to demonstrate the applicability of the approach.

Keywords

Social Engineering Attacks (SEAs), Human Factors, Security Investment (SI), Security incident, Return on Information Security Investment (ROISI).

1. Introduction

Providing a strong security posture is crucial for business continuity. Currently with great threats of cyber attacks and virtual terrorism, security must be given adequate consideration. If they are not, everyday organizational activities will be grounded with real possibilities of loss, punitive financial fines and damaged reputation. SEAs undermine organizations' efforts to deal with security in an effective way. There are several malicious practices such as Advanced Persistent Attack that create security breaches in organizations (Siponen et al. 2010). Janczewski and Fu (2010) defined the SEAs with two distinct methods; the "Human-Based and Technology-Based" attacks. However, the role of people and certain human factors are contributing greatly to SEAs. The attackers crack the security of an information system by exploitation of human weaknesses. SEAs increase risks of financial loss, legal fees and reputational loss for organizations. It is a challenging task for organizations to deal with SEAs because they are human-oriented activities and human factors are difficult to deal with. This paper contributes to the link between the main human factors, which have been identified in previous study (Alavi et al. 2013) and SEAs with consideration of security investment. In particular, the paper proposes a language to analyze the attacks caused by human factors. This paper has adopted the Secure Tropos methodology to identify and analyze security concepts and extend it with these human factors and Security Investment (SI) so that appropriate justification can be taken into consideration in preventing such attacks (Mouratidis and Giorgini, 2004). Finally, the study considers a case study from a real security incident to demonstrate the applicability of the approach.

2. Related Works

There have been a number of works that focus on analyzing SEA attacks. This section includes the works that are relevant to the study's approach. Janczewski & Fu (2010) provided a conceptual model in order to understand SEAs impacts on individuals and businesses and present a defensive approach to mitigate these risks. The study focused on IT departments and a more abstract view of SEAs without considering SEAs concepts related to human factors and their relationships to the concept of SI. Greitzer et al (2014) looked at the insider threat that derives from SEAs. The study considered some related human factors but concentrated mainly on unintentional insider threats whilst observing psychological and social characteristic of people. Karpati et al (2012) used a comparison study between mal-activity diagram and misuse cases and presented two modeling techniques. This study attempted to provide a conceptual comparison in order to find the advantages and efficiency of each approach. It provided three main concepts; risk, asset-related and risk-treatment concepts. Although the paper concentrated on SEAs and provided a concrete discussion in the validity of the study, it did not embrace SI and actors such as human and security systems. In addition, the paper distinguished between information security assets and business assets, which can potentially be a confusing issue when it comes to SI. Some other studies concentrated on specific attacks such as phishing attacks (Finn & Jakobsson 2005) or advanced persistent attacks (Shakarian et al 2013).

All the above-mentioned works contribute towards investigating SEAs. However, none of these works explicitly focus on human factors, which are one of the main reasons for SEAs. In particular, SEAs require a systematic approach to analyze the complex human factors and solutions in order to address any issues relating to them. Security markets are dominated with technical solutions promising much in security efficiency whilst brushing aside human elements despite overwhelming evidence to the contrary. This work contributes in analyzing human factors and proposes solutions and security investment in these solutions so that an organization can make the right decision relating to information security.

3. Social Engineering

3.1. Social Engineering Attack

Social engineering is the act of manipulating a person to take an action that may or may not be in the target's best interest which include obtaining information, gaining access or getting the target to take a certain action (Hadnagy and Wilson, 2010). Responding to the threats of SEAs using technological resources and tools would not be enough to deal with the associated risks because people are at the centre of such attacks and they play a vital role in it. Organizations may use various tools such as web server security to detect and minimize SEAs but they have difficulty in preventing and responding to human actions and behavior in socially engineered incidences. SEAs resulted mainly in the exploitation of many related issues of human factors. There are specific factors, which were identified, in the previous study and play important roles in such attacks (Alavi et al., 2013): Lack of awareness and ample set of skills, inadequate communication skills, Lack of supervision and sufficient involvement of management. Therefore, it can be concluded that human factors and human social interactions can be engineered for exploitation in gaining access to an organization's assets. The lack of, or an inadequate control mechanism leaves human factors open to exploitation. Attackers generally use different deceptive methods to exploit users who have a lack of awareness about the system and its surrounding context.

3.2. Reasons for Social Engineering Attacks

Human factors remain essential to any SEAs because no matter how many training programs or control mechanisms are deployed; people are the weakest link in security (Hadnagy 2011). SEAs can cause a great deal of disruption to everyday business activities and create financial, social and technical mayhem in which the impacts may go beyond geographical borders and organizational boundaries. Therefore, dealing with SEAs would be in the best interest of any organization. According to the (Verizon 2014) report, human factors are the main sources of SEAs. People can be easily socially engineered which leads to compromise of information systems in organizations. Even when attackers use complex and sophisticated technical hacking methods they would consider using people as a main tool in delivering their malicious software. For example they use e-mail attachments, which can easily mislead people and deliver the payloads of malicious program in order to gain access to a system. This type of attack is just one example out of hundreds of methods, which has worked both with big organizations and central governments. Janczewski and Fu (2010) identified five main causes of SEAs, i.e., people, lack of security awareness, psychological weaknesses, technology, and defenses and attack methods.

3.3. Social Engineering Attacks Taxonomies

There are certain concepts which must be considered to provide adequate defense mechanism against SEAs either detective or preventive. These include the style of attacks with consideration of human factors, the expected result of attacks and the possible impacts. This study developed SEA taxonomy in order to identify the main concepts and their attributes of the proposed language. Figure 1 shows how an attacker can plan an attack, which has variable impacts such as disclosure of data and theft of resources. The impact/s fulfils the goals and objectives of the attacker whether financial, personal, or political gain.

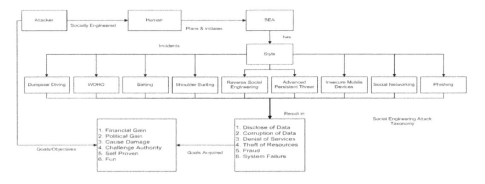

Figure 1: Social Engineering Attack Taxonomy

4. Language for Managing Social Engineering Attacks

4.1. Framing concepts

The process of securing information has become more critical than ever. When security is mission-critical and tied to revenue chains and compliance, then it has significant bottom-line impact. Security, cannot tolerate any performance delays by protection mechanisms, and require extra attention to ensure its success and at the lowest possible cost. Most research has concentrated on the success of security without consideration to cost that has an impact on the overall Return on Information Security Investment (ROISI). However, both security concepts of ISMS process and cost concepts of ROISI process have the same goal which includes the protection of information assets to prevent extra cost as a result of financial and reputational losses. Adopting a combined framework would enable us to address both security and investment concepts. The novelty of this work is a language that combines the concepts from security, risks and investment to support defense mechanism against SEAs and to assist in the calculation of return of SI considering human factors. The paper adopted Security Tropos to analyze security concepts such as actor, security goal, vulnerability, threat and plan and extended it with risks and SI from which ROISI can then be appropriately calculated in future study (Mouratidis and Giorgini, 2004). These concepts equip security architecture to establish the security-investment relationship and the systematically reasoning of them. This section lays out an overview of the concepts used in the Metamodel.

Actor: is the central concept of the proposed language. It represents an entity that has strategic goals and intentions within a system and organizational settings. An actor in this case can be human or the ISMS. In particular, human actor includes several factors such as awareness, communication and the involvement of management. ISMS actor has properties such as security policy and physical security.

Goal: is a stakeholder (Actor) objective or strategic interest for a system and its surrounding environment. The strategic objective of actor is to achieve goal and does not care how it is achieved but goal satisfaction should be formulated in agreement of shared development amongst all actors. The proposed language differentiates between security and organizational goals. Organizational goals represent goals that are important at an organizational level. Such goals include profitability, compliance, continuity, reputation and performance. Security goals support security needs. This means a secure goal serves actors' and concerns associated with goal (Giorgini et al, 2006). Confidentiality, integrity, availability, auditability and authenticity are the security goals. An adequate security balance can be obtained by exchanging security requirements and other functional/non-functional requirements of the security system that is equipped according to the goal.

Risk: Risk is the potential damage of consequence of a security incident. The incident arises from information process in organizations that may be maliciously exploited. SEA is an example of such exploitation. Risk is present in every aspect of information process and poses a possible loss within an organization. The proposed language has three different types of risks including; **financial loss**: A risk, which is difficult to quantify. However, this risk can be a direct loss of financial accounts or a loss as a result of disruption of business. **Legal fines:** A risk of organizations in receiving a fine as result of a security incident which violates legal obligations. **Reputational loss**: This is a risk, which traditionally was a result of reporting to the regulator. The risk of reputational loss could be the loss of attracting new customers and in some cases could affect credit rating.

Security incident: In the proposed language SEAs create threats that are caused by actors using different types (Figure 1). The possible threats can be: Internal system compromise, stolen customer data, phony transaction, insider attack and DoS attacks.

Vulnerabilities: A weakness in ISMS procedures, design, implementation, or internal controls that could be exercised and result in a security breach. Despite being patched by control mechanism a system always has vulnerabilities. This concept can be addressed by the vulnerability assessment which provides guidelines for protection mechanism. It consists of defining and classifying system resources, assigning levels of importance to the resources, identifying potential threats to each individual resource, developing countermeasure strategy and implementing methods to minimize the consequences of SEAs.

Security investment (SI): the concept of SI is defined as the capital that is being made available for security solutions via protection mechanism in supporting a goal. SI in this case is not a direct measure of the profit but prevents or at least, lessens the loss that could occur from human related security incidents. Therefore SI should consider technical and non-technical cost implications. The reason for this is that the cost of preventive measures of SEAs is varied whilst the landscape of threats and consequently the risks are changing. At the same time other attributes require attention. They can be business impact analysis (BIA), threat description, vulnerability assessment, risk evaluation and treatment.

Plan: is a workable long-term (strategic) mid-term (tactical) and short-term (operational), actions for reasoning and achieving goal must be utilized and adoptable for actors. Protect mechanism requires a plan to achieve ISMS security and organizational goals by ensuring strategic security and SI improvements. Long-term strategy entails issues related to human factors portfolio (involvement of senior management) and risk analysis. Mid-term (tactical) plan also concerns a human factors portfolio (awareness and communication) and tactical improvements such as maintenance and communication. The short-term (operational) phase of the plan is about allocation of critical IT assets, human factors portfolio and security implementation practice.

Protect mechanism: is the real control for addressing strategy and supporting plan. It can be detective or preventive for SEAs. It also protects information assets and assists patch system vulnerabilities. They can be either technical or non-technical and are listed as part of SI.

The goal, actor and plan used and defined is based on the entities of Secure Tropos. The security-risk language and other related concepts are adopted from ISMS principles whilst SEA incidents are defined based on wider SE concepts. The SI relies on ROISI process that was briefly explained earlier and will be followed by future study. Figure 2 presents the Metamodel, which is the combination of the above concepts, linked with some of the Secure Tropos security concepts.

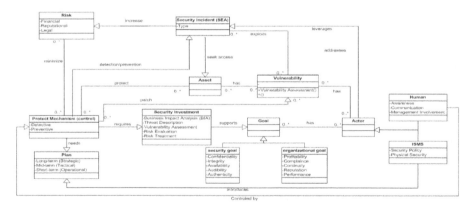

Figure 2: Proposed Metamodel

This paper approaches the concepts of security incidents, SI and humans as actor all play a major role whilst the protect mechanism is the core concept. Protect mechanism relies on strategic planning in providing detective and preventive methods for security incidents. It assists patching vulnerabilities and assets protection, which are mainly information (soft) assets. Once SI is configured, then detective and preventive control mechanism could potentially mitigate financial, reputational and legal risks. The mid and long-term plan strategy also supports protect mechanism in addressing awareness, communication and management support of actor (human) entities. Actor has vulnerabilities which can be exploited and influence security incidents. The identified detective and preventive controls create a set of consequences in the system. The consequences require validating against security incidents and SI to establish the leverage of the incident and actor in the system. If this is not justified then protect mechanism must be equipped to replace the gap requirements of planning and investment.

5. Case study

To demonstrate the applicability of the proposed approach, the paper deployed the proposed language through a case study scenario. The following description is a real and successful SEA incident that happened in a financial institution within the UK. This incident was an isolated but, successful case and the organization did not publicize it. One of the authors of this study had access to the incident log and therefore the company's name cannot be revealed.

Scenario

An employee received an email from one of the managers' referencing an invoice hosted on a cloud file sharing service. A few minutes later, the same employee received a phone call from another manager within the organization, instructing her to examine and process the invoice. However, the invoice was a fake and the manager who called the employee was an attacker. The apparent invoice was in fact a Remote Access Trojan (RAT) that was designed to contact and command-and-control (C&C) the server. By using the RAT, the attacker took control of the employee's computer instantly. The attacker managed to breach a part of the server as the multi-layered encrypted server prevented him from getting access to all the servers. This attacker used a socially engineered attack for financial gain. Before the attack was stopped they succeeded in getting a financial incentive in the region of £50,000.00.

Actors: The main actors involved in the scenario are:

- **Employee**: The employee here is the target victim. She was exposed with malicious pretexting and an identity theft by the attacker. She was a victim of a malicious and successful pretexting method.
- **Employee Manager**: The scenario also includes a victim target whom was a manager as an employee of the organization. The manager was a victim of impersonation. The attacker used the victim's defined organizational authority.
- **Attacker**: The attacker was an ex-contractor who previously carried out some network maintenance and had some insider knowledge from the target

company. However, the attacker needed to elicit his knowledge so he used various sources such as, the organization's web site and social media for this purpose. The attacker implemented some SE techniques in order to be confident enough to run the attack. He exploited various weaknesses of the target victims, such as lack of authentication in the communication process and the skill of the target employee. The attacker manipulated the employee to behave in certain ways in order that the attacker accomplished his goal, which was to access financial data for financial gain.

- **ISMS**: is a target system and provides security policy and physical security to ensure security is sound. The nature of this attack reveals that an employee is easily tricked. Something which security policy should re-adjust itself to. The re-training program lacks adequate phone calls and E-mail authentications' procedures.

Goals: The following goals have been observed:

- **Financial gain**: The attacker's goal is to obtain financial information in order to gain financial reward.
- **Perform duty**: The victim employee's goal is to perform their duty and follow the ISMS practice of the organization. In addition, the target victim employee's desire is to protect her employment contract that can be in line for review because it has been breached.
- **Organization goal**: the victim target organization requires continuity, performance and profitability needs to be maintained whilst the reputation and its compliance objectives are preserved.

Security Incident: The incident was mainly exploited by a phishing attack in which the attacker impersonated one of the managers. The main reason the attack was successful was because the employee followed the existing ISMS practice but the authentication process was not adequate in identification checks over the phone.

Vulnerabilities: The attacker mostly followed different elicitation methods to consolidate information before making the attack. The main weakness was the lack of an authorization mechanism for phone call verification.

Risk: The incident posed several possible risks in context.

- Financial loss: Attacker successfully obtained financial gain which is estimated at £50,000.00,
- Classified data leakage: There was a specific data related invoice that helped the attacker exploit the attack. This means that there was a violation of the Data Protection Act by the organization.

Plan: In this scenario the lack of improvements in the three stages of planning including long, medium and short-term is clear. The human factors portfolio raises major concerns whilst some technical improvements in authentication of communication seems necessary.

Protect mechanism: The study observed following protection mechanism for mitigating root causes of the incident so that the chance of success of such attacks can be minimized in future. Therefore, if the control mechanism was adequate enough to detect socially engineered activities then the attack could have been detected and dealt with adequately. This could have been done through a detailed training program as a soft control measure. A hard (technical) measure could have been established for the authentication of phone communication where such requests in accessing sensitive data require a password. This helps to establish an authenticated communication channel. This mechanism requires investment in updating security policy and providing new training reminders that seeks management support. Because the attacker was an ex-contractor, a review of access control measures is required to ensure unauthorized access is denied to the use of out dated credentials.

Security Investment (SI): intends to identify the investment that organizations require in order to deal with all security incidents effectively and adequately. The following questions could help in reaching the right decision of the executive management team: What obligations is the organization bound by in terms of compliance? What sanctions in information management in this scenario have been hit? Does the organization feel over-retention is a concern or is a necessary price to pay for compliance? Future study should look at the quantification of ROISI to response to the above questions. As far as this study is concerned, investment could more than cover the loss involved in an incident and is the main part of the proposed language. For the purpose of this study, the paper introduced the preliminary expected cost to cover the loss arising from incidents from the following parameters: External Services Cost ES(C), Purchasing Cost P(C), Employee Cost E(C), Administrative Cost A(C), Legal Costs L(C). Therefore the total expected cost of new and updating control mechanism would be: TEC(T) =ES(C) + P(C) + E(C) + A(C) + L(C). Future study should look at other parameters of investment concepts such as, Single Expected Attack Loss, Insurance Claim, Revenue Loss (from existing/potential clients) and Average Margin.

6. Discussion

The paper presents a SEAs risks-based language considering human factors and security investment. It includes several concepts such as goal, actor, SI, incident, risk, and protection mechanism that allow the analysis of SEA incidents and proposes appropriate control in a structured manner. The main reason for the discussed incident was because of the way in which employees were deceived with infected E-mail and hoax phone calls. This timely work contributes in addressing the challenge of managing human factors and security investment, so that possible risks can be mitigated. The study demonstrates the concepts through case study. This paper's observation is that the organization's current protection mechanism lack consistency. There are two important issues that have not been considered. Firstly there is the nature of attacks in which employees are easily tricked. Secondly that controls are needed by the application of patching. Employees are required to be trained in dealing with email and phone authentication processes, to distinguish between genuine and invalid hoax communications. Without knowing how much organizations would get in return from extra and new investment, it is a little like walking blind folded along a path. The concepts of language support analyzing the factors with realistic proposed solutions to control SEA based on SI. CISOs in organizations are the main beneficiary of this language in addressing security policy and security related human factors. There are certain limitations in this study. However the most important consideration is the nature of a business as well as the differences in organizational, culture and risk appetite.

7. Conclusions

With the rapid grown of information technology and the subsequent rise of an information society, the cost of information security and consequently the return of any investments in this area become one of the major concerns of organizations and governments. The objective of this work is to present a language that provides an understanding in the relationship between various concepts involved in SEA incidents considering human factors. These concepts systematically support analyzing SEAs and identifying appropriate mechanisms and investment for a mechanism to protect SEAs. The study then illustrated the use of this language in a real-life circumstance within a case study. The ROISI process which will be developed in future study will provide a valuation of annual expectancy in loss and SI. To develop a model from this language further research is required.

8. References

Alavi, R., Islam, S., Jahankhani, H. & Al-Nemrat, A. 2013. Analyzing Human Factors for an Effective Information Security Management System. International Journal Of Secure Software Engineering (IJSSE) 4, 50-75.

Alavi, R., Islam, S., Mouratidis, H. 2014. A Conceptual Framework to Analyze Human Factors of Information Security Management System (ISMS) in Organizations. Human Aspects of Information Security, Privacy, and Trust. T. Tryfonas and I. Askoxylakis, Springer International Publishing. 8533: 297-305.

Hadnagy, C. 2011. Social Engineering: The Art of Human Hacking. Indianapolis, Wiley Publishing Inc.

Hadnagy, C. & Wilson, P. 2010. Social Engineering: The Art of Human Hacking, Wiley.

Janczewski, L. & Fu, L. 2010. Social Engineering-Based attacks: Model and New Zealand Perspective. Computer Science and Information Technology, 847-853.

Mouratidis, H., Giorgini, P. 2004. Enhancing Secure Tropos to Effectively Deal with Security Requirements in the Development of Multiagent Systems. 1st International Workshop on Safety and Security in Multiagent Systems. N.Y. USA.

Verizon Enterprise Solutions. 2014. 2014 Data Breach Investigations Report (DBIR). Available: http://www.verizonenterprise.com/DBIR/2014/ [Accessed 01/10/2014].

Siponen, M., Pahnila, S. & Mahmood, M. A. 2010. Compliance with Information Security Policies: An Empirical Investigation. Computer, 43, 64-71.

Finn, P. and Jakobsson, M. 2005. Designing and conducting phishing experiments. IEEE Technology and Society Magazine, Special Issue on Usability and Security.

Shakarian, P., Shakarian, J., & Ruef, A. 2013. Introduction to cyber-warfare: A multidisciplinary approach. Maryland Heights: Syngress Publishing.

Greitzer, F. L., Strozer, J. R., Cohen, S., Moore, A. P., Mundie, D. & Cowley, J. Analysis of Unintentional Insider Threats Deriving from Social Engineering Exploits. Security and Privacy Workshops (SPW), 2014 IEEE, 17-18 May 2014. 236-250.

Karpati, P., Sindre, G., S. & Matulevicius, R. 2012. Comparing Misuse Case and Mal-Activity Diagrams for Modelling Social Engineering Attacks. International Journal of Secure Software Engineering (IJSSE), 3, 54-73.

Mismorphism: a Semiotic Model of Computer Security Circumvention

S. Smith[1], R. Koppel[2], J. Blythe[3] and V. Kothari[1]

[1]Dartmouth College, United States
[2]University of Pennsylvania, , United States
[3]Information Sciences Institute, University of South California
e-mail: sws@cs.dartmouth.edu

Abstract

In real world domains, from healthcare to power to finance, computer systems are deployed with the intention of streamlining and improving the activities of human agents in the corresponding non-cyber worlds. However, talking to actual users (instead of just computer security experts) reveals endemic circumvention of the computer-embedded rules. Well-intentioned users, trying to get their jobs done, systematically work around security and other controls embedded in their IT systems. This paper reports on our work compiling a large corpus of such incidents and developing a model based on *semiotic triads* to examine security circumvention. This model suggests that *mismorphisms*—mappings that *fail* to preserve structure—lie at the heart of circumvention scenarios; differential perceptions and needs explain users' actions. This paper supports this claim with empirical data from the corpus.

Keywords

Circumvention, authentication, authorization, usability.

1. Introduction

Users systematically work around security controls. The security community can pretend this does not happen, but it does. This paper reports on research addressing this problem via observation and grounded theory (Bernard and Ryan, 2010; Charmaz, 2003; Pettigrew, 2000). Rather than assuming that users behave perfectly or that only bad users do bad things, this approach instead observes and records what really goes on compared to the various expectations. Then, after data items are reviewed, structure and models are developed, and additional data is brought in to support, reject, and refine these models. Over the last several years, via interviews, observations, surveys, and literature searches, the authors have explored the often-tenuous relationship among computer rules, users' needs, and designers' goals of computer systems. A corpus of hundreds of circumvention and unusability scenarios has been collected and analyzed. This corpus cataloged close to 300 examples of these "misunderstandings" and the circumventions users undertook to accomplish their needed tasks. The examples were derived from 285 different sources and categorized into 60 fine-grained codes. Because several examples reflect multiple codes, there were 646 applications of the codes linked to the examples.

Semiotic triads, proposed almost a century ago (e.g., Ogden and Richards, 1927), offer models to help understand why human agents so often circumvent computer-embedded rules. Our research suggests that these triads provide a framework to illuminate, organize, and analyze circumvention problems.

This paper presents these ideas and supports them with examples. Our longer technical report (Smith et al., 2015) provides a far more exhaustive presentation of examples. When this paper does not cite a source, the example came from interviews with parties who wish to remain anonymous. As this research focuses on developing a typology rather than supporting a hypothesis, many of the usual factors in confirmation bias to do not apply

2. A Semiotic Model for IT Usability Trouble

Our previous paper (Smith and Koppel, 2014), organizing an earlier corpus of usability problems in health IT into a coherent typology, considered three sets: the mental model of the clinician working with the patient and the health IT system; the representation of medical reality in the health IT system; and the actual medical reality of patients. Usability problems organized nicely according to mismatches between the expressiveness of the representation "language" and the details of reality–between how a clinician's mental model works with the representations and reality.

However, this tripartite framework goes back almost a century. In their seminal 1920s work on the meaning of language, Ogden and Richards (1927) constructed what is sometimes called the *semiotic triad*. The vertices are the three principal objects: what the speaker (or listener/reader) *thinks*; the *symbol* they use; and the actual item to which they are *referring*.

Much of Ogden and Richard's analysis stems from the observation that there is not a direct connection from symbol to referent. Rather, when speaking or writing, the referent maps into the mental model of the speaker and then into the symbol; when reading (or listening), the symbol maps into the reader's (listener's) mental model, which then projects to a referent, but not necessarily the same one. For example, Alice may think of "Mexico" when she writes "this country," but when Bob reads those works, he thinks of "Canada"—and (besides not being Mexico) his imagined Canada may differ substantially from the real one.

As our research moves from health IT usability to consider a new corpus of scenarios in security circumvention and other authentication misadventures, this framework also applies. Each scenario has at least one IT system. Each system serves a set of users, and mediates access between these users and a cross-product of actions and resources. Each system has an IT administrator who worries about the security configuration—as well as users who worry about trying to use the resulting system for their actual work. For different systems, the user sets are not necessarily disjoint.

The interaction between the reality, the IT representation, and the mental models correspond to the vertices in Ogden and Richards' triad:

- Thought: the mental model a party has about the actions users can and cannot (or should and should not) do with resources.
- Symbol (i.e. configuration): the representation of security policy within the IT system itself; the built-in functionality of the IT system, intended to express the correct workflow. (Here, "policy" refers to the actual machine-actionable expression of administrator intention, not a published instructional document.)
- Referent (i.e. reality): the actions users can and cannot do with the resources, in reality; the de facto allowed workflow.

Figure 1-a sketches this basic triad. In this framework, the primary mappings are counterclockwise:

- *Referent → thought*: the administrator constructs a mental model of what she imagines are the actual enterprise workflow requirements.
- *Thought → symbol*: the administrator reasons about security and work goals and construct a system configuration that she believes achieves these goals.
- *Symbol → referent*: this configuration in practice then generates some actual reality.

Thanks to the connection of IT and reality, there now exists a direct symbol-referent connection, improving on (or at least complicating) the merely linguistic world Ogden and Richards explored. Note however, that ordinary users also participate in this triad, and that mappings in the other direction can also be interesting: e.g., investment bankers trying to infer which of their entitlements are actually necessary in their daily job (symbol-thought, then thought-referent).

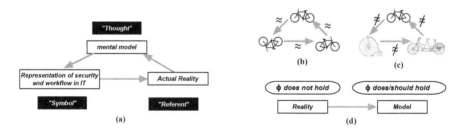

Figure 1: (a) The basic Ogden-Richards triad, moved into 21st-century IT; the arrows indicate the main direction of mappings. (b) Standard semiotics considers structure-preserving mappings between the nodes of the triad; (c) circumvention semiotics considers mappings that fail to preserve structure. (d) the generated reality fails to embody a property the user regards as critical.

3. Extending this Model to Security Circumvention

To illustrate the role of semiotic triads, consider of *de-authentication* and proximity detectors for *computers-on-wheels (COWs)* in a hospital. One triad characterizes the creation of the security policy. The administrator perceives a reality (*referent*) where clinicians are walking away from logged-in sessions, and thus creating data exposure and corruption risk. The administrator then constructs a mental model (*thought*) where COWs automatically log out sessions when users walk away. Deciding that this is a better reality, the administrator crafts an IT configuration (*symbol*) intended to implement this policy—in this case, by installing a proximity detector on each COW, and choosing a timeout threshold (triggered by the clinician moving away from the COW) after which lack of proximity effects the logout.

However, the hospital IT system has another set of actors: the clinicians who are the users. The triad involving IT configuration, user, and reality then characterizes the emergence of the workaround. The administrator's new IT configuration (*symbol*) generates a *reality* (*referent*) where proximity detectors cause appropriate logouts. However, the clinicians perceive this reality as not matching their desired workflow (*thought*), where clinicians often must walk away from the COW to examine a patient, to observe readings on a device, to find a document, and to speak with another clinician. Consequently, the clinicians generate their own addition (*symbol*) to the IT configuration—inverted styrofoam cups placed over the detectors that defeat their function—to modify the generated reality (*referent*) to one closer to their liking and need. Furthermore, unless the administrator "closes the loop" by observing the disabled proximity detectors, the administrator may never realize that the eventual result of this security improvement (automatic timeout) is an *increase* in exposure, because previously timed logouts are now indefinitely postponed.

The semiotics of language and the effective communication of meaning focus on *morphisms*—"structure-preserving mappings"—between nodes of the triad. However, with IT usability problems one is concerned instead with ineffective communication—and hence focus on what our research calls *mismorphisms*: mappings that *fail* to preserve important structure when we go from z in one node of the triad to its corresponding z' in another (Figure 1-b,c). Indeed, one may hypothesize that mismorphisms lie at the heart of circumvention, because they characterize the scenarios that frustrate users—and often the resulting circumvention itself.

The styrofoam cup scenario above provides examples of several types: the reality generated by the new IT configuration failed to preserve the workflow features desired by the users; the administrator imagined that "dialing up" security configuration—by adding a timeout—would *increase* security; but when mapped to reality, the change *decreased* security; the users' additions of styrofoam cups caused the emergent reality to lose the security properties the administrators imagined.

4. Loss of Static Properties

Many troublesome scenarios arise when a mapping from one triad node to another fails to preserve some critical property. For clarity of presentation, this paper will treat this property as some Boolean predicate. More precisely, when z in one node of the triad maps to z' in another, it may be that $\Phi(z) = true$ but $\Phi(z') = false$, for some crucial predicate Φ. (E.g., see Figure 1-d.)

Lost Workflow Properties In many common incarnations of this type of mismorphism, the reality generated by the administrator's IT configuration does not match the workflow the users perceive as necessary. E.g., a vendor of power grid equipment had a marketing slide showing their default password and the default passwords of all the competitors. The slide was intended to show how secure this vendor was, since they used a more secure default password. However, a deeper issue here is that access to equipment during an emergency is critical, since availability of the grid is far more important than other classical security aspects. Any scheme to replace default passwords with a stronger scheme must preserve this availability. Here, two predicates are at play: password authentication with well-known defaults generates a reality that fails to preserve the basic security properties in the administrator's mental model; but password authentication without well-known defaults generates a reality that fails to preserve the availability required in the domain expert's mental model.

In a particularly ironic twist, sometimes the technology itself, in the setting in which it is being applied, causes the mismorphism. E.g., knowledge-based authentication at one credit bureau failed for one of the authors when he was the victim of identity theft, because the bureau assumed that the information (e.g., past addresses) in their record was accurate. However, identity thieves corrupted this information, so the genuine user was not able to correctly answer questions about it. (There were similar problems with trying to correct the "current" address, since none of the choices it gave were correct.) Here, the mapping loses the property that "the bona fide user can authenticate himself to system" precisely because this choice of authentication technology fails when the user has been the victim of identity theft.

Failure to preserve some critical property can also develop over time. For one example, one often sees *citogenesis*: when some artifact of the IT causes a spurious change to reality's representation, which then gets interpreted by all users as genuinely representing the real world, e.g: medical personnel tell of *chart ghosts*: when information mistakenly gets added to a patient's record, it becomes real. It can retroactively change many other parts of the patient's record—and clinicians may take the multiple occurrences of this information as confirmation that it must be true.

Circumvention as Compensation When the generated IT fails to have some property the users regard as critical, a standard circumvention response is for users to customize the IT configuration to compensate. One standard way is to add functionality. This can include all the standard ways users share credentials (thus causing the "1-1 credential-person" property in an administrator's mental model to fail in reality): sticky notes with passwords; shared PINs; a senior professor sharing his NSF password with a staffer; in one banking scenario, employees routinely used the credential of an employee appropriately authorized but deceased. Sometimes users compensate for the loss of a critical property by *removing* functionality: in multiple industries, security officers have told us that senior staffers insist on not patching their compromised machines, sometimes by disconnecting them during remediation.

Alternatively, users can establish *shadow systems*, sometimes using functionality already inadvertently present in the system—and this inadvertent presence itself can sometimes be seen as a mismorphism: the administrators would probably have not allowed this pathway had they seen how it would undermine policy. E.g.: in trading, employees perform desired exfiltration, despite data exfiltration guards, by scanning documents, turning them into images, then embedding the images in PDFs—rendering the text opaque to the online guards. (In a different industry employees screen-scraped medical images into Powerpoint, for similar reasons.)

Mismorphism as Circumvention Mismorphism can be a vector of circumvention, as well as a cause. One category seen is *intentional distortion.* A human user, striving to get the IT to generate the desired real-world functionality, intentionally alters one of the triad mappings, making it less correct. Sometimes, the user aspires to later undo this distortion; sometimes, she does not. E.g. in one medical scenario, one EHR prevents the doctor treating a patient with predicted risks of clotting from leaving the software until the doctor orders a blood thinner. If the patient is already on blood thinners, the double dose may kill her. The workaround is for the doctor to order the second, lethal dose, then go back into the system and cancel the original dose. That is, to leave the EHR, the clinician must make the "EHR reflects needed dose, not lethal dose" invariant temporarily false.

Breaking the Workaround Sometimes, there exists a second round of mismorphisms: the IT loses the property that the workaround works. E.g. in an EHR, a doctor could not find an appropriate place to record the medication he thought was needed (missing property). But he found a box that he thought would be seen and recorded it there (workaround). However, the box was not visible to subsequent users of this record; the order was not seen, and the patient was in crisis (failure to preserve the workaround).

Provisioning When it comes to access control specifically, a particular challenge is the difficulty of what some industries call *provisioning*: the mapping of an administrator's mental model of "correct" access control to an IT policy configuration that generates a real-world system enforcing that model. Problems with provisioning are central to many scenarios of security engineering and circumvention trouble, but these problems themselves are consequences of mismorphism: failure of the mapping between the triad nodes to preserve certain structure. E.g. a figurative "greybeard" in computer security tells of giving a room full of experienced Unix system administrators the problem of devising a scheme in

Unix filesystem access controls to match a relatively simple enterprise organization model. Each system administrator would very quickly come up with a solution. But each solution was wrong. Even for those understanding the provisioning technology did not come up with an IT configuration that generated a reality matching their goal.

The reverse mapping—from IT policy to mental model—is also problematic. An investment bank had "entitlement review" in which employees reviewed their privileges and gave up ones they did not think they needed—except then they had to ask for them back (Sinclair, 2013). In real-world organizations (as opposed to computer security textbooks), provisioning using standard technology can be dauntingly complex.

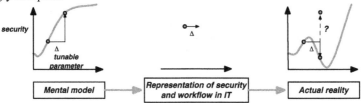

Figure 2: In *uncanny descent*, the mental model shows dialing up security improves security; but when mapped into reality, security actually decreases.

5. Loss of Functional Properties

Both the administrators officially configuring IT systems and the users unofficially reconfiguring them are practicing a form of security engineering: trying to optimize some overall property of the system by adjusting a human-settable parameter. However, this process implicitly assumes that a functional relationship exists from the parameter to the property, and that the morphisms between nodes of the triad preserve that relationship. In many circumvention scenarios, both the causes—and sometimes the negative security consequences—stem from morphisms failing to preserve this relationship.

More specifically, in questions of security design, implementation, and use, there implicitly exists some function S taking a tunable parameter (e.g., password length) to the level of security achieved. The intention of the human is to tune the parameter x so as to maximize $S(x)$. However, if the mappings across the triad nodes fail to preserve crucial properties of this x versus $S(x)$ curve, unfortunate things can happen. This paper discusses three properties in particular.

Loss of Monotonicity In one node, the function S can be *monotonic*: for $\Delta > 0$, $S(x+\Delta) > S(x)$. However, when mapped into another node, the function loses monotonicity: $S'(x+\Delta) < S'(x)$.

Computer graphics offers the term "uncanny valley" for when dialing up realism makes things worse before it makes things better. Security scenarios show many variations of such uncanniness. The timeout/styrofoam scenario is a good example of what we call *uncanny descent*: dialing up security in the IT configuration (from x to $x+\Delta$) instead leads to a decrease in security in the system itself: although the administrator imagined $S(x+\Delta) > S(x)$, the reality has $S(x+\Delta) < S(x)$ instead (Figure 2).

"Best practices" for password-based authentication are notorious for exhibiting the loss of monotonicity when going from the administrator's mental model through the IT configuration into the generated reality: dialing security up can make it worse instead. E.g., when one of our universities established requirements that made passwords hard to remember, many users reported relying instead on regularly resetting it via security questions that were easy to guess. (Our full report discusses many other examples.)

Fieldwork also reveals incidents of *faux uncanny descent*: dialing up security led to an incorrect perception that actual security decreased. For example, changing an EMR to make it easier for clinicians to record when medications were given at the wrong time led to an increase in the reports of mistimed medications—which managers interpreted as a decrease in quality of service.

A different consequence of the loss of monotonicity is what we call *uncanny ascent*: dialing *down* the security controls can also counter-intuitively lead to an *increase* in actual security. Once again, the map from the administrator's mental model through the IT to reality does not preserve the shape of the setting/security curve. Two examples:

- A security officer for a large pharmaceutical reported a nice example of this. Concerned that senior executives were illicitly sharing their work account passwords with assistants and staff, he instituted a rule that executives use the same password for both their work accounts and their personal salary and benefit information. Eliminating unique passwords (which is "bad") led to a reduction in sharing (which is "good"). $S(x-\Delta) < S(x)$ but in fact $S'(x-\Delta) > S'(x)$.
- A common belief is that making passwords longer makes them more secure. However, a student exploring gmail's password strength meter discovered that it considered "*qwertyqwerty* to be a weak password, *qwertyqwert* to be a fair password, and *qwertyqwer* to be a good password." Shortening the password made Google consider it to be stronger. (Our work has also found sequences of lengthened passwords that change from strong to good to strong to good to weak—the assumed monotonic curve can in fact become rather bumpy!)

Loss of Continuity In one node, the function S may be *continuous*: for any $\epsilon > 0$, there is a $\delta > 0$ so if $|x - y| < \delta$, then $|S(x) - S(y)| < \epsilon$. When mapped into another node, the function may lose continuity: the difference $|S'(x) - S'(y)|$ may be significantly large.

Circumvention scenarios often arise because the morphisms across the triad nodes fail to be continuous. Amusingly tangible examples here are the regular occurrences of when an innocuous photo reveals a password which users have posted on paper—the small change of a photo yields to a dramatic change in who can authenticate.

Domain and Range Trouble Another property that can be lost to mismorphism is the nature of S as a function. In a mental model, $S : D \rightarrow R$ can be a well-defined function taking some x *in D* to $S(x)$ *in R*. However, mapping to the generated reality, loses these properties. Instead, perhaps S' depends on other parameters besides x' *in D'*; or perhaps changing to x' to $x' + \delta$ changes more than just items in R', so that the mapped range loses important information.

In the former case, the mapping loses the morphological property of *locality of control*. The administrator A_1 of system S_1 implicitly assumes that de facto security of S_1 depends only on the de jure configuration A_1 puts together—or, at worst, also on the behavior of the users. A user U of a system may believe his actions only affect his portion of the system, and not those of other users. However, given that the same user can use multiple systems, and that the same system can be used by multiple users, effects of actions can reach unexpectedly far. Such *cross-channel effects* between apparently unrelated nodes can both lead to, as well as exacerbate, the consequences of circumvention.

For example, one often sees "action at a distance"—when the security of a system S_1 is reduced because of the actions of an administrator A_2 of a different system S_2. E.g. an energy trader set up an SSL server, for security, but used a self-signed certificate—thus leaving his own service vulnerable to man-in-the-middle attacks, but also training all his users to accept self-signed certificates on SSL sessions, thus increasing the exposure of all the other SSL services—banks, credit cards, medical sites—they use. The security of these other sites, in practice, decreased because of the actions of a careless administrator on an apparently unrelated site. Without changing their own x, $S'(x)$ suddenly declines. Password practices at one site—good and bad—can create risks at other sites, as our full report discusses.

6. Related Work

The classic work of Ogden and Richards (1927) generated some subsequent scholarship relevant to computer systems including the use of formal semiotic models to examine user interfaces and human access to the underlying computational functionality (e.g., Ferreira et al., 2005; Goguen, 1999; de Souza et al., 2001). More recently, several researchers have investigated the effects of user mental models on their security decision-making (e.g. Wash, 2010; Camp, 2009; Olembo et al., 2013). An understanding of mental models may help predict human behavior that would otherwise seem irrational but is rational in the context of a faulty model (Johnson-Laird, 1986). Our longer technical report (Smith et al., 2015) surveys our earlier work exploring aspects of this space.

7. Conclusion

This paper has presented our model looking at computer/workflow usage as an Ogden-Richards semiotic triad, but considering instead how the mappings fail to preserve structure: static properties, correspondence of "security setting" to "security achieved," continuity, control. To support this model, this paper cited many examples of distortions and unwanted effects arising from mismorphisms among users' needs, computer-embedded rules, and the (mis)understandings of computer system administrators; our full report catalogs many, many more examples. Building this topology also highlights the necessity for observation of use in reality, rather than as reflected in the system's blueprint or initial design.

In future work, we plan to distill this model into design principles for better security engineering. One may start by looking at mismatches as while moving around the triad and then considering where "shape" fails to be preserved, perhaps via feedback loops, regular discussions, and explicit monitoring. Alternatively, growing this corpus may allow us to create a database that security personnel can consult for design patterns. Discovering circumventions and analyzing their causes can improve system design so that users can get their jobs done without working around the rules.

8. Acknowledgements

This material is based in part upon work supported by the Army Research Office under Award No. W911NF-13-1-0086.

9. References

Bernard, H. R. and Ryan, G. W. (2010). *Analyzing Qualitative Data: Systematic Approaches.* Sage Publications.

Camp, L. (2009). Mental models of privacy and security. *IEEE Technology And Society Magazine*, 28(3).

Charmaz, K. (2003). Grounded theory. In *The SAGE Encyclopedia of Social Science Research Methods*, pages 440–444.

de Souza, C. S., Barbosa, S. D. J., and Prates, R. O. (2001). A semiotic engineering approach to user interface design. *Knowledge-Based Systems*, 14(8):461–465.

Ferreira, J., Barr, P., and Noble, J. (2005). The semiotics of user interface redesign. In *Proceedings of the Sixth Australasian Conference on User Interface - Volume 40*, AUIC '05, pages 47–53.

Goguen, J. (1999). An introduction to algebraic semiotics, with application to user interface design. In Nehaniv, C. L., editor, *Computation for Metaphors, Analogy, and Agents*, pages 242–291. Springer-Verlag.

Johnson-Laird, P. (1986). *Mental models: towards a cognitive science of language, inference, and consciousness.* Harvard University Press.

Ogden, C. and Richards, I. (1927). *The Meaning of Meaning.* Harcourt, Brace and Company.
Olembo, M. M., Bartsch, S., and Volkamer, M. (2013). Mental models of verifiability in voting.

In Heather, J., Schneider, S., and Teague, V., editors, *E-Voting and Identify*, volume 7985 of

Lecture Notes in Computer Science, pages 142–155. Springer Berlin Heidelberg.

Pettigrew, S. F. (2000). Ethnography and Grounded Theory: a Happy Marriage? In *NA Advances in Consumer Research*, volume 27, pages 256 – 260. Association for Consumer Research.

Sinclair, S. (2013). *Access Control In and For the Real World*. PhD thesis, Department of Computer Science, Dartmouth College.

Smith, S. and Koppel, R. (2014). Healthcare information technology's relativity problems: a typology of how patients' physical reality, clinicians' mental models, and healthcare information technology differ. *Journal of the American Medical Informatics Association*, 21:117–131.

Smith, S., Koppel, R., Blythe, J., and Kothari, V. (2015). *Mismorphism: a Semiotic Model of Computer Security Circumvention (Extended Version)*. Computer Science Technical Report TR 2015-768, Dartmouth College. www.cs.dartmouth.edu/reports/TR2015-768.pdf

Wash, R. (2010). Folk models of home computer security. In *Proc Symposium on Usable Privacy and Security*.

Perceived Information Security Risk as a Function of Probability and Severity

T.Sommestad, H.Karlzén, P.Nilsson and J.Hallberg

Swedish Defence Research Agency, Linköping, Sweden
e-mail: teodor.sommestad@foi.se

Abstract

Information security risks are frequently assessed in terms of the *probability* that a threat will be realized and the *severity* of the consequences of a realized threat. In methods and manuals, the product of this probability and severity is often thought of as the *risk* to consider and manage. However, studies of human behavior and intentions in the field of information security suggest that in general, this is not the way security is perceived. In fact, few studies have found an interaction (i.e., a multiplicative relationship) between probability and severity. This paper describes a study where the ratings of risk and the two variables probability and severity were collected on 105 security threats from ten individuals together with information about the respondents' expertise and cognitive style. These ten individuals do not assess risk as the product of probability and severity, regardless of expertise and cognitive style. Depending on how risk is measured, an additive model explains 54.0% or 38.4% of the variance in risk. If a multiplicative term is added, the mean increased variance is only 1.5% or 2.4%, and for most of the individuals the contribution of the multiplicative term is statistically insignificant.

Keywords

Information security risk assessment, Risk perception, Perceived severity, Perceived probability

1. Introduction

It is widely accepted and uncontroversial to view information security in terms of perceived risks. Information security risks are, in many of the most widely accepted definitions, assessed in terms of the *probability* that a threat will be realized and the *severity* of the consequences of a realized threat. For instance, the following literature describe security risk as a combination of probability (in other contexts termed likelihood or frequency) and consequence (or impact or magnitude) (NIST, 2012)(Club de la Sécurité de l'Information Français, 2011)(Karabacak and Sogukpinar, 2005) and (Lund et al., 2011).

In the literature the relationship between severity, probability and risk is also clear – risk is defined as the product of the severity and the probability. Thus, rational and balanced security decisions require that risk is assessed as the product of probability and severity. The rationale for this is clearest in the extreme cases – with no negative effect (severity zero) the probability should be irrelevant, and with no possibility of happening (probability zero) the severity should be irrelevant. But it is also clear in-between these extremes – if a bad thing is twice as likely or twice as severe as another bad thing, the expected costs will be twice as large.

A multiplicative relationship is well established in decision making theory regarding information security. However, results from both information security and from other domains suggest that people do not multiply the two in practice. For example, in the original formulation of the Protection Motivation Theory it was proposed that an interaction of perceived vulnerability and perceived severity influenced behavioral intentions (Maddux and Rogers, 1983; Rogers, 1983). However, this interaction has been abandoned for a simpler additive model on empirical grounds – empirical data does not offer firm support of a multiplicative relationship (Das et al., 2003)(Pechmann et al., 2003)(Cismaru and Lavack, 2007). One possible explanation for these results is that humans are incapable or unwilling to adhere to reason and mathematical stringency and prefer to simply combine (add) a percentage with a cost into a risk value. Another possible explanation is that studies fail to observe the multiplicative relation for one reason or another. There are several reasons to expect that this is the case.

First, some studies have measured the intentions to engage in protective behaviour rather than assessing actual risk. Clearly, the effectiveness and costs of the protective behavior is also a factor to consider in such protective decisions, and this may have distorted the results – at least when both factors are present. Second, the scales to measure probability and severity used in many of the studies of information security behavior (e.g., (Posey et al., 2011)) are not suited for multiplication. A multiplicative operation requires that two ratio scales are used, which is seldom the case in the research. For instance, a Likert scale with questions asking if the respondent *Completely Agree* or *Completely Disagree* does not produce a ratio, and multiplications with such variables are questionable if not outright invalid. Third, it is possible that some persons multiply probability and severity to calculate risk and others do not or that some interpret scales differently and, e.g., do not start their severity ratings at 0 but do start at 0 for probability and risk. This would distort the results of between-subject designs. Fourth, when a fairly homogenous group of respondents are asked to assess one or few incidents in a between-subject design, a large portion of the variance may be because of measurement errors, i.e., it comes from unreliable responses rather actual differences in perceptions. To discover an interaction term when most of the observed variance between subjects' perceptions is due to error requires considerable sample size. Fifth, the incidents may be too homogenous resulting in only part of the scales being used.

Only one study was found that addresses the relationship between probability, severity and risk while isolating risks from remedies, using scales allowing multiplication, and using a within-subject-design. This study, by Weinstein (2000), comprised a convenience sample of 12 individuals who assessed 201 health risks, covering the entire probability-severity matrix, on two occasions. The respondents first assessed risk (R) by prioritizing events and valuing hypothetical insurances. After 1 to 2 weeks they assessed probability (P) and severity (S) for the same events. A clear multiplicative effect was found in the sample. A function with only a multiplicative term (i.e., R=P*S) explained approximately 90% of the variance explained by a function that also included the additive terms (i.e., R=P+S+P*S), i.e., the additive function did not add much. However, the interaction between probability and severity appears to vary with the magnitude of these two. For example, considering events with high probability and high severity, the severity matters most, but for events with low probability and high severity, the multiplicative relationship is highly significant. The results also suggest that there are considerable individual differences between how people assess health risks. For instance the respondents are, on average, insensitive to health risks with moderate to high (P>40%) probability, but the sensitivity varies between respondents.

This paper performs a study similar to Weinstein's (2000), but in the information security domain. A within-subject design is used and meaningful scales are used to test the risk equation in the minds of ten individuals. More specifically, the following hypothesis is tested.

H1: Perceived information security risk is determined as the product of its perceived probability of occurrence and perceived severity.

In addition, it is reasonable to suspect that people who are more used to the subject matter will be more inclined to multiply. Thus, the present study adds a between-subject design by investigating if the tendency to multiply severity and probability to obtain risk is higher among respondents who 1) are proficient in risk assessments, 2) possess information security expertise, or 3) have a rational decision making style rather than an intuitive one. The following hypotheses are tested.

H2: The tendency to assess risk as a product of probability and severity is related to risk assessments experience.

H3: The tendency to assess risk as a product of probability and severity is related to information security expertise.

H4: The tendency to assess risk as a product of probability and severity is related to cognitive decision making style.

Section 2 of the paper describes the method. Section 3 describes the results and section 4 discusses these results.

2. Method

The study design is heavily influenced by the one used by Weinstein (2000). The sections below describe the participants, the survey instrument and the data collection procedure.

2.1. Participants

The survey was distributed to a strategic sample of 10 researchers active in the areas of information security, IT security, IT management or human factors. All respondents are from the Swedish Defence Research Agency (as are the authors of this paper), possess university degrees, are in the age range 29-54 and work as researchers. In order to test H2 and H3, pertaining to security expertise and experience in risk assessments, five of the respondents were drawn from the information security research group and five of the respondents were drawn from the research group called "Human, technology organization", which specializes in requirements engineering and human-machine-interaction. Thus, whereas the participants are a convenience sample drawn from the authors' own organization, the sample is designed to test the hypotheses in question. Furthermore, the questionnaire had all participants answer questions on both probability and severity rather than separating the two factors. This reflects the common situation where experts conduct the entire risk analysis process from threat elicitation to countermeasure recommendations. Thus, stakeholders might be involved with asset elicitation but are unlikely concerned with specific threats, or qualified to determine potential consequences.

2.2. Material and scales

Two paper based questionnaires were used to conduct the study. The first questionnaire comprised two parts: one part asking questions about the respondent and one part asking the respondent to assess the probability and severity of 105 incidents. The second questionnaire repeated some of the probability and severity questions in the first questionnaire to allow reliability tests, but focused on measuring the perceived risk associated with the 105 incidents.

2.2.1. Incidents and scenarios

The 105 potential incidents (or scenarios) were designed to be meaningful for the target population. For example, they used information objects and threats that are relevant for the organization. Some examples include:

- "A computer virus extracts all documents related to cooperation with foreign states in the office network and shares this with a foreign intelligence service."
- "Spyware is introduced into the organization's office network by an international defence corporation".
- "Employees intentionally violate policies related to the storage of secret documents."
- "A scientist's USB-stick with five years of collected (unclassified) material is stolen at an international conference."

The incidents were constructed to cover the whole range of possible assessments. In other words, they were designed to be assessed as all combinations of low probability, high probability, low severity, and high severity. Fortunately, identifying incidents of high probability and severity turned out to be difficult.

2.2.2. Perceived probability and severity

In the first questionnaire, the respondents were asked to provide the severity and probability of each incident. The perceived *severity* of incidents was indicated by marking a line stretching from 0 (Minimal, no harm at all) to 10 (Greatest harm). In the questionnaire, it was emphasized that the worst of all 105 incidents should be rated a 10 and that other ratings should be proportional to this (e.g., that 5 is half as harmful a 10). The perceived *probability* of an incident occurring during the next ten years was provided by marking a line with endpoints 0% (Minimal, completely unlikely) to 100% (Maximal, guaranteed to happen).

Anchors were present along this line, however, respondents were free to mark any point on the line. The corresponding value (e.g., severity 1.6 or probability 16%) was measured using a ruler. To enable tests of reliability, i.e., that answers were stable over time, the second questionnaire asked the respondents to provide probability and severity assessments for twelve randomly selected incidents a second time.

2.2.3. Perceived risk

In the second questionnaire, the respondents were asked to provide the overall perceived risks associated with the incidents in two ways to increase confidence in the results. Both of these methods are supposed to reflect the perceived risk associated with an incident, without considering how easy or difficult it would be to lower the risk.

First, the respondents were presented with the hypothetical scenario that they would have the power to eliminate some of the risks corresponding to the 105 incidents. They were asked to mark the *priority* of eliminating the risks by putting a mark on a line stretching from 0 (Not at all prioritized) to 10 (Absolutely highest priority). Second, the respondents were asked to indicate the *expected costs* of the incident in monetary terms. More concretely, respondents were asked to write how much they would be prepared to pay to insure the organization against the risk if they were in charge of the budget. As in the study by Weinstein (2000), an anchor and an upper limit were used to simplify the assessment. The respondents were told that no risk was worth more than 10 million SEK (approximately 1 million EUR) and that protection against incidents involving lost or stolen USB-sticks ever happening (this is an acceptable deviation of the standard definition of insurance, also shared by Weinstein (2000)) was worth about 30% of the maximum amount.

2.2.4. Decision making style

Cognitive style was measured using eight items. These items are direct translations of the items presented by (McShane, 2006), which in turn is inspired by (Scott and Bruce, 1995) and the Cognitive Style Index (Allinson and Hayes, 1996). Four items measure the tendency to be rational, i.e., to ignore gut instinct when it contradicts objective information and to make decision based on facts and logical analysis. Four items measure the tendency to be intuitive, i.e., to make decision based on inner feelings or instinct rather than to rely on rational choices conflicting with intuition.

2.2.5. Expertise and experience

Expertise and experiences were obtained from self-ratings by the respondents, which were validated against dichotomous classifications made by the investigators based on organisational department. Self-ratings were provided on the format "Completely agree" to "Completely disagree" for the following statements: "I work with security assessments or risk assessments", "I work with information security", and "My colleagues think that I am an IT-security expert or information security expert".

2.3. Data collection procedure

Respondents were provided the second questionnaire one to two weeks after they had answered the first questionnaire. One week was expected to remove the opportunity of simply recollect their previous responses and multiply them to obtain responses for the second questionnaire. In addition, after the first questionnaire they were asked to remove all copies or notes related to their responses. Furthermore, to avoid influencing the respondents' risk assessment procedure (or combination procedure) they were not told what the test actually was about. They were only told that the aim was to investigate how risk perceptions vary between people and why they vary.

2.4. Validity and reliability measurement

In the study, the items on cognitive style had a Cronbach's alpha of 0.810 and the items on security expertise had a Cronbach's alpha of 0.962, i.e., they were highly internally consistent. As expected, the five participants who belonged to the information security research group considered themselves to have high security expertise while the other five participants evaluated themselves much lower (means 4.533 compared to 1.733 on the scale 1-5).

The repeated questions of the second survey showed 8 participants to be highly reliable with Pearson correlations larger than 0.767 ($p<0.001$), whereas the reliability of two participants was statistically non-significant. Thus, the tests and retests suggests that all but two respondents reasoned about incidents in a similar way when answering questions on probability and consequence and questions about risk. Furthermore, the two measures for risk used in the second questionnaire were highly internally consistent with an overall standardized Cronbach's alpha of 0.776, with the figure for each respondent being above 0.7, i.e., showing sufficient consistency for all respondents.

3. Results

The risk equation used by the respondents is inferred within-subjects and presented in section 3.1, which presents the test of H1. As will be seen, the results of this test made it difficult to test H2-H4. Section 3.2 describes this further.

3.1. The risk equation

As by Weinstein (2000), the hypothesis is tested by modeling the relationship between answers in the first questionnaire (on probability and severity) as predictor variables for answers in the second questionnaire (on priority and insurance premium) in a linear regression model. Table provides the figures of the regression models for risk as priority (upper half of the table) and risk as insurance premium (lower half of the table). $R^2(S, P)$ is the coefficient of determination for the linear (non-interaction) model, indicating the fit of that model. $\Delta R^2(SxP)$ describes how much the fit improves when considering an interaction model (multiplicative term). Four rows (p) indicate the significance (*) or non-significance (ns) of R^2, the severity (S), the probability (P) and ΔR^2, respectively.

As the table shows, few of the respondents show a tendency to multiply probability and severity to obtain the remediation priority or the insurance fee, and thus there is little support for H1. Considering the priority, the interaction-term is significant for three of the respondents; considering the insurance premium, the interaction-term is significant for two of the respondents. Furthermore, the contribution of the interaction term is small in the regression models for all respondents. At most, the interaction term adds 0.096 (statistically non-significant) explained variance to a regression model which explains 0.193 of the variance (participant #5) and 0.082 (statistically significant) of explained variance to a model which explains 0.453 of the variance (participant #8). Overall, the mean additional variance obtained by introducing the interaction term is 0.015 for priority and 0.024 for insurance premium. This should be related to an additive model, which explains 0.540 and 0.384 of the variance.

Participant	1	2	3	4	5	6	7	8	9	10	Mean
R^2(S, P)	0.381	0.683	0.493	0.545	0.352	0.724	0.544	0.540	0.434	0.544	0.540
pR^2	*	*	*	*	*	*	*	*	*	*	
pS	*	*	*	*	*	*	*	*	*	*	
pP	ns	ns	*	*	ns	ns	*	ns	ns	*	
ΔR^2(SxP)	0.003	0.018	0.008	0.015	0.000	0.014	0.009	0.072	0.000	0.008	0.015
$p\Delta R^2$	ns	*	ns	ns	ns	*	ns	*	ns	ns	
R^2(S, P)	0.108	0.464	0.505	0.357	0.193	0.657	0.406	0.453	0.281	0.415	0.384
pR^2	*	*	*	*	*	*	*	*	*	*	
pS	ns	*	*	*	*	*	*	*	*	*	
pP	ns	ns	ns	ns	ns	ns	*	*	*	*	
ΔR^2(SxP)	0.000	0.013	0.007	0.014	0.096	0.003	0.004	0.082	0.024	0.001	0.024
$p\Delta R^2$	ns	ns	ns	ns	ns	*	ns	*	ns	ns	

(Row groups labelled "Risk as priority" (upper) and "Risk as insurance premium" (lower).)

Table 1: Regression analyses with linear and interaction models

It should be added that the insignificance of the multiplicative term is not because the additive terms are present. The mean variance in risk (priority) explained by a model with only the multiplicative term is 0.049, and it is only statistically significant for the three respondents (as it was with the additive terms in the model). Furthermore, it is worth noting that these results hold within all quadrants of the probability-severity-spectrum, i.e. for high/low, low/high or low/low probability and severity.

3.2. Variables related to the tendency to multiply

There were no statistically significant correlations between expertise and either risk as priority or risk as insurance. Nor were there any statistically significant correlations between cognitive style and either risk as priority or risk as insurance. However, as described above, there was no general tendency to multiply probability and consequence in the studied population. As a consequence, identifying variables that relate to this tendency (i.e., H2-H4) is doomed to fail.

4. Discussion and Conclusions

Most of the respondents seem to have an idea of probabilities and severities associated with information security incidents. For eight out of ten respondents, the responses provided at different weeks had very strong correlations (>0.75). This idea is also, to some extent, shared among the respondents. Between-subjects correlations are above 0.50 for both probabilities and severities. Thus, their responses seem to stem from some partially shared perception of the information security threats. This suggests that the survey is able to measure the perceptions it set out to measure. Nevertheless, there are many possible reasons for the fact that our result – in contrast to Weinstein (2000) – does not support a multiplicative relationship between severity and probability in people's minds when calculating risk. The results indicate that information security risk assessments are determined by the severity.

Similarly to Weinstein we used a limited sample non-random sample. Our participants were more homogenous in terms of profession and slightly more homogenous in terms of age and gender than the sample of Weinstein. Any of these factors may explain the focus on incident severity and the insignificance of the multiplicative terms in this test. However, it is unclear to the authors why they should. On the contrary, it is hard to see how and why a population of researchers, of which many had considerable risk assessment experience, should be unable or unwilling see risk as a product of probability and severity.

The scales and measurement procedure used in this test is different from the ones used by Weinstein (2000) in several ways. First, Weinstein's first survey concerned (compound) risk where he let half of the participants prioritise the incidents and the other half estimate the insurance premiums. We instead measured (compound) risk in the second survey, with probability and severity in the first. This may have caused our participants to be more prone to thinking of risk as a product of probability and severity, so this is not an issue considering our results. Second, we let all the participants rate risk both by priority and insurance premium. This made it possible to verify that the two measurements correlated strongly and it is hard to see why this will remove the tendency to multiply probability and severity. Third, we measured priority with the slightly different phrasing "stop the incidents from happening or render them harmless if they do". While this phrasing is different form Weinstein's ("If you purchase insurance against a particular problem, you are guaranteed that it will never happen to you"), it is unclear to us why this would remove the tendency to multiply. Fourth, it is possible that it was harder for our participants to reason in terms of monetary loss for an organization rather than hundreds of dollars for a personal insurance premium. However, as risk as priority and risk as insurance premium correlated, it is hard to see this as a possible reasons for the insignificant multiplicative term. Also, there were no substantial differences between those of our respondents used monetary risk and relative risk, so difficulties understanding scales is unlikely to be an issue. Fifth, we further imposed restrictions on risk as priority and severity, with both max values defined by the "worst" among our incidents for risk and severity respectively. But this would only lead to our measurements being off by a (scale-converting) constant, which is no problem in regression models.

Perhaps the most important difference between our study and Weinstein's (2000) study – and indeed between information security and health – are the topics of the incidents. In our case, the incidents relate to the participants' organisation rather than the participants themselves and our incidents are less well-known than say pneumonia or rash from poison ivy. Weinstein partly based his incidents on a standard compendium of diseases, while we constructed our own. This may have led to incidents that were more difficult to interpret with greater variance between subjects. However, our results suggest that the respondents' assessments agreed and the performed test-retests suggest that most respondents understood the questions well enough to answer them similarly. Thus, the scenarios were clearly comprehendible. Also, the answers for each respondent showed no more absolute correlation between probability and severity than those Weinstein reported (-0.56). This correlation should be expected to be negative, as few incidents have high values for both probability and severity.

Another significant difference to Weinstein's (2000) survey is probabilities were (implicitly) restricted in that incidents should happen in the respondents' remaining lifetime. For an organisation, there is no natural upper time limit so to avoid infinite possibilities. We used a ten year limitation, and we do not anticipate any issues with our results due to this.

In conclusion, it is doubtful that information security experts are any better at risk assessments than novices, at least concerning the combination of severity and probability to form risk. For this reason, it is straightforward to recommend appropriate risk matrices which force the assessor to adhere to the established definition of risk as the mathematical product of probability and severity.

5. Acknowledgements

The authors would like to thank Neil Weinstein for his thoughts on why the multiplicative relationship is hard to detect.

This research was funded by the Swedish Civil Contingencies Agency.

6. References

Allinson, C. W., & Hayes, J. (1996). The Cognitive Style Index: A Measure of Intuition-Analysis For Organizational Research. *Journal of Management Studies*, *33*(1), 119–135.

Cismaru, M., & Lavack, a. M. (2007). Interaction effects and combinatorial rules governing Protection Motivation Theory variables: a new model. *Marketing Theory*, *7*(3), 249–270.

Club de la Sécurité de l'Information Français. (2011). MEHARI 2010 Processing guide for risk analysis and management. Paris: Club de la Sécurité de l'Information Français.

Das, E. H. H. J., de Wit, J. B. F., & Stroebe, W. (2003). Fear appeals motivate acceptance of action recommendations: evidence for a positive bias in the processing of persuasive messages. *Personality & Social Psychology Bulletin*, *29*(5), 650–64.

Karabacak, B., & Sogukpinar, I. (2005). ISRAM: information security risk analysis method. *Computers & Security*, *24*(2), 147–159.

Lund, M. S., Solhaug, B., & Stolen, K. (2011). *Model-driven risk analysis: the CORAS approach. Media*. Springer Verlag.

Maddux, J. E., & Rogers, R. W. (1983). Protection motivation and self-efficacy: A revised theory of fear appeals and attitude change. *Journal of Experimental Social Psychology*, *19*(5), 469–479.

McShane, S. L. (2006). Activity 8.8: Decision Making Style Inventory. In *Canadian Organizational Behaviour* (Sixth edit.). McGraw-Hill Education. Retrieved from http://highered.mheducation.com/sites/0070876940/student_view0/chapter8/activity_8_8.html

NIST. (2012). NIST Special Publication 800-30 Revision 1 Guide for Conducting Risk Assessments. Gaithersburg, USA: NIST.

Pechmann, C., Zhao, G., Goldberg, M. E., & Reibling, E. T. (2003). What to Convey in Antismoking Advertisements for Adolescents:The Use of Protection Motivation Theory to Identify Effective Message Themes. *Journal of Marketing*, *67*(2), 1–18.

Posey, C., Roberts, T., Lowry, P. B., Courtney, J., & Bennett, R. J. (2011). Motivating the insider to protect organizational information assets: Evidence from protection motivation theory and rival explanations. In *Proceedings of the Dewald Roode Workshop in Information Systems Security 2011* (pp. 1–51). Blacksburg, Virginia, September 22–23, pp.: IFIP WG 8.11 / 11.13.

Rogers, R. W. (1983). Cognitive and physiological processes in fear appeals and attitude change: A revised theory of protection motivation. In J. Cacioppo & R. Petty (Eds.), *Social Psychophysiology*. New York, New York, USA: Guilford Press.

Scott, S. G., & Bruce, R. A. (1995). Decision-Making Style: The Development and Assessment of a New Measure. *Educational and Psychological Measurement*, *55*(5), 818–831.

Weinstein, N. D. (2000). Perceived probability, perceived severity, and health-protective behavior. *Health Psychology : Official Journal of the Division of Health Psychology, American Psychological Association*, *19*(1), 65–74.

Understanding User Knowledge of Computer Security and Risk: A Comparative Study

C. Thurlby, C. Langensiepen, J. Haggerty and R. Ranson

School of Science and Technology, Nottingham Trent University, Clifton Campus, Clifton Lane, Nottingham, NG11 8NS, United Kingdom
e-mail: criag.thurlby@ntu.ac.uk

Abstract

Academic institutions have to cope with thousands of new students every year, with a wide range of knowledge of computer security. This can potentially lead to many breaches, with resultant impact on availability and cost to fix. In this paper we report on a survey of a group of new first year undergraduate students. Their replies show that 18 year olds use computers very heavily, but their understanding of what computer security means can range from the sophisticated to the worrying. In addition, their emphasis is often on their personal security and privacy within social media rather than any impact on the machines they use at university. We discuss their responses in detail and make some recommendations regarding further analysis.

Keywords

Risk, Computer Security, Security Education

1. Introduction

The Verizon 2015 breach investigations report states that 61 educational institutions who replied to the survey suffered 165 security incidents with 80% of threats coming from external actors. The results demonstrate that all organisations and institutions are vulnerable to malicious attacks and should not ignore strengthening their network and employees.

The purpose of this study is to gain an understanding of how individual students perceive risk by analysing their level of knowledge when related to computer use to better understand how knowledgeable the individual is when introduced into an institution's environment. This forms part of a larger study into behavioural profiling of university students and will eventually be combined with various network data to enable a fuller picture of user network behaviour. It is important to gain both security knowledge and attitude from the students to better understand why certain breaches are more prevalent than others and how this could potentially contribute to problems for the IT department within the University. The questionnaire will build the foundation to better understand the student and ultimately educate the student by grouping these findings into appropriate classifications of security training.

To start with a clean slate, the respondents of the survey conducted were first year undergraduate students attending their university inductions. This selection of students were chosen because of their limited knowledge of the university's IT systems which ensured the capture of a more neutral and balanced set of results. This selection also assumes that they have a more casual approach to the way they work; another reason why they were chosen.

This paper is organized as follows. Section 2 discusses related work. Section 3 presents the methodology used for the comparative survey. Section 4 presents the results of the survey. Finally, we make our conclusions and discuss further work.

2. Related Work

Security education needs to address the organisation as well as the individual within it. Tsohou et al (2013) comments on how security awareness research has mostly focused on the individual or organisation level with limited studies examining both. The inclusion of institutional IT changes would deliver a more relevant training plan to the end user due to having exposure to changes of the organisation's infrastructure.

Within any organisation employees demonstrate different behaviours and attitudes to their roles and Parsons et al (2014) suggest the production of an empirically validated instrument (HAIS-Q). This tool could be used to measure employee knowledge, attitude, and behaviour to provide management with a benchmark. The need to combine both the understanding and benchmarking of all employee attitudes and behaviours is an important factor to enable the profiling of an employee knowledge base. This would provide direct education that complements the employee knowledge. Szilagyi et al (1990) state that the group, made up of individuals, develops unique characteristics beyond those of the person and his personal contributions. Groups need to be examined independently and not just as the individuals that comprise them.

The study by Bulgurcu et al (2010) suggests that employees who use the information and technology resources of their organisations assume certain roles and are responsible for safeguarding those resources. Within an educational environment consisting of employees and students both parties need to be educated to enable responsibility for the resources that are used. Siponen et al (1990) suggests trying to understand the different ways people respond to different methods and actions used to increase information security awareness.

It is important that all users within an institution are engaged when an Information Security induction is performed to avoid a malicious attack on the organisation or the user. Shropshire et al (2015) state that the greatest threat to information security lies not behind the security perimeter, but rather with the careless or malicious actions of internal users. Tampoe et al (1993) suggest that it would be wrong to assume that users were all interested in the same motivators or that their preferences met the generalized model.

Within the educational context, knowledge-sharing plays a pivotal part of an employee's education and Tagliaventi et al (2006) defines networks of practice that are sets of individuals who share common values and ways of doing things; that is, practices and knowledge sharing through subject matter. The ability to search for a common motivator between students would be of great benefit by forming grouping of individuals from the analysis of common subject areas, thus enabling the sharing of knowledge long after an information security induction has occurred.

For the implementation of a successful information security awareness programme it is imperative that the employees' education is effective and informs all of the employees. Thomson et al (1998) states that the technical development of the computer and associated disciplines has played a large part in the profile and involvement of the user with Harris et al (1999) suggesting that successful end-user computing is therefore dependant on the behaviour of individual end users.

User behaviour dictates the attitude towards end-user computing within the organisation with Pahnila et al (2007) suggesting that attitude, normative beliefs and habits have significant effect on intention to comply with IS security policies and Dhillon et al (2001) indicating that informal controls, perhaps the most cost-effective type of controls, essentially centre around increasing awareness of employees.

In the next section, we present the methodology of a survey of undergraduate students to discover the attitudes towards risk and understanding of computer security.

3. Survey Methodology

To deliver a varied set of results, a questionnaire containing 14 questions targeted a mixed cohort of 97 students who would be attending a range of courses, e.g. Computing, Social Sciences, Psychology and Education. All participants completed a questionnaire that related to their own and observed perception of risk when using computers. The survey sets out to answer what risk means to the individual student, their knowledge of computer related risk and their daily exposure to computer usage.

The survey received 97 responses of mixed gender and all were first year undergraduate students with a varied set of subject knowledge. This research criteria was intentionally chosen to enable a more balanced set of results. The 14 questions were graded by a point scale system of 1 to 3.

When grading the answers for all questions within this paper, an independent examination will be carried out to prevent any preconceptions of the individual's knowledge and academic course. Not all questions contained in the questionnaire have been included for this paper; only the questions that relate to risk and computer usage were chosen to deliver a more directed set of results for the benefit of this paper.

4. Survey Results

The following subsections present and discuss the participants' answers that focus on Computer Security and Risk. The questionnaire required the student to answer 14 questions related to their use of computers and perception of computer risk.

The first question selected for study is: "Briefly explain what you are studying at university". Although not directly related to the question of risk it is of vital importance that an understanding of an individual student's background when related to the use of computers.

A total of 38% of the students who answered the questionnaire were studying an academic subject that did not directly involve the use of computers as their core study area. These subjects included: Psychology, Forensic Science, Education, Criminology and Surveying. The remaining 59% represented those students who have a direct interaction with an academic computing subject area that included subjects: Computer Science, Software Engineering and Computer Systems. Further study of the results demonstrated that the 38% of students from non-computing subjects was more weighted with female participants compared to the 68% that held more male responses.

What part have computers played in your life up to now?

This question provided an insight into the individual student's personal experience of computer use.

Played a little part in my life	3%
Played a general part in my life	30%
Played a big part in my life	63%

Table 1: Personal Experience of Computer Use

Analysis of table 1 shows a higher percentage of students where computers have played a major part in their everyday life compared to only 3% who have limited interaction. For the non-computing group, the following comments were recorded:

"very big part. Socially (Facebook, Twitter, tumblr), for entertainment (YouTube, Netflix)"

"major part, use computer everyday, so do my children"

"a significant part, for both social and educational purposes".

The first question represented 38% of students who were studying a non- computing subject and involved modules that were less computer-intensive. However from the examination of table 1, the results present the opposite when taking into account that

30% of individuals have a general daily interaction with computers and 63% have a lot of interaction from the combined groups.

From the observation for non-computing students, 38% agreed that computers played a major part with a recurring answer that related to the use of social media and 13% having a general usage commenting on the usage of social media and delivering an overall total of 51%.

The result for the computing group showed 68% were of high usage and 51% were of general usage. Responses were:

"I have been using computers since I was 4, for gaming, learning and literally everything"

"a massive part, I use them everyday they are my passion, I love them and enjoy using them".

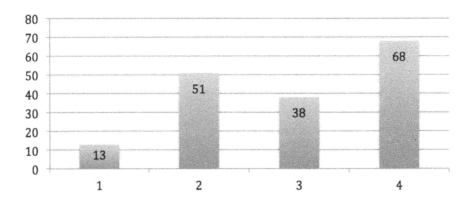

Figure 1: Computer Usage Amongst the Participants

The study of these results shows that all students with a non-computing background have more exposure to computers than was first assumed. From the analysis of the computing group's results, a combined total of only 23% of students with high and general use mentioned social media and a combined total of 75% of the responses for high and general referring to computer related activities.

Study of the results has showed that the non-computing group may still be susceptible to a malicious attack in the guise of a phishing attack due to their regular usage of social media applications for communication compared to the computing group whose answers are directed to the use of computing in relation to programming, gaming, 3D modelling and the building of computers. Also of interest is the split between genders where the majority of female students mentioned the use of social media compared to the more technical side from the computing group. Also of note is the amount of exposure both groups have and the definite separation of how computers are used in the conventional way with the first group having large amounts of exposure from the use of social media.

What does computer security mean to you?

This was asked to form an understanding of the individual student's perception of Computer Security in relation to their everyday life. This was a 3-point scale ranging from 'a little knowledge' to 'a lot' with all answers being examined independently.

Have little knowledge	22%
Have a general knowledge	46%
Have a lot of knowledge	32%

Table 2: Perception of Computer Security

The study of table 2 shows 22% of individuals had a limited knowledge of computer security with 46% having a general understanding and 32% demonstrating a lot of knowledge. Dividing the results into their relevant groups, 21% of the non-computing individuals showed a lack of knowledge, 51% had a general knowledge and 22% a lot of knowledge. The 46% of students commented:

"I take my computer security very seriously as I bank online and purchase products regularly"

"after getting a few (like 50) viruses on my laptop. It is the most important thing when downloading items online"

"making sure that all my private information is safe and secure. Also that by having security ensures I don't get any viruses".

The computing group who claimed a general knowledge delivered similar comments:

"not getting viruses and your information being private"

"staying safe when using computers, like dodging viruses and keeping data secure and safe".

Those who claimed more knowledge showed this in their answers – for example:

"Privacy, knowing that I am the only one who can access/view/modify my work. Security, preventing unauthorised access which could lead to a breach of privacy"

"To ensure a computer or system is secure from both malicious and accidental attacks, whether it be physical or cyber-based".

The responses for the more knowledge group demonstrated an understanding of threats that occur both internally and externally and dominated by the computing group compared with the non-computing group's responses that presented a more insular view on computer security with concerns relating to their personal computers and private work. The comparison between the two groups demonstrate a definite split between the perception of computer security with a more secure rounded approach coming from the computing group due to the inclusion of external threats. The study of the non- computing comments demonstrated a high response related to the protection from viruses, demonstrating knowledge of personal protection but no responses related to external threats. This is by no means a negative aspect as both groups showed a good grasp of computer security. Again analysing both of the groups' responses to determine which group could be more vulnerable to a malicious attack, the non-computing group, based on responses, would be the most at risk due to the insular nature of their responses.

What risk have you taken when using computers and would you take the same risk now?

From the results of the previous questions the assumption is that the non-computing group will focus more on the internal experience compared to the computing group who will understand both internal and external risk. A 3-point scale was used from 'no risk' to 'high risk' and all answers being examined independently.

No Risk	27%
General level of Risk	30%
High level of risk	41%

Table 3: Participants risk appetite

From the study of the table findings there is a fairly even spread of students who take no risk to students that are classed as taking a general risk with only 3% difference. The separation of results into the two respective groups showed a shared percentage for all three scales for non-computing at 33% with answers to for medium risk consisting of:

"posting pictures online and details of holidays, and no I wouldn't"

"used to use the same password which was very obvious. And I would never take that risk again"

Comments for the high risk group stating that:

"I have used computers when they still had a virus. I wouldn't do it again as I ended up loosing all my photos"

"downloaded fake updates that put viruses on my PC. No don't download much now."

The results of the 32% of the computing group answers for medium risk consisted of:

"using computers in public without protecting my passwords or data. No I wouldn't do it again"

"Downloading from untrusted websites, and no."

Non-computing students concentrated on the downloading of files or leaving their accounts logged on which is in total contrast to the computing groups focus, directed at using open networks, having their personal data stored on shared computers and accessing untrusted websites which demonstrates the understanding of what an external threat is.

For the Computing students answers for high risk, 54% fell into this category and responses to the question consisted of:

"downloaded unsafe software, torrenting"

"Sourcing unsafe software. No I would not take that risk again" "downloading software from dodgy websites. Most likely not."

From the study of these results, it is evident that the majority of the computing group have a good understanding of the risk that they have taken with the majority of answers involving the downloading of software from non-reliable sources and descriptions of methods and sites they have used and visited. Although the risk and consequence of this activity is understood the individuals still decide to carry out the activity. If compared with the non-computing group, the risk, acknowledgement and avoidance have been acknowledged. The study of both groups demonstrates that the non-computing delivers the less risk due to the internal nature of responses that were provided, again the risk is related to the student's personal work and PC. The computing group understands the risk they are taking which could increase the chances of a malicious attack due to their knowledge of external entities.

5. Conclusions and further work

From the study of the questionnaire on risk and computer security, it can be observed that there is a need to adapt the way that computer security education is delivered to users. Tracing through the questions that were asked and answered, there is a definite split on the way that students perceive computer security.

From the analysis of the answers it establishes the way that different interpretations of usage and risk are perceived. The analysis of question 2 "What part have computers played in your life up to now" demonstrates the perception of usage between the two groups of students with one being the usage of social media and the other with usage of computer based software. The author has discovered that the perception of what computer use represents is no longer the traditional view of sitting at a computer producing work; it also associated with the use of social media. Both sets of groups have good exposure to computers but from completely different sides of how IT is used.

The study of question 3 "What does computer security mean to you?" demonstrates the different perceptions that both groups deliver with the non-computing group presenting an internal perception and the computing group presenting the internal and external perception. From the study of this question, it is evident that the first group is more focused on their personal work within the internal environment. The comment of viruses and anti-virus software were mentioned throughout the non-computing group's answers but do the group understand what a virus is or how it is propagated compared to group 2 who included external influences in their responses. In the second phase of research work will be performed to discover how much knowledge of external threats the students truly understand to enable a fuller understanding of student security knowledge.

The initial assumptions until question 4 were that the non-computing students would be the biggest threat from a malicious attack to the institution until the responses from "What risk have you taken when using computers and would you take the same risk now?" The students within group 2 identified the risk and also understood the risk that was being taken which when compared to the responses of the computing group was more reckless in relation to the non-computing group due to the level of knowledge that these students hold.

The results from this questionnaire have highlighted that further work is needed within the field of information security training. From the analysis of four questions, the research has highlighted the levels of knowledge that exists between users and more importantly the groupings of users. Observation of the collected data has highlighted a definite trend when related to knowledge and usage between different groupings of students and the importance of further study in this area. When designing an effective training plan, the classification of groups with the same background and knowledge base could minimize the need to address individual users with targeted training by developing separate computer security groups to ensure full engagement and understanding of the security information that is being delivered.

Also of importance is the student interpretation of risk along with the acceptance of computer risk. The study of the results showed those students who had a greater knowledge of computers were more likely to take the bigger risks that could potentially cause greater issues to the organisation's IT systems. Further studies will be carried out on how confident students are when using computers and if this confidence can influence the student into taking greater risks.

The next stage of the research is to investigate the students' perception of risk further, with more work on the influence of their peers attitudes and actions towards risk, along with the study into their knowledge of external threats and understanding of how this could have an effect on an organisation's IT system. These new questions combined with the present set would enable a fuller student profile to be developed that would assist in developing a relevant security training programme for new students.

6. References

Bulgurcu, B., Cavusoglu, H., & Benbasat, I. (2010). Information Security Policy Compliance: An Empiracal Study of Rationality-Based Beliefs and Information Security Awareness. MIS Quarterly, 34(3), 523–548

Dhillon, G., & Moores, S. (2001). Computer crimes: Theorizing about the enemy within. Computers and Security, 20(8), 715–723.

Harris, R. W. (1999). Attitudes towards end-user computing: A structural equation model. Behaviour & Information Technology, 18(2), 109–125.

Pahnila, S., Siponen, M., Mahmood, A., Box, P. O., Oulun, F.-, & Siponen, E. M. (2007). Employees ' Behavior towards IS Security Policy Compliance University of Oulu , Department of Information Processing. October, 1–10.

Parsons, K., McCormac, A., Butavicius, M., Pattinson, M., & Jerram, C. (2014). Determining employee awareness using the Human Aspects of Information Security Questionnaire (HAIS-Q). Computers and Security, 42, 165–176.

Shropshire, J., Warkentin, M., & Sharma, S. (2015). Personality, attitudes, and intentions: Predicting initial adoption of information security behavior. Computers & Security, 49, 177–191.

Siponen, M. T. (1991). A conceptual foundation for organizational information security awareness. Information Management & Computer Security, (Table I), 31–41.

Szilagyi AD, Wallace MJ. Organizational behavior and performance. 5th ed. Illinois: Scott, Foresman and Company; 1990.

Tagliaventi, M. R. (2006). The role of networks of practice, value sharing, and operational proximity in knowledge flows between professional groups. Human Relations, 59(3), 291–319.

Tampoe, M. (1993). Motivating knowledge workers—The challenge for the 1990s. Long Range Planning, 26(3), 49–55. doi:10.1016/0024-6301(93)90006-2

Thomson , M. E., & Solms , R. Von . (1998). Information security awareness: educating your users effectively. Information Management & Computer Security, 6(4), 167–173.

Tsohou, A., Karyda, M., Kokolakis, S., & Kiountouzis, E. (2013). Managing the introduction of information security awareness programmes in organisations. European Journal of Information Systems, 24(1), 38–58.

Verizon Business. (2014).2014 Data Breach Investigations Report. Verizon Business Journal, 2014(1), 1–60.

Tracking Risky Behavior On The Web: Distinguishing Between What Users 'Say' And 'Do'

T. Kelley and B. I. Bertenthal

Developmental Cognitive Neuroscience Laboratory
Department of Psychology and Brain Sciences, Indiana University, Bloomington
Indiana, United States of America
e-mail: kelleyt@indiana.edu

Abstract

Modern browsers are designed to inform users as to whether or not it is secure to login to a website, but most users are not aware of this information and even those that are sometimes ignore it. The goal of this research is to assess users' knowledge of security warnings communicated via browser indicators (e.g., https, lock icon in the status bar), and the likelihood that their online decision making adheres to this knowledge. A large sample of participants was recruited from Amazon's Mechanical Turk and their knowledge of cybersecurity was assessed with an online survey. These participants were also instructed to visit a series of secure and insecure websites, and decide as quickly and as accurately as possible whether or not it was safe to login. The results revealed that knowledge of cybersecurity was not necessarily a good predictor of decisions regarding whether or not to sign-in to a website. Moreover, these decisions were modulated by attention to security indicators, familiarity of the website, and psychosocial stress induced by bonus payments determined by response times and accuracy. We suggest that even individuals with security knowledge are unable to draw the necessary conclusions about digital risks while browsing the web. Users are being educated through daily use to ignore recommended security indicators and we surmise that the lack of conformity in website conventions contributes to this behavior.

Keywords

Information security, browser login, security expertise, Mechanical Turk, experiment

1. Introduction

Users on the Internet are regularly confronted with complex security decisions that can affect their privacy. They must decide whether it is safe to enter their username, password, credit card details, and other personal information on websites with very different interfaces and only a few visual clues on whether it is safe to do so. These security indicators include the protocol used, the domain name, the SSL/TLS certificate, and visual elements in the browser window. Very few users understand the technical details of these various indicators.

Not surprisingly, users often get it wrong, either ignoring security indicators completely or misunderstanding them. Many popular websites' are designed in such a way that these indicators are displayed in a suboptimal way, further complicating users' decision making process (Stebila 2010). Moreover, these websites can appear confusing, because they include no or only partial encryption, but users will treat them as secure even without security indicators if they have been previously visited (Hazim *et al.* 2014). This confusion is due to the manner in which security information is typically deployed, i.e., as communication between technical experts (Garg and Camp 2012).

While several studies have evaluated whether users correctly use security indicators, there has been very little work investigating whether their knowledge of these indicators will predict their behavior (Schechter *et al.* 2007). One reason for this predicament is that it is challenging to design behavioral studies that will realistically simulate the conditions that a user would experience on the Internet (Arianezhad *et al.* 2013).

One real-world condition that is particularly difficult to replicate in an experimental environment is the experience of risk. Many studies ask participants to assume the role of someone else to avoid exposing participants to real risks (Schechter *et al.* 2007, Sunshine *et al.* 2009). Other studies use priming—alerting participants to the fact the study is interested in behaviour related to security—to induce secure-like behaviour (Whalen and Inkpen 2005). It is unlikely, however, that participants playing roles behave as securely as they would when they are personally at risk.

A different strategy is to use monetary incentives and penalties as a method for creating risky decisions. We utilize participants' assumed goal of maximizing payment to put pressure on the participant to act as quickly as possible by offering participants a bonus payment that decreases as the total elapsed time increases.

2. Methodology

By introducing a performance bonus based on both speed and accuracy in completing the task (Figure 1), we sought to increase the motivation and risk taking behaviour of participants (Petzold *et al.* 2010). Our primary question was whether users would ignore or simply miss security indicators when pressed for time. In order to address this question, we wanted a relatively large sample with a broad distribution of knowledge concerning security indicators.

Screen Clock

Figure 1: Screenshot of top of experimental task instructions. Note the presence of the sample clock resting on top of the simulated browser chrome

2.1. Participants

The sample consisted of 173 participants ranging in age from 18- to 76-years-old *(M = 32.6, SD = 9.58)* recruited from Amazon's Mechanical Turk (AMT). Studies have shown that AMT provides more diverse study populations and robust findings in numerous psychological paradigms (Buhrmester *et al.* 2011, Crump *et al.* 2013). There were 100 males and 73 females, primarily Caucasian. Most participants listed Firefox *(N = 84)* or Google Chrome *(N = 81)* as their primary browser.

2.2. Stimuli

Each trial simulated websites appearing on a Firefox browser. In order to standardize all websites, logins always appeared on the second page of the website. All websites were manipulated in a graphical editing program and presented to participants in a popup window with disabled user interface chrome to minimize confusion between the proxy websites' chrome and their actual browser chrome. This also prevented participants from manipulating the experiment by reloading pages or navigating back and forward outside of our simulated website user interface.

2.3. Procedure

Participants were instructed to decide whether or not to login to a series of websites depending on whether or not they were judged to be secure. The goal was to visit all the websites as quickly as possible, and the pay for completing this task was contingent on how quickly it was completed. If a participant clicked to login to a secure website, the screen advanced to the next one. If a participant did not click to login to a secure website and instead pressed the back button, a penalty screen was displayed for 20 sec and that time was added to their cumulative time. If a participant pressed the back button and the website was insecure, the screen advanced to the next website. If, however, a participant clicked to login to an insecure website, the penalty screen was displayed for 10 sec and that time was added to their cumulative time.

An online survey assessing participants' knowledge concerning security indicators was administered after the experimental task so as not to bias participants' performance. There were three categories of questions: 1) Demographic information (e.g., age, gender, education level), 2) Applied security knowledge (e.g., security indicators, password behaviour), and 3) Technical security knowledge (e.g., DDoS, Phishing, Firewalls).

2.4. Design

This study addressed two questions: 1) Do web security indicators affect participants' behaviour when discerning the safety of encrypted vs. unencrypted websites, and 2) Do web security indicators affect participants' ability to discern between spoofed vs. not spoofed websites. The first question was tested by manipulating whether the security indicators included http or https (https/http manipulation). The second question was tested by manipulating whether or not the website was spoofed with an incorrect domain name (no-spoof/spoof manipulation). There are four different levels of encryption information displayed by web security indicators:

1. Extended Validation (EV) – green lock and https – full encryption; Extended vetting by certificate authority
2. Full Encryption (FE) – grey lock and https – full encryption; domain validation only
3. Partial Encryption (PE) – triangle with exclamation mark; some (unknown) elements of website encrypted
4. No Encryption (NE) – globe; no encryption of the displayed page

For the spoof manipulation we included all four levels for both spoof and no-spoof websites, but this was not possible for the https/http manipulation because unencrypted websites (http) only display a globe (NE), whereas the encrypted websites (https) display the three other security symbols listed above (1-3). Thus the https/http and no-spoof/spoof manipulations were analysed separately in this study.

Each participant was presented with 16 trials, 8 corresponding to each security manipulation condition (https/http vs. no spoof/spoof). Four trials corresponded to secure websites (https/no spoof) and 4 corresponded to insecure websites (http/spoof). For the https/http manipulation, each secure website included 1 of the 3 valid levels of encryption information (EV, FE, or PE), whereas each insecure website included only the NE indicator. For the spoof/no spoof manipulation, the 4 secure and 4 insecure trials each corresponded to one of the 4 encryption information levels. The secure and insecure websites were counterbalanced between participants and the presentation order of the websites was randomized.

2.5. Metrics and Data Reduction

Applied security knowledge was computed from the number of correct and incorrect security indicators identified in the survey $(\# \ correct \ indicators + 1)/(\# \ incorrect \ indicators + 1)$ resulting in an indicator score ranging from [0.2, 4.0], with a log-normal distribution $\ln N(M - 0.14, SD = 0.58)$.

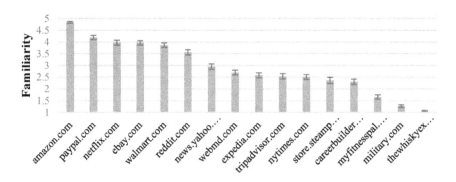

Figure 2: Mean familiarity for each website used in our study

Technical security knowledge was scored from 1 to 5 depending on the number of survey questions answered correctly (0%-20%=1, 21%-40%=2.....). Participants scoring greater than 60% ($N = 50$) were identified as "High Technical Security Knowledge" (Hi-Knowledge) and participants scoring 60% or less ($N = 123$) were identified as "Low Technical Security Knowledge" (Lo-Knowledge).

Familiarity of the websites was rated on a 5-point Likert scale. The mean rating was 2.90, and it ranged from a low of 1.00 to a high of 5.00 (Figure 2).

3. Results

The primary question concerned how frequently participants would login to insecure websites. Overall, they were more accurate responding to encrypted than to unencrypted websites (*Mdiff* = 0.55, *95% HDI* = 0.45, 0.69) and to non-spoofed than to spoofed websites (*Mdiff* = 0.46, *95% HDI* = 0.37, 0.57). Critically, the results revealed a strong response bias to login regardless of available security indicators (Figure 3). Participants' lack of sensitivity to the available stimuli was reflected in the relatively low d' in both the https/http manipulation ($M = 0.41$, $SD = 0.66$) and the no spoof/spoof manipulation (M = 0.34, SD = 0.67).

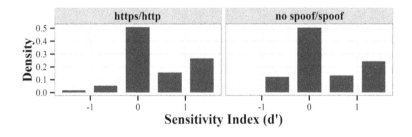

Figure 3: Participants' response bias towards login

Participants performance on the http/https websites was analysed by assessing the percent of accurate logins as a function of technical security knowledge (lo vs. hi) and security manipulation (http vs. https). A 2 x 2 repeated measures analysis of variance (ANOVA) revealed significant main effects for both security manipulation $(F(1,1368) = 382.5, p < 0.001$ and technical security knowledge , $F(1,1368) = 3.88, p < 0.05$. As can be seen in Figure there was also a significant interaction between manipulation and technical security knowledge $F(1,1368) = 6.94, p < 0.01$, because participants with high knowledge were more accurate than those with low knowledge in the https condition *(Mdiff = 0.12, 95% CI = 0.02, 0.21, p < 0.01)*, but technical security knowledge had no effect in the http condition *(Mdiff = -0.02, 95% CI = -0.11, 0.08, p > 0.96)*.

In a separate analysis of encryption information in the https condition, encryption was found to have a main effect $F(1,676) = 19.56, p < 0.001$, but was not involved in any interactions. As can be seen in Figure 4, participants were more accurate in the lock than the no lock encryption condition, The presence of encryption information (FE and EV) led participants to be more accurate *(Mdiff = 0.12, 95% CI = 0.06, 0.18, p < 0.001)*, as seen in Figure .

Participants' performance on the no spoof/spoof websites was analysed similarly, but included level of encryption information as a third independent variable. An ANOVA revealed a main effect for manipulation (no spoof vs. spoof), $F(1,1352) = 342.42, p < 0.001$ and technical security knowledge (Hi vs. Lo) $F(1,1352) = 41.28, p < 0.001$, but not encryption information, $F(3,1352) = 0.79, p > 0.37$. Encryption information, however, did interact with security manipulation $F(1,1352) = 36.78, p < 0.00$, and there was also an interaction between security manipulation and technical security knowledge, $F(1,1352) = 12.89, p < 0.001$.

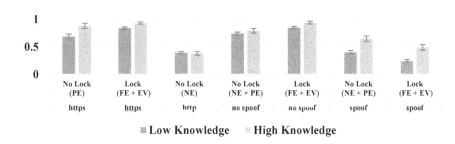

Figure 4: Differences in accuracy by manipulation (https/http and no spoof/spoof), and technical security knowledge

As can be seen in Figure 4, the two-way interaction is accounted for by participants performing more accurately in the no lock than lock conditions at the spoof websites which is opposite their performance at the no spoof websites. The presence of a lock (FE + EV) led to greater accuracy than the lack of a lock (PE + NE) *(Mdiff = 0.12, 95% CI = 0.035, 0.20, p < 0.05)*, but that the presence of a lock in the no spoof condition negatively impacted participants' accuracy *(Mdiff = -0.16, 95% CI = -0.24,*

0.08, $p < 0.001$). The second interaction shows that those with high technical security knowledge were, in general, more accurate than those with low knowledge *(Mdiff =* 0.16, *95% CI* = 0.11, 0.21, $p < 0.001$), but the difference in accuracy due to knowledge did not occur in the no spoof condition *(Mdiff* = 0.07, *95% CI* = -0.02, 0.16, $p > 0.18$), rather, it was found in the spoof condition *(Mdiff* = 0.25, *95% CI* = 0.16, 0.34, $p < 0.001$).

3.1. Effects of Indicator Scores and Website Familiarity

In order to assess whether knowledge of web browser security indicators or website familiarity interacted with participants decisions to login to secure and insecure websites, we added two covariates (indicator score and website familiarity) to the previous analyses.

For the https/http manipulation, the only covariate that had a main effect was indicator score $F(1,1368)$ = 4.42, $p < 0.05$, with a higher indicator score correlated with higher accuracy $r_\tau(398)$ = 0.05, $p < 0.05$. There was also a two-way interaction between familiarity and manipulation $F(1,1368)$ = 16.52, $p < 0.001$. Familiarity increased accuracy in the https manipulation, but decreased it in the http manipulation (Figure 6). These patterns were modulated by technical security knowledge, leading to a four-way interaction between security knowledge, https/http manipulation, and both indicator score and familiarity, $F(1,1368)$ = 4.22, $p < 0.05$. Knowledge of security indicators increased accuracy in the http condition, while familiarity decreased it. Accuracy was unaffected, or reduced, by indicator score in the https condition depending on the presence of encryption information (Lock (FE + EV) vs. No Lock (PE)). Familiarity increased accuracy in the https condition, particularly for lo-knowledge participants, with encryption information present (FE + EV) (Figures 5 and 6).

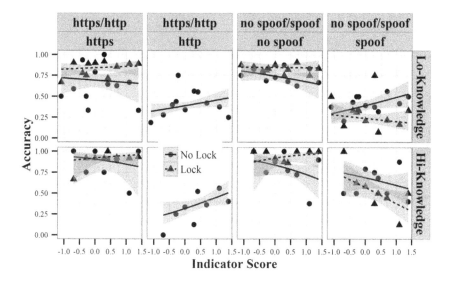

Figure 5: Relationship between participants' use of security indicators and their proportion of correct responses

For the no-spoof/spoof manipulation, there was a main effect of familiarity, $F(1,1352) = 11.61$, $p < 0.01$. Familiarity also interacted with manipulation, $F(1,1352) = 6.42$, $p < 0.05$, as well as with both manipulation and technical security knowledge $F(1,1352) = 7.24$, $p < 0.01$, and there was a four-way interaction with manipulation, technical security knowledge, and encryption information $F(1,1352) = 4.64$, $p < 0.05$.

As observed with the https/http manipulation, familiarity drives logins, but unlike the https/http manipulation, it generally increased accuracy in the spoof condition for the more knowledgeable group. Participants' with high technical security knowledge are better able to take advantage of their familiarity $r_\tau(398) = 0.11$, $p < 0.05$, but this was not true for lo-knowledge participants, especially for the spoof websites. We hypothesize that hi-knowledge participants are more likely to detect spoof websites (i.e., wrong domain names) as their familiarity increases, whereas this detection process does not apply to lo-knowledge participants.

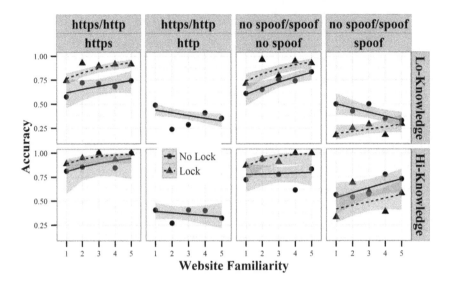

**Figure 6: Relationship between participants' proportion of correct responses
and their familiarity with the given website.**

Participants' indicator scores interacted with no-spoof/spoof manipulation and encryption information $F(1,1352) = 6.91$, $p < 0.01$. In the no-spoof condition, knowledge of indicators improves participants' accuracy, but, in the spoof condition, rather than improving accuracy, attention to indicators, specifically when encryption information was present, reduces participants' accuracy (Figure 5).

4. Discussion & Conclusions

Although these results suggest that security knowledge is related to a decrease in risky behavior, it would be a gross exaggeration to suggest that security knowledge is sufficient to ensure secure and safe behavior on the web. Limiting our analysis to just those participants who scored correctly on at least 80% of the technical security questions (n = 32), we find that they scored correctly on 88% of the secure logins, but just 59% of the insecure logins across both studies.

These results clearly reveal that there is no simple relationship between security knowledge and the likelihood of logging into insecure websites. Although this result might have been predicted for non-experts, we expected that experts would show a lower likelihood of logging in to insecure websites. Given that this study was designed to increase both risk-taking and stress by motivating participants to respond as quickly as possible in order to maximize their pay-off, it is possible that either factor or both inflated the number of errors that were shown by experts. Familiarity of the websites may have also contributed to participants being less likely to check security indicators because they were more likely to revert to habitual behaviour of logging in to familiar websites. In theory, this should have made all participants more vulnerable to the no spoof/spoof manipulation, but the performance of experts, in particular, was more complex than expected.

Experts are better than non-experts at detecting spoofed websites, but no better at detecting sites without encryption information. One possible explanation for this phenomenon is that experts primarily use the domain name highlighting feature available in modern browsers when identifying insecure websites, while non-experts do not. Assuming that the spoofed URLs are not particularly clever, then modest familiarity of an authentic URL—but not user interface—should expose a fraudulent website if one is aware of domain highlighting. This hypothesis would help explain why experts are good at identifying fraudulent websites, but no better than non-experts when it comes to logging into websites with no encryption. Experts' choices rely on more than familiarity. The presence of security indicators appears to diminish their accuracy when detecting spoofed websites. This suggests that experts find that security cues obscure the presence of an inauthentic URL, leading to a reduction in accuracy when dealing with spoofed websites with encryption information present.

These results clearly suggest that education alone will not be sufficient to change risky behaviors on the web. Just like in our study, a typical Internet user will often be asked to make security decisions against best-practice recommendations on security indicators. In essence, users are being educated through daily use to ignore recommended security indicators. These indicators are also used in an inconsistent fashion, where it is often necessary to have some familiarity with the website to know whether a partial or no encryption indicator is tantamount to commerce on an insecure site. Some of this confusion could be reduced if website designers conformed to the same set of conventions regarding security indicators. This would at the very least give users a better chance to identify insecure and spoof websites where their credentials and financial information can be hijacked.

5. Acknowledgements

Research was sponsored by the Army Research Laboratory and was accomplished under Cooperative Agreement Number W911NF-13-2-0045 (ARL Cyber Security CRA). The views and conclusions contained in this document are those of the authors and should not be interpreted as representing the official policies, either expressed or implied, of the Army Research Laboratory or the U.S. Government. The U.S. Government is authorized to reproduce and distribute reprints for Government purposes notwithstanding any copyright notation here on. The authors would also like to acknowledge the following people for their assistance: L. Jean Camp, Prashanth Rajivan, Rachel Huss, and Tom Denning.

6. References

Arianezhad, M., Camp, L.J., Kelley, T., and Stebila, D., 2013. Comparative eye tracking of experts and novices in web single sign-on. *In: Proceedings of the third ACM conference on*

Data and application security and privacy - *CODASPY '13*. New York, New York, USA: ACM Press, 105.

Buhrmester, M., Kwang, T., and Gosling, S.D., 2011. Amazon's Mechanical Turk: A New Source of Inexpensive, Yet High-Quality, Data? *Perspectives on Psychological Science*, 6 (1), 3–5.

Crump, M.J.C., McDonnell, J. V, and Gureckis, T.M., 2013. Evaluating Amazon's Mechanical Turk as a tool for experimental behavioral research. *PloS one*, 8 (3), e57410.

Garg, V. and Camp, J., 2012. End User Perception of Online Risk under Uncertainty. *In: 2012 45th Hawaii International Conference on System Sciences*. IEEE, 3278–3287.

Hazim, A., Felt, A.P., Reeder, R.W., and Consolvo, S., 2014. Your Reputation Precedes You: History, Reputation, and the Chrome Malware Warning. *In: Symposium on Usable Privacy and Security (SOUPS)*.

Kruschke, J.K., 2013. Bayesian estimation supersedes the t test. *Journal of experimental psychology. General*, 142 (2), 573–603.

Petzold, A., Plessow, F., Goschke, T., and Kirschbaum, C., 2010. Stress reduces use of negative feedback in a feedback-based learning task. *Behavioral neuroscience*, 124 (2), 248–255.

Schechter, S.E., Dhamija, R., Ozment, A., and Fischer, I., 2007. The emperor's new security indicators an evaluation of website authentication and the effect of role playing on usability studies. *In: Proceedings - IEEE Symposium on Security and Privacy*. Oakland/Berkley, CA, USA: IEEE, 51–65.

Stebila, D., 2010. Reinforcing bad behaviour. *In: Proceedings of the 22nd Conference of the Computer-Human Interaction Special Interest Group of Australia on Computer-Human Interaction - OZCHI '10*. New York, New York, USA: ACM Press, 248.

Sunshine, J., Egelman, S., Almuhimedi, H., Atri, N., and Cranor, L.F., 2009. Crying Wolf: An Empirical Study of SSL Warning Effectiveness. *In: Proc. 18th USENIX Security Symposium*.

Tukey, J.W., 1949. Comparing individual means in the analysis of variance. *Biometrics*, 5 (2), 99–114.

Whalen, T. and Inkpen, K.M., 2005. Gathering evidence: use of visual security cues in web browsers. *In: Proceedings of Graphics Interface 2005*. 137–144.

Cyber Threat Incident Handling Procedure for South African Schools

N. Sonhera[1], E. Kritzinger[2] and M. Loock[2]

[1]ICT Department, Vaal University of Technology, Ekurhuleni Campus
[2]School of Computing, University of South Africa (UNISA), South Africa
e-mail: nausonhera@yahoo.com; {kritze; loockm}@unisa.ac.za

Abstract

With the increase of networks and electronic tools, the online antisocial behaviours have increased and cyber threats have consequently became prevalent world-wide. The new technologies are challenging current networking practices, and this has given rise to cyber threats in South African schools. Learners are not aware of what they should do when threatened online. There is a lack of procedures that can be consistently followed by South African schools, governing boards and educators. As a result, many learners remain vulnerable to the negative effects of these threats. A lack of fixed reporting procedures when dealing with incidents of cyber threats in South African schools, the potential legal obligations and the lack of research in this area has prompted this research. This paper proposes a cyber threat incident handling procedure for South African schools, based on already existing cyber safety guidelines for schools in other countries like Australia and Canada. The proposed procedure will contribute to these existing guidelines by determining and implementing characteristics specific for South African schools.

Keywords

Learner, cyber threats, incident handling procedure, cyber space, role players, cyber safety

1. Introduction

Both the academics and practitioners of the 21st century have applauded the paradigm shift in schools of encouraging learners to be computer literate (Li 2008). With the right to have and use this technology also come responsibilities on how to use it responsibly in a way that ensures no harm is caused to other learners. However access to new technology has led to an increase in misuse and abuse of technology and this has brought about many incidents of threatening, harassing, embarrassing and humiliating behaviours and actions online (Popovac & Leoschut 2012). The misuse and abuse has become a concern for parents, social psychologists, authorities of schools, colleges and universities (Fisher 2013; Kite, Gable & Filippelli 2013; Oosterwyk & Kyobe 2013). On the other hand, these behaviours are placing learners' psychological health, safety, and well-being at risk (Popovac & Leoschut 2012). This could cause low self-esteem, anger, school failure, avoidance, school violence or suicide among learners (Li 2008; Willard 2006).

This article, therefore proposes a procedure that could assist learners, who are threatened online, to alert respective role players. The procedural approach could also assist educators and parents who do not know how to deal with learners who are threatened online. The article is divided into two sections; the first section is about role players involved in the incident handling procedure. The second section is about an incident handling procedure which could help learners to be confident about alerting respective role players when they feel unsafe online.

2. Background of the study

Today's learners are no longer the learners the educational system was designed to teach. They have changed radically; they represent a first generation which is growing up with new technology. They spent their entire lives surrounded by and using computers, iPods, MP3 players, Androids, tablets, Play stations, Smart phones, and other tools of the digital age (Herther 2009). The 21st century has brought with it a different revolution; learners who are on the cutting edge of technological proficiency (Gouws 2014). They are exposed to new-age technologies, various social networking sites, unlimited access to the internet and chat rooms, and phone communications (Badenhorst 2011); (Tokunaga 2010). Their social landscape has changed completely; they constitute a generation of people who know more about technology than their parents, grandparents and, in most cases, their educators and lecturers (Gouws 2014).

As a result of this ubiquitous environment and the volume of learners' interaction with it, today's learners think and process information fundamentally differently from their predecessors. On the other hand, some adults who were born in the non-digital world have adopted many aspects of the new technology and are called Digital Immigrants (Prensky 2001). Unfortunately for Digital Immigrant educators, the people sitting in their classes grew up in the environment of hypertext, downloaded music, phones in their pockets, library on their laptops and, beamed messages and instant messaging. Digital Immigrant educators, who speak an out-dated language, are struggling to solve the cyber problems of a population that speaks an entirely new language (Herther 2009). Many educators continue to prepare learners for a world which has long since disappeared.

If educators teach today's learners as they taught yesterday learners, then they are robbing them of tomorrow – John Dewey (1859-1952).

Online threats takes place off the radar screen of educators and parents, this makes it difficult to detect in schools and more impossible to monitor off school premises (Steeves & Wing 2005). Discipline has been a problem in South African schools. Research has found that educators lack a repertoire of effective methods of maintaining discipline (Mawdsley, Ralph, Smit, Marius, & Wolhuter 2013).

With these increases in technological usage, cyber threats are also on the rise and have become a major concern in South African schools. Unfortunately, there are increasing reports of learners using these technologies to post damaging text or images that raise concern of an act of violence toward others or themselves, to cyber threaten their peers or engage in other aggressive behaviour. Victims of these horrific acts are usually school learners (Oosterwyk & Parker 2010). Therefore it is increasingly important to research in the South African context on the changing life of the learners. More focus should be on how the victims can be helped, with particular attention on how role players can support learners in coping with the demands and challenges posed by technological advances (Gouws 2014).

3. Problem Statement and Research Questions

3.1. Problem Statement

In South Africa there is a lack of structure or guidance for schools on how to deal with cyber threats. There are no clear procedures that are consistently followed by schools, governing boards and educators (Bailey 2012). As a result, many learners remain vulnerable to the negative effects of cyber threats. An example is that of a Krugersdorp High School girl who was attacked after a cyber-threat ordeal. Threats were reported by the learner to the school management yet no clear procedures were followed to assist the learner until the physical attack occurred. The gap which exists now makes educators feel unsupported and so they ignore these unethical violations rather than to follow ill-defined and unenforced policies (Pruitt-Mentle 2000). This lack of support sometimes deters learners from reporting cyber threat incidents.

3.2. Research Questions

This study seeks to understand how cyber threat incidents are handled in schools and the contribution from the role players. The article examines this new phenomenon guided by the following questions:

- What is the prevalence of cyber threats among learners within South African schools?
- How do learners react after they have been cyber threatened?
- To what extent are role players concerned about cyber threats in schools?
- What are the prevention and intervention techniques for cyber threat incidents which can be identified?
- What are the responsibilities of the role players in cyber safety?
- How can an incident handling procedure assist learners to report incidents of cyber threats?

4. Literature Review

The literature review focuses on what has been documented by other researchers in terms of the prevalence and effects of cyber threats in schools. Existing conference papers, journals, articles, books, online sources, dissertations, theses, educational and governmental documents will be examined. This section is also aimed at highlighting some incidents of cyber threats in South Africa which are online articles or anecdotal cases which have been reported by the media.

4.1. Cyber Threats Incidents

Cyber threats are direct online threats or "distressing material" – general statements that make it sound like the writer is emotionally upset and may be considering harming someone else, harming himself or herself, or committing suicide (Willard 2005). New technologies have resulted in an increase in cyber threats in South African schools (Jansen van Vuuren, Grobler & Zaaiman 2012). One example is of a 16-year-old girl who attends a school in Port Elizabeth, she commented that parents do not know how bad the issue of cyber threat is. This is because a learner being threatened is only known to those on a specific Facebook or BBM (BlackBerry Messenger) group (Alexander & Harvey 2012). Alexander and Harvey (2012) reported that some learners read news on websites and what most people consider as horrific stories they see them as comic and humorous. They then draw inspiration from these violent stories and do the same to hurt other learners. A new type of forum or chat room that has attracted the attention of learners in Cape Town schools called "Outoilet" - http://outoilet.wen.su/ - allows learners to post mean and hurtful things about their friends.

4.2. Efforts for Structures, Guidance and Procedures

Generally, most of the countries worldwide are addressing the problem of cyber threat incidents in schools. In Australia, a number of schools, Department of Education, different groups and organisations have focused on cyber ethics, cyber safety and cyber security in education (Department of Education and Children's Services 2009). Epstein and Kazmierczak (2007) suggest that it is necessary to conduct periodic surveys to assess the degree of cyber threats. Bhat (2008) added that role players should address cyber threats in schools. Campbell (2007) recommends that victims need to be empowered and not to be blamed.

In South Africa, the Cabinet approved a National Cyber Security Policy Framework with some challenges on how to bridge the gap between law and technology (Minister of State Security 2012). The Policy Framework acknowledges that the South African Cyber Security Legal Framework is scattered across various pieces of legislation and is therefore administered by different government departments (Badenhorst 2011). The South African government has also promulgated a number of acts on cyber threats (Kganyago 2012). As an initiative towards cyber safety, the DBE (Department of Basic Education) has developed guidelines on electronic safety in schools (Department of Basic Education 2010). Additionally, the Centre for Justice and Crime Prevention and the DBE (2013) have produced the school safety framework which is mainly focusing on bullying in general.

The case of Le Roux v Dey is the only court ruling by South African courts involving learners' use of cyberspace (Constitutional Court of South Africa 2011). In this case Hendrick Pieter Le Roux (1st defendant) had created a computer image at his home in which the faces of the principals and deputy principal of his school were super-imposed on an image of two naked gay bodybuilders sitting in a sexually suggestive posture. This image was shared with the whole school. Understandably, the principal and deputy principal were embarrassed and felt particularly aggrieved by this. However, despite the disciplinary steps against the learners, the tag "Dey is gay" was heard in the corridors of the school which perpetuated untrue rumours and continued to infringe the deputy principal's dignity. There is a growing tendency in South African schools to challenge the status and authority of educators with a concomitant breakdown in discipline.

4.3. Gap Identified in the Literature

Although South Africa has publicised a number of acts on cyber security and safety, there is a lack of processes in place which can be used for cyber threat incident reporting in schools. There are no fixed procedures within the schools to handle cyber threats incidents. Burton and Mutongwizo (2009) state that currently there are no specific procedures that directly addresses cyber aggression and cyber safety of learners both online and in the realm of cellular technologies. As a result of all this, the learners are facing a lot of online challenges.

The challenges are that learners are no longer safe at school or in their homes since there are no barriers for threats found online (Kite et al. 2013). An example is of a 39-year-old educator who has been suspended from Hyde Park High School after a mother had revealed that he had been sending her 16-year-old son pornographic material (Neille 2013a). On the other hand school personnel do not know how to deal with learners who are cyber threatened because of the absence of cyber threat handling procedures (Bailey 2012; Tokunaga 2010). From learners' point of view, most of the time when they do report these threats, nothing is done by the School Management Board (Alexander & Harvey 2012). It is also reported that the trend involving school learners filming their peers being beaten or bullied in order to gain notoriety is becoming increasingly apparent in South African schools (Neille 2013b). On the other hand, according to Mogotlane, Chauke and van Rensburg (2010), there is now a new family structure called a child-headed household in South Africa. As indicated by Mudhovozi (2013), aggressors often come from these families. This also implies that there is often a lack of monitoring and supervision of these children by adults. This allows cyber threats to occur unnoticed and for an extended period of time without any intervention.

5. Research Methodology

The literature study was undertaken to provide sufficient background on the existence of cyber threat incidents in South African schools. It also highlighted a lack of procedures that could be consistently followed by South African schools, governing boards and educators when handling cyber threat incidents.

This collection of theoretically valid and reliable evidence, contributed to a better understanding of learners' interactions in cyber space and how much help they get when they are in trouble. The explanatory nature of this research was aiming at revealing a wide range of opinions and experiences of cyber threat incidents in schools. This information has been utilised to help develop empirically driven prevention and intervention procedure to ensure the safety and psychological well-being of learners (Campbell 2005; Lodge & Frydenberg 2007).

6. Research Structure

This article is focusing on developing and proposing a cyber threat incident handling procedure which could help a learner who has been threatened online to alert respective role players. The procedural approach could assist the respective role players with procedure which could be taken to intervene. This article is therefore divided into two sections, namely the "Role Players" and "The Incident Handling Procedure".

6.1. Section 1- Role Players for the Framework

This section seeks to equip all role players with guidelines and ability to recognise potential dangers and to be discerning enough to avoid them. Figure 1 summarises how the role players fit together.

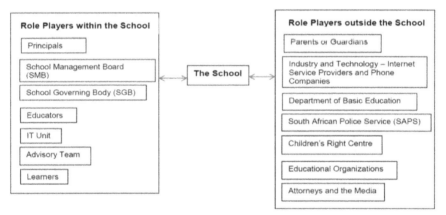

Figure 1: A summary of how the role players fit together

The responsibility of the school is to incorporate technology as a valuable learning tool, and to equip learners to be discerning, responsible and ethical participants in the information age (Department of Basic Education 2010). Schools should develop their own Information and Communication Technology (ICT) policies; since learners are bringing sophisticated range of handheld devices to school that give them separate access to online content that is not necessarily appropriate. The school may suspend or suspend pending exclusion the leaner(s) involved in cyber threat incidents. School do not exist in isolation; they are driven by role players, within and outside the school.

6.1.1. Role Players within the School

Role players within the school community have responsibilities in creating a school environment free from cyber threats (Centre for Justice and Crime Prevention and the DoBE 2013). Preventing and addressing these threats requires a collaborate effort and given below are the responsibilities of role players within the school.

- Responsibilities of the Principals

The principals should approve the posting of any information on school web sites, news groups, web-based forums, and should ensure that it conforms to minimum cyber safety standards (Department of Education and Children's Services 2009). They should take action if posted material might disrupt school safety. It is important that school administrators carefully assess the situation and provide evidence justifying any disciplinary action. Principals should also ensure that the school's private information is not accessible to the public on the school's websites.

- Responsibilities of the School Management Board (SMB) and the School Governing Board (SGB)

The principal, SMB and SGB should contribute to developing an ICT policy and should meet and consider what additional rules or guidelines staff and learners may need that are specific to their own school situation. This team should develop a mandatory acceptable use agreement for all staff and learners and should put in place management protocols so that any cyber threat incidents are responded to, in an appropriate and consistent manner (Department of Education and Children's Services 2009). The team should be responsible for the behaviour management.

- Responsibilities of the Educators

Educators should be able to understand the concept of the 21st century learner, especially to ensure that their teaching strategy is in line with the devices their learners use (Department of Basic Education 2010). During their teaching, educators should keep up to date with the relative risk and educational benefits of online activities in learning programmes. They should be aware of the steps to take and advice to give if learners notify them of inappropriate or unwelcome online activities by other learners or members of the public (Department of Education and Children's Services 2009).

- Responsibilities of Information Technology Unit

The Information Technology Unit should consist of the ICT Coordinator, an SGB representative, an SMB representative, a Network administrator, an ICT educator, a librarian and an RCL (Representative Council of Learners) - learner representative. The function of the team is to develop an ICT policy for the school with attendant penalties for breach of the policy. The policy should be approved by legal professionals to ensure that it does not contradict or impinge on other legislation, and also that child protection procedures are correctly followed.

- Responsibilities of Advisory Team

This team should be the first point of call for any cyber threat incident. This team can be composed of; the principal, a counsellor / psychologist, the ICT coordinator and a Life Orientation educator.

- Responsibilities of Learners

Learners should be able to select the most appropriate communication tool to resolve issues and not to create them, and to be responsible for their own behaviour (Department of Basic Education 2010). They should use the school's internet facilities only for learning related activities that are approved by the educators and not to access or distribute inappropriate material. Learners should be confident about alerting the adults when they feel unsafe, threatened, bullied or exposed to inappropriate material online. If cyber threats become serious, the learner(s) should contact the school Advisory Team or the SAPS and file a report. Learners who are victims of cyber threats should block or limit all communications with the accused parties and should save the harassing messages and forward them to the school Advisory Team or the SAPS.

6.1.2. Role Players outside the School

Sometime more serious or repeat cyber incidents might involve external role-players. Given below are some of the responsibilities for role players outside the school.

- Responsibilities of Parents or Guardians

Parents should monitor their children's activities on social sites by checking the content, and having clear internet and cell phone agreements with their children (The Alannah and Madeline Foundation 2007). It is vital that parents or guardians understand cyber threats and the mechanics of cyber threats. When parents discover that their children are being threatened, it is always best to contact the School Management or School Advisory Team. They should work closely with the schools for cyber threats to be prevented and early intervention measurers to be taken.

- Responsibilities of Industry and Technology – Internet Service Providers and Phone Companies

Internet Service Providers should track instant messaging and these messages could be used as evidence in a court of law (Campbell 2007). They should work with the DBE and schools in a proactive and educational way which will help make all the school stakeholders and parents aware of the cyber threats, how to prevent them and what to do whenever they occur. If threat messages are coming through mobile devices, a phone company should be able to trace the source of the message and warn the aggressor that he may lose his cell number and access to the network if the threats persist. The up-to-date filters and other useful technologies should be developed by industry and be freely accessible to schools and parents, and be easy to implement.

- Department of Basic Education

The DBE should outline the policies and repercussions of online behaviour for schools. The DBE together with the industry should adequately resource and support schools to implement cyber safety strategies. Educational laws should include guidelines for safe and emotional free environment for learners. The DBE should provide assistance in determining appropriate measures to be taken when any ICT is misused.

- The South African Police Service (SAPS)

If there is evidence of a crime and has been captured on a cell phone or other electronic device, the device should be confiscated and kept securely until handed to the investigating police officer. Criminal charges should then be laid, and the police should do the necessary investigations, in order to get hold of the necessary evidence.

- Children's Rights Centre

If a threat is a suspected child protection issue, then a violence or suicide risk assessment should be done in accordance with DBE process. The Child Protection and Abuse Organisation should be contacted for help. It should be mandatory for educators to notify the Child Abuse or Child Protection Unit if they suspect child abuse and neglect. These organisations should educate the government about areas of specific concern for learners in cyber space (The Right Times 2012).

- Responsibilities of Educational Organizations

Educational Organizations should continue to hold workshops, do research and give presentations on cyber safety topics in order to help school communities. On the 19 August 2011, the Centre for Justice and Crime Prevention (CJCP) hosted a roundtable discussion about the nature of cyber violence in South Africa and the legislative and policy framework available pertaining to cyber threats (Centre for Justice and Crime Prevention 2011). The presentations were from the Nelson Mandela Metropolitan University (NMMU, University of Cape and Films and Publication Board (FPB). Based on FPB's research results, it was found that there are no structures in place for parents and guardians to refer to when a case of cyber threats emerges. It was evident that the cyber aggression scourge in South Africa needs to be controlled. CJCP delineated that responses to cyber threat aggressors, are fragmented and rely on the various sections in the legislation, including common law definition of crimes and civil law.

- Attorneys and the Media

The attorneys can be of assistance in terms of pending civil action that could be taken against the aggressors. They should be able to provide a parent with sound legal advice on how to open a possible criminal case and how to get restraining orders against the accused (Cellphone Safety 2011). Exposing an aggressor in the media, should never be a first resort because a victim would be horrified at the thought of a parent going public about him being threatened and the shame that goes with it. It can however be a valuable weapon if no other options are available to parents (Cellphone Safety 2011).

6.2. Section 2 - A Proposed Incident Handling Structure

Role players need a procedure to refer to when handling cyber threat incidents. The focus of this section is to explore ways to intervene in cyber threat cases in schools after they have occurred. The article is proposing an incident handling procedure which will assist learners in reporting incidents of cyber threats and help respective role players to handle these threats. Figure 2 outlines the decision making process that should be followed. An incident handling procedure explains each step which should be considered when helping learners. It is critical that the safety and welfare of learners are considered as paramount throughout the process.

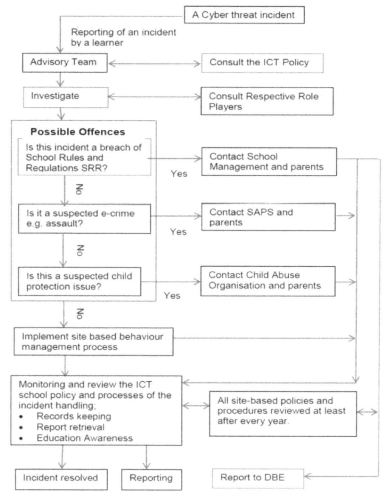

Figure 2: A decision making process

6.2.1. Incident Handling Procedure

Advisory Team

This team can be composed of; the principal, a counsellor or psychologist, an ICT coordinator and a Life Orientation educator. This is the first point of call for learners to report cyber threat incidents. All learners should be made aware that they can report anonymously or confidentially. Optionally, if a school has a website, an online report feature on a school home page could also be considered with the provision of a Uniform Resource Locater (URL). In this case all members of the team should have the rights to override the URL filters in order to have access to records during their investigations. If a cyber threat appears to present a legitimate imminent threat of violence and danger to others learners or self then an Advisory Team should advise the School Management Board to contact law enforcement and initiate a protective response. It is also necessary for the Advisory Team to continue with the following evidence gathering steps.

Investigate

i. *Gather Evidence and preserve it*
All evidence gathered should be preserved. Parents, learners and staff should be advised to preserve evidence and a record of threats on computers or devices. Phone messages, record of instant message conversations, screen-grab of social network pages should be printed, saved and forwarded to the member of the Advisory Team.

ii. *Determine the identity of the aggressor*
The identity of the aggressor may be difficult to identify because aggressors can post their threats anonymously or impersonate someone. The advice of an ICT Coordinator could be of value in this circumstance. If there are any anonymous cyber threats or concerns of impersonation, and there be reasons to suspect that other learners could be involved, then a search of internet use records of learners should be conducted. If a criminal action is involved, law enforcement mechanisms have greater abilities to identify anonymous creators.

iii. *Search for Additional harmful material or interactions*
An ICT Coordinator and a librarian should assist. A search should include all suspected participants. A search of files and internet use records should be done, even if the threat appears to be an out of school activity. Conduct an additional search on the online environment where initial material appeared, and a search engine should be used to find out the name of a learner, friends, enemies, or the school name. Related activities at school should also be investigated.

iv. *Review of the Investigation*
Review all the material and evidence gathered. Identify a learner that could be causing harm, at school or online. Determine the roles which different learners could be playing and whether their threats are a continuation of previous threats or retaliation.

6.2.2. Possible Offences

After the investigation has been done an appropriate intervention should be considered based on the severity and history of the cyber threat incident and the learners involved. The rehabilitative measures could be considered as one of the first possible ways to help the learners involved. This may involve external role-players such as counsellors, health or social work professionals for specialised assistance. Parents or guardians should be invited to be part of measures to resolve the issue. Stated below are some of the offences which may be committed by cyber threat aggressors.

i. *A Breach of School Rules and Regulations (SRR)*

Determine the nature of the evidence to see if there is any substantial threat or disruption. If it is a nuisance activity, ignore it, but if it is something of substantial harm then the School Management Board should impose formal discipline and get to the root of the problem. It should convene an independent tribunal to assess the case, and depending on its findings, determine appropriate sanctions. The School Management Board is responsible for recommending to the Provincial Head of Department to consider suspension or expulsion of a learner. Suspensions and expulsions should be avoided unless there are school safety concerns. More focus should be put on a restorative justice response. Fully documented evidence, decision making process, and rationale for formal discipline response should be produced and kept for future references.

ii. *A Suspected E-Crime*

In some instances a cyber threat crosses a line between a behavioural issue to be dealt with by school staff and parents to a criminal one that may involve the police. If the online material appears to present a legitimate imminent threat of violence and danger to others, contact law enforcement (SAPS) and a protective response should be initiated.

iii. *Child Protection Issue*

A violence or suicide risk assessment should be done by the member of the Advisory Team (the Life Orientation educator) to determine if the evidence gathered raises concerns that learner(s) may pose a risk of harm to others or self. If it is a suspected child protection issue then a violence or suicide risk assessment should be done in accordance with DBE process and then the Child Protection and Abuse Organisation should be contacted.

7. ICT Polices, Supervision, Monitoring and Review

Possible offences should be addressed in accordance to the ICT Policy document. Department of Basic Education (2010)'s Draft Guidelines on e-Safety states that the ICT policy should be developed and include a clear statement of actions which a school should take if a policy is breached. An ICT policy should be reviewed and updated regularly to ensure its appropriateness and effectiveness. Campbell (2005) believes that each school should adopt its own policy and guidelines that are tailored to its individual requirements and context. The school's ICT resources should be monitored and supervised to ensure that users are secure and in conformity with the school's ICT policy. The frequent change of technology requires that policies, procedures and agreements be updated and reviewed yearly. This change in technology is also a call for the introduction of Education Awareness Programs schools.

8. Education Awareness Programs

All school officials should be trained about cyber threats. Educators, coaches, after school supervisors and transport drivers, should be made aware of cyber threats and how to watch out for them. They should know how to respond to the triggers and how to reinforce positive problem solving. Teaching aids like posters, pamphlets, wallet booklets, digital literacy lesson plans and child friendly sites could be used. Other awareness programmes should include teaching parents on how cyber threats can be prevented in the home and how they can respond to incidents. Offering conferences, information sessions and workshops about cyber threats could be another way to educate the older generation on current cyberspace practices so that they can begin to understand their children's cyber world.

9. Conclusion

The advantage of an incident handling procedure is that; dialogue, both verbal and nonverbal, can help learners to feel connected and cared for. If the learners know that the people around them care, it makes going to school worthwhile for both the victims and aggressors. Among the learners, this will result in caring and respectful behaviours during learner-to-learner exchanges, safe and nurturing environments for the healthy development of identity and citizenship and tolerance and impartiality. Implementing policies and practices that encourage learners to respect each other, whether online or face-to face remains an important responsibility of the school.

The cyber threat is a phenomenon that has been considered as a worldwide concern especially in first world countries. These online threats are becoming surprisingly prevalent across many different communities throughout the world. The United Nations (UN) child convention rights are part of the international legal framework which protects children and young people. They state that children and young people should be viewed and treated as human instead of passive objects of care and charity. The Government should undertake to ensure that such protection and care is necessary for their well-being (General Assembly 1989). With the increase of cyber threats in South African schools, the call to action against these threats is even more urgent. South African schools are putting a lot of effort into using ICT to support learners' learning. With this comes a responsibility to ensure that learning takes place in an environment where safe and responsible use of ICT is modelled and taught. The development of cyber threat incident handling procedure is a step ahead in trying to protect South African learners. This will ensure that learners are protected from emotional harm to the greatest degree possible. Empirical research should continue to be conducted in order to understand the cyber threat handling phenomenon in South African schools as well as evidence-based intervention programmes to control and combat cyber threats. The essential challenge is to have this procedure communicated to all stakeholders involved.

For future developments, the researcher will continue to explore ways of using a qualitative research method and research design to collect data from the role players with the intention of coming up with a cyber threat framework to help learners in cyber space. A qualitative phenomenological method will be intended to approach the role players in order to understand, describe and explain a cyber threat social phenomenon in South African schools. It will seek to unpack what role players are doing or what is happening to them in terms that are meaningful and offer rich insights (Gibbs 2007). Data collection will be done through group and individual interviews. This will be done to gain an in depth understanding into role players' perceptions of the nature, impact and successful intervention strategies for cyber threat incidents.

10. References

Alexander, W. & Harvey, J., 2012. Cyber bullying scourge. *Weekend Post*. Available at: http://myportelizabeth.co.za/cyber-bullying-scourge/ [Accessed September 12, 2013].

Badenhorst, C., 2011. Legal responses to cyber bullying and sexting in South Africa. *Centre for Justice and Crime Prevention*, (CJCP Issue paper No. 10). Available at: http://www.cjcp.org.za/articlesPDF/32/Issue Paper 10-1.pdf [Accessed September 8, 2013].

Bailey, C., 2012. Girl attacked after cyberbully ordeal: teen, 15, taunted on Facebook and BBM. *The Star*. Available at: http://www.genderlinks.org.za/article/girl-attacked-after-cyberbully-ordeal-teen-15-taunted-on-facebook-and-bbm-2012-02-29 [Accessed September 3, 2013].

Bhat, C.S., 2008. Cyber Bullying: Overview and Strategies for School Counsellors, Guidance Officers, and All School Personnel. *Australian Journal of Guidance and Counselling*, 18(1), pp.53–66. Available at: http://www.recoveryonpurpose.com/upload/Cyberbullying Overview and Strategies Australia.pdf [Accessed July 19, 2012].

Burton, P. & Mutongwizo, T., 2009. Inescapable violence: Cyber bullying and electronic violence against young people in South Africa. *CJCP*, 2012(March). Available at: http://www.cjcp.skinthecat.co.za/articlesPDF/30/Issue Paper 8 - Inescapable Violence - Cyber aggression.pdf [Accessed May 4, 2013].

Campbell, M., 2007. Cyber bullying and young people: Treatment principles not simplistic advice. *www.scientist-practitioner.com (paper of the week), 23 Feb.*, 2007(February). Available at: http://eprints.qut.edu.au/14903/1/14903.pdf [Accessed May 12, 2012].

Campbell, M.A., 2005. Cyber bullying: An old problem in a new guise? . *Australian Journal of Guidance and Counselling*, 15(1), p.68.

Cellphone Safety, 2011. Cyber bullying 3 of 3: When all else fails. Available at: http://www.cellphonesafety.co.za/cyber-bullying-3-of-3-when-all-else-fails.html [Accessed March 24, 2012].

Centre for Justice and Crime Prevention, 2011. *Cyber bullying and "sexting" roundtable report*, Newlands, South Africa. Available at: http://cyberbullying.ezipezi.com/downloads/CJCPRoundtable-cyberbullying-report_19Aug2011.pdf.

Centre for Justice and Crime Prevention and the DoBE, 2013. School Safety Framework; Addressing Bullying in Schools - Course Reader.

Department of Basic Education, 2010. *Guidelines on e-Safety in Schools: Educating towards responsible, accountable and ethical use of ICT in education*, South Africa.

Department of Education and Children's Services, 2009. Cyber-Safety. Keeping Children Safe in a Connected World.A Guidelines for Schools and Preschools. South Australia. , 2011(July

15), pp.1–20. Available at: http://www.decd.sa.gov.au/docs/documents/1/ CyberSafetyKeepingChildre.pdf [Accessed July 15, 2011].

Epstein, A. & Kazmierczak, J., 2007. Cyber bullying: What Teachers, Social Workers, and Administrators Should Know. *Illinois child welfare*, (3), pp.41–51.

Fisher, E.J., 2013. From Cyber Bullying to Cyber Coping: The Misuse of Mobile Technology and Social Media and Their Effects on People's Lives. *Business and Economic Research*, 3(2), p.127. Available at: http://www.macrothink.org/journal/index.php/ber/article/view/4176 [Accessed April 17, 2014].

General Assembly, 1989. Convention on the Rights of the Child. *General Assembly resolution*. Available at: http://www.ohchr.org/en/professionalinterest/pages/crc.aspx.

Gibbs, G., 2007. What is qualitative research? In U. Flick, ed. *Analyzing Qualitative Data*. London: SAGE Publications Ltd, pp. x – xi.

Gouws, F., 2014. The Changing Life World of the Adolescent: A Focus on Technological Advances. *J Communication*, 5(1), pp.9–16. Available at: http://www.krepublishers.com/02-Journals/JC/JC-05-0-000-14-Web/JC-05-1-000-14-Abst-PDF/JC-5-1-009-14-103-Gouws-F-E/JC-5-1-009-14-103-Gouws-F-E-Tx[2].pdf.

Herther, N.K., 2009. "Digital Natives and Immigrants: What Brain Research Tells Us" | Questia, Your Online Research Library. *Online*, 33(6), pp.14 – 21. Available at: http://www.questia.com/library/1P3-1895898431/digital-natives-and-immigrants-what-brain-research [Accessed June 3, 2014].

Jansen van Vuuren, J., Grobler, M. & Zaaiman, J., 2012. The influence of cyber security levels of South African citizens on national security. In Academic Conferences Limited, p. 138. Available at: http://researchspace.csir.co.za/dspace/bitstream/10204/5832/1/Grobler_2012.pdf [Accessed November 19, 2013].

Kganyago, K., 2012. Information Security Discussion by Microsoft South Africa's Chief Security Advisor. Available at: kganyago.org/tag/cybersecurity [Accessed December 12, 1BC].

Kite, S.L., Gable, R.K. & Filippelli, L.P., 2013. Cyber threats: a study of what middle and high school student know about threatening behaviours and internet safety. *International Journal of Social Media and Interactive Learning Environments*, 1(3), pp.240 – 254. Available   at: http://www.jwu.edu/uploadedFiles/Providence_Campus/News_and_Events/Employee_News/I nside_Providence/KiteGableCyberThreats.pdf [Accessed April 19, 2014].

Li, Q., 2008. Cyberbullying in schools: An examination of preservice teachers' perception. *Canadian Journal of Learning and Technology*, 34(2), pp.75–90.

Lodge, J. & Frydenberg, E., 2007. Cyber-bullying in Australian schools: Profiles of adolescent coping and insights for school practitioners. *The Australian Educational and Developmental Psychologist*, 24(1), pp.45–58.

Mawdsley, Ralph D, Smit, Marius H, & Wolhuter & Charl, 2013. Students, websites, and freedom of expression in the United States and South Africa. *De Jure*, 46(1), pp.132–161. Available at: http://www.scielo.org.za/scielo.php?pid=S2225-71602013000100009&script= sci_arttext&tlng=en.

Minister of State Security, 2012. Statement on the Approval by Cabinet of the Cyber Security Policy Framework for South Africa. Available at: www.info.gov.za/speech/DynamicAction?pageid=461&tid=59794 [Accessed March 8, 2014].

Mogotlane, S.M., Chauke, M.E. & van Rensburg, G.H., 2010. A situational analysis of child-headed households in South Africa. *Curationis*, 33(3), pp.24–32. Available at: http://www.curationis.org.za/index.php/curationis/article/viewFile/4/7 [Accessed May 10, 2014].

Mudhovozi, P., 2013. Bullies and victims at a public secondary school: The educators' perspective. *Presentations*. Available at: http://proz.ontodo.org/presentations/196239/index.html [Accessed May 21, 2014].

Neille, D., 2013a. Hyde Park High sex pest case reveals more sexual assaults. *ENCA.Com*. Available at: http://www.enca.com/south-africa/hyde-park-high-sex-pest-case-reveals-more-sexual-assaults [Accessed June 12, 2014].

Neille, D., 2013b. Voyeurism fuelling school violence. *ecna.com*. Available at: http://www.enca.com/south-africa/voyeurism-fuelling-school-violence-analyst [Accessed June 12, 2014].

Oosterwyk, G. & Kyobe, M., 2013. Mobile Bullying in South Africa - Exploring its Nature, Influencing Factors and Implications. In *Proceedings of the European Conference on Informations Warfare*. p. 201. Available at: http://connection.ebscohost.com/c/articles/88849609/mobile-bullying-south-africa-exploring-nature-influencing-factors-implications [Accessed April 19, 2014].

Oosterwyk, G. & Parker, M., 2010. Investigating bullying via the mobile web in Cape Town schools. In A. Koch & P. Van Brakel, eds. *12th ANNUAL CONFERENCE ON WORLD WIDE WEB APPLICATIONS*. Durban, South Africa: ZA WWW 2010. Available at: http://www.zaw3.co.za.

Popovac, M. & Leoschut, L., 2012. Cyber bullying in South Africa: Impact and responses. *Centre for Justice and Crime Prevention*, (CJCP Issue Paper No. 13). Available at: http://cjcp.skinthecat.co.za/articlesPDF/63/IssuePaper13-Cyberbullying-SA-Impact_Responses.pdf [Accessed August 4, 2013].

Prensky, M., 2001. Digital Natives, Digital Immigrants. *On the Horizon*, 9(5), pp.1–6. Available at: http://www.marcprensky.com/writing/Prensky - Digital Natives, Digital Immigrants - Part1.pdf [Accessed June 3, 2014].

Pruitt-Mentle, D., 2000. C3 Framework Cyberethics, Cybersafety and Cybersecurity Promoting Responsible Use. Educational Technology Policy, Research and Outreach. , 2010(March 13). Available at: http://www.edtechpolicy.org/cyberk12/Documents/C3Awareness/C3_framework_full_final.pdf .

Steeves, V. & Wing, C., 2005. Young Canadians in a Wired World, Media Awareness Network. *Industry Canada's SchoolNet program and CANARIE*. Available at: http://www.media-awareness.ca/english/research/YCWW/phaseII/.

The Alannah and Madeline Foundation, 2007. The Alannah and Madeline Foundation, in consultation with the National Coalition Against Bullying and Center for Strategic Education. In *Cyber-Safety Symposium Report*. Canterbury, Melbourne.

The Right Times, 2012. The National Cyber Security Policy Framework for South Africa. , 2012(May 21). Available at: http://childrensrights.org.za/magazine/index.php//the-national-cyber-security-policy-framework-for-south-africa [Accessed September 4, 2013].

Tokunaga, R.S., 2010. Following you home from school: A critical review and synthesis of research on cyberbullying victimization. *Computers in Human Behavior*, 26(3), pp.277–287. Available at: http://www.sciencedirect.com/science/article/pii/S074756320900185X [Accessed March 19, 2014].

Willard, N., 2006. *An Educator ' s Guide to Cyberbullying and Cyberthreats : Responding to the Challenge of Online Social Aggression , Threats , and Distress*, Available at: http://miketullylaw.com/library/cbcteducator.pdf [Accessed March 21, 2011].

Ethical Dilemmas and Dimensions in Penetration Testing

S. Faily[1], J. McAlaney[1] and C. Iacob[2]

[1]Bournemouth University, UK
[2]University of East London, UK
e-mail: {sfaily,jmcalaney}@bournemouth.ac.uk; c.iacob@uel.ac.uk

Abstract

Penetration testers are required to attack systems to evaluate their security, but without engaging in unethical behaviour while doing so. Despite work on hacker values and studies into security practice, there is little literature devoted to the ethical pressures associated with penetration testing. This paper presents several ethical dilemmas and dimensions associated with penetration testing; these shed light on the ethical positions taken by penetration testers, and help identify potential fallacies and biases associated with each position.

Keywords

Penetration Testing, Ethics, Dilemmas, Fallacies, Biases

1. Introduction

Penetration testers attack systems to evaluate their security in the face of realistic threats. These attacks take the form of authorised *penetration tests* that probe a system's defenses; these defenses are then breached to evaluate the impact of any weaknesses; the results of these tests are used to improve a system's security, making them resilient to further attacks.

Hacking a system requires technical prowess, creativity, and ingenuity to find unexpected ways of appropriating it (Geer and Harthorne, 2002). Penetration testing requires all of this, with the added constraint that finding and exploiting vulnerabilities should neither harm the system nor encroach on the dignity of those affected by it. Unfortunately, commercial pressures mean that penetration testers face pressure to discover insecurity without themselves engaging in unethical behaviour before, during, and after a penetration test. For example, consider the following scenario: *An investment bank is considering whether to enter a long-term contract for information assurance services with a security consultancy. As a pilot project, the bank commissions the firm to evaluate whether a policy forbidding the plugging in of unauthorised USB devices into workstations is being adhered to. The IT staff at the bank want the firm to adapt a known piece of banking malware that, when installed on a USB stick which is plugged into one of the bank's workstations, will email a selection of spreadsheet files on a shared working directory to an email account owned by the firm. This simple test will help the bank evaluate who in the company is violating the policy.*

Such a test may be legal if the exfiltrated data was not personal, but this legality may be questionable depending on the legal jurisdiction where the test takes place. There are also question marks about the morality associated with employing malware, and engaging with markets where the malware is acquired might also have ethical implications based on the nature of the exploit or the system under evaluation (Egelman et al., 2013). Finally, is the use of deception and de-anonymisation of employees acceptable, particularly where a policy is intentionally violated to achieve critical productivity goals (Adams and Sasse, 1999)?

Previous work (Chiesa et al., 2009; Holt, 2010) has started to glean an understanding of hacker values, but has focused on hackers trying to compromise systems, rather than 'ethical' hackers trying to protect them. These studies indicate that the morality of many hacker's actions, and whether or not they exceed the ethical parameters of a given situation, varies based on mood or other factors. Although there have been studies of different types of security practitioners (Haber and Bailey, 2007; Werlinger et al., 2009), the social and ethical challenges faced by penetration testers remains an unexplored area. A better understanding of these challenges might provide directions for improving the techniques and tools used to penetration test systems.

In this paper, we present several ethical dilemmas and dimensions faced by penetration testers; these shed light on how penetration testers value the role of ethics, justify ethical decisions, and shape perceptions around their clients and practices. We consider the relationship between ethics and penetration testing in Section 2 before describing our approach in Section 3. We present the ethical dilemmas and dimensions found in Section 4, and illustrate its use in unpacking fallacies and biases, before concluding in Section 5.

2. Ethics and Penetration Testing

Ethics is the study of morality (Tavani, 2006). By providing principles and theories about different viewpoints about what is meant to be 'right', ethics helps classify arguments, defend a position or better understand the position others take and, in doing so, helps determine an appropriate course of action. Penetration testing vivifies ethics, forcing practitioners to think about the consequences of a variety of situations, ranging from agreeing the parameters of a test, to deciding which techniques should or should not be allowed during a test (Bishop, 2007). Unfortunately, as the previous section illustrated, many dilemmas are more sophisticated and fall within a grey area where a response may be legal, but potentially unethical. While the necessity to attend to ethical considerations is broadly accepted, guidance on how to do so is not. For example, the Open Source Security Testing Methodology Manual (OSSTM) states that, when evaluating the security posture of a target, "business and industry ethics policies" that influence security and privacy requirements should be identified (Hertzog, 2010). However, the objective of undertaking such a review is to scope any testing activity and identify vulnerabilities that might lead to inappropriate disclosure of private information. OSSTM puts emphasis on what should be evaluated rather than the techniques used to carry out an evaluation; it is non-prescriptive about how such policies should be identified and analysed.

Although some of the ethical implications of hacking are understood (Spafford, 1992), the implications of *ethical* hacking are comparatively ill-explored. Moreover, while the role of ethics is discussed in computing degree courses, there are inconsistent options in what should be taught to students to prepare them for their professional careers (Hall, 2014). Consequently, professional penetration testers inevitably fall back on professional codes to provide advice on their conduct; such codes need to be broad enough to cover ethical conflicts and concerns, yet specific enough to guide decision-making in actual situations (Perlman and Varma, 2002). There have been several examples of the security community drawing up such codes for ethical hackers. For example, the Council of Registered Ethical Security Testers (CREST) provides their members with a code of conduct (CREST, 2014). This code not only stipulates a code of ethics, but is also an aide-memoire for good practice; these include the need to evaluate the impact of new techniques and tools, and requirements to explain project deliverables to clients, and keep up to date with new standards and regulations. However, such codes are often framed as constraints and rules rather than providing specific guidance. Not only do such codes give the false impression that locating and following a directive is both necessary and sufficient to behave ethically, they also fail to provide advice on how to deal with conflicts of ethical significance (Ladd, 1985).

Penetration testers are expected to make informed decisions based on their understanding of the situation at hand, supported by any procedural, ethical, and technical training they may have undertaken (Xynos ct al., 2010). Although there is a plethora of books and events that provide technical training, there is little to describe the form that ethical training might take. Moreover, Xynos and his colleagues claim that ambiguity associated with penetration testing practices raise a number of other questions about how penetration testers demonstrate professionalism, how clients can be confident that a penetration testing team can be trusted to complete their assignment, and their work is fit for purpose?

(Pierce et al., 2006) have proposed a conceptual model of penetration testing ethics, which is centered on the role of integrity. It considers the avoidance of conflicts of interest, false positives and negatives, and binding ethical and legal agreements influences professional integrity, which, in turn, helps protect the interests of clients and the security profession in general. This model is grounded in technical literature of penetration testing, and codes of practice, which encompass it. The role of the model purports to provide guidelines for what it means for ethical hackers to behave ethically. The issues at stake are, however, greyer than suggested by this framework. For example, Pierce et al. claim that if penetration testers refuse to engage with criminal hackers then they are using their skills only for commissioned tests and are upholding the profession. However, there are numerous ways that penetration testers might fail to uphold the profession. Moreover, the framework implies that behaving legally is synonymous with behaving ethically. This fails to recognise scenarios of legal ambiguity; penetration testers must unpack these to determine the right thing to do.

3. Approach

To understand the relationship between penetration testing and ethics, we interviewed eight professional penetration testers. While largely unstructured, the interviews sought responses to some of the questions raised by the related work (Pierce et al., 2006; Xynos et al., 2010; CREST, 2014). These were structured around the following four areas.

- Responsibilities: What are your professional responsibilities, and how do you ensure you that you and your team behave responsibly?

- Practices: How do you assess the legal and ethical import of your everyday practice?

    •Ethics: What ethical codes of practice do you rely on, and how do you resolve any ethical dilemmas you might face?

- Assurance: What assurances do you provide of your professionalism, and how can clients be confident that you can be trusted to complete your engagement?

To ensure a consistent level of professional expertise, all interviewees either held qualifications awarded by CREST, or an equivalent qualification recognised by the UK government's CHECK scheme (CESG, 2014). Interviewees either worked for security practices recognised as CREST member companies or, in some cases, UK government teams with a responsibility for penetrating government systems and installations. During the interviews, interviewees were encouraged to talk about their own experiences carrying out penetration tests. Given the broadness of the term `penetration test' these ranged from office-based white and black box evaluations of a client's product, through to open-scope `red team' tests. Client confidentiality and lack of security clearance made it difficult for interviewees to talk precisely about specific examples. In such cases, interviewees were presented with hypothetical ethical dilemmas (similar to that presented in Section 1) and asked to describe how they would address them.

Each interview took place at the workplace of the interviewees, and each interview lasted between 45 minutes to an hour. Transcripts from the interviews were subject to open and axial coding (Corbin and Strauss, 2008). From this coding exercise, 34 refined thematic concepts were identified, together with 34 relationships between these concepts. From this emerging model, a set of propositions was written that summarised each of the 34 conceptual relationships. These propositions were written on post-it notes, and subject to affinity diagramming to identify themed groupings of categories.

4. Results

4.1. Dilemmas

While the interviewees claimed they rarely faced moral dilemmas, we found evidence of two forms of dilemma faced by penetration testers. The first dilemma concerned managing penetration testing clients, and the tension between doing the right thing for the client company (the whole), and the right thing for its staff (the individual). While it was generally accepted that any form of activity that involved deception risks breaking the trust between the company and its staff, some interviewees believed that a company's security policy justified the use of human testing, irrespective of the legality or morality of the policy itself. The second dilemma concerned managing testing practices, and the tension between choosing a structured and carefully considered strategy (structured), over a strategy that was unstructured and contingent (unstructured). The former approach entails structuring an engagement such that ethical concerns are designed out. However, if the scope of a test expands or emergent technology is evaluated, there is a need to be more creative, and less bound by convention.

Based on the affinity diagramming exercise, we found two clusters of thematic concepts. One cluster corresponded with penetration testing behaviour that resolved these dilemmas by taking an individual/unstructured position (IU); the other cluster corresponded with a whole/structured position (WS). Both positions are not mutually exclusive, and we do not consider any position more virtuous than the other.

4.2. Dimensions

On considering the themes associated with the IU and WS positions, we found the following four additional groupings of category; these groupings provide insight into how penetration testers holding each position reflect on different concerns of ethical import. We consider these issues as ethical dimensions (Figure 1), and define these as follows:

- Value of ethics: the value penetration testers see in ethics.

- Ethical appeal: the means used by penetration testers to establish the credibility of their ethical position.

- Client focus: the emphasis placed on responsibly managing clients.

- Practice focus: the emphasis placed on providing assurance about penetration testing practices.

Dimension	Dilemma Positions	
	Individual / Unstructured (IU)	Whole / Structured (WS)
Value of ethics	Interpersonal skills	Legal sense
Ethical appeal	Common sense	Contingency
Client focus	Individual	Collective
Practice focus	Data and tool assurance	Information management

Figure 1: Perspectives adopted by dilemma positions for each dimension

4.2.1. Value of Ethics

For most interviewees, being ethical marked them out as professionals. For example, one interviewee (I4) observed: *"We all have to adhere to the CREST code of ethics, so we all rigorously adhere to that. I think I always go with the mentality that if the client is happy with what you're doing then you're along the right lines. Whenever I try and make a decision, you need to justify whether or not it's going to be beneficial for the client."* For this reason, some interviewees stated that either they or their companies would avoid testing activities, such as social engineering, for fear that these might be easily construed as unethical. Such activities not only jeopardise the well being of deceived clients, but also their career should problems occurred during testing. In some cases, however, such testing was deemed acceptable when undertaken as part of a `red team' test that evaluates a client's broader security posture.

In considering the more specific value of ethics taken by each position, we noted that the IU position considered ethics as a learned, interpersonal skill. When faced with a dilemma, juniors may defer responsibility for tackling ethical hazards to seniors or even their client. However, it is unclear who would be in the best position to tackle the dilemma. While the less senior tester has the most contextual knowledge, they may not necessarily know who is best placed to deal with it. The WS position of ethics is that of a vehicle for legality, and a means for honing legal senses. This standpoint claims that legal and moral issues are treated as one and the same, and that debate takes place in teams when moral issues are found. Testers subscribing to this perspective eschew anything morally ambiguous because it is understood that legal nuances are difficult to unpack.

4.2.2. Ethical appeal

Most interviewees claimed that the appeal used to resolve ethical issues was situational in some way, or – as characterized by I2 – " *The more you test, the more you get a sense of what is risky to do.* "

The justification taken by those adopting an IU position is that being ethical is 'common sense'. One interviewee claimed that the ease with which the law can be broken, and the implications to their career of breaking the law keeps testers honest. Junior penetration testers hone their penetration testing 'common sense' by shadowing more senior testers to understand how adopting an adversarial perspective can identify what would be hitherto ignored vulnerabilities. While the primary purpose of such shadowing is to glean an understanding of the technical detail of penetration testing, junior testers develop their understanding of professional penetration testing in the process. The justification taken by those taking a WS position is that being ethical means appealing to contingency and putting any ethical dilemma in context. By placing any prospective ethical issue in context, the risks associated with it become obvious when the right questions are asked at the right time; this ability to identify and address risks in context is developed as testers become more experienced.

4.2.3. Client focus

While no interviewees were asked to carry out activities that breached the UK Computer Misuse Act, some interviewees had been asked to consider engaging in activities that might have been in breach of Article 8 of the Human Rights Act. As such, interviewees were mindful of the need to do the right thing for the client with respect to their own legal and moral obligations. For example, I3 notes: *"the major thing for us is to always remember why you're there, and keep within that scope so not to go and explore the network for the sake of exploring the network. We're not there to read people's emails and that kind of thing."*

The IU position is shaped by the need to reactively manage individual contacts within the client organisation. While few interviewees reported active hostility towards them, conflict between penetration testing "red" teams and client infrastructure "blue" teams was not uncommon, particularly in companies where the managerial contact was inexperienced or lack credibility within their organisation. For example, one interviewee stated that, when testing web apps at a client site, any unavailability of the web app would typically be blamed on the testers. In other cases, conflict arose as a response to some form of criticism, be this in the design of software or the infrastructure. The WS position is shaped by the duty to provide value to the client organisation as a whole. This includes keeping the organisation appraised throughout a penetration test, implicitly educating clients about the value of penetration tests, and collaborating in such a way that clients are well placed to fix any problems identified once a final report is delivered. In some cases, this obligation is so strong that some testers addressed dilemmas by focusing initially on the impact to the client, rather than by starting to consider the social and technical implications of the dilemma first. Some interviewees felt obliged to proactively address potential conflict. For example, one interviewee described how he would engage client staff by encouraging them to raise problems with him in such a way that, when highlighted in the final report, recommendations could be stated that address them.

4.2.4. Practice focus

The interviewees unanimously cared about their security practices, and the perceptions people hold about penetration testers. They believed that their association with a professional body, such as CREST, provided some assurance that their work practices are trustworthy. For example, I4 expressed concern that bad practice or low standards potentially undermine their entire industry: *"you have to adhere to all of your ethical guidance and you need to ... if you find those vulnerabilities you need to tell them about them immediately. As security experts, we have to do that otherwise the security industry as a whole... there wouldn't be any faith in it, or any trust."*

The responsibility to penetration testing practice is manifest by the IU and WS positions in different ways. The IU position is concerned with providing assurance about both the tools used, and any findings resulting from tool usage. Several interviewees noted that research into a potential tool's provenance was strongly encouraged by their firms, and internal training courses and seminars are used to share knowledge team members had discovered about new tools. Although some interviewees noted that job interview questions touched upon ethical practice, it was acknowledged that little staff development time was spent on what was described as 'soft consultancy stuff' like ethics. The WS position is shaped by the need to provide assurance about how information is managed. This position focuses on the integrity of information managed and delivered to the client. While this integrity is a product of the tools used to provide input into the report, referring to raw data and logs was considered as something only required as a last resort. Those adopting this position believe that factual information should always be defended, and evidence from different sources is sanitised before use. This level of assurance allays any apprehension that clients might have about what a penetration testing team has been doing.

4.3. Using the model to unpack fallacies and biases

By creating a model of ethical dilemmas and dimensions, it becomes possible to spot fallacies resulting from each position. For example, within the IU position, it is acknowledged that adopting an adversarial perspective, and shadowing more senior colleagues can hone the senses of more junior penetration testers. However, it is a fallacy to assume that ethical behaviour will always follow in such a situation. If the more senior colleague's behaviour is morally ambiguous then a junior tester may not appreciate that practices gleaned are equally ambiguous. Moreover, when adopting an adversarial and unstructured position then there is also a danger that behaviour that seems common sense may become legally ambiguous as well.

Potential biases are also evident when considering tensions between concepts. Within the WS position, educating the client about penetration testing is important, as is the need for clients to accept responsibility for remedying any problems found. When a report has been delivered to the client, positive feedback and the lack of further correspondence may indicate that the report has been accepted and its recommendations actioned. It is, however, equally possible that the client may have sought the test only to obtain some form of accreditation, and may action few of the recommendations made. Should testers believe the report is being actioned then they may be subject to the fundamental attribution bias; this refers to the tendency of people to ignore possible external causes of the behaviour of others and to assume that their behaviour is a reflection of internal dispositions (Gilbert and Malone, 1995). As such, testers may underestimate how the role of external constraints and requirements shape the behaviour of those around them, and in turn overestimate how much their actions are determined by their personality, values and beliefs. This bias is also evident by the tendency of testers to assume that they are in fact better at understanding the importance of external factors in the behaviour of others than their peers (van Boven et al., 2003).

5. Conclusion

This paper has presented several ethical dilemmas and dimensions faced by penetration testers. In doing so, we have made two contributions. First, we have shown how the differences associated with the dilemmas identified are manifest across different ethical dilemmas. Second, we have briefly illustrated how both these differences and the model can be used to unpack possible fallacies and biases that affect ethical decision making before, during, or after a penetration test. A limitation of this work is that only UK practitioners were interviewed. However, given the experience level of the testers, there is little reason to assume these results do not scale when considering other testers with an equivalent level of professional experience, particularly those that engage with other professional bodies.

6. Acknowledgements

The research described in this paper was funded by the Bournemouth University FIF project Bournemouth European Network in Cyber Security.

7. References

Adams, A. and Sasse, M. A. (1999). Users are not the enemy. Communications of the ACM, 42:41–46.

Bishop, M. (2007). About penetration testing. Security & Privacy, IEEE, 5(6):84–87.

van Boven, L., White, K., Kamada, A., and Gilovich, T. (2003). Intuitions about situational correction in self and others. Journal of Personality and Social Psychology, 85(2):249–258.

CESG (2014). What is CHECK? Available from http://www.cesg.gov.uk

Chiesa, R., Ducci, S., and Ciappi, S. (2009). Profiling hackers: the science of criminal profiling as applied to the world of hacking. Auerbach Publications.

Corbin, J. M. and Strauss, A. L. (2008). Basics of qualitative research: techniques and procedures for developing grounded theory. Sage Publications, Inc., 3rd edition.

CREST (2014). Code of Conduct for CREST Qualified Individuals. Available from http://www.crest-approved.org

Egelman, S., Herley, C., and van Oorschot, P. C. (2013). Markets for zero-day exploits: Ethics and implications. In Proceedings of the 2013 Workshop on New Security Paradigms Workshop, NSPW '13, pages 41–46. ACM.

Geer, D. and Harthorne, J. (2002). Penetration testing: a duet. In Computer Security Applications Conference, 2002. Proceedings. 18th Annual, pages 185– 195.

Gilbert, D. T. and Malone, P. S. (1995). The correspondence bias. Psychological Bulletin, 117(1):21–38.

Haber, E. M. and Bailey, J. (2007). Design guidelines for system administration tools developed through ethnographic field studies. In Proceedings of the 2007 symposium on Computer human interaction for the management of information technology, CHIMIT '07. ACM.

Hall, B. R. (2014). A synthesized definition of computer ethics. SIGCAS Comput. Soc., 44(3):21–35.

Hertzog, P. (2010). OSSTMM 3 - The Open Source Security Testing Methodology Manual. ISECOM.

Holt, T. (2010). Examining the role of technology in the formation of deviant subcultures. Social Science Computer Review, 28(4):466–481.

Ladd, J. (1985). The quest for a code of professional ethics: An intellectual and moral confusion. In Johnson, D. G. and Snapper, J. W., editors, Ethical Issues in the Use of Computers, pages 8–13. Wadsworth Publ. Co.

Perlman, B. and Varma, R. (2002). Improving ethical engineering practice. Technology and Society Magazine, IEEE, 21(1):40–47.

Pierce, J., Jones, A., and Warren, M. (2006). Penetration testing professional ethics: a conceptual model and taxonomy. Australasian Journal of Information Systems, 13(2):193–200.

Spafford, E. H. (1992). Are computer hacker break-ins ethical? Journal of Systems and Software, 17(1):41–47.

Tavani, H. T. (2006). Ethics and Technology: Ethical Issues in an Age of Information and Communication Technology. John Wiley & Sons, Inc., New York, NY, USA.

Werlinger, R., Hawkey, K., Botta, D., and Beznosov, K. (2009). Security practitioners in context: Their activities and interactions with other stakeholders within organizations. International Journal of Human Computer Studies, 67(7):584–606.

Xynos, K., Sutherland, I., Read, H., Everitt, E., and Blyth, A. J. C. (2010). Penetration Testing and Vulnerability Assessments: A Professional Approach. In Proceedings of the 1st International Cyber Resilience Conference, pages 126–132.

The Relationship Between Privacy, Information Security and the Trustworthiness of a Crowdsourcing System in a Smart City

L. Cilliers and S. Flowerday

University of Fort Hare, South Africa
lcilliers@ufh.ac.za; sflowerday@ufh.ac.za

Abstract

With the growing number of people living in cities, the challenges faced by governments in providing an acceptable standard of service delivery are immense. 'Smart cities' is a new and innovative approach that has been formulated over the past few years in order to use current infrastructure and resources more effectively and efficiently. For a smart city to work, large amounts of information must be collected from the citizens, which may cause privacy concerns. Information security influences the perceived trustworthiness of the crowdsourcing system which, in turn, increases the participation of citizens in smart city projects. This paper investigates the relationship between the privacy, information security and perceived trustworthiness of a crowdsourcing system in a smart city. The study made use of a quantitative approach using a survey design. A questionnaire was completed by 361 participants in a public safety project hosted in East London, South Africa. The results indicated there is a positive relationship between the information security in and the perceived trustworthiness of a crowdsourcing system. Therefore, the privacy concerns of citizens making use of a crowdsourcing system can be alleviated by increasing the perceived trustworthiness and the information security of the system.

Keywords

Smart city; trustworthiness; information security; privacy

1. Introduction

More than half of the world's population is now living in cities, with this trend towards urbanisation expected to continue in the future (Balta-Ozkan, Davidson, Bicket, & Whitmarsh, 2013). It is thus incumbent on local government to provide public services for this increasing population; however, city infrastructure and resources often have not increased in line with the growing population. This suggests that local governments must find alternative ways of using existing resources more efficiently and effectively (Fuzile, 2011; Harrison & Donnelly, 2011). In order to accomplish these goals and address some of the problems of urbanisation, cities have to become 'smarter' (Karadağ, 2013; Buhl & Jetter, 2009).

Smart cities make use of information and communication technologies (ICT) in order to integrate and connect city services so that the services provided are sustainable and ultimately improve the citizens' quality of life (Dimitriou, 2012). There are a variety of areas in the city that can be improved by making use of the smart city concept. These include the economy, energy, e-governance, mobility, environment and the quality of citizens' lives (Chourabi, et al., 2012).

Smart cities depend on large amounts of information being collected from either the city infrastructure or the citizens in order to be able to make intelligent decisions about city management. The data that is collected can then be analysed in order to anticipate problems or isolate trouble spots (Introna, 1997). There are two types of crowdsourcing method that can be used to collect data from citizens. The first is opportunistic data gathering which takes place when citizens provide information making use of sensors connected to their mobile phones. This type of data gathering is involuntary and the participant does not have control over what data is collected, the time frame for collecting the data, or the location where data will be collected. This data collection method raises serious privacy concerns for citizens who often decline of participate in opportunistic data gathering smart city campaigns (Christin, Kanhere, Reinhardt, & Hollick, 2011; Mehta, 2011).

By contrast, participatory crowdsourcing is a voluntary data gathering method where individuals can choose what they want to report. This approach is particularly useful for unusual events such as accidents or other public safety related problems because citizens can report what they observe in their immediate environment (Halder, 2014). As the person involved can choose what data is reported to a participatory crowdsourcing system, privacy concerns are minimal. However, once the person has reported the information to the crowdsourcing system, they have no control over what is done with it (Bhaveer & Flowerday, 2013). Therefore, information security controls must be in place to ensure that the information reported to the crowdsourcing system remains confidential, maintains integrity and is available to the correct stakeholders (Whitman & Mattord, 2009). Wang, Huang and Louis (2012) report that there is often no transparency concerning the information security controls in crowdsourcing systems, meaning that citizens have no idea whether their data is properly secured. These concerns affect the perceived trustworthiness of the crowdsourcing system and the citizens' participation rate. However, since trust is a subjective term, it is difficult to manage it effectively (Sarwar & Khan, 2013). Consequently, this paper sets out to investigate what the major privacy, information security and trust issues are in current smart cities and how the relationship between these factors influences the decisions of citizens to participate in smart city projects.

The paper is structured as follows: The next section provides a discussion about the privacy concerns of citizens when reporting data to a crowdsourcing system. Then, the concept of information security is discussed with particular reference to the trustworthiness of a crowdsourcing system, after which a brief overview is provided of the methodology used in this study. Next, the results of the study are discussed as they relate to increased citizen participation in a smart city.

2. Privacy

Privacy has been identified as one of the most important considerations for citizens in deciding whether they are willing to participate in smart city initiatives (Pew

Research Centre, 2014). Citizens are becoming more concerned about their privacy as the ability of local government to collect information about them increases. The data that is collected from a citizen can be used to record and track the individual's activities and, coupled with other personally identifiable information, can be viewed as an intrusion of user privacy. As a result, citizens may refrain from participating in smart city projects in order to avert the Big Brother effect (Halder, 2014; Dimitriou, 2012; Chourabi et al., 2012; Christin et al., 2011).

The definition of information privacy that is most relevant to a smart city is that of Westin (1967, p. 1): "Information privacy relates to the person's right to determine when, how and to what extent information about him or her is communicated to others." There are three different concerns when one considers privacy in a smart city. These concerns include the right of the citizen to be left alone, the right of the citizen to control the information collected about them and how the information is used, disclosed to third parties or retained, and the right to be aware what harm may be caused if personally identifiable information is made available to unauthorised parties (Sarwar & Khan, 2013).

Cilliers and Flowerday (2014) reported that the majority of citizens expected detrimental consequences if the information reported to the crowdsourcing system were to be made available to unauthorised parties and they therefore chose to remain anonymous when reporting information to the system. There are four possible consequences for the individual if the information reported to a crowdsourcing system were to be used for malicious purposes (Chourabi et al., 2012). These include intrusion upon one's private affairs; public disclosure of embarrassing private facts about the individual; defamation of character arising from having "private facts" misrepresented in public; and identity appropriation or theft for personal gain by others (Westin, 1967). Therefore, the decision to participate in smart city projects will be determined by the level of privacy and information security that the crowdsourcing system affords citizens (Pew Research Centre, 2014). The next section will discuss the information security necessary in a smart city.

3. Information Security

Information security makes use of proactive measures in order to manage the risks, threats and vulnerabilities related to private information (Parakkattu & Kunnathur, 2010). These measures can protect the privacy of citizens and the information provided to the crowdsourcing system, as they make provision for access controls, retention and storage of information, as well as incident response and recovery procedures (Pearson, 2012).

Whitman and Mattord (2009) report that the most commonly used framework in information security is called the 'C-I-A triad', which refers to the confidentiality, integrity and availability of the information reported to the crowdsourcing system. Confidentiality entails the prevention of any unauthorised disclosure of information reported to the crowdsourcing system, while integrity refers to the protection of the reported information from unauthorised amendment or deletion. The availability of the information is concerned with the ability of all who are authorised to access the information to do so reliably and without undue delay (Suna, Chang, Suna, & Wanga, 2011; Whitman & Mattord, 2009).

Most of the information security problems reported by citizens in a participatory crowdsourcing project can be divided into two categories. The first category considers hardware risks and includes the device that is used to report information to the crowdsourcing system. Mobile devices can be stolen and are vulnerable to security breaches, as the devices lack the computational capacity of personal computers (Wang et al., 2012). Furthermore, once the information is reported, the citizen has to trust that it will be stored securely. The second category has to do with the information that is reported to the crowdsourcing system. Sarwar and Khan (2013) state that the citizen has no control over the ownership of the information once it is reported to the crowdsourcing system; this means that the information can be stolen, used for a different purpose than that originally agreed on, or made available to unauthorised parties. There is also a lack of transparency about the physical location of storage, the security profiles of the site, ownership of the information and what can be done with it (Pearson, 2012). The next section will elaborate on the concept of trust and information security in crowdsourcing systems.

4. Trust

Trust is considered to be a complex social phenomenon (Huang & Nicol, 2014). While there is no universally accepted scholarly definition, trust is understood as a psychological state where an individual has the intention to accept vulnerability or risk based on the positive expectation of the intention or behaviour of another (Pearson, 2012).

There are three characteristics that will determine the perceived trustworthiness of a crowdsourcing system. These are the ability, the benevolence and the integrity of the system (Mayer, Davis, & Schoorman, 1995). The first characteristic, ability, indicates the competency of the crowdsourcing system in performing the expected functions efficiently and consistently (Mallalieu, 2005). In a crowdsourcing system, the ability of the system to record the information reported by the participants correctly will influence this characteristic (Cilliers & Flowerday, 2014). The second characteristic, benevolence, is defined as the extent to which the trustee, that is, local government, is believed to want to act in the trustors', or citizens', best interests. In this study, benevolence refers to the intention of local government to use the information reported to the crowdsourcing system in the best interests of the citizens (Mayer et al., 1995). The last characteristic, integrity, is defined as the perception that, in order to be useful, the information that is reported in a crowdsourcing system must be complete, accurate and current (Cilliers & Flowerday, 2014).

Furthermore, trust can be divided into two categories that will determine the level of perceived trustworthiness of the crowdsourcing system. The first considers preventative security measures that are put in place from a technical point of view (Varadharajan, 2009). These 'hard trust' mechanisms are used to determine the crowdsourcing system's security measures, making use of authenticity controls, encryption, algorithms and audits (Pearson, 2012). Hard trust is often fairly static and the trustworthiness of a system is perceived solely on the basis of the evidence provided by these security measures (Varadharajan, 2009).

The second type of trust is called 'soft trust' and takes into consideration human emotion, perception and experience (Varadharajan, 2009). Unlike hard trust, soft trust is not based on evidence of security credentials, but depends on past interaction with the crowdsourcing system and the recommendations of fellow citizens. Soft security attributes such as the reliability, dependability, benevolence and perceived competence of the crowdsourcing system will all determine how trustworthy the citizens perceive the system to be (Suna et al., 2011). While no crowdsourcing system can be made 100% secure with hard trust mechanisms, soft trust can be used to complement these mechanisms to improve the trustworthiness of the crowdsourcing system (Ling & Masao, 2011).

Information security controls, or hard trust mechanisms, are put in place to protect the information the citizen reports to the crowdsourcing system (Flowerday & Von Solms, 2006). However, the level of trustworthiness will be affected by the perception of how adequate the citizens perceive the security controls that are in place to protect this information to be (soft trust) (Pearson, 2012).

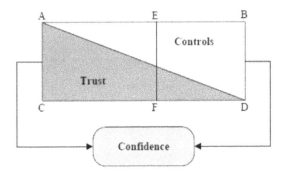

Figure 1: The relationship between trust and controls in a crowdsourcing system (Flowerday & Von Solms, 2006)

Figure 1 illustrates how trust and information security can work together to influence a citizen's decision to participate in a crowdsourcing project. The rectangular area, A, B, D, C, represents the interaction between the citizen and the participatory crowdsourcing system, while triangle A, B, D represents the controls that are inherent to the crowdsourcing system (hard trust). Triangle A, D, C represents the trust that the citizen has that the system will protect their privacy (soft trust). The line E–F is the hypothetical positioning of the citizen's risk appetite, the position of which can be influenced by the individual's propensity to accept risk. When considering the risk appetite line it is clear that the white area is protected by the information security controls and the dark area, which presents risk, is influenced by the perceived trustworthiness of the crowdsourcing system. This means that a citizen's confidence in the crowdsourcing system can be influenced by both trust and information security controls. However, the extent of this confidence will depend on the risk appetite line of the individual (Ling & Masao, 2011).

5. Research Methodology

A positivistic, quantitative study design was used in this project. The study population consisted of citizens living in East London, South Africa. The current East London population is estimated to be 440 000 people (StatsSA, 2011). The general socioeconomic conditions are considered to be poor with the unemployment rate at 28%; in addition, 57% of the population is reported to be living below the poverty line (Managa, 2012).

The University of Fort Hare, in conjunction with IBM, developed an Interactive Voice Response (IVR) system and mobi site which allowed members of the public to report public safety concerns in their immediate environment. The reported data was used in predictive analysis in order to identify problem areas in East London where, if deployed, the limited public safety resources would have the biggest impact.

An IVR system is suitable for developing countries because the existing telephone infrastructure can be used, citizens unfamiliar with the technology can report public safety matters at their own pace, and the IVR system would not exclude illiterate citizens from the project (Whitman & Mattord, 2009). Owing to the high cost of telephone calls in South Africa, the mobi site was introduced as a suitable alternative to the IVR system. During the survey that followed the introduction of the IVR system, citizens indicated no preference for either the mobi site or IVR system when reporting public safety matters. Residents were recruited to participate in this project through marketing in the local newspapers, social media and the distribution of flyers. Figure 2 provides a graphical representation of the project.

PUBLIC SAFETY

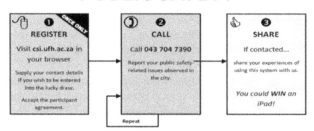

The Crowdsourcing Safety Initiative (CSI)
Helping you to help your city...

Figure 2: Steps in the crowdsourcing system

A total of 485 people registered for the project and were subsequently sent a questionnaire to complete at the end of it. The questionnaire was compiled making use of previously published material in the area of information security and trust. Information security was tested making use of 3 variables: Availability, Confidentiality and Integrity of the crowdsourcing system while the trustworthiness of the system was tested making use of 3 variables: Benevolence, Integrity and Ability of the system to accurately reflect the public safety concerns of the citizens of East London (Refer Table 1 for questions). A total of 361 questionnaires were completed and returned. Thus, the response rate was 81.2%. The Cronbach's alpha coefficient was computed and was found to be 0.9, which is considered to indicate good test reliability. Ethical approval for the study was obtained from the Research Ethics Committee of the University of Fort Hare.

6. Results and Discussion

This paper discussed the relationship between privacy, information security and the perceived trustworthiness of a crowdsourcing system in a smart city. The study sample consisted of 219 (60.7%) males and 142 (39.3%) females. Seventy-one per cent of the participants were younger than 40 years of age. The 40 to 49 year age group consisted of 14.7% of the study sample, while the two oldest age groups, 50 to 59 and 60+ were the smallest groups with percentages of 10.2 and 3.3%, respectively.

Correlation analysis tests were conducted to determine whether relationships existed between the different factors identified for these two constructs in the literature section. The correlation coefficients provide an indication of whether the relationship is a positive relationship (changes to constructs increase or decrease in the same direction) or a negative relationship (constructs respond in opposite directions). The results for the information security factors (confidentiality, integrity and availability) and the trust factors (integrity, benevolence and ability) are displayed below.

As shown in Table 1, Pearson's correlation coefficient was used to investigate the relationship between the factors contributing to information security and the trustworthiness of the crowdsourcing system. A p-value of less than 0.001 was chosen to indicate statistical significance.

The relationships between the information security and the trustworthiness of the crowdsourcing system were found to be statistically significant, as positive correlations are shown with a p-value smaller than 0.001. These findings illustrate that it can be anticipated that information security will increase the perceived trustworthiness of a crowdsourcing system among citizens, which in turn will increase participation in smart city projects.

			Confidentiality	Integrity	Availability
			I prefer to provide information anonymously	I do not worry that the information I provided will be modified in any way	The IVR system must be available 100% of the time in order to be useful
Integrity	The information that is reported in a participatory crowdsourcing system must be complete, accurate and current in order to be useful	Pearson Correlation	164.573	97.067	375.730
		Sig. (2-tailed)	0.00	0.00	0.00
		N	361	361	361
Benevolence	I do not worry if the information provided will be used for something other than the intended purpose	Pearson Correlation	98.509	205.753	66.704
		Sig. (2-tailed)	0.00	0.00	0.00
		N	361	361	361
Ability	I trust the system to reflect my public safety matter correctly	Pearson Correlation	183.632	70.912	393.119
		Sig. (2-tailed)	0.00	0.00	0.00
		N	361	361	361

Table 1: Correlation between information security and trust factors

From the statistical tests conducted in this section, it is clear that there is a direct correlation between the trustworthiness of a crowdsourcing system and information security in place to protect the privacy of the citizens. The information security controls in a crowdsourcing system are not always transparent, meaning that the majority of the citizens (72.6%) preferred to remain anonymous when reporting information to the system (confidentiality). The citizens also agreed that for the system to be useful, it must be available all the time (86.6%). The integrity of the system was more of a concern for citizens, however, as more than a third (37.5%) raised concerns that the information could be modified in some way.

The citizens did believe that the crowdsourcing system would be able to reflect their public safety concerns correctly (84.0%), while 86.6% agreed that the information reported must be complete and accurate in order to be useful. This is especially important in the public safety context as the information will be used to determine the correct response to emergency situations. The citizens were concerned about the intended purpose of the information reported, with 42.2% reporting that they were concerned that the information may be used inappropriately.

7. Conclusion

In view of the resource constraints experienced by local authorities in developing countries, they must find ways to make use of existing resources more effectively and efficiently. Accordingly, smart cities make use of ICT to collect data that can be analysed to predict where resources will be needed or will have the biggest impact. In view of the fact that large amounts of data have to be collected, citizens participating in these projects have certain privacy concerns. One of the ways in which to address these privacy concerns, and subsequently increase the participation of citizens in smart city projects, is to enhance the perceived trustworthiness of the crowdsourcing making use of information security controls. This study found that there is a positive relationship between the privacy concerns and perceived trustworthiness of the crowdsourcing system. The trustworthiness of a crowdsourcing system can be increased by implementing appropriate information security controls. Consequently, further research in the field needs to investigate the specific influence that either soft and hard trust mechanisms have on the perceived trustworthiness of the crowdsourcing system. Appropriate feedback mechanisms should also be investigated to find the most appropriate mechanism for the public safety context.

8. References

ACOPEA. (2012). African Child Online Protection Education \& Awareness Centre. available online from: http://www.cto.int/media/events/pst-ev/2013/CTO%20Forum/African%20Child%20Online%20Protection%20Education%20\&%20Awareness%20Centre.pdf, Accessed on [12 November 2013].

Antwi-bekoe, E., & Nimako, S. G. (2012). Computer Security Awareness and Vulnerabilities : An Exploratory Study for Two Public Higher Institutions in Ghana. Journal of Science and Technology , 1, 358-375.

Atkinson, S., Furnell, S., & Phippen, A. (2009). Securing the next generation: enhancing e-safety awareness among young people . Computer Fraud \& Security , 2009 (7), 13-19.

Ayodele, T., Shoniregun, C., & Akmayeva, G. (2012). Anti-Phishing Prevention Measure for Email Systems. Internet Security (WorldCIS), (pp. 208-211). Guelph.

Balta-Ozkan, N., Davidson, R., Bicket , M., & Whitmarsh, L. (2013). Social barriers to the adoption of smart homes. Energy Policy, 63 , 363-374.

Becta. (2009). AUPs in context: Establishing safe and responsible online behaviours. available online from: http://education.qld.gov.au/studentservices/behaviour/qsaav/docs/establishing-safe-responsible-online-behaviours.pdf, Accessed on [10 November 2013].

Bhaveer, B., & Flowerday, S. (2013). Using participatory crowdsourcing in South Africa to create a safer living environment. International Journal of Distriuted Sensor Networks , 1-13.

Buhl, H. U., & Jetter, M. (2009). BISE's Responsibility for our Planet. Business and Information Systems Engineering, 1(4) , pp. 273-276.

Byron, T. (2008). Safer Children in a Digital World. available online from: http://webarchive.nationalarchives.gov.uk/20130401151715/https://www.education.gov.uk/pu blications/eOrderingDownload/DCSF-00334-2008.pdf, Accessed on [5 November 2013].

Caragliu, A., Del Bo, C., & Nijkamp, P. (2009). Smart Cities in Europe. Series Research Memoranda 0048. Amsterdam: University of Amsterdam, Faculty of Economics, Business Administration and Econometrics.

Chen, J., & Guo, C. (2006). Online Detection and Prevention of Phishing Attacks. Communications and Networking in China, 2006. ChinaCom '06. First International Conference, (pp. 1-7). Beijing.

Chourabi, H., Nam, T., Walker , S., Gil-Garcia, J., Mellouli, S., Nahon, K., et al. (2012). Understanding Smart Cities: An Integrative Framework. 45th System Science (HICSS) Hawaii International Conference (pp. 2289-2297). Hawaii: HICSS.

Christin, D. (2010). Impenetrable Obscurity vs Informed Decisions: Privacy Solutions for Participatory Sensing. In Proceedings of the 8th IEEE International Conference on Pervasive Computing and Communications (pp. 847-848). Mannheim: IEEE.

Christin, D., Kanhere, S., Reinhardt, A., & Hollick , M. (2011). A Survey on Privacy in Mobile Participatory Sensing Applications. Journal of Systems and Software, 84(11) , 1928-1946.

Cilliers, L., & Flowerday , S. (2014). Information security in a public safety, participatory crowdsourcing smart city project. World CIS Conference (pp. 1-5). London: World CIS.

Cole, K., Chetty, M., Larosa, C., Rietta, F., Schmitt, D. K., & Goodman, S. E. (2008). Cybersecurity in Africa : An Assessment. available online from: http://s3.amazonaws.com/zanran_storage/www.cistp.gatech.edu/ContentPages/43945844.pdf, Accessed on [22 November 2013].

de Lange, M., & von Solms, R. (2012). An e-Safety Educational Framework in South Africa. Proceesing of the Southern Africa Telecommunication Networks and Applications Conference (SATNAC) .

Dimitriou, T. (2012). Smart Internet of things in future cities (with emphasis on security). Berlin: Germany.

Dlamini, I., Taute, B., & Radebe, J. (2011). Framework for an African policy towards creating cyber security awareness. Proceedings of Southern African Cyber Security Awareness Workshop (SACSAW) , 15-31.

e4Africa. (2011). Technology in schools – for better or for worse. available online from: http://www.e4africa.co.za/?p=3516, Accessed on [20 November 2013].

Flowerday, S., & Vol Solms, R. (2006). Trust: An Element of Information Security. SEC .

Furnell, S. (2005). Why users cannot use security. Computers & Security (24), 274-279.

Fuzile, L. (2011). Local Government budgets and expenditure. Pretoria: National Treasury.

Grobler, M., & Dlamini, Z. (2012). Global Cyber Trends a South African Reality. IST-Africa 2012 Conference Proceedings .

Halder, B. (2014). Evolution of crowdsourcing: potential data protection, privacy and security concerns under the new Media Age. Democracia Digital eGoverno Electronico , 337-393.

Harrison, C., & Donnelly, I. (2011). A theory of smart cities. Proceedings of the 55th Annual Meeting of the ISSS. London: University of Hull Business School.

Huang, J., & Nicol, D. (2014). Evidence-based trust reasoning. HotSoS2014 (pp. 1-2). Raleigh: ACM.

IBM. (2010). Smarter Thinking for a Smarter Planet. Retrieved February 28, 2013 from IBM: http://www.ibm.com/smarterplanet/global/files/us_en_us_1oud_ibmlbn0041_transtasman_boo k.pdf

Introna, L. (1997). Privacy and the computer: why we need privacy in the Information Society. Metaphilosophy, 28(3) , 259-275.

Jagatic, T., Johnson, N., Jakobsson, M., & Menczer, F. (2005, December 15). Social Phishing. Bloomington.

Janssen, C. (n.d.). Spear Phishing. Retrieved April 29, 2013 from Techopedia: http://www.techopedia.com/definition/4121/spear-phishing

Jisc. (2012). A guide to open educational resources. available online from: http://www.jisc.ac.uk/publications/programmerelated/2013/Openeducationalresources.aspx Accessed on [20 November 2013].

Kanyesigye, F. (n.d.). New drive to fight hackers, New Times. available online from: http://www.newtimes.co.rw/news/index.php?a=66437&i=15343, Accessed on [22 November 2013]. , 2013.

Karadağ, T. (2013). An evolution of the Smart City Approach. Middle East Technical University.

Kortjan, N., & von Solms, R. (2013). Cyber Security Education in Developing Countries: A South African Perspective. Lecture Notes of the Institute for Computer Sciences, Social Informatics and Telecommunications Engineering , 119, 289-297.

Kritzinger, E. (2011). Cyber Awareness Implementation Plan (CAIP) for schools. Presentation for Southern African Cyber Security Awareness Workshop (SACSAW) .

Ling, A., & Masao, M. (2011). Smart grid information security (IS) functional requirements. arXiv preprint arXiv:1109.4474, 2011.

Mallalieu, L. (2005). An examination of the role of customer attributions in understanding trust loss and recovery in buyer-seller relationships. Supply Chain Forum: an International Journal, 6(2) , 68-80.

Managa, S. (2012). Unfulfilled Promises and their Consequences: A Reflection on Local Goverment Performance and the Critical Issue of Poor Service Delivery in South Africa . Africa Insitute of South Africa , 76, 1-8.

Mars, M., & Erasmus, L. (2012). Telemedicine can lower health care costs in Africa. Innovate , 7, 32-33.

Mayer, R., Davis, J., & Schoorman, F. (1995). An integrative model of organizational trust. Academy of Management Review , 20 (3), pp. 709-734.

Mehta, S. M. (2011, August 25). Mobile 311: a framework for 311 services with mobile technology. San Diego: San Diego State University.

Migrant. (2013). M-PESA International Money Transfer Service, Safaricom. available online from:
http://www.ilo.org/dyn/migpractice/migmain.showPractice?p_lang=en\&p_practice_id=70, Accessed on [12 November 2013].

Miles, D. (2011). Youth protection: Digital citizenship - Principles and new resources. Second Worldwide Cybersecurity Summit (WCS), (pp. 1-3).

OER_Africa.   (2013).   Understanding   OER.   available   online   from: http://www.oerafrica.org/understandingoer/UnderstandingOER/tabid/56/Default.aspx, Accessed on [20 November 2013].

Parakkattu, S., & Kunnathur, A. (2010). A framework for research in infomration security management. Northeast Decision Sciences Institute Proceedings , 318-323.

Pearson, S. (2012). Privacy, security and trust in cloud computing. New York: IBM.

Pew Research Centre. (2014). Emerging nations embrace the Internet. Washington: Mobile Technology.

PWC. (2012). Telecoms in Africa: innovating and inspiring. Communications Review .

Reed, M. (2012). Press release: Africa mobile subscriptions count to cross 750 million mark in fourth quarter of 2012. Informa Telecoms \& Media .

Safaricom. (2012). iCow. available online from: http://www.safaricom.co.ke/personal/value-added-services/social-innovation/icow, Accessed on [12 November 2013].

Safaricom.   (2012).   Relax,   you've   got   M-Pesa.   available   online   from: http://www.safaricom.co.ke/personal/m-pesa/m-pesa-services-tariffs/relax-you-have-got-m-pesa, Accessed on [12 November 2013].

Sarwar, A., & Khan, M. (2013). A review of trust aspects in cloud computing security. International Journal of Cloud Computing and Services Science , 116-122.

Sato, N. (2013). ICT stakeholders discuss emerging issues on African cyber security. available online   from: http://www.humanipo.com/news/32773/ict-stakeholders-discuss-emerging-issues-on-cyber-security, Accessed on [21 November 2013].

Spamhaus. (2010, January). Whitepapers: Effective filtering. Retrieved July 16, 2013 from Spamhaus: http://www.spamhaus.org/whitepapers/effective_filtering/

StatsSA. (2011). Key results: Census 2011. Retrieved January 21, 2015 from Stats South Africa: www.statssa.gov.za/Census2011/.../Census_2011_Key_results.pdf

Suna, D., Chang, G., Suna, L., & Wanga, X. (2011). Advanced in Control Engineering and Information Science surveying and analysing security, privacy and trust issues in cloud computing environments. Procedia Engineering , 2852-2856.

TeleGeography. (2013). Africa's international bandwidth growth to lead the world. TeleGeography: Global Bandwidth Forecast Service .

Think_U_Know. (2008). Welcome to Hector's World. available online from: http://www.thinkuknow.co.uk/5_7/hectorsworld/, Accessed on [15 November 2013].

Varadharajan, V. (2009). A note on trust-enhanced security. IEEE Security and Privacy, 7 , 57-59.

Wang, Y., Huang, Y., & Louis, C. (2012). Respecting user privacy in mobile crowdsourcing. ASE2012 (pp. 1-15). London: ASE.

Westin, A. (1967). Privacy and Freedom. New York: Atheneum Publishers.

Whitman, B., & Mattord, H. (2009). Principles of information security. Boston : Thomson Course Technology.

Online Fraud Defence by Context Based Micro Training

J. Kävrestad and M. Nohlberg

The School of informatics, Högskolan i Skövde, Skövde, Sweden
e-mail: {joakim.kavrestad; marcus.nohlberg}@his.se

Abstract

Online frauds are a category of Internet crime that has been increasing globally over the past years. Online fraudsters use a lot of different arenas and methods to commit their crimes and that is making defence against online fraudsters a difficult task. Today we see continuous warnings in the daily press and both researchers and governmental web-pages propose that Internet users gather knowledge about online frauds in order to avoid victimisation. In this paper we suggest a framework for presenting this knowledge to the Internet users when they are about to enter a situation where they need it. We provide an evaluation of the framework that indicates that it can both make users less prone to fraudulent ads and more trusting towards legitimate ads. This is done with a survey containing 117 participants over two groups where the participants were asked to rate the trustworthiness of fraudulent and legitimate ads.. One groups used the framework before the rating and the other group did not. The results showed that, in our study, the participants using the framework put less trust in fraudulent ads and more trust in legitimate ads.

Keywords

Online fraud, fraud defence, awareness, micro training

1. Introduction

Over the past years online fraud has evolved to be an increasing crime that is targeting a large portion of the Internet users. This fact is being reported in many countries including Sweden and the USA (Brottsförebyggande rådet,2013; IC3, 2013). As one example it was estimated that one third of the American adults experience victimization annually (Pratt, Holtfreter, & Reisig, 2010). Online frauds come in many different forms and are occurring in several different arenas including e-mail, social networks, online auction houses and telephones. The great variety of the modus operandi of the fraudsters makes online fraud defense a difficult task.

Previous research makes it clear that online fraud is not a crime that target specific groups of Internet users. Rather, it seems as if anyone that is present on the arenas were frauds are being executed faces the risk of not only being targeted by a fraudster, but also to fall for the fraudsters actions. This is shown in the research by Wilsem (2013).

The common suggestion on how to defend yourself against online fraudsters in to gather the knowledge and skills you need to avoid being defrauded before you encounter a fraudster, as exemplified by usa.gov (2013) *"The best way to fight Internet fraud is to learn how to avoid becoming a victim".*

Today, this knowledge is often presented on governmental and business webpages and the users are expected to identify and make use of the information on their own. This puts the responsibility of defense on the users rather than the actors hosting the arenas were the frauds can take place.

In this paper we suggest a model for online fraud defense that aims at educating users that are encountering a potentially fraudulent situation. The education is taking place in the moment were the fraud may be executed and is tailored to learn the user about the specific fraud attack he is currently in the risk of facing. This methodology is influenced by the concept of situated learning as described by Herrington & Oliver (1995).

With this approach we believe that the users will make use of the information because it is relevant for their current situation. It has also been discussed that when you acquire knowledge in a situation where you use that knowledge, the overall learning process provides are better result compared to if you are learning in a theoretic manner, i.e. by reading from a book or webpage (Brown et al, 1989). Further, as shown by Davinson & Sillence (2010), being aware of the possibility of being defrauded will reduce the risk of being victimized. It is our belief that presenting information about online frauds just before the user enters an arena where frauds are being executed will make the user more aware and thus further reducing the risk of victimization. Similar effect was discussed by Davinson & Sillence (2010) who researched the effects of anti-phishing training. They discussed if the users behaviour was enhanced due to actual training or due to that the users awareness was increased just by being confronted with a training program.

Within this paper we also present an evaluation of the defense model that indicates that it can change user behavior in potentially fraudulent situations. The evaluation is done in an online auction house scenario.

The remainder of this paper presents our suggested defense model and our evaluation of the model

2. Proposed defence mechanism

Several researchers argue that knowledge is the best defense against online fraudsters. In example see Arachchilage and Love(2014) and Garg and Nilizadeh (2013). The same is stated by several governmental web pages including usa.gov (2013). While we do not argue with this fact we have seen that this knowledge often comes in the form of informational websites, thus creating a situation where the potential victims are required to acquire the knowledge they need before they encounter a potentially fraudulent situation.

We also believe that knowledge is the best countermeasure to online fraud but in our opinion the current situation introduces the following three issues:

- The potential victims are expected to gather knowledge before they encounter a potentially fraudulent situation. This implies that common Internet users must gather knowledge about something they may not be aware of.

- Internet users are supposed to read about online frauds in a context were the knowledge is not usable.

- The responsibility is put on the users rather than on the owners who hots the arenas were online frauds are taking place.

With our defense mechanism we make use of the ideas of situated learning that states that a learning experience is more meaningful if the learning is taking place in a context were the information is immediately useful (Herrington & Oliver, 1995). We call our approach context based micro training.

With context based micro training we developed a framework for introducing precise and tailored knowledge to Internet users in the situation were they may need it. To make the information as useful as possible to the users, the framework states the following about the information that is presented to the user:

- Relevant in the users current situation, i.e. if a user is entering an online auction house, where frauds has taken place, he will receive information about how to identify and avoid fraudsters in online auction houses.

- Interactive information meaning that the information module will require active participation from the users. As stated by Herrington & Oliver (1995) this approach increases the users awareness

The processes in the framework are shown in Figure 1.

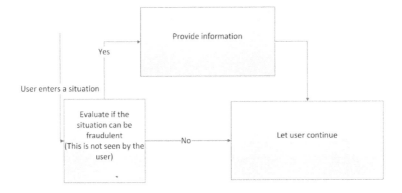

Figure 1: Overview of the processes in our framework

With this approach we aim to put precise information into a user's mind just before the users enters a potentially fraudulent situation. Since the information is tailored to the users current situation and requires participation from the user we believe that users that make use of this framework will be educated and prepared for the situation they enter and they will also be more aware of online frauds.

3. Research aim and limitations

The aim of this study is to evaluate the presented defense mechanism for use against online fraudsters. As described, the aim of the model is to provide knowledge "in the moment" and for that reason long time effects of the mechanism is not in the scope of the study. Rather, this study aims at providing a proof of concept for the direct effects of the proposed defense mechanism. Further, this study evaluates the defense mechanism in an online auction house environment. While we strongly believe that it can be used in other environments as well, effects of the mechanism in other environments is beyond the scope of this study and could be explored in the future. Also, this study does not provide a technical solution for how to implement the mechanism. While the actual implementation is not in the scope of this study we suggest that the mechanism can, for instance, be implemented in the following ways:

- As an interactive game or questionnaire when a user in an online auction house is entering a category of goods where the owner of the auction house is currently aware of ongoing frauds.

- As a way of countering telephone related frauds by warning users that are calling or receiving calls from numbers that are related to fraudulent behavior. This can be accomplished by matching incoming calls to a database of numbers that has been reported for fraudulent actions.

The aim of this study was reached by exploring the following questions in a controlled environment:

Q1: Can the defense mechanism help users identify fraudulent ads?

Q2: Will the mechanism make the users more likely to falsely identify legitimate ads as fraudulent?

4. Research model

To generate truly reliable results one could argue that this research is best conducted with a real-world approach by testing user's behavior in authentic situations. However, it is hard to conduct such study in an ethically appropriate manner. As example see Dittrich & Kenneally (2011) and Schrittwieser, Mulazzani & Weippl (2013). The guidelines proposed in those articles were followed in this study.

Instead, the research questions were explored in a survey-style environment. A central point in conducting a survey is that the sample of participants should represent the characteristics of the surveys intended population (May, 2001). In this case the intended population was everyone, in Sweden, that uses the Internet. May (2001) argues that the only way to generalize from the results of a survey is to use a probability sample. However May (2001) also states that using this kind of sample is not always possible. One requirement that a sample must fulfill in order to be called a probability sample is that every person in the population has an equal chance of participating in the survey. In this survey that is impossible because of the size of the population that holds a large portion of the Swedish population. A more convenient way of sampling would be to use a convenience sample where the sample is taken from people close to the researcher (Robson, 2011). Using such a sample will, however, generate less generalizable results (Robson, 2011). Since it was not feasible to use a probability sample in this study the aim was to get participants from different geographical places and with different demographic attributes. In order to achieve this, the surveys was be marketed over the Internet through social networks. This did not generate a probability sample but the sample did likely contain respondents with different backgrounds resulting in a more generalizable result than if convenience sampling where to be used.

In the survey, the participants were presented to six ads from a Swedish online auction house called Tradera.se. Three of the ads were known to be fraudulent and three were supposedly legitimate. The fraudulent ads were supplied by the Swedish online auction house Tradera and the other ads were randomly chosen from the same site. The participants was asked to rate the trustworthiness of each ad on a sex-graded scale were 1 meant that the ad was not trustworthy at all and 6 meant that the ad was completely trustworthy. The participants were guided to a website containing the survey and were randomly assigned to one of two groups called DM and non-DM. A total of 117 participants went through the full survey, 70 in the non-DM group and 47 in the DM group. The participants in the different groups performed the following tasks:

- DM: The participants in this group went through three learning modules designed according to the proposed defense mechanism before rating the ads. The learning modules were in the form of slideshows that presented a dialogue between a buyer and a seller. The participants were asked to decide if the buyer was in a potentially fraudulent situation or not. Based on the participants answer they received feedback describing if the buyers behavior was insecure and in that case why.

- Non-DM: The participants in this group rated the ads without going through the defense mechanism or being presented to any training.

5. Results

This section provides the results from the survey and conclusions related to the research questions. Figure 2 shows the average answers from both groups for the fraudulent ads. The column names are formatted in the following way: *"question number – group"*

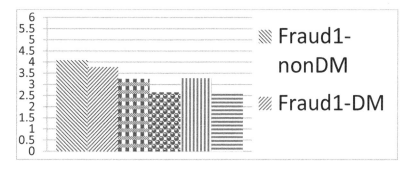

Figure 2: Overview of results for the fraudulent ads

As seen in the figure the participants in the DM group rated all three fraudulent ads as less trustworthy compared to the rating from the group non-DM. This result does show that the defense mechanism can, in a controlled environment, make users better at detecting fraudulent ads. This is the answer to Q1: Can the defense mechanism help users identify fraudulent ads?

Figure 3: overview of the results for the legitimate ads

Figure 3 reflects the average answers for the randomly chosen supposedly non-fraudulent ad.

As seen in the figure the participants in the group DM rated these ads as more trustworthy than the participants in the non-DM group. Thus, based on the results from this study the answer to Q2 "Will the mechanism make the users more likely to falsely identify legitimate ads as fraudulent?" appears to be no. On the contrary the participants who used the defense mechanism actually placed more trust in the supposedly legitimate ads than the participants who didn't.

To summarize; this survey indicates that using the defense mechanism we propose in an online auction house environment can make the users less susceptible to fraudulent ads. Moreover the results indicate that the users will also put more trust in legitimate ads. However it must be said that there was a great spread in the answers for all groups over all ads. This is shown in Table 1 that presents the standard deviation for each ad and group. This shows that with or without training it is hard to distinguish a fraudulent ad from a legitimate with only the actual ad as information.

Question	Standard deviation
Fraud1-nonDM	1,48
Fraud1-DM	1,56
Fraud2-nonDM	1,51
Fraud2-DM	1,35
Fraud3-nonDM	1,64
Fraud3-DM	1,38
Fraud4-nonDM	1,60
Fraud4-DM	1,56
Fraud5-nonDM	1,65
Fraud5-DM	1,73
Fraud6-nonDM	1,68
Fraud6-DM	1,37

Table 1: Standard deviation for all survey questions

6. Discussion

This study presented a framework for defense against online fraudsters and provided a proof of concept for that framework by testing it in a controlled environment. In this particular study the framework was tested in an online auction house environment. For that reason it is not possible to tell about the effects of the framework in another setting. Furthermore we want to mention that making this kind of studies in a controlled environment is troublesome since several factors that are present in a real world situation are difficult to imitate. After all, the participants in this study did never face any real risk of actually being defrauded. Also, they did not have all the opportunities to really investigate the seller that you would have in a real situation. For one, calling the seller and offer to meet and conduct the transaction in person can be an effective way of avoiding fraudsters.

With that said the study does provide the results that we set out to find by generating a proof of concept for the defense mechanism that we propose. This is done by showing that in our test:

- A person who uses the mechanism is better at identifying a fraudulent ad than a person who does not use it and,

- A person who uses the mechanism does not falsely identify legitimate ads as fraudulent more frequently than a person who does not use it. On the contrary the results actually indicated that a person using the mechanism places more trust in legitimate ads than a person that does not use the mechanism.

7. Future work

One could argue that to generate really strong results when researching online fraud you would have to conduct research in real life scenarios. Since this would involve actually tricking real persons without their knowledge and consent it is of course impossible without breaking many of the ethical guidelines set by the research community.

Even with these problems we acknowledge that conducting studies that imitates real life scenarios is crucial in order to generate a strong basis of research with reliable results. It is our understanding that more research within the area of online fraud prevention with a focus on the users behaviors is necessary. For future research within this domain we suggest that researchers make use of gamification as a part of the methodology. While we cannot recreate a real life situation using surveys or likewise we believe that making the actual study into a game, where the participants are encouraged to do good in order to get a high score or likewise, can make the participants feel the same risks as they would in a real life situation.

8. References

Arachchilage, N.A.G. and Love, S. (2014), "Security awareness of computer users: A phishing threat avoidance perspective." *Computers in Human Behavior*, Vol. 38,pp304-312.

Brottsförebyggande rådet (2013), "Bedrägerier och ekobrott.", http://www.bra.se/bra/brott--statistik/bedragerier-och-ekobrott.html, (Accessed 1 may 2014)

Brown, J.S., Collins, A. and Duguid, P. (1989), "Situated cognition and the culture of learning.", *Educational researcher*, Vol. 18, No. 1, pp32-42.

Davinson, N. and Sillence, E. (2010), "It won't happen to me: Promoting secure behaviour among internet users." *Computers in Human Behavior*, Vol. 26, No. 6, pp1739-1747.

Dittrich, D. and Kenneally, E. (2011), "The Menlo Report: Ethical Principles Guiding Information and Communication Technology Research", *US Department of Homeland Security.*

Garg, V. and Nilizadeh, S. (2013), "Craigslist scams and community composition: Investigating online fraud victimization." *Security and Privacy Workshops (SPW), 2013 IEEE* pp. 123-126.

Herrington, J. and Oliver, R. (1995), "Critical Characteristics of Situated Learning: Implications for the Instructional Design of Multimedia.", *ASCILITE 1995 Conference,* pp253-262.

IC3. (2013), "2012 - Internet Crime Report", https://www.ic3.gov/media/annualreport/2012_IC3Report.pdf (Accessed 30 marsh 2015)

Pratt, T.C., Holtfreter, K. and Reisig, M.D. (2010). "Routine Online Activity and Internet Fraud Targeting: Extending the Generality of Routine Activity Theory.", *Journal of Research in Crime and Delinquency*, Vol. 47, No. 3, pp267-296.

Schrittwieser, S., Mulazzani, M., & Weippl, E. (2013), "Ethics in Security Research - Which Lines Should Not Be Crossed?", *Security and Privacy Workshops (SPW), 2013 IEEE*, pp1-4.

USA.gov. (2013),"Internet Fraud", http://www.usa.gov/Citizen/Topics/Internet-Fraud.shtml, (Accessed 1 may 2014).

Wilsem, J.V. (2013), "'Bought it, but Never Got it' Assessing Risk Factors for Online Consumer Fraud Victimization.", *European sociological review*, Vol. 29, No. 2, pp168-178.

Proceedings of the Ninth International Symposium on
Human Aspects of Information Security & Assurance (HAISA 2015)

Human factors related to the performance of intrusion detection operators

P. Lif and T. Sommestad

Department of Information and Aeronautics Systems, Swedish Defence Research Agency (FOI)
e-mail: patrik.lif@foi.se

Abstract

Intrusion detection systems are common in contemporary enterprises. These systems are sometimes operated by a single individual as a part time activity; they are sometimes operated by cyber security operation centres in which a group of technology experts with the sole task of monitoring, detecting, analysing and responding to threatening events in the computer network. In either case, human factors and ergonomics should be expected to influence the intrusion detection capability. In this paper, Wickens' model of information processing and human factors concepts and tests are related to the tasks of intrusion detection operators. This model is used to identify both environmental conditions and human capabilities that are relevant for operators' performance as well as experimental setups that can test hypotheses related to these factors. Based on this analysis, it is proposed that the most important factors are attention, vigilance, automation, multitasking and mental workload and tests and measures such as NASA-TLX and eye-movements, should be useful.

Keywords

Human factors, intrusion detection system, system operator, cyber security.

1. Introduction

Intrusion detection systems (IDS) continue to be a promising technology which attracts researchers. It is safe to say that vast majority of this research focuses on improvements of the technical solutions, without considering the human factors related to them. The extant research on human factors related to IDSs is mainly qualitative and descriptive, describing current practice and issues associated with it. In fact, the only quantitative studies found in the literature are the test by Sommestad and Hunstad (2013) , the test by Sawyer et al. (Sawyer et al., 2014) and the test by Ben-Asher and Gonzalez (2015). Sommestad and Hunstad found that intrusion detection operators screening the output of an IDS significantly reduces the portion of false alarms without significantly decreasing the probability that an attack is detected; Sawyer et al. who found that it is more difficult to detect correlations when relevant information is available for less time and when frequently and attacks are rare; Ben-Asher and Gonzalez found that situated knowledge helped operators detecting attacks and that knowledge in cyber security helps the operator to identify the attack type (i.e. the root cause of the attack).

This paper suggests that more experimental research should be focused on intrusion detection operators to further understand their role and factors that determine their efficacy. In addition, it is recommended that this research utilize established methods and tests from the *Human Factors and Ergonomics* domain.

Section two of the paper provide an overview of the work intrusion detection operators and relates this work to Wickens' model of information processing, a model commonly used in the human factors and ergonomics research. Section three relates the work of intrusion detection operators to theories within human factors and ergonomics research and with associated measurement procedures. Section four summarizes the result and present conclusions from the analysis.

2. Operation of intrusion detection systems

This paper is concerned with the activities carried out by intrusion detection operators who focus on identifying analyzing threats to cyber security. Overall, work on intrusion detection can be said to aim at identifying threats and ongoing attacks against the monitored systems and devising a suitable response. It is a subset of the activities usually carried out by operators in cyber security operation centers (Zimmerman, 2014) or a task placed on system security administrators (Werlinger et al., 2008). This section provides a general description of the activities intrusion detection operators carry out in intrusion detection work, based on the three phases for intrusion detection identified by Goodall et al. (2004): monitoring (section 2.1), analysis (section 2.2) and response (section 2.3). In addition, the section describes previous research of human performance in relation to these phases. We relate these tasks to Wickens model of information processing (Wickens, 2013), depicted in Figure 1

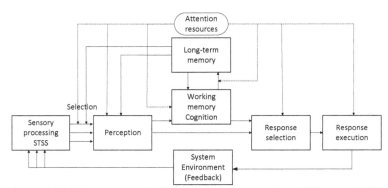

Figure 1: Wickens' model of information processing (Wickens, 2013).

The model describes typical stages or mental operations characterized by the flow of information when humans perform tasks. Events are first processed by our senses, which for IDS-operators is mostly visual. The information may be held in a short term sensory store for up to one second. From the sensation humans only perceive parts of the information available. Perceiving involves determining the meaning of the event. This is affected by past experiences that are stored in our long-term memories. From perception, the models show two possible paths: one meaning a direct response and one where the information goes to working memory. From working memory the information may be transferred to long term memory for later use and used to select a response. Wickens' four-stage plus memory model also contains a feedback loop: an executed response may change the environment and thereby affect future sensory input. Also of great importance is attention, which act as a filter that selects some elements for further processing and block other elements. Also, attention acts as the "fuel that provides mental resources or energy to the various stages of information processing" (Wickens, 2013).

2.1. The monitoring task

Monitoring is the mundane task of identifying anomalies, irregularities and other signs of active threats in a stream of alerts. This includes, in addition to visual inspections of the output from log systems, keeping track of ongoing threats such as new malware and new software vulnerabilities. In a cyber-security operation center, where tasks are divided among personnel, this is a phase that the tier one typically takes care of (Zimmerman, 2014).

Much of the work performed in the monitoring phase keeping up with the information that flows in and dealing with false positives and false negatives from sensors (e.g. network based IDSs). In Wicken's model, this means that the operator will have to be able to perceive the alerts and decide if this alert (along with related alerts) is worthy to investigate further. Because of this, it has been suggested that the monitoring task bares the signature of a vigilance problem (Mancuso et al., 2014). Thompson et al. (2006) found that intrusion detection alerts is the key resource in the task. This is in line with the findings by Goodall et al. (2004), who just as Thompson et al. (2006), identified that efforts are made to configure the sensors' rulesets so that the right alerts and the right amount of alerts are raised. Other information used to effectively monitor the security posture includes information about ongoing threats (e.g. from email lists and feeds) and situational knowledge related to the own environment (e.g. vulnerability scans, normal business and network configurations) (Goodall et al., 2004).

An operator's performance in this phase can be seen as the ability to identify actual attacks (i.e. alerts worthy of further investigation) without spending much time on events that are benign or not threatening.). The only quantitative study on this phase found in the literature is the one by Sawyer et al. (2014). Sawyer et al. used *NASA Task Load Index* to assess the mental workload during a task pertaining to matching IP-addresses in two columns of a table. They found that, as one would expect, it is more difficult to detect correlations when the table with IP-addresses were rearranged frequently and attacks are rare. The implications from this test on intrusion detection work are not clear, especially since the task does not resemble any monitoring activity performed by those who perform intrusion detection.

2.2. The analysis task

In the analysis phase, the analyst starts with the events that were found to be worthy of further investigation during the triage performed in the monitoring phase. These are analyzed further in order to successfully diagnose it and determine if a response is needed. However, the activity is more unpredictable in terms of duration and frequency than the continuously ongoing monitoring phase.

The information passed from monitoring to analysis, which usually is an alert from a sensor, is during analysis fused together with other information that can help in this work in a deeper analysis aiming at determining if the root cause of the alerts is a threat to the organization. In terms of Wicken's model, the operator will iterate through a series of loops to sense, perceive, decide and act on information. Actions will mainly involve collection of new information sources (e.g. network scans, machine states and traffic logs) and tools to feed this information to (e.g. malware scanners). This will produce new things (e.g. tool output) to perceive and make decision based on. Alternatives will be explored and hypotheses will be tested before a final decision is reached concerning the root cause. According to Goodall et al. (2004), system administrators mainly use knowledge related to intrusion detection (e.g. the sensors), general security expertise and local knowledge about the own environment. Furthermore, other types of system logs are often used in this process (Thompson et al., 2006).

An operator's performance in this phase can be seen as the ability to identify actual attacks along with root causes within a short period of time. This includes the ability to dismiss false alarms and, when possible, identify the root cause for the false alarm. Sommestad and Hunstad (2013) tested an intrusion detection operator's ability to filter out relevant alerts in an experiment based on synthetic data. These results suggest that an operator can reduce the portion of false alarms significantly, while not missing that many actual attacks. Ben-Asher and Gonzalez (2015) performed an experiment where subjects had the task of determining if a system state (e.g. certain network loads and active services) posed a security threat or not. In this simplified IDS task, they found that more knowledge in cyber security facilitated the correct detection of malicious events, decreased the false classification of benign events as malicious and helped operators to identify the type of threat causing the state.

2.3. The response task

In the response phase the operator device a suitable response to the events that were detected during the monitoring phase and analyzed during the analysis phase. The most common forms of responses are: interventions, feedback and reporting (Goodall et al., 2004). Examples of interventions include pulling a network plug, reconfiguring a network, reinstalling a machine or patching a software; feedback usually means tuning the signature ruleset of the IDS; examples of reporting includes letting other know about the threat or escalating the matter to even more in depth analysis (e.g. to collect forensic evidence and pursue legal action). Which of these types of interventions that is suitable depends not only on the event as such, but also on the operator's role in the organization and the operator's constituency.

Because the proper response is contingent on the cause of the incident and on the operator's authority/responsibility, it is difficult to define an overall performance marker for this activity. It could be that also this phase involves a number of iterations of perceive-decide-act-respond, e.g. where the operator contact asset owners to collect more information and to discuss alternatives. In the end, the action will be the response used. Cichonski et al. (2012) state that the criteria for determining the right containment strategy include: potential damage, need for evidence preservation, availability requirements, the cost of the strategy, and the effectiveness of the strategy. While it seems quite possible to study humans in the response phase there are, to the authors' knowledge, no empirical studies in the extant literature.

3. Human factors and intrusion detection

It is clear that the intrusion detection operator and his/her interaction with the IDS are important for the detection capabilities in most organizations. Human factors methods could be used to understand the operator's role and variables that determine the overall intrusion detection capability. In intrusion detection research, overall intrusion detection capability is typically using signal detection theory, which allows four possible outcomes: hit, miss, false alarm and correct rejection. The purpose with this chapter is to exemplify human factors issues that are relevant in information processing for IDS-operators, and are likely to influence the overall intrusion detection capability. Our analysis suggests that the established concepts and test from human factors research depicted in in Figure should be considered highly relevant. These will be further presented in sections 3.1 to 3.6.

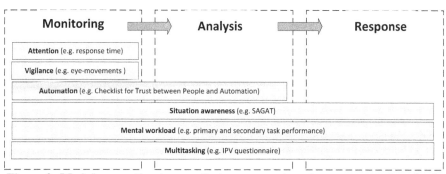

Figure 2: Model presenting human factors concepts and measurement methods that can be used in IDS-operators during monitoring, analysis, and response.

3.1. Attention

As seen in Figure 2 *attention* (Wickens, 2013) affects IDS-operators in three (of four) information processing stages: perception, response selection and response execution. Limitations in human attention are well known and can be described in three categories: 1) selective attention, 2) focused attention, and 3) divided attention (Wickens, Hollands, Banburry, & Parasuraman, 2013). Selective attention is when we select and process the wrong information; focused attention is when we fail to focus on one task, even when we know we should (i.e. we get distracted); divided attention is when we want or need to focus on multiple tasks but it is not possible, i.e. the IDS-operator has to handle information from two sources simultaneously. Visual and auditory attention is different, and should be used with the strength and weaknesses. Visual attention can be improved in the design process of displays, e.g. by close proximity in space or color (Wickens et al., 2013). Auditory attention is different from visual attention since it is omnidirectional and can be used in darkness or even during sleep. Attention could be measured in terms of response time and eye movements. For instance, response time could be measured as the time it takes for the operator to see some alert that he/she is set to look for and eye movement measurements could be used to measure if the operator continuously looks for new alerts on the computer screen.

3.2. Vigilance

Within the vigilance paradigm, an operator is required to work during a long time and detect signals that are intermittent, rare, unexpected and often of low salience (Wickens et al., 2013). As noted by Mancuso ct al. (Mancuso et al., 2014), *vigilance* is likely to be important to IDS-operators. IDS-operators' vigilance could be manipulated and tested to better understand its relevance in the monitoring task, and thereby enable optimization of the IDS-system from a human factors perspective. To measure vigilance; psychophysiological methods (e.g. heart rate and skin conductance), response time (e.g. time to answer an alarm), eye-movements (to analyze search patterns, what subjects look at, and what they missed) and NASA-TLX (a subjective workload assessment tool for ratings of operators mental workload in man-machine systems).

3.3. Automation

Experience shows that IDS-operators cannot possibly handle all alarms produced by today's sensors, and some level of *automation* will be necessary. Implemented correct, automation can generate substantial benefits in the monitoring process. However, it may also have negative effects and thereby lower the overall detection capability by suppressing true alerts from the alert feed. In many situations a task analysis should be conducted to weight costs and benefits of automation to determine how and if automation should be implemented. In complex systems it can be hard, or impossible for the operator to understand how automation is done in the system at hand, e.g. how rulesets of the IDS works. Experience from other domains suggests that one important factor is operators' possibility to override automated functions and that another important part of automation is *trust*. An operator's trust on a system and automation is affected when he/she will conduct actions suggested by the alarm. Depending of the system performance trust is built over time. If there are too many false alarms, it is possible that the operator will completely ignore the alarm and seek other information and act according to experience or other information sources (Wickens et al., 2013). Automation is not all or none, but a continuum from fully manual to full automation. To get an understanding of a system at the level of automation Sheridans & Verplank (1978) developed a scale with ten levels. Also trust between people and systems can be investigated using the Checklist for Trust between People and Automation (Jian, Bisantz, Drury, & Llinas, 2000).

3.4. Situation Awareness

The analysis task is typically solved using a complex process where alternatives are explored and hypotheses are tested. As noted above, this includes keeping track of current and previous alerts, other logs, and the monitored system as well as its environment. Thus, in this process, *situation awareness* (SA) (Endsley, 1995a, 1995b) appears to be necessary for IDS-operators to perform well. SA can be seen as an internal mental model where incoming data from systems, the environment, and co-workers should be integrated. This integrated picture can be used for decision making and actions (in the response phase), but in a complex and dynamic situations it is necessary to update situations awareness continuous.

Good SA for IDS-operators may be problematic for operators supervising huge data sets in very complex network systems that often are geographically distributed. SA is divided in three levels: perception, understanding and prediction. These three levels appear to match well with the level of awareness required during the monitoring (perception), analysis (understanding) and response (prediction) phases. It is applicable to IDS-operators that must perceive attacks, value if it is a real attack, and also be prepared for future attacks.

While SA is often referred to in cyber security research, it is typically used as conceptual tool without explicit measurements of the level of SA (see Franke and Brynielsson (2014). The experiment by Stevens-Adams et al. (Stevens-Adams et al., 2013) is an exception, where participants ability to answer questions concerning attacks and the overall system state was measured using a method developed by the experimenters. More established SA measures can be divided in: requirement analysis, freeze probe recall, real-time probe, post-trial subjective ratings, observer rating, process indices and team SA. Two popular methods are SAGAT (freeze probe technique) and SART (self-rating technique). In SAGAT, participants are interrupted and excluded from sensor information at certain (randomly selected) points in time and asked to state the current and/or future state of system. For example, with SAGAT, the IDS-operator's screen could be shut and the operator could be asked how much traffic that is coming in through the external firewall, which users that are logged on and/or if there is any machine that has been involved in multiple alerts the last 10 minutes. SART is a questionnaire developed for air traffic control for retrospectively measuring ten dimensions of SA: familiarity of the situation, focusing of attention, information quantity, information quality, instability of the situation, concentration of attention, complexity of the situation, variability of the situation, arousal, and spare mental capacity. Questionnaires like SART uses a 7-grade rating scale that operators answer and this could be adapted to IDS-work, or used as-is.

3.5. Multitasking

In the response task, *multitasking* is likely to be an issue. Multitasking is closely connected to attention, but it has more emphasis on the actual execution of the task and the interaction between perceptual, cognitive and motor processes is in focus in multitasking. This interaction may cause interference, and system effectiveness may be reduced since the operator cannot handle all tasks or process the information available. Perhaps the most obvious interruption is perceptual or motor (e.g moving the mouse or hit buttons), when an operator only can focus on one screen and normally only handle one motor task at a time. Cognitive interruptions are more subtle, but as for perceptual and motor processes, our resources to handle tasks are limited (Wickens et al., 2013). Also for cognitive tasks, interference occurs when the same resources are needed for cognitive processes (Wickens, 2008). By analyzing the operators tasks in a continuum, from tasks taking a couple of seconds to tasks that demands focus for perhaps twenty minutes, the operators work situation can be improved. It is often easy to shift between tasks that take a couple of seconds, but a forced interruption of the primary task is not optimal. Interruptions during task with high *mental workload* (see below) is harder to recover from than during tasks with low mental workload (Stanton et al., 2013). The literature reveals that there is some confusion of how to measure multitasking performance, but speed and error rates are sometimes used. Two standard questionnaires have been used: the Inventory of Polychronic Values (IPV) and Modified Plychronic Attitude Index 3 (MPAI3) (König & Waller, 2010; Poposki & Oswald, 2010).

3.6. Mental workload

Mental workload is an established concept and there is a large body of literature on the topic (Tsang & Wilson, 1997). The important and underlying theoretical assumption is operators limited capacity to process information (Kahneman, 1973). With greater task difficulty and complexity increasing mental workload is acquired and when demands exceed capacity task performance will decrease. Another known phenomena is that interruptions during task with high *mental workload* are harder to recover from than during tasks with low mental workload (Stanton et al., 2013).

Measuring workload requires reliable and valid metrics but since there are multiple methods it is not always obvious which method to choice. Methods differ in sensitivity and must therefore be matched to the situation in hand (Matthews, Reinerman-Jones, Barber, & Abich, 2015). Some examples of methods to measure mental workload are: 1) primary and secondary task performance (performing two tasks to evaluate spare capacity), 2) psychophysiological measures (e.g. heart rate), and 3) NASA-TLX (subjective ratings of operators mental workload). Often these measures can be combined and sometimes simplified versions of these methods are used.

4. Summary and conclusions

Previous research has found that IDS-operators play an important role and face several challenging tasks when they 1) monitor systems, 2) analyse events and 3) respond to events. In terms of established concepts from human factors research, the success in all these phases appears to be related to situational awareness, mental workload and multitasking; issues pertaining to automation appear to be relevant for phases of monitoring and analysis; the operator's attention and vigilance appears to be important in the monitoring phase.

Although IDS-operators are known to be important and IDS are important cyber security tools, the extant literature contains few quantitative tests on IDS-operators or the challenges they face. Established measurement techniques of both objective and subjective types could be used to better understand how these concepts relate to, and influence, the efficacy of IDS-operators. For example, eye-trackers would give us valuable information about search pattern and how to focus attention to the right information; self-ratings of mental workload (e.g. from NASA-TLX) could be used to measure mental workload and understand how it relates to performance; the importance of different types of situational awareness could be measured using SAGAT. These, and other established methods from human factors research, ought to be leveraged in further research on IDS-operators. Next we plan to validate the model (Figure 2) in a two-step process. First we will conduct further discussions and interviews with IDS-operators, and second we will run experiments with IDS-operators. In the second part human factors concepts and measures will be used (e.g. SA, multitasking, vigilance, mental workload) to get a better understanding of IDS-operators and their work situation.

5. References

Ben-Asher, N., & Gonzalez, C. (2015). Effects of cyber security knowledge on attack detection. Computers in Human Behavior, 48(0), 51-61.

Endsley, M. (1995a). Measurement of Situation Awareness in Dynamic Systems. Human Factors, 37(1), 65-84.

Endsley, M. (1995b). Toward a Theory of Situational Awareness in Dynamic Systems. Human Factors, 37(1), 32-64.

Franke, U., & Brynielsson, J. (2014). Cyber situational awareness – A systematic review of the literature. Computers & Security, 46(0), 18-31.

Goodall, J., R., Lutters, W., G., & Komplodi, A. (2004). The Work of Intrusion Detection: Rethinking the Role of Security Analysts. Paper presented at the Proceedings of the Tenth Americas Conference on Information Systems, New York, US.

Jian, J.-Y., Bisantz, A. M., Drury, C. G., & Llinas, J. (2000). Foundations for an empirically determined scale of trust in automated systems. Dayton, OH, US.: Wright-Patterson Air Force Base.

Kahneman, D. (1973). Attention and effort. Englewood, NJ: Prentice Hall.

König, C. J., & Waller, M. J. (2010). Time for Reflection: A Critical Examination of Polychronicity. Human Performance, 23(2), 173-190. doi: 10.1080/08959281003621703

Mancuso, V. F., Christensen, J. C., Cowley, J., Finomore, V., Gonzalez, C., & Knott, B. (2014). Human Factors in Cyber Warfare II: Emerging Perspectives. Proceedings of the Human Factors and Ergonomics Society Annual Meeting, 58(1), 415-418.

Matthews, G., Reinerman-Jones, L. E., Barber, D. J., & Abich, J. (2015). The Psychometrics of Mental Workload: Multiple Measures Are Sensitive but Divergent. Human Factors: The Journal of the Human Factors and Ergonomics Society, 57(1), 125-143.

Poposki, E. M., & Oswald, F. L. (2010). The Multitasking Preference Inventory: Toward an Improved Measure of Individual Differences in Polychronicity. Human Performance, 23(3), 247-264.

Sawyer, B. D., Finomore, V. S., Funke, G. J., Mancuso, V. F., Funke, M. E., Matthews, G., & Warm, J. S. (2014). Cyber Vigilance: Effects of Signal Probability and Event Rate. Proceedings of the Human Factors and Ergonomics Society Annual Meeting, 58(1), 1771-1775.

Sheridan, T. B., & Verplank, W. (1978). Human and Computer Control of Undersea Teleoperators. Cambridge, MA: Man-Machine Systems Laboratory, Department of Mechanical Engineering, MIT. .

Sommestad, T., & Hunstad, A. (2013). Intrusion detection and the role of the system administrator. Information Management & Computer Security, 21(1), 30-40.

Stanton, N., Salmon, P., Rafferty, L., Walker, G., Baber, C., & Jenkins, D. (2013). Human Factors Methods. Surrey, England: Ashgate Publishing Limited.

Stevens-Adams, S., Carbajal, A., Silva, A., Nauer, K., Anderson, B., Reed, T., & Forsythe, C. (2013). Enhanced Training for Cyber Situational Awareness, Foundations of Augmented Cognition (Vol. 8027, pp. 90-99): Springer Berlin Heidelberg.

Thompson, R. S., Rantanen, E. M., & Yurcik, W. (2006). Network Intrusion Detection Cognitive Task Analysis: Textual and Visual Tool Usage and Recommendations. Proceedings of the Human Factors and Ergonomics Society Annual Meeting, 50(5), 669-673.

Tsang, P., & Wilson, G. F. (1997). Mental workload. In G. Salvendy (Ed.), Handbook of Human Factors and Ergonomics (Second edition ed.). New York, U.S.: John Wiley & Sons, Inc.

Werlinger, R., Hawkey, K., Muldner, K., Jaferian, P., & Beznosov, K. (2008). The challenges of using an intrusion detection system: is it worth the effort? Paper presented at the Proceedings of the 4th symposium on Usable privacy and security, Pittsburgh, Pennsylvania, USA.

Wickens, C. (2008). Multiple Resources and Mental Workload. Human Factors, 50(3), 449-455.

Wickens, C. (2013). Attention. In D. N. Lee & A. Kirlik (Eds.), The Oxford Handbook of Cognitive Engineering. Oxford, U.K.: Oxford University Press.

Wickens, C., Hollands, J., Banburry, S., & Parasuraman, R. (2013). Engineering Psychology and Human Performance. New York: Pearson Education Inc.

Zimmerman, C. (2014). Ten Strategies of a World-Class Cynersecurity Operations Center. Bedford, MA, U.S.: The Mitre Corporation.

Digital Rights Management: The Four Perspectives of Developers, Distributors, Users, and Lawyers

N. McDonald, S. Faily, M. Favale and C. Gatzidis

Bournemouth University, United Kingdom
e-mail: {nmcdonald,sfaily,mfavale,cgatzidis}@bourenmouth.ac.uk

Abstract

Digital Rights Management (DRM) refers to a collection of security mechanisms that are widely deployed on a number of copyright-protected digital assets. However, despite the existence of a number of studies of the technical architectures of rights management security systems, there is little scholarly/academic literature dedicated to the human aspects associated with circumvention of DRM security. Using videogames as a case study, this paper discusses how DRM is perceived differently depending on where one's stake in the use of DRM security lies. This paper concludes by posing questions that could be used to aid content distributors and security practitioners in the creation of a fairer DRM framework.

Keywords

Digital Rights Management, Human Aspects, Privacy and Fairness, Game Security.

1. Introduction

Copyright infringements and the evolution of digital rights management (DRM) have been among the most antagonistic points of the digital age (Anderson, 2008). It is questionable whether a flawless rights protection system can ever be accomplished when drawing on the analogy that, in the traditional sense of security, you are protecting your asset from an attacker, but in DRM scenarios the authorised user and attacker may well be the same individual. Therefore, there is surprisingly little literature around the human aspects that influence this area of rights protection circumvention. In software development security requirements should be addressed as early in the design process as possible. However, all too often, security is considered an after-thought (Adams, A and Sasse, M. A. 1999) and DRM security is often added to protected content after the development phase is complete.

Computer/video games outsold video and music content during 2014. For example, the UK games market grew by 7.5% to reach £2.5bn, while video decreased by 1.4% to reach £2.2bn and music fell by 1.6% to reach £1billion (Butler 2014). Because games currently have the largest market share compared to these other aforementioned creative industries, our research is centred on game DRM. (Butler 2014). The debate surrounding the effectiveness and future of rights protection mechanisms has been closely aligned to the subjects of interoperability, user privacy, user acceptance and maintenance of secure systems. Some of the lesser explored areas have been the human aspects of DRM from the involved stakeholder groups: a) the game developer; b) the game rights holder/distributor; c) the games user and; d) the legal profession. The remainder of this paper is organized as follows: Section 2 explores the background of game security circumvention; Section 3 introduces the justification for research. Section 4 introduces the methodology. Section 5 discusses the DRM stakeholder groups. Section 6 discusses the need for balance, Section 7 introduces the human difficulties, and, finally, Section 8 concludes this paper.

2. Background

Piracy is the use of a copyrighted material without paying for it (Nagesh, 2011). Digital piracy occurs regardless of what type of media is being developed or for what distribution platform it is intended for. The factors influencing the user's desire to circumvent DRM in acts of piracy can be construed as a social problem driven by human aspects such as intent, motive, moral judgement and social consensus. Possible reasons behind the circumvention of DRM go beyond any technological weaknesses of the security into the human aspects of security. The growth of online gaming, the uptake of faster internet connections along with the rise of initiatives such as the 'Occupy Movement' against corporatism and economic inequality (Townsend, 2015) have provided opponents to DRM with more ways to present themselves in terms of the justification for their circumvention actions. Organisations distributing games view DRM as a necessary instrument in the fight against copyright violation. However, the critics of DRM allege that it stifles innovation and fair competition by quashing lawful uses of digital content, and, as such, is creating economic and social inequality regardless of the context of the intended use. (Litlow, 2012)

Because of this perceived economic and social inequality between rights holders and users of games, it becomes imperative for the legal system to ensure that there is fairness for all in the event of a legal dispute. Fairness is achieved when people restrain their liberty in ways necessary to yield advantages for all (Hart, 1955). Fairness in the English legal system is underpinned by the principle of Equity. This is described as "the means by which a system of law balances the need for sufficient judicial discretion to achieve fairness in individual factual circumstances" (Hudson, 2012). Because of the perceived bias towards the rights holders, it is essential that justice should be seen to involve procedural fairness and fair decisions being reached by an objective decision-maker, whilst protecting the rights of individuals and promoting public confidence in the legal process (Chang, 2007)

Perhaps the most serious drawback to the debate surrounding the effectiveness and future of DRM is that fairness for all, as defined by Hart, may never be achievable across groups serving such different interests. Consequently, "the monopoly on restrictions of use sought by many distributors extends beyond any concept of a monopoly in intellectual property and is often at the expense of user satisfaction" (Darroch, 2012). Because of these restrictions, DRM can seem inequitable and unfair when applying Hart's principle of fairness. This apparent lack of fairness and bias in the direction of rights-holding organisations "results in DRM, gaining a large share of attention from copyright scholars, the content industry, and the media" (Diehl, 2012). It is questionable whether game developers should be leaving DRM to the publisher to deploy. There is need for clarity in regard to DRM responsibility; after all, the developer cannot be expected to have the market knowledge of a distributor/publisher.

3. Justification for Research

This paper is part of a larger study on DRM security identifying and communicating how game developers make sense of DRM technology when developing video games. The worldwide DRM market is said to be worth 2.9 billion US dollars and is estimated to grow at a compounded annual growth rate of around 16% between 2015-2020 (Egar 2015). While this has obvious positive consequences for growth and innovation, such an expansion should be matched by a period of extended attention to the fundamental values and the social interactions impacted by these technologies. The perspectives in this paper are limited to games, but the questions posed in this paper could potentially be applied to any type of rights protected digital content.

4. Methodology

This paper is part of a project building empirical evidence on the way content producers "make sense" of DRM. The human aspects revolving around content protection will be identified and analysed. To this end, the project will first review the discussion surrounding fairness and DRM from the point of view of the main stakeholders groups. Data was retrieved from Scopus, IEEE's Xplore, book chapters, journal articles and the conference proceedings of the ACM Digital Library. The data selection utilised Google Scholar and Scopus to identify the most frequently cited material. 22 journal articles, 11 conference papers, 3 case reports and 2 working papers were coded into the NVivo qualitative analysis software using an open coding technique with a hierarchal structure with four master codes of Developer view, Distributor view, User view and Legal view. The sub-code structure was then broken down into: a) Constraints of DRM, b) interoperability of DRM, c) opinions on DRM, and, finally, d) reasons for DRM. This socio-legal approach identifies and explores the elements of law and the human behavioural aspects in rights protection security by exploring the perspectives and opinions of the stakeholder groups.

5. The DRM Stakeholder Groups

The selected scholarly literature highlights four main DRM stakeholder groups. The chosen business model and financial situation of the stakeholder will influence the level of reliance on DRM. Despite the potential financial impact of the business model on DRM, there is little literature to the best of the authors' knowledge dedicated to the relationship between business model choice and DRM deployment. In essence, "DRM requires a complex system of technical, organisational and social elements" (Mayer-Schonberger, 2006). The practical implications of stakeholder opinions and interaction towards DRM security needs to be carefully considered and may go some way towards the creation of a fairer, more equitable DRM framework.

5.1. Game Developers

The developer's interests are the first part of DRM. Although not a game specific statistic, digital content developers only accounted in total for "6.7% of lobby meeting requests with the evaluation rapporteur of the EU Parliament Copyright Directive 2001/29/EC" (Reda, 2015). It is inevitable that some users will try to use digital content without paying the appropriate fee, unless they are prevented from doing so by societal rules and social consensus (Mayer-Schonberger, 2006). However, there is very little work on precisely which societal rules might be used to prevent the social perception that circumvention of DRM security in acts of piracy is a fair or a victimless act. Additionally, the game developer's perception of DRM may be influenced by what business model they are basing their business on. One question that should be addressed is the following; do content developers view the content they produce as a product that will generate a recurring income stream or as a product that can be traded at a one-off price to a distributor, who will then take ownership of the rights and entitlement to the recurring income stream, in return for distribution of the product to a much wider audience than the developer alone could reach? Many developers are nascent and often backed by external investors who have a financial interest in DRM deployment in order to maximise the return on investment. Additionally, the practical implications of these ever-changing business models need to be carefully measured in relation to the wider DRM debate centred on the effectiveness and future of game security. This raises the following questions, are developers creating products with a business model clearly defined from the outset and if so, are they considering future industry changes when developing? During the last two decades the digital content industry has undergone a period of significant change in both social and business strategy (Reda, 2015), and, as such, the current legislation in the area of content rights protection may still be some years behind the industry in terms of development.

5.2. Game Distributors

The selection of literature reviewed shows the distributors to have the strongest interests in DRM deployment. Developers have seemingly "given distributors unprecedented levels of power and control over the use and distribution of their works" (Darroch, 2012). For developers to advance the gameplay experience continually, they need a recurrent income stream or a large preliminary investment from a content distributor with a large market reach. Consumers now have a greater than ever choice of content through multiple merchants such as Google's Google Play, Apple's App Store, Microsoft's Xbox Live etc. As a consequence, one of the emerging business models for games is the 'freemium model' where the core game content is offered for free but value is added by optional in-game purchases such as in-game characters, extra content, cheats or game customizations. Because of the growth of this model, the consumer of games should no longer be considered a mere submissive receiver of products through an initial one-time purchase. The freemium model appears to eliminate the need for DRM in the traditional anti-piracy sense, as wider distribution of the core free game content targets a wider market share of potential customers resulting in a higher probability of in-game purchases. However, under the traditional purchase business model, the distributor appears to be shouldering the entire burden of rights protection and security.

If DRM is considered as a collection of security mechanisms designed to protect the game assets, then the developers are basically saying that the distributor takes full responsibility and, as a consequence, liability for the security of the game. If this is the case, distributors are seemingly accepting responsibility for any possible security vulnerability associated with the development code, the game engine, or indeed any aspect of the game. Distributors may see this differently in terms of their vicarious liability, and this then raises the issue of who should be liable for security breaches, if the distributor is able to absolve themselves from vicarious liability through the use of contractual terms in place with the game developer upon agreement to distribute the content.

5.3. Game Users

DRM is a variety of security mechanisms designed to prevent users from carrying out action that may breach rights protected by copyright and IP law (Qun, 2010). However, this system of restrictions often fails to account for the permitted copyright exceptions granted to users in the EU or the fair use allowances granted in users in the USA (Favale, 2008). Both of these rights permit backup copies for personal use, or for the purposes of educational use. Users of rights protected content accounted for only 20% of the total lobby meeting requests with the evaluating rapporteur of the EU European Parliament Copyright Directive 2001/29/EC (Reda, 2015). Regardless of the size of the stakeholder's interest in DRM there is an underlying sense of an imbalance of power with the bias falling in the direction of rights holders. The rights holders appear to be free to undermine a number of lawful copyright exceptions granted in law to the users. For example, the game World of Warcraft (prior to the freemium model version) could not be successfully bought used, because of a DRM-based one-time installation key policy. (Dusollier, 2003) The literature suggests that overly restrictive DRM systems are likely to be counter-productive as they provide little in the way of an incentive for users to purchase legitimate, paid-for content (Darroch, 2012). It may be the case that the financial motives for user piracy or circumvention of DRM would be less prominent, if the pricing policies set by the content distributors were more aligned with the current economic climate. At present, these distributors have unprecedented levels of power over the distribution methods of the products in the portfolio. This power has had a negative impact on the user's attitude towards the use of and acceptance DRM technologies from a consumer perspective (Darroch, 2012).

5.4. The Lawyers

From a legal perspective the existence of DRM can create a variety of different fee-earning disputes including copyright, IP, privacy, contract and which legal jurisdiction should ultimately apply in a dispute. Advances in the future user acceptance of DRM will be determined not only by technology implications, but also by the current and emerging economic and legal developments. (Heileman and

Jamkhedkar, 2005) Additionally, changes in the game development market, such as the development of new hardware platforms, different distribution methods and new payment technologies all carry risks and legal challenges that require access to legal professionals for those involved in disputes involving DRM. When markets go through rapid change such as the gaming sector has, it takes time for legislation and regulations to catch up (Samuelson, 2003). These market factors aid the need for legal professionals specialising in these disputes. Furthermore, the business models of the stakeholders involved in disputes around rights protection will also have an influence on the legal outcome and access to justice. For example, the complexity of disputes in copyright law, along with the nebulousness of the fair use exceptions, combined with the struggle of negotiating licensing agreements, mean that non-experts such as fledgling game developers are often at an informational disadvantage when they face a dispute involving DRM. In any type of legal dispute access to high quality legal advice is vital but also dependent on having the financial means to defend one's position and seek the necessary expert guidance prior to litigation. Financial health and the ability to seek high quality legal advice is more commonly found in larger more established organisations than smaller nascent organisations (Davies, 2006). Consequently, the lack of a clear definition between fair uses and acts that would constitute copyright infringements does not help the status of DRM security. Although some uses are clearly fair and others clearly not fair, there is essentially a large grey area of uses that may or may not be conceived as fair and could only ever be settled with the assistance of a court ruling. Even a well-accomplished copyright lawyer cannot say with absolute certainty where the line between fair and unfair use is really found. (Felten, 2003) The very existence of DRM security and the complex legal arguments DRM can create add to the justification and commercial viability for legal professionals working in this field of practice.

6. The Need for Balance

If the future acceptance levels of DRM are to be viewed as effective, it is vital that a greater degree of balance needs to be struck between the stakeholders (Dusollier 2003). As can be seen from the discussion in this paper, rights protection security is a complex topic with multiple viewpoints and social arguments for and against its implementation. As far as the law is concerned, the issue of DRM has been examined at the highest level with regard to circumvention on games consoles. This circumvention is sometimes achieved through the use of modified chips ('mod chips') which allow the user to play unauthorised games.

The European Court held that the protection of 'effective' Technological Protective Measures (TPMs) can be extended to external hardware devices such as mod chips because there is nothing in the Information Society Directive 2001/29/EC of the European Parliament that forbids it, especially when considering the broad definition of TPMs provided by the directive. The Court however specified that a number of conditions need to be satisfied in order to allow the protection of TPMs. In particular, a) the aim pursued by the manufacturer implementing TPMs must be legitimate (e.g. it must seek copyright protection and not competition hindrance); b) TPMs must be suitable for the task (e.g. 'effective'); c) certain proportionality criteria must be met, which includes a number of considerations: the volume of infringing behaviours compared to legitimate behaviours, and whether a different protection technology 'could cause less interference' with legitimate uses.

It is unlikely that DRM systems will ever be able to accurately predict or read human intent and, as such, there is a very fine line between legitimate fair use actions (i.e. hardware modifications to allow bespoke home-brewed content to run or be used for backup purposes) and those actions that have a secondary purpose that can carry out unlawful circumvention of DRM and breach TPMs. Ultimately, the DRM system cannot ever know enough about the circumstances outside of the computer (Felten, 2003). However, human intent is only one part of the problem. Copyright infringement can be determined objectively, irrespective of the human intent, when the unlawful acts are clarified by law. As this is not the case currently, legislative reform in this area is urgently needed.

7. The Human Difficulties

The human-related social difficulties of DRM are notably less discussed in the literature than the technical aspects (e.g. effectiveness) but nonetheless appear to be an underlying theme running through the debate surrounding DRM. It should come as no surprise that language difficulties between developers, lawyers and rights holders appear to be another problematic area that is less well-studied. Terms and conditions of use for rights-protected content are often written using legalistic language and there is an apparent disengagement by content users of anything that appears written in that manner. In many cases the contractual relationship and legal terms that the user enters into with the rights holder are not given a second glance. Another difficulty is the use of abbreviations in language used by stakeholder groups. In the legal sector the abbreviation TPM stands for Technological Protective Measure, but in the field of software development TPM is the abbreviation for Trusted Platform Module which "is a crypto-graphic coprocessor chip that has been included on most enterprise-class PC and laptop motherboards produced in the past decade" (Challener, 2013). This is but one example of language difficulties across the stakeholder groups.

8. Conclusions

Legal norms and social behaviours are some of the human aspects surrounding the effectiveness and future of DRM security. Understanding the human perspectives behind the circumvention of games security may have a significant impact on how DRM technical issues are addressed in future. Further exploration of the human behavioural aspects influencing DRM would help unravel the complexities of the interaction of rights protection security and law. Although there have already been projects on the acceptability of rights protection security by consumers e.g. The Informed Dialogue About Consumer Acceptability of DRM Solutions in Europe (INDICARE) (Böhle, 2008), it is shown that there are multiple stakeholder views, from different viewpoints, associated with DRM security. While other papers have investigated the impact of DRM from the perspective of consumer acceptance and, whether certain acts which are permitted in law are being adversely affected by the use of DRM (Akester, 2009), this paper, as part of an ongoing project, adds to research in this field with the exploration of the different stakeholders human centric perspectives of what DRM should be and whose interests DRM should primarily serve. It is evident that a greater degree of balance and fairness needs to be present in any DRM framework developed for use in the videogame marketplace. Developers of content should ask the following human-centric questions to guide problematic and complex human aspects of deploying DRM security. The data analysed in this part of the project so far has produced the following questions:

- What are the users' motives for circumvention of current DRM?
- What is the incentive for user circumvention?
- Can this incentive be combated through fair use/copyright exceptions or pricing structure or business model changes?
- What is the motive for deployment of DRM in this scenario?
- Is this motive for deployment sufficiently valuable or can value be added to the content in other ways e.g. in game purchases, extra content?
- Are the terms and conditions and end user license agreement of this rights protected content undermining legislation (e.g. copyright law, privacy norms, competition law, etc.?)
- Is enforcement of this DRM solution legally viable?
- Are the fair use/copyright exceptions entitlements properly designed for the type of protection technologies we arc deploying?

9. Acknowledgements

The research described in this paper was funded by Bournemouth University Fusion Investment Fund MADRIGAL project.

10. References

Adams, A and Sasse, M. A. (1999). Users are not the enemy. Communications of the ACM. 42 (12), p41-46.

Akester, P (2006). Digital Rights Management in the 21st Century. European Intellectual Property Review. 28 (3), p159-168.

Anderson R (2008). Security Engineering. 2nd ed. Hoboken: Wiley. p679-725.

Böhle, K.. (2008). Informed Dialogue about Consumer Acceptability of DRM Solutions in Europe. Available: http://www.indicare.org/tiki-page.php?pageName=Downloads. Last accessed 10/04/2015.

Butler L. (2014). ERA UK Market Statistics. Available: http://www.gera-europe.org/info-stats/overview.aspx. Last accessed 16/04/2015.

Challener, J. 2013. Trusted Platform Module Evolution. John Hopkins APL Technical Digest, 32(2), p 1.

Chang, Y-L, (2007). Who should own access rights? A game-theoretical approach to striking the optimal balance in the debate over Digital Rights Management. Artificial Intelligence and Law, 15(4), p323-356.

Darroch, C. (2012). Problems and Progress in the Protection of Videogames: A Legal and Sociological Perspective. The Manchester Review of Law, Crime and Ethics, 1(1), p136-172.

Davies, W. and Withers, K. (2006). Public Innovation. Intellectual Property in a Digital Age. Institute for Policy Research. p48.

Diehl, E. (2012). Securing Digital Video. 1st ed. New York: Springer p4-5.

Dusollier, S. (2003) Tipping the Scale in Favour of the Right Holders: The European Anti-Circumvention Provisions' Springer-Verlag, Berlin p462-478.

Eggar, C. (2015). Digital Rights Management Market Outlook 2020. Available: http://www.reportlinker.com/p02975947-summary/Digital-Rights-Management-Market-Outlook.html. Last accessed 26/05/2015.

Favale, M. (2008) Approximation and DRM: Can digital locks respect copyright exceptions?. International Journal of Law and Information Technology 19 (4) p306-323.

Felten, E. (2003). A sceptical view of DRM and fair use. Communications of the ACM. 46 (4), p56-59.

Hart, H., (1955). Are there any natural rights. The Philosophical Review, 64(2), p175 -191.

Heileman G and Jamkhedkar.P (2005). DRM interoperability analysis from the perspective of a layered framework. Proceedings of the 5th ACM workshop on Digital rights management, 05 (1). p17-26.

Hudson, A. (2012) Equity and Trusts. 7th ed. Oxford: Routledge, p5-6.

Litlow, B. (2012) DRM's Rights Protection Capability: a review. The First International Conference on Computational Science and Information Management, Volume 1 (2012), p12-17.

Mayer-Schonberger, V. (2006) Beyond Copyright: Managing Information Rights with DRM. Denver University Law Review, 84(1), p181.

Nagesh, G. (2011) 24% of Web Traffic Involves Piracy. Hillicon Valley Blog, the Hill. Available: http://thehill.com/policy/technology/141509-study-24-percent-of-web-traffic-involves-piracy Last accessed 10/04/2015.

Qun, G., (2010). Digital Contents Interoperability between Diverse DRM Systems. Shandong, Intelligent Computing and Intelligent Systems (ICIS)(2) p170-173

Reda J. (2015). EU copyright evaluation report – explained .Available: https://juliareda.eu/2015/01/report-eu-copyright-rules-maladapted-to-the-web/. Last accessed 09/04/2015.

Samuelson, P. (2003). DRM {and, or, vs.} the law. Communications of the ACM, 46(4), p41 - 45.

Townsend, M. (2015). Parliament Square fence crushes protest rights, says Occupy Democracy. Available at: http://www.theguardian.com/uk-news/2015/jan/03/boris-johnson-occupy-democracy-london-protest-fence Last accessed 15/04/2015.

Author Index

www.ingramcontent.com/pod-product-compliance
Lightning Source LLC
Chambersburg PA
CBHW051046050326
40690CB00006B/612